C000270586

An Encyclopaedia of

European Sports & GT Cars

from 1961

Graham Robson

ISBN 0 85429 256 X

© **Graham Robson 1980**

First published 1980, Reprinted 1984.

All rights reserved. No part of this book may be reproduced or transmitted in any form or by any means electronic or mechanical, including photocopying, recording or by any information storage or retrieval system, without permission of the copyright holder

A FOULIS Motoring Book

Published by
Haynes Publishing Group
Sparkford, Yeovil, Somerset BA22 7JJ, England

Distributed in North America by
Haynes Publications Inc
861 Lawrence Drive, Newbury Park, California 91320 USA

Editor Rod Grainger
Dust jacket design Phil Jennings
Printed in England by Haynes Publishing Group

Contents

Introduction

I know I ought to start this book with a couple of neat definitions, but I find that impossible. Just what *is* a sports car? And what constitutes a Grand Touring machine? Like other more eminent writers before me, I cannot really tell you. Indeed, it was not until I began to gather material for this book that I realised that my own personal concepts were not accurately developed.

It is true, of course, that the problem is more difficult nowadays than it used to be. In the last generation an army of dedicated product planners and publicists have managed to debase the 'GT' label by applying it to some very unworthy cars. On the other hand, clever engineers and stylists have found ways of evolving sporting machines from the basic layout of a mundane touring car. Both have succeeded in bringing rather more prestigious motoring to more people than ever before. For these, and for many other reasons, I decided to leave definitions to a professor of philosophy who is also a motoring enthusiast.

Somehow it was never too difficult to decide if a car qualified for inclusion in the book, but I was often in trouble over its place in the scheme of things. Although I was never likely to include a Renault Caravelle, I felt I had to include the very sporting Gordinis. Some coupe versions of saloon designs (the Sunbeam Rapier and the Opel Manta both spring to mind) didn't qualify by my standards, but Ford's Capri, which was entirely special, did. I felt that I could include Jaguar's XJ-S without a qualm, but not the XJ 5.3C 'coupe'. I knew it would have been quite wrong to leave out the potentially fierce Escort RS1800s and Fiat 131 Abarths, but I decided I couldn't stretch a point to include RS2000s and Mirafiori Sports as well. I spent a lot of time worrying about the place of cars like the MGB GT and the Volvo 1800ES in the scheme of things; were they sports? Or GT? or both? I also decided that special-bodied cars (by renowed coach-builders) could only qualify if they were officially approved by the manufacturer of the chassis – which cut out lots of beautiful Italian 'specials' and a selection of fast-looking machines on mundane underframes. It also eliminated several Abarths and similar cars which were no more than heavily-modified Fiats. In British terms, therefore, a Lotus-Cortina qualifies as a budget-price GT car, but a Cortina-Savage, which is a nicely-engineered conversion, does not.

In the field of Supercars, there was rarely a problem in deciding which cars should be included, but here again some really fast European saloons had to be eliminated. I felt sure that neither Jaguar nor Mercedes would mind that their 5.3-litre and 6.9-litre saloons were not called Supercars, and that the Fiat 130, for all that it had a Ferrari-derived vee-6 engine, would not be offended either.

I thought that, to keep the list to manageable proportions, all cars included must either have been, or intended to be, in production according to the standards of the companies building them. A Ferrari 275LM, therefore, qualifies even though only a few were built. At the other end of the scale, in status terms, the rare Ford Escort RS1800 is certainly a production car. 'Cars which got away' like the Monica, have not been included, while those (like Marcos's Mantis) which were killed by circumstances get a mention.

In this volume we cover the years from 1961 to date. Some well known cars like Jaguar's XK150, which went out of production in 1961, have not been included here, but will obviously find a home in the next volume, which will cover the period 1945 to 1960. Cars like the MGA, and the AC Ace only have those models described which were in production from 1961 on.

But, please what *is* a sports car? Will someone invent the true definition?

Graham Robson

Chapter One

Into the 1960s –
The Sporting Scene

By the beginning of the 1960s, the European scene had settled down after its postwar upheaval. Immediately after the end of that war, when the European motor manufacturers struggled to re-convert their factories from building tanks, guns and aeroplanes, back to private cars, almost every 'new' model was based on the designs of the late 1930s. The supply of new cars was so restricted that almost anything on four wheels could be sold. Outdated models like MG's TC were snapped up as soon as they rolled off the production line.

All over Europe the shortages had eased by the middle of the 1950s, and a normal supply-demand balance returned. It was at about this time that the car makers stopped looking so hard for exports, stopped making the cars which were simple and straightforward, and began to look ahead. It was predictable that at about this time all manner of strange chassis layouts, styles, and marketing combinations were tried.

By the mid-1950s, too, the sports car revolution had got under way. For the first ten years after the end of the war, most sports cars had been in short supply, had been expensive, and had certainly not been aimed at a large market. Cars like the TR2, the Austin-Healey 100, the MGA and the Alfa Romeo Giulietta Sprint changed all that. By the end of the decade, therefore, the supply of sporting cars was larger than ever before, as was the choice between models. Most important of all, there was usually a sports car for every customer – rich or not so rich, conventionally-minded or technically adventurous.

By 1961, too, almost every basic layout which we now recognise as feasible for a sporting car had already been tried, though the concept of a mid-engined machine with a transversely-positioned engine was no more than a twinkle in the eye of designers already bedazzled by the brilliance of Alec Issigonis's new Mini. Even in chassis design, every layout worth pursuing had also been tried.

If the engine is the heart and soul of a sporting car, then the chassis frame and its related structure is the essential skeleton. It was in chassis design, rather than in engine layouts, where the greatest changes had occurred in the 1950s, and which would set the acceptable standards in the 1960s. In the 1930s and the 1940s almost every sporting car

11

in the world had been built around a simple ladder-type chassis frame, usually with independent front suspension (unless it was British, where such new-fangled ideas took longer to be accepted), almost always with a beam rear axle, and often with less-than-rigid side members. Post-war designs, at least, acknowledge the superiority of box-section members in terms of beam *and* torsional rigidity, but were otherwise completely recognisable descendants of 10 or 20 years earlier.

Mass-production models like the Triumph TR2 and the Austin-Healey 100 had been designed around box-section conventional frames, mainly because such components were easily developed, cheap to manufacture, and likely to be trouble-free in service. The changes – the revolution, even – came insidiously, but dramatically, by way of one-off and limited-production competition cars. Four different types of frame had evolved – three being suitable for small-scale manufacture in series, and one only possible for the manufacturer with great capital and press-tool resources available. These types were the large-section tubular chassis, the 'space frame' type, the platform frame – and the unit-construction shell often rather inaccurately known as a 'monocoque.'

I should dispose of the space-frame concept at once. Those with relatively short memories might suggest that it was Colin Chapman (and his Lotus cars) which started this trend, but the truth is rather more prosaic. Multi-tube frames had evolved for aeroplane structures during the second world war, to a very sophisticated degree, and these were no more than modern developments of the frames which had been in use in air-frames for many years.

For a car therefore, the concept of a space-frame was not a new engineering idea, but merely an interesting adaptation of aeronautical practice. For a car, too, the basic requirement of a space-frame usually had to be abandoned, because of practical requirements. To be truly efficient a space-frame had to be completely three-dimensional, with straight tubes from junction to junction, on which bending stresses or torsional forces were never applied. In the complicated environment of a car's structure, this was never practically possible, due to the need to install (and, subsequently, extract) bulky engines and those boring necessities called passengers!

The first demonstrably successful space-frame car was the Mercedes-Benz 300SL sports-racing car of 1952, which was refined and put into production as the legendary 'gullwing' model of 1954. Colin Chapman's Lotus 6 of the early 1950s was by no means as 'pure' a concept; his Lotus 7 road car was more advanced, but the uncompromised space-frame layouts were confined to sports-racing machines like the Lotus 9/11/15 models, and to copycat cars like the little Lolas which followed.

When the 300SL went into production, the pundits suggested that it would start a trend. They were quite wrong. Even the mighty Mercedes-Benz organisation soon realised that they had backed the wrong concept, modified their design (for the 300SL Roadster of 1957) to make the car more practical, and laid plans to replace it with something more versatile in the 1960s. At the start of the 1960s, therefore, the 300SL, which was still in production, was the only example of a space-frame road car, though there were several small-production machines (like Britain's Gilbern) which offered cheap imitations of the layout, where the niceties of stress distribution were severely compromised by practical considerations.

The large-tube type of frame, on the other hand, found many friends, because it had already been shown to be extremely cheap and simple to build. Traditional frames, after all, relied on channel or box section members being prepared on press-tools by specialist suppliers. A tubular frame, on the other hand, could be knocked up on the simplest of jigs, from easily available supplies of straight seamless tubes. Any concern with simple bending fixtures, welding gear, and skilled mechanics, could tackle such things – and many of them did.

Large-tube frames even had the patina of racing respectability for a time (until Mercedes-Benz and – in another technological direction – Jaguar came along to change everything). Alfa-Romeo's Type 158/159 models, and the Ferraris which eventually overwhelmed them, both used simple tubular frames, and it was only the more advanced three-dimensional frames of the later 1950s (which on Ferrari, Lancia and Maserati Grand Prix cars were decidedly *not* space frames) which ousted them.

By that time, racing sports cars like the Aston Martin DB3S, the big Maseratis, and the vee-12 Ferraris, had all shown that such simple frames could do an extremely adequate job. More and more limited-production road cars came to be built in this manner. Indeed, the large-diameter tubular frame almost became the hallmark of the Italian (or Italian-derived) sporting car of the early 1960s. All Ferrari and Maserati road cars, the Facel Vegas, and models like the AC Ace (which had evolved from the *original* concept of an Italian racing sports car), used such frames. To this day there are new-model Supercars being built around such layouts – the Ferrari Dino 308 cars being perfect examples.

Platform-type chassis were something of a half-way house between the simple tubular frame, and the unit-construction bodyshell. In some cases they appeared as a result of direct *ad hoc* improvement of a tubular frame from an old model, and in others they were laid out from scratch. In all cases, however, their makers were conscious of the need to allow for coach-built bodyshells, or perhaps glass-fibre shells of their own manufacture, to be mounted on this base, so the rolling chassis of a platform-framed car had to be self-supporting in every sense.

Such frames were at the same time more complex, more expensive to prepare for production, and more rigid than a simple tubular frame, and in many cases they could also be arranged to give a lower seating position and therefore the possibility of a lower and sleeker body style. The perfect example of a platform chassis was provided by Porsche in quantity-production terms, or by Jensen in the bespoke sector. The Porsche platform, inspired by the VW Beetle layout, was a pressed-steel structure for the 356 range, while the Jensen layout relied to some extent on large-diameter tubing. It is significant that wherever a marque has carried on through the 1960s and 1970s, relying on separate or coachbuilt bodies, in most cases the platform-style of chassis has been preferred.

Even at the end of the 1950s, when tooling costs were already high but not yet astronomical, the decision to use a chassisless layout on a new model was not to be taken lightly. I use the term 'chassisless' because 'monocoque' really refers to shells where even the skin is fully stressed, and where cut-outs for access to the engine bay or the passenger compartment are tiny; most unit-construction shells of the day (and even those of later years) are considerably less than perfect in this respect.

Not only did the question of considerable investment have to be weighed carefully at project definition stage, but there was also the consideration of becoming 'locked in' by this investment to a given chassis layout or body style for a considerable body style. Sports car customers, their likes and dislikes, and their somewhat volatile loyalties, were still thought to be somewhat variable, and no manufacturer liked to be in a situation where he had to go on selling the same type of car for a long period to get his money back.

Even among the quantity-production machines, therefore, the first years of the

1960s showed widely differing approaches to this problem. Although BMC still made the MGA with a massive separate chassis frame, they already had a unit-construction MGB model under development, and they had been building Sprites with such a form of body/chassis unit since 1958. They were, however, about to re-style the Sprite at considerable cost on what was almost a self-supporting platform frame; on the other hand, they knew that the Austin-Healey 3000 would have to be replaced and not merely re-styled, as its combined chassis and body (the two, of effectively separate design, were welded securely together on assembly) was not easily modifiable.

Alfa Romeo, with the Giulietta variants, Volvo with the P1800, and Sunbeam with the new Alpine, had already taken the decision to use a pressed-steel body shell, but in the case of the Alfa-Romeo an extra complication had been drawn in. The Italian manufacturers — Alfa Romeo and Lancia in particular — designed their pressed-steel structures to be built with more than one superstructure. Giuliettas, Appias, 2000s and Flaminias all relied on a mundane touring car underframe, with the pressed-steel superstructures being provided by the styling *and* production efforts of one or other of the Italian coachbuilding specialists.

In many ways Triumph was the 'odd man out' at this time. Their TR3A, which was still selling very well in North America, was due to be replaced by a new model before long, but this was to have a separate chassis (and this, in turn, would be replaced by an entirely new frame in 1965), while a new small Triumph sports car, the Spitfire, was also being developed around a separate backbone style frame.

On the other hand, Jaguar were about to jump from a classic frame layout on the XK150 to a complex tubular and unit-construction assembly for the sensational new E-Type, which was logical, while Lotus were thinking of abandoning their Elite's glass-fibre monocoque for a new and more simple backbone frame for the Elan.

It seemed to be generally agreed, however, that the days of the old-fashioned box-section chassis frame were numbered, and unless the company concerned was either very backward-looking or very traditional for good marketing reasons, they were expected to disappear during the 1960s. If Daimler's SP250 had carried on into another model we might have expected them to abandon their TR3A look-alike frame for something more advanced, but we would undoubtedly have been shocked if Morgan had ever proposed to drop their age-old layout in which the side members were not even boxed, but of a Z-section.

Just for the moment there was not much innovation apparent regarding engine and driveline layouts, where the classic front-engine/rear-drive system was dominant. Even though, at the beginning of the 1960s, every modern competition car maker was busily evolving a rear-engined or mid-engined car (even Ferrari were proposing to run mid-engined single-seaters in 1961), makers of road cars were not in such a hurry to change.

Even at that time it was clear to any engineer who specialised in laying out the bare bones of a new model that a mid-engine would take away a good deal of the space he needed for passenger or luggage accommodation, and it was equally clear that to hang a heavy engine out in the tail might lead to all manner of serious roadholding and stability problems.

The rear-engined cars in existence existed by courtesy of the mass-production cars from which they drew their units. Tiny competition machines like the Abarths only used rear engines because they used Fiat 600 components modified at times almost out of all recognition, while the newly-formed Alpine-Renault concern relied on the rear-engined Renault 4CV and Dauphine models for their major items.

The vast majority of companies, however, put their engines in the nose, gearboxes in unit with engines, and final drives either in beam axles or as chassis-mounted units if de Dion or independent rear suspension was provided. It was not that many would not have wanted to put their gearboxes at the rear (in Alfetta or Porsche 924/928 style), but that they simply could not find these in mass-production and easily-available quantities. Independent firms like Jensen had to rely on the gearbox which came with the engine — in their case an Austin — while quantity-production types like MG, Alfa-Romeo, Triumph and Jaguar all used modified (in some cases not even that) versions of touring car components. Then, as now, the 'building block' approach to economical design was well-developed.

The gearboxes themselves were almost invariably four-speed designs with unsynchronised 'crash' first gears, though a five-speed cluster would sometimes be a high-cost feature of the design and usually an extra at that. Alfa-Romeo liked five-speed gearboxes at an early stage, and never even looked at electrically controlled overdrives, which were a very popular alternative for which a quick-witted manufacturer might charge a great deal of money as an optional extra. Automatic transmissions, even as extras, were rarely seen except on cars like the Jaguar XK150, for which transatlantic sales mattered so very much. On the smaller-engined, cheaper, quantity-production machines such a fitting was usually brushed aside with horror.

All cars had independent front suspension (not until Panther produced their strange J72s, which were anachronisms in many ways, did a beam front axle come back), but surprisingly few had independent rear suspension to match. In the case of the budget-priced machines this was a matter of cost-control, and in the case of many others it was because the engineers had not the time nor the inclination to develop their own schemes. It did not help that the Supercars like Aston Martin's DB4 or Ferrari's 250GT made do with heavy live axles and often simple methods of locating them. Experience gained in the 1970s convinced many eminent engineers that a really properly-located live axle could provide roadholding and ride which was superior to many mediocre or casually-designed independent systems; at the beginning of the 1960s, however, many cars were supplied with live axles merely because their rivals had one, and because the product could be sold in this state.

Very few cars were being supplied with a choice of engines, though several were on offer in more than one state of tune. Tune-up firms prospered all over Europe, so that the purchaser — say — of a Fiat, Renault, VW, Ford or BMC-engined car could spend money to have his engine made more powerful, less reliable, and more profligate with its fuel. You could buy a Giulietta, an XK150, a Sprite, an Elite or a Porsche with more than one engine tune; the cars offering a choice of complete engines were usually to be found relying on proprietary designs, though Triumph (2.0 or 2.2-litre units), AC (AC or Bristol units), MG (pushrod or twin-cam engines) and Austin-Healey (normal or supercharged Sprites) were honourable quantity-production exceptions. The concept of the Capri (1.3-litre to 3.0-litre engines, in straight or vee-formation) was still years ahead.

Several companies were still able to make and use their own engines, but as the investment involved in machine tools was rising fast (and engines themselves were becoming more complex) the number of *new* designs under development was slowing down fast. Lotus, as ever, were proving to be as inventive as anyone else, by proposing to convert a Ford pushrod unit to twin overhead camshafts; on this occasion, however, they had not invented a new process, as Abarth had already thought of this for their own purposes.

15

It was still possible, however, for AC to make a small number of cars fitted with the light-alloy six-cylinder 2-litre engine of their own manufacture, and for Bristol to supply their own needs and those of AC with six-cylinder 2-litre units. Aston Martin had only recently revealed a brand-new and extremely powerful 3.7-litre straight-six, while Daimler were building the SP250 with an exquisite but only partly tooled 2.55-litre vee-8. Facel Vega were just taking the first steps towards making their own (twin-cam) engines for the very first time, and could not know that this was shortly to lead them towards bankruptcy.

While, on the one hand, Ferrari and Maserati seemed to be able to make enormously powerful and technically advanced engines on the very minimum of tooling, firms like Bristol and Jensen were beginning to look round desperately for new sources of increased power. Packaged power from Detroit was a concept often talked about, but not yet adopted. The Gordon GT prototype, with its Chevrolet Corvette vee-8 engine, was a pointer to the future.

In terms of body construction, coachbuilding by traditional methods (of steel or light-alloy panelling on a framework of wood or sometimes of steel) was on the decline, that of coachbuilding on a more methodical and partly tooled basis was on the up and up, while the idea of using glass-fibre bodyshells instead was definitely on the increase. The problem with using glass-fibre, however, was not one of strength (Lotus, with their monocoque Elite had already disproved that one), and not entirely one of the considerable space required to allow curing of new shells, but one of 'image'. Too many cars had been built in the 1950s with flimsy and scruffy glass-fibre shells, particularly in Britain, and any car maker with established traditions did not want to 'step down', as he thought, to the twilight world of glass-fibre construction. Lotus, however, Alpine-Renault, TVR, Daimler and Jensen were all well on the way to altering that 'image' problem, and would soon be joined by Reliant, and even by Morgan for a time, to confirm the acceptability of the material. But it would not be for more than ten years before the truly patrician Supercar manufacturers like Ferrari and BMW adopted glass-fibre coachwork.

A good few cars were being sold in kit form, especially where this could be done at a cheaper selling price to attract more sales. In effect, a car supplied as a kit of parts had fewer man-hours of assembly built in to its costs, and in Britain at least it could also be sold without the imposition of purchase (sales) taxes. Most such cars, however, were of the lower-priced and mechanically simple variety. It is easy to see why the self-assembly of a Lotus Elite or a TVR was a practical proposition, but that (even had it been possible) the building of a Ferrari or an Aston-Martin in one's own garage would be an entirely different and rather perilous proposition. At best the kit-car business only appealed to those people who probably could not afford the model in question if it had been supplied completely ready for the road, and this meant that some cars were only supplied to a rather marginal market.

The technical, marketing and legislative revolution, however, was yet to come. Although the BMC Mini had heralded the front-wheel-drive revolution, and Ford were not to take an active interest in motor sport until 1962/1963, the first stirrings of a 'consumers' movement' were afoot in North America, and the Japanese continued to expand their motor industry and its interests at a disturbing rate. The complacency often shown by the Europeans, who thought that they, and they alone, had a right to make popular sports cars, was about to be shattered.

Chapter Two

The Breed Evolves – 20 years of progress

For the sports car, the miracle of the 1960s and 1970s was that it managed to survive at all as a species. There were times when everything – economic, political, moral and legislative – seemed to be against this. In a sombre world where the motor car was rapidly becoming known only as a working machine, and not as a thing of pleasure, the self-indulgent purchase of a sporting car made no logical sense at all. How, for instance, could the use of a 170mph two-seater Ferrari or Lamborghini be balanced against the need to squeeze whole families into miserable little 30bhp saloon cars?

Hundreds of thousands of customers, fortunately, either didn't realise this or didn't care, and bought one anyway. Now, as the 1980s begin, sports car sales are strong precisely *because* such machines are usually neither utilitarian nor space- and fuel-efficient. To buy a sports car is a motorist's red-blooded reaction against an unfrivolous world and its grey-faced politicians.

Nevertheless, in the last 20 years there have been great changes on the sporting scene, in Europe and elsewhere, not least in the type and make of cars being built. In 1961 a sports car, to carry any real cachet, had to be designed and built in Europe, preferably with an open top, only two seats, and came from a relatively small and independent concern. Today's sports car, which is more numerous and more effective in almost every way, often comes from Japan, usually has a fixed coupe roof, sometimes has four seats, and may be built under the auspices of one of the world's industrial giants. For the 1960s and 1970s, if not totally destructive of the type, were the years in which specialisation and hand-building was almost squeezed out, and in which real quantity-production and multi-model product planning came in. If the single-model MGA or Triumph TR2 was typical of the 1950s, it is the huge range of Ford Capris or even Porsche 911s which is typical of the later years. And as the ranges widened, so did the tuning business contract.

Before trying to trace the more important skeins of development through the period covered by this book, it is worth emphasising just how much of the change has been due to the legislative burden, and particularly due to the special requirements of the United States. It should never be forgotten that without the existence of the potentially enormous North American market for sports cars, many European manufacturers would have been out of business years ago. The real dollar-conscious makers like MG, Triumph, Jaguar, and Alfa-Romeo make no secret of this.

The modern trend towards ecology-consciousness began in North America, and began to crystallise in terms of new laws at the beginning of the 1960s. By 1967 the stranglehold of exhaust emission control, ushered in by one or other of Congress's 'Clean Air' acts, had been established, and with very few pauses was steadily made more severe with each passing year. It was not long before eminent engineers were proclaiming, without exaggeration, that they were being asked to ensure that their engines exhausted cleaner air than had been inhaled in the first place!

At the same time, an over-zealous legislature, spurred on by the noisy and at times only half-accurate pronouncements of Ralph Nader's disciples, began to pass ream after ream of laws controlling everything from visibility standards to crash resistance, from the marking of tyres to the performance of brakes, and from lighting standards to the flammability of materials used in the seats. By the end of the 1970s it seemed that design departments were becoming subservient to the legal specialists in their companies, and it became necessary to learn the United States laws even before the styling of a new car commenced.

In the short term this led to some very strange interim machines being sold in North America (the bumper standards, requiring a 'no damage' performance in 5mph accidents, produced some fearsomely ugly new protruberances at first), and in all cases it led to the performance being sharply reduced. The problem was that it was difficult to convince the domestic buyer that his sports car had to be subservient to North American requirements, because a British, French, German or Italian enthusiast could not always accept that many more machines were sold on the other side of the Atlantic, and that it was only reasonable that a new model should be designed with that in mind.

Although the basic shape of most European sports cars changed along with motoring fashions (and, in particular, took account of the wedge profile as both aerodynamically desirable and potentially attractive), and to look after the new North American laws, the almost complete disappearance of the truly open sports car came about for several reasons.

To own an open car, in which the hood, side windows (or screens) *and* the windscreen could all be taken down, had seemed very desirable in the 1930s and even in the 1940s, when cruising speeds were normally no more than 60mph, and when traffic densities were thin. Even by the middle of the 1950s, however, when motorways (in Europe at least, if not yet in Britain) were spreading across the land, when performance had raised many cars' cruising pace to at least 80mph, and when a good deal more obnoxious exhaust fumes were being pumped out in heavy traffic, the magic of a truly open car began to disappear. At 50 or 60mph, it might have been pleasant enough for your girlfriend's hair to be blown about in the slipstream; at 80mph or even more, it could be purgatory.

At about the same time, sports car owners began to demand the same standards of heating and ventilation as those enjoyed by buyers of mere GT or even touring cars. No longer were they prepared to swathe themselves in bulky layers of clothing in winter, or to swelter in the heat of a Riviera summer. Open cars could never acclimatise their interior in a satisfactory manner, even when equipped with wind-up windows, and as a halfway house a large number of models were sold with an optional hardtop, supplied either by the factory or by one of several proprietary concerns.

18   Although it was not strictly necessary for a unit-construction shell to have a fixed

metal roof, it helped, and this together with the demands of the new safety laws helped to bring the fixed head coupe into prominence. At one time, at the end of the 1960s, it looked as if proposed North American laws concerning passenger protection in roll-over accidents would effectively outlaw the open top sports car for ever. New models like the Triumph TR7, the Fiat X1/9 and the Lancia Monte Carlo/Scorpion (and, from Japan, the Datsun 240Z) were all designed with fixed tops at first. These laws, however, were not completely enacted, and those manufacturers locked into expensive tooling for coupe models cursed their luck.

Already, however, an ingenious halfway house towards open-car motoring had been developed, which gave the fresh air without the draughts, and without the aggravation of a fold-away hood and sticks; this, quite wrongly, has now become known as the 'Targa' roof. In fact the idea of selling a car with a coupe style in which the entire centre roof panel could be removed by unscrewing a few bolts had been invented by Triumph in 1962!

It was the Michelotti-styled TR4, with its optional 'Surrey' top feature, which first provided the customer with the choice of having a snug closed coupe, or of having the roof panel off (and, in Triumph's case, replaced at will by the PVC 'Surrey' top). For reasons still unknown to Triumph, this idea never really caught on, so that when Porsche introduced their 'Targa' version of the 911s in 1967 it was hailed as a great and thoughtful German invention.

More and more cars – the Fiat X1/9, the Lancia Monte Carlo, the Beta Spider are all good examples – adopted this feature, or at least offered the luxury of a good steel sliding sun roof.

The fixed head coupe sports car, however, had come to stay, and had really been heralded by nothing less important than the Giulietta Sprint of 1954. Almost every new sporting car of the 1970s had a fixed roof, and the famine in open-top cars was such that obviously obsolete models like the MGB and the Fiat 124 Sport Spider continue to sell in large numbers due to the lack of competition. The Triumph TR7, which has now been re-engineered in soft-top form, is likely to upset that delicate balance.

The boundary between a fixed-roof sports car and the load-carrying car began to be blurred way back in the 1950s, when Aston-Martin introduced their DB2/4 in 1953, in which the 2 + 2 seating was combined with a fastback style, and an opening rear window which gave access to the 'boot' or loading area. This innovation, however, did not start a trend, and it was not until 1961 and the arrival of the sensationally-sleek Jaguar E-Type coupe that the DB2/4 had an imitator. Even then it was worth noting that the E-Type was originally only to have been an open car, and that the sweeping lines of the coupe evolved relatively late in the development programme.

The next two imitators were British – one, the MGB GT, having Pininfarina touches to a basically Abingdon design, and the other, Triumph's GT6, being very much of a mini-E-Type in Triumph's thoughts. Both had upward-opening hatches, and loading platforms behind their seats, but it was still not the time for the world of motoring to take notice.

The breakthrough came in 1968, with the launch of the Reliant Scimitar GTE. This new model, designed by Reliant's styling consultants, Ogle, combined all the grace of a limited-production sporting coupe with the practicality of a load-carrier. Not only did the car look smart and sporting, but its roof line was carried back horizontally without dipping sharply down towards the rear bumper, and was linked to a near-vertical loading hatch which incorporated the rear window; it also had folding rear seats to allow the loading area to be increased still more.

European Sports & GT Cars

This was the new model which had been needed, and it was soon copied by Volvo, who converted their 1800E coupe into an 1800ES 'sporting estate'. The true accolades, however, followed with the announcement of the Ford Capri Mk 2s (which were so much more versatile that the original mini-Mustang models they replaced), by the Alfetta coupes, and by the Lancia Beta HPE, all of which did the same thing but with considerably more style and panache. Even cars on the verge of the Supercar class − like the Lotus Elite − have now taken to the hatchback theme.

In the period under study, styles have gradually and noticeably become sleeker and more wind-cheating (North American legislation permitting), and have progressed through a rounded and superficially more aerodynamically efficient phase to a more sharp-edge, often wedge-shaped motif. It came as a shock to many of us to learn from Jaguar that the XJ-S of 1975 had a better drag coefficient than the wind-tunnel-evolved Jaguar E-Type which it 'replaced', but the performance capabilities of comparable models back up this claim. Styling tended to follow fashion in motor racing, and it is a straightforward and fairly instructive business to compare cars like the De Tomaso Mangusta and Pantera models with the Ford GT40s from which they seemed to draw their inspiration, and the wedge-styled TR7s, X1/9s and Ferrari 308s from the many such chisel-nosed sports racing cars of the early 1970s.

It was a surprise that virtually no-one copied the exaggerated but undeniably effective lines of the E-Type Jaguar, but it was no surprise at all to find many designers hanging on every hint, flourish and change in emphasis of the Italian styling houses. Firms like Pininfarina, Bertone and − in the 1970s − Italdesign, had an enormous influence on the European scene, if not through direct consultation at project stage, then at the many motor shows where their 'dream' cars were first shown. Some dream cars without marketing intent finished up in production as a result of their first showing − Bertone's Lancia Stratos and Italdesign's Lotus Esprit being perfect examples.

But a firm with a saleable theme often found a sale for it in more than one place. At the beginning of the 1960s Bertone's coupes for NSU, Simca and ASA (the mini-Ferrari) were all obvious derivatives of the same style, while someone like Frua might actually be using the same basic framework for shells provided in small numbers to Maserati and AC.

In the field of aerodynamics, it took time for the discovery that a well-shaped but blunt obstruction under the nose might actually improve the under-body aerodynamics (and wasn't it a tiny British 'tuning shop' which first proved this on bread and butter cars?), and that a tail spoiler could not only trim the rear-end lift, but also improve the drag characteristics and bring a little *machismo* into the life of a car. Only one car − the BMW 3.0CSL Coupe − actually brought extreme drag-cheating aids to the showrooms, and was soon warned off by the safety-conscious and spoil-sport West German authorities.

There was a gradual but persistent move away from making pure two-seater cars, to providing at least 2 + 2 accommodation. When Ferrari first showed their 250GT 2 + 2 in 1961 it made such seating layouts respectable. Quite soon, cars like the Lamborghini 350GT and the AC 428 began to look like self-indulgent anachronisms. In the 1970s, therefore, the only all-new cars to offer simple two-seater accommodation were either inflicted with an old-fashioned chassis which could not accommodate more, were backward-looking in a nostalgic sort of way, or had mid-engined layouts, which made everything more difficult.

The structure to support the developing style in bodies − so vitally interesting to the engineer and the technical journalist, but much less vital to the customer and the marketing man — changed gradually but firmly from the use of a separate chassis to a self-supporting pressed-steel structure, either in the shape of a complete unit-construction bodyshell or at least as a platform frame. I have already noted the links between the types in my opening chapter on the cars which were sold at the beginning of the period.

Apart from the more efficient use of materials, of computer analysis to determine stress paths and to optimise sections to match these, and of (not before time) some deep thought directed at anti-corrosion treatment, there were no radically new structural developments in the 1960s and 1970s. By the end of the 1970s, it is true, a unit-construction shell was much more sparing of material in areas which could not benefit beam or torsional rigidity, but weight gains had often been nullified by the compulsory addition of massive beams inside the doors and monstrous roll-over and bumper support structures to satisfy North American legislation. The economics of body production usually meant that cars for sale in Europe had to be built with USA-style bodyshells.

In regard to suspensions and steering, it became clear that most motorists demanded four-wheel independent suspension, even though some very experienced engineers were sure that this meant sacrificing the best in ride and handling at the rear. As with the disc brakes of the 1950s, and the horsepower claims of any era, an all-independent suspension layout was something which the marketing men could trumpet to the skies. It comes as a shock to many of us to realise that for some years in the 1960s the Ferrari Supercars had the crudest possible beam axle rear suspension, and that best-selling modern designs like Ford's Capri still do.

Putting the engine in the tail, or putting a gearbox in unit with the final drive, automatically meant that a more sophisticated layout was needed, so cars like the Porsche 924s, 928s, and Alfetta GTs all benefitted from this. Cars with classic layouts, no matter how expensive, sometimes still kept well clear of independent rear suspension — Aston Martin's Vantage and their Lagonda being typical, though their de Dion layout was a good compromise. But once Ferrari had adopted an all-wishbone layout for the 275GTB of 1964, and had been aped by Maserati, Lamborghini, and other equally precocious Supercars, the trend was obvious. Fiat's X1/9, Lancia's Betas and the Monte Carlo all joined in, so that by the middle of the 1970s a car like the MGB was not only beginning to look, but to feel, old-fashioned. Among the many gaffes committed by Triumph, in marketing if not in technical terms, was to equip their all-new TR7 with a live rear axle; in competition with the Datsun 240Z, one wonders how they dared to do it?

As to steering, the story is simple. Those who had not already adopted rack-and-pinion steering, a system not only mechanically efficient, but extremely precise, and very sparing of space in the front suspension area, usually hastened to do so. If the car was so heavy as to need power assistance, then it was usually provided — and one is proud to note that this development was a credit to the British motor industry. It remains a mystery as to the continuing popularity of recirculating ball or worm-and-nut steering in some quarters, as such installations are invariably more costly, more bulky *and* less effective than the rack-and-pinion alternative. The change from one to the other layout in mid-model run is rarely made, so the adoption of rack-and-pinion by Rolls-Royce for their Camargue in 1977 was something of an event.

The story of braking changes is equally straightforward. Disc brakes had been introduced on European road cars by Citroen in 1955, and on sports cars by Triumph (on the TR3) just a year later. By the beginning of the 1960s many British, and a growing number of European, sports cars had adopted disc brakes in quantity-production. Jensen (first, in tiny numbers) and Jaguar made four-wheel discs popular, and both Lancia and Renault surprised us all by fitting four-wheel-discs to their very mundane new models at the beginning of the 1960s. Companies like Porsche (who demanded meticulous testing of anything before they would adopt it) and Ferrari (who couldn't be bothered, it seemed) were strangely reluctant to join the trend, but by the mid-1960s no proper sports or sporting car was sold without having discs, at least on its front wheels.

Because the size of roadwheels continued to trend persistently downwards, and rim widths inexorably widened, it meant that the new-fangled brakes were at one and the same time limited in size, and in the amount of cooling ventilation they received. It was not long, therefore, before the ventilated and drilled discs seen on out-and-out sports racing cars of the 1960s became standard wear for sports cars with a great deal of performance in the 1970s. Times, indeed, have changed, for ventilated front discs are now found on vehicles as mundane and work-a-day as the heavier Ford Transit commercial vehicles!

After initial flirtations with rear disc brakes, which proved to be unnecessary on many not-very-fast machines, and for which it was often difficult to provide an effective pad-operated handbrake, most smaller and relatively slow sporting cars settled for front discs and rear drums, while those cars retaining rear wheel disc brakes often matched those with tiny drum brakes, under separate handbrake control, in the hub of the discs.

As the performance of the Supercars continued to rise (membership of the Supercar league demanded a 140mph maximum in 1960, a 160mph maximum by 1970, and the ability to maintain this speed in spite of exhaust emission controls by the end of the decade), along with the expectations of road behaviour, the performance of tyres had to keep pace. Not many cars had high-speed radial-ply tyres in 1961 – and, indeed, the only people making radial-ply tyres of any sort were Michelin (the pioneers, with their X) and Pirelli (with the Cintura). High-speed crossplys were neither as grippy, as forgiving, or as compliant as they should have been.

Paradoxically enough, radial-ply tyres were adopted on quantity-production and specialist models before they found favour on more expensive and faster cars. This was because there were then certain problems of noise and vibration transmission which the makers of cheaper cars found easier to reconcile than did the makers of Supercars. By the closing years of the 1960s, however, it was a stubborn and inward-looking firm which had not begun to fit radials to its cars; in Britain, Jensen came late to this standard, and so did Rolls-Royce, while for years Aston Martin saw fit to insist that its own choice of high-speed Avons were better than anything else.

On conventional front engined cars wheel rims were invariably of the same width at front and rear, but on cars with a big rearward weight bias (and a suitably high performance) it was usually found that bigger tyres and fatter rims would be specified at the rear. It is an instructive business to chart the development and the trend in rim widths and tyre sizes on cars which have been in production (and have been updated at regular intervals) for many years. A comparison between the wheels and tyres fitted to the Porsche 911 Turbo of 1979 with the spindly equivalents of the 1964 911 is startling, and in this case the wheelarches and the entire tail have had to be re-styled to make the changes possible. On a Supercar, particularly a mid-engined model, space for stowage was usually at a premium, and to reconcile this with the need for a spare wheel and tyre many models are now sold with the flimsiest possible 'space-saver' type of spare. It is a frighteningly expensive thought, too, that the tyres capable of looking after a 170mph maximum speed are so delicately put together that they must be renewed and not repaired, after a puncture!

During the 1960s there was a rapid switch away from wire-spoke wheels towards sculptured pressed-steel disc wheels, or – on the more expensive and exotic cars – to the use of cast-alloy wheels. One remembers that when the MG TD had been announced in 1950 with disc wheels instead of the wires used on the obsolete TC, there had been an outcry from the traditionalists. In the 1960s however, there was no such outcry; as with the decline of the open-top car, so with that of the wire-spoke wheel. Performance had risen so much, and the demands on the suspension become so much greater, that a wire-spoke wheel was no longer rigid enough to do a proper job. Not only was it flexible, and likely to go 'out of round', but it was also a real pig to keep clean.

Wire wheels, therefore, hung on for many models with which they were inextricably linked (like, for instance, the Austin-Healey 3000), but even cars like the MGB and the TR6 changed their allegiance in mid-model run. Not only were cast-alloy wheels light in weight and very rigid, but they were yet another detail for the stylists to ply their wares upon, and they had the functional advantage of being able to conduct heat from the brakes very rapidly away from the scene. As in so many cases, it had been motor racing which precipitated this development, with cars like the Jaguar D-Type, being equipped with centre-lock pressed-alloy wheels, and with F1 cars adopting light-alloy wheels just a few years later. Ferrari, the great traditionalist, was the last to stick to wire-spoke wheels on his single-seaters, but had fallen into line with fashion by 1963.

I have already touched on the question of the basic engine position in the previous section, but it is an appropriate moment to trace the significant moves in the 1960s. When they opened, the majority of cars had front-mounted engines, invariably in line with the chassis, though a significant minority had engine/transmission installations in the tail, because these had been taken from mass-production cars already using such a layout.

At the time, there were no mid-engined cars in production, although Grand Prix racing was already dominated by cars like the Coopers and Ferraris; after 1960, no Grand Prix was won by a front-engined car, and this led the trend-conscious sports car manufacturers to think.

Few, however, were willing to go for a rear-engined car, as they could usually not afford to build an engine which was light enough to live in that position, nor find a suitable proprietary unit. Porsche dominated the rear-engined sports car scene for many years (as, indeed, they still do with the 911 models), but only because of their design philosophy then lined-up with having a rear-mounted engine, and because many design and development man-hours were poured in to making the system at least tolerable. In general, however, the problem of weight distribution and handling was insuperable.

In the 1960s and early 1970s, many manufacturers investigated the problem of developing cars with mid-mounted engines (in other words, with engines ahead of the line of the rear wheels, but behind the seats), though few of these projects came to fruition. MG's experience, of laying out the bare bones of a Maxi-engined mid-engined car to replace their MGB, but of abandoning it, was probably typical. Apart from the little Unipower GT, which was no more than a hand-built 'special' using BMC Mini parts, the Matra-Bonnet Djet was probably the first to sell in any numbers, while the Lamborghini Miura was the first such Supercar, and the Lotus Europa was the first to be delivered in rather greater quantities. By 1970, however, there were mid-engined production cars from Ferrari (the Dino), Matra (the M530 models) and from de Tomaso (the Mangusta), but all of these paled into insignificance compared with the Porsche 914 models which had been announced in 1969.

It is probably not going too far to suggest that the fortunes of the 914 probably put back the acceptance of the mid-engined car by the sports-car buying public by a few years, and those of the Lancia Monte Carlo in recent years have not helped. In each case, although there was nothing basically wrong with the engineering of the cars, they had to sell alongside (and against) less advanced creations — the 911s and the Betas respectively. In each case the public decided that they could not put up with the severe lack of space for themselves or for their luggage, the inability to carry more than two people — not even a dog or a small child could find space — nor with the seemingly inescapable losses in refinement and behaviour which the layout brought with it. In each case the mid-engined cars were withdrawn, and the internal competition forged ahead undaunted.

Such a failure to penetrate would have been bad enough if it had not been emphasised by Porsche's gradual rejection of the rear-engined philosophy completely. After the 914 had gone, the 924 arrived; the change of just one digit in the title meant a complete turn-round in their thinking. Out went the adherence to mid-mounted air-cooled engines, and in came a new model with water-cooling and a front-mounted unit. When the 928 Supercar followed the 924, it merely rubbed further salt into the wound.

Although the delicious little Fiat X1/9 continues to make mincemeat of all sweeping statements about the type, it is a fact that no other manufacturer has seen fit to try to make and sell so many cars with a mid-mounted engine, and one doubts if anyone will. If the X1/9 was any more than a tiny but nicely detailed toy, it might have a much harder time.

In twenty years, there was gradual but not very spectacular improvement in the engines fitted to European sporting cars. Felix Wankel's revolutionary (in more senses than one) engine was only fitted into the NSU Wankel Spider as a trial run for the Ro80, and has not been repeated by that firm, while the Mercedes-Benz C111 models were only publicity-conscious prototypes, and never intended to be anything else.

Nor has any dramatic new type of piston engine been ushered in during the 1960s and 1970s, as both Alfa-Romeo and Jaguar had already made the twin-cam cylinder head layout commonplace by then, and Ferrari's vee-12s were well-enough known if in rather limited numbers. Fuel injection — first on a few Maseratis and rather more Mercedes-Benz 300SLs, later on Porsche 911s and TR5/TR6 models — later spread to cars as diverse as Alfa Romeo's USA-specification models, the Renault 17TS/Gordini cars, the Volvo 1800E and to thousands of Porsches, but surprisingly enough has not often been found essential as a means to meeting pollution-control standards.

Also surprising, in a period when specific power outputs continued to rise steadily, and when such things were adopted rapidly in Grand Prix engines, was the fact that four-valve cylinder head breathing layouts never made a proper breakthrough. Such engines were to be found in limited numbers in the Ford Escort RS1600/RS1800, Vauxhall Chevette 2300HS and Fiat 131 Abarth 'homologation specials', but the current 2.0-litre Lotus engine is the only proper production unit in this category. Surprisingly, not even the TR7 (where such a derivative of its engine is already in production for the Dolomite Sprint saloon) has yet been given a 16-valve engine.

Turbocharging, of course, provided a real talking point during the 1970s. By the end of the 1950s, and throughout the 1960s, supercharging (i.e., a mechanically-driven blower installation) was effectively dead, as such things were very wasteful of petrol due to the amount of useful power needed to drive them. The turbocharger, however, which was driven by the 'power for free' in the exhaust gases, was potentially a different matter.

Known, and extensively developed, first for heavy truck Diesels, and later for Indianapolis racing cars, turbochargers were first taken up in Europe by BMW for their very special BMW 2002TIK cars in 1969. Porsche also developed turbocharged versions of their flat-six air-cooled engines at the beginning of the 1970s, also for racing purposes, and the use of turbocharging as a 'tuning shop' speciality was just about to take off when the world was hit by the Suez crisis and the hoist in fuel prices in 1973-1974.

Almost at the same time, however, BMW had revealed their BMW 2002 Turbo, and it was followed just a year later by the Porsche Turbo, which had a 260bhp 3.0-litre engine. But even since then, there has been no gadarene rush to adopt turbocharging. Other Porsches – the 924 and (soon, reputedly) the 928 – and TVR have been joined by Saab (with a car which does not qualify for inclusion in this book), while there are already turbocharged diesel-engined cars from Peugeot and Mercedes-Benz. The rush to turbocharge other sporting cars will surely not be delayed for long, and by the end of the 1980s such installations may be commonplace.

If you discount the growing adoption of transversely-positioned in-line engines (a stance made necessary if mass-production front-wheel-drive power packs are to be modified – for instance in Fiats and Lancias), then there was no single startling development in engine configurations during the 1960s. Porsche chose a flat-six air-cooled engine for their 911 range, which was not very surprising as their 356 range had a flat-four cooled by air, but this layout was not taken up by any other company. Ferrari's monoply of vee-12 engines disappeared in 1963 when Lamborghini joined in, and their dominance in numbers built was quickly destroyed by Jaguar in 1971 with their own 5.3-litre vee-12. Twelve cylinders, however, was at least four too many for almost everyone else, who thought they could do the same job at lower cost. And so, in factual terms, they could, but they were always to be at an 'image' disadvantage compared with these three magnificent units.

It is true that some splendid specialised vee-8s were developed, and built in relatively large numbers – Mercedes-Benz and Porsche from Germany, Aston Martin from Britain, and Ferrari and Maserati from Italy all making their names in the Supercar category with such engines. The surprise about the Porsche 928 engine was not that it was a vee-8 and not that it was water-cooled, but that it was mounted in the front of the car.

Vee-6 units, as used exclusively by Lancia in the 1950s, became very popular from many quarters. Although a vee-6 is never as smooth as a straight-six, it is much more compact, and because of the advance in engine mounting design and in balancing techniques can be made smooth enough. Ford's mass-production vee-6 units were not only invaluable in their own Capris, but in several specialist cars like the Reliant and the TVR. Renault's own new vee-6 (produced co-operatively for Peugeot and Volvo) found a home in the latest Alpine Renault A310.

The two most famous vee-6 engines, however, were Italian – one from Ferrari and one from Maserati. The Ferrari Dino vee-6 had its roots, and its strange 65-degree angle between cylinder banks, in the F2 and F1 engines of the 1950s, but it did not find a home in a production car until 1966, when it was adopted by Fiat for their front-engined Dino models. The same engine (in 2.0-litre form for both cars) was also fitted to the mid-engined Ferrari Dino, where it had the distinction of being mounted transversely across the chassis. From 1969 the engine was enlarged to 2.4-litres and given a cast-iron cylinder block, after which it was built in even greater numbers, and was also fitted to the Lancia Stratos 'homologation special.'

Maserati's vee-6, originally a 2.7-litre unit, and finally enlarged to 3.0-litres, also had a strange cylinder bank angle – 90 degrees – which came about because it was an engine speedily developed from the bare bones of the celebrated Maserati vee-8 unit! In Italy, where speed of execution is more important than a mere technical nicety, such things as ideal cylinder bank angles are not considered important! That engine, incidentally, was used not only in the Maserati Merak, but also in the Citroen SM, and in the Ligier JS2.

The development story of transmissions in the 1960s and 1970s is not nearly as complicated. In summary, use of electrically controlled overdrives declined, all-synchromesh manual gearboxes became universal, and many self-respecting sporting cars found that five forward speeds were essential. In spite of the fact that diehards said that automatic transmission had no place in a sporting car, a surprising number were offered with that extra during the 1970s. Ferrari's adoption of such systems was something of an accolade, though Mercedes-Benz and Jaguar were forced to adopt an automatic box as they had no suitably strong manual gearbox to fit in its place.

In view of the fact that maximum speeds could at times be approaching 180mph, it is surprising that no-one has yet dared to offer a six-speed gearbox, though there would be nothing more daunting than cost in the way of such features. Perhaps, indeed, it will never happen, and that a two-speed axle (as already well known on commercial vehicles) might be linked to a three-speed manual box instead.

Putting the gearbox in unit with the final drive was inevitable where a front-wheel-drive or a rear/mid-engined car was designed, but the trend to a rear-mounted gearbox in unit with the final drive when a front engine is retained is now obvious. Alfa Romeo (with the Alfetta) and Porsche (with the 924 and the 928) are the most important of what may be a growing number of adherents to this layout, though we musn't forget that Ferrari, with the 275GTB, way back in 1964, pre-dated the trend by some years.

In passing, it is worth noting that no-one else has emulated Lamborghini, who put into production a car (the Miura) in which even reverse gear was synchronised!

Will there be as much technical advance in the next twenty years as we have seen since 1960? Or will proper mechanical development be stifled by the need to meet more and yet more legislation, or to counter zooming fuel prices? Will we look back from 1990 and find that the big changes were in the realms of aerodynamics and in ultra-precise carburation? Is the age of the true sports car already drawing to a close?

Surely not. After all, the Porsche 928 is a markedly better and more sensible car than the 911s which it supplements, and the BMW M1 is surely one of the most exciting Supercars ever revealed? It is true that the ranks of the Supercar manufacturers is thinning all the time, but on the other hand sales of more budget-priced sporting cars are booming.

But, above all, this is a book of record, and not of forecast. What follows is a list of all the significant cars built in Europe between 1961 and 1979, and the story of all of them is fascinating.

Chapter Three

The Specialists

There is nothing easy or simple about the successful marketing of a new high-performance car, and the world of motoring is littered with the wreckage of businesses — and personalities — who thought otherwise. It is not merely a question of providing for flashing performance, which in engineering terms is not difficult, nor of providing an adequate chassis, which presents many more problems. Neither is it merely enough to throw man-power, money or time at a project, as several large concerns have discovered in the past. Because many such cars, and companies, are already successfully established, the one thing, above all, which a new design needs is *character*.

Developing that character, offering an attractive visual and functional package, and finding a dash of that undefinable 'something' — style — a new design of car needs real expertise from its designers, a real love for the type, and preferably a great deal of flair. No one, however, can go to school or university to learn about flair. It cannot be learned from books. Neither is it acquired by observation. In the same way that great musicians and great artists are born, so do great designers become prominent. There are not many Colin Chapmans in the world.

By definition, too, it is apparent that such cars can often only combine high performance and great character with higher prices, and this means that they will almost certainly not sell in large numbers. All over Europe, therefore, famous companies have evolved, which have gained and retained their reputations by building limited numbers of fine cars with real character, which sell at very reasonable prices. Without these specialists, indeed, the sports and GT scene would be a much less exciting affair.

In the early days of motoring, of course, nearly every car maker quali'
'specialist', and due to the economic conditions which then prevailed
Europe, these makers could take on a great deal of their own manufacti'
Even in the inflationary postwar years, most have tried to
independence. The dictionary definition of 'specialise', after al'
or individual', which these firms still try to do. Certainly whei

a prospective customer, they have usually tried to steer clear of using commonplace items, and each tries to make his own design unique and readily recognisable. But for many years now the cost, and complication of producing one's own engines and transmissions has been too much for 'most specialists; they usually place a good deal of reliance on mass-production concerns for such supplies.

Because capital commitments can be kept to a minimum, a large number of firms have tried to get into this market sector, but it is a sad fact that many of them have only had a very short life. Of the twenty-five marques I list in this category, which have featured since 1960, no fewer than thirteen are now out of business, or out of the sporting-car market. Such firms have flared into prominence all over Europe, with radically different products, for completely different customers. How can I group Clan, ASA, and Facel Vega under the same heading?

However, I must now try to define the cars and manufacturers which qualify for inclusion in this section. First of all — and this is very significant — several specialist manufacturers do not feature here because they concentrate on Supercars; in this case, their cars are to be found in Section 6. To confuse things a little, however, I have to point out that firms like Jensen have made Supercars *and* other types; this explains why only the 541S model is listed here, and why the Jensen-Healey is defined as a quantity-production type. Secondly, I have had to make my own decisions about the difference between specialist cars in relatively large-scale production (Lotus, for example), and quantity-production machines (like the Jensen-Healey) which were somewhat more numerous. The dividing line, as I explain more fully in the prologue to Section 4, really comes when a manufacturer takes a deep breath and arranges for his new product to have a pressed-steel bodyshell, perhaps even of the chassisless type.

Many small firms, however, do not figure at all, and this is for a very simple reason. I refuse to admit as a viable marque, any car which is merely a modified version of another, or which merely rebodies a quantity-production machine, unless it has been done specifically by encouragement of the original concern. No sports car or coupe, however sleek, gains a place here, for instance, if it is based on something like a VW Beetle underframe. On the other hand, a car like the Bond Equipe gets my vote because it evolved with the encouragement of the Triumph company (on whose Herald/Vitesse chassis it was based) and was sold through their dealerships. In the 'homologation special' category of Section 5, therefore, I include Lotus-Cortinas but eliminate other more or less special Fords.

I have also had to draw the line somewhere when considering what is, or is not, a true production car, of however small a scale, and what is, or is not, a road car. Without doubt there are dozens, perhaps scores, of marques, which were adequately special, but were never really put into production.

It is interesting, for a moment, to look at a few more statistics. When the 1960s opened, just ten marques were already in existence. Only six of them lasted throughout the next two decades, of which five — Alpine-Renault, Lotus, Matra (really Matra-Simca), Morgan and TVR — can really be described as thriving. It is perhaps significant that two of them — Alpine-Renault and Matra — are now subsidiaries of larger combines — and that one (Lotus) is now industrially so large that it is teetering moving out of this category either into the ranks of the quantity-production makers, become a purveyor of Supercars.

fewer than eight of the twenty-five marques have, at one time or another, done heir business by selling their cars in 'knocked-down' kits of parts. Lotus, of above such things at the beginning of the 1970s, and their current range of cars is of an entirely different character than the kit-cars of old. Five of these manufacturers — Clan, Elva, Fairthorpe, Gilbern and Marcos — all disappeared as a direct consequence of the collapse of the kit-car market, which was a combination of changing motoring fashions and government legislation with regard to taxation.

I don't think I have been biassed in favour of the British by including seventeen of them, compared with only eight from the rest of Europe. Even today, a survey of active car makers shows that most of the specialist concerns are British based; there are several Italian marques, it is true, but four of them — Ferrari, Lamborghini, Maserati and de Tomaso — all make Supercars. Saab only qualify because I cannot count the two Sonett production cars as anything other than 'specialist', and I find it very interesting that there is not a single German car in the list. Apart from Britain and Italy, France — with Alpine-Renault, Facel-Vega and Matra — is the most prominent host country for the specialists.

Without exception, of course, the specialists make their own bodywork, and it is surely of great technical significance that all but three chose separate chassis frames; it is in this way that they were able to make their offerings attractive, and obviously different from the run-of-the-mill machinery sold at lower prices, and in greater numbers.

Before the second world war, and for a time after it, any specialist car worth its reputation had a hand-built body, with steel and sometimes light-alloy body panels. Since the end of the 1950s, however, the availability of glass-fibre shells has been a real boon. Of the twenty-five marques listed, no fewer than twenty — at one time or another — have offered cars with glass-fibre coachwork, either open or in coupe form. Some — like AC, Jensen, Morgan and Panther — changed over to glass-fibre after years of experience with metal coachbuilt bodies. Only Morgan, having built a run of Plus Four Plus models, reverted to more traditional methods of construction.

For most of the companies in this group, glass-fibre offers an ideal solution to the problem of providing a distinctive and stylish body shell without having to expend huge capital sums in tooling, or to put up with lengthy and expensive hand-working of individual bodyshells. Its principal drawback — that a newly-made shell requires a long time to cure — can safely be ignored by a concern which is making perhaps 1000 cars a year.

There were good reasons for each of the three firms to get away without using a separate chassis. Clan used a glass-fibre monoque (original Lotus Elite style), the Innocenti sports car was really a rebodied Sprite/Midget, while the Saab Sonetts used a glass-fibre superstructure on the underframe and mechanical assemblies of a quantity-production Saab saloon.

In many cases the chassis were tubular, in some instances multi-tubular, but in no case did they approach the theoretical ideal of a true 'space' frame. AC, Bizzarini, Ginetta, and Panther, widely differing cars for different classes of customer, have all relied on the simple virtues of large-diameter tubular frames. So, too, did Facel Vega, but it was welded to an all-steel body on assembly from new. Pressed box-section, combined in some cases with fabricated sections, has been found on Bonds, Jensens, Reliants and Tridents. The most ambitious multi-tubular frames feature in Gilberns, TVRs and Warwicks. Morgan, with their Z-section frame of ancient origins, and Lotus, with their backbone and tubular frames are well away from the mainstream of chassis engineering, as is Alpine-Renault (steel backbone) and Ligier (pressed-steel platform).

There is no denying that this group includes some strange marques. How, for instance, can one match the ASA 1000, with its Ferrari-designed four-cylinder engine, against the Sbarro, which is nothing more than a extremely carefully copied replica style of the prewar BMW 328? Is a Facel-Vega Facellia, however unsuccessful, but with its own special engine, transmission and body/chassis unit, more or less to be admired than a Reliant Scimitar GTE, where only the chassis and the bodyshell are truly special? No matter. For that, surely is the attraction of the specialists?

Because their investment can be low, and because they are usually able to react speedily to alter an unsatisfactory design, specialist cars have often been the pioneers of engineering features only adopted by the quantity-production makers years later. I have already mentioned that Lotus were *the* first to sell a car with a glass-fibre monocoque, and their Europa of 1966 was the first true road car to have a mid-engined layout (with apologies to Unipower, whose production achievements were small). The AC Cobra was one of the first to combine North American brute horsepower with a lightweight structure – though there is nothing historically new in that, as Railton proved in the 1930s, and Allard in the 1940s; it was merely that AC did it in such an exciting and full-blooded way. Marcos were the first – and still the only – to utilise marine construction methods, with a boxed wooden frame under a glass-fibre bodyshell. Morgan were the first to show that a specialist firm could continue to prosper by *never* changing the basic looks of their cars; many of their competitors will be happy if they can ever aspire to such a reputation. To Reliant, of course, goes the accolade for inventing the 'sport hatch', or the sporting estate car, and it is to their credit that Ford, Opel, Toyota, Lancia, and others, have not been able to extinguish their early reputation.

Unless the weight of new legislation becomes unbearable. I have no doubt that there will be many more new models to come in this sector of the market, though whether the climate will ever again be right for new firms to emerge is another question altogether.

AC Ace series

Built: Thames Ditton, England, 1953 to 1963

By the time the 1960s opened, the AC Ace sports car family had been on the market for several years, but it was still popular and still the mainstay of the AC concern's production. Further, in a couple of years it would be transformed, and gain an even greater reputation, as the AC Cobra. It was at the same time elegant, practical, fast and mechanically simple. It was everything, indeed, which we would have expected of a specialist concern with great traditions.

The Ace had evolved in the 1950s from John Tojeiro designs, the Cooper-MG and the Tojeiro which followed it. AC, looking round for a successor to their obsolete and stodgy 2-litre saloon, took this up, and made a success of it. The basis of the Cooper-MG had been a simple ladder-type tubular frame and an open two-seater sports car style of Barchetta type, inspired by a Ferrari of the day.

As taken up by AC, the Ace (which revived a famous AC model name of the 1930s) used the Thames Ditton company's old but technically interesting overhead-camshaft six-cylinder engine, matched to the gearbox previously fitted to the 2-litre, and to an ENV axle. The chassis featured two large section (3-inches diameter) steel tubes, and there was all-independent suspension by transverse leaf springs and lower wishbones. In comparison with the old AC chassis design, it was entirely new, of much more modern layout, and had great potential. In the first years four wheel drum brakes had, naturally, been used, but front wheel discs were adopted later in the 1950s. The engine was set back in the chassis, so that weight distribution was ideal for sporting purposes, and the attractive body style was immediately popular.

With great respect to the fabulous old AC engine, however, it *had* been introduced soon after the first world war, and was not capable of great improvement, so it was entirely reasonable to expect that AC would seek alternative power units for this very

AC Aceca, 1961

promising model. By the beginning of the 1960s, therefore, the Bristol 2-litre engine had been available for some years, and it was in this form that the AC Ace was most popular and most successful in competitions. However, when Bristol themselves abandoned their own engine in 1961, to use Chrysler vee-8 engines in their new model, it was clear that supplies to AC could not last long. It was for this reason that the Ace was again re-engined, with a much-modified six-cylinder Ford Zephyr engine, to become the AC 2.6 or Ace-Zephyr. Very few of these cars were made, however, as the entire Ace programme was soon to be abandoned in favour of the very popular AC Cobra, which took its place on the Thames Ditton assembly line.

Two types of two-seater were available until production ran out – the open Ace sports car, and the fastback Aceca sports coupe, which were mechanically identical. Coupes had a higher top speed because of superior aerodynamics, but Aces had better acceleration because they were significantly lighter.

Specification

Engine and transmission: Six-cylinders, in-line, with single-overhead-camshaft cylinder head. Bore, stroke and capacity, 65 × 100mm, 1991cc. Maximum power 102bhp (net) at 5000rpm; maximum torque 120lb.ft. at 3000rpm. Four speed manual gearbox and optional overdrive, in unit with engine. Hypoid bevel final drive.

Chassis: Front engine, rear drive. Separate chassis frame, with tubular members. Independent front suspension by transverse leaf spring and lower wishbones. Rack and pionion steering. Independent rear suspension by transverse leaf spring and lower wishbones. Front wheel disc brakes, rear drums.

Bodywork: Light-alloy coachbuilt bodyshell, in two-door, two-seater, open (Ace) or fastback coupe (Aceca) styles. Length 12ft. 8in.; width 4ft. 11.5in.; height (Ace) 4ft. 1in, (Aceca) 4ft. 4in. Unladen weight (Ace) 1720lb., (Aceca) 1990lb.

Performance: (Aceca-Bristol) Maximum speed 116mph. 0-60mph 10.3sec. Standing ¼-mile 17.8sec. Typical fuel consumption 22mpg. **(Ace-Bristol):** Maximum sped 117mph. 0-60mph 9.1sec. Standing ¼-mile 16.5sec. Typical fuel consumption 23mpg. **(Aceca-AC engine):** Maximum speed 102mph. 0-60mph 13.4sec. Standing ¼-mile 19.1sec. Typical fuel consumption 22mpg.

Note: Alternative engine had six-cylinders in-line, with pushrod-operated overhead-valve cylinder head, manufactured by Bristol. Bore, stroke and capacity, 66 × 96mm, 1971cc. Maximum power 125bhp (net) at 6000rpm.; maximum torque 132lb.ft. at 4500rpm. Cars thus fitted have unladen weights (Ace) of 1700lb., and (Aceca) 1970lb.

Specification of Ace-Zephyr

Specification as for Ace except for: Six-cylinder overhead-valve engine, manufactured by Ford, and modified by Ruddspeed. Bore, stroke and capacity 82.55 × 79.5mm, 2553cc. Maximum power (most powerful version) 170bhp (gross) at 5500rpm. Maximum torque 154lb.ft. at 3000rpm. Unladen weight 1745lb.

AC Cobra

Built: Thames Ditton, England and Venice, USA, 1962-1968

Carroll Shelby first approached AC with the idea of mating Ford parts and the AC Ace structure, in the autumn of 1961. The first prototype was built early in 1962, and the first batch of 100 cars were dispatched to the United States for completion in the autumn. It was the start of one of the most remarkable success stories in modern sports car history.

AC Cobra 289, 1966

There were two basically different Cobras − fitted with 4.2/4.7 engines, and with 7-litre engines, respectively − but all cars used the same ruggedly attractive body style, directly developed from that of the 1953-1963 Ace, and the chassis evolved from that same layout. In every case, the result was colossal performance, made possible by the high outputs and surprisingly low weights of the two different Ford vee-8 engines.

The last of the Cobras, however, was very little like the AC Ace from which it evolved. Most importantly, the chassis and suspension was completely changed. The original Ace chassis had had to be strengthened, right from the start, but early in 1963 a fundamental change saw the adoption of rack and pinion steering in place of the Ace's worm-and-sector. Later, from the spring of 1965, Shelby's connections with Ford of Detroit led to the design of new front and rear suspensions; the transverse leaf spring layout was dropped, and combined coil spring/damper units allied to double wishbone geometry took its place. Further stiffening was needed for the later 7-litre cars, and of course wheels and tyres were also entirely different.

The Ace body shell also underwent considerable change, including the addition of wing vents to aid under-bonnet air circulation, a repositioned fuel tank, modified boot lid arrangements, and flared wheel arches to accommodate the larger wheels and tyres. All cars, however, were sold with the open style of bodywork, the Aceca style not being considered suitable for the North American market.

At first the car was given a 4.2-litre Ford vee-8 engine (the same type, incidentally, as that which the later Sunbeam Tiger would use), but this was changed for the more famous 4.7-litre version after 75 cars had been built. Later the standard Ford gearbox was modified to include Pontiac gears. From 1965, however, the phenomenal 7-litre Cobra, with the entirely different 6989cc Ford engine, arrived, and though it was sold with 'only' 345bhp (net), it could also be tuned to give well over 400bhp, and the most electrifying performance. Though the engine was different, and physically somewhat larger, than the 4.7-litre unit, it still fitted fairly comfortably under the bonnet, and – if kept adequately cooled – was very reliable and docile.

It is worth noting that the car seemed to have various names during its life. The original car, according to AC, was an AC Cobra, but according to the Shelby organisation was a Shelby Cobra. Later, in the United States, they became known colloquially as Ford Cobras, and they were homologated as Shelby American Cobras. Once the car became available on the British market, the 4.7-litre device became an AC289, which meant that AC427 was sometimes applied to the 7-litre car! The AC 427 incidentally, was only ever intended for sale in North America.

The Cobra was raced with great success, particularly by the Shelby concern in special 'Daytona' coupe-bodied form, and was good enough to win the 1964 GT Manufacturers' Championship.

The Cobra ran out of production before the end of the 1960s, but the basic design of the 7-litre car carried over, in more civilised and stylish form, in AC's own 428, which is described later.

Specification

Engine and transmission: Eight-cylinders, in 90-degree vee-formation, with pushrod-operated overhead-valve cylinder heads, manufactured by Ford USA. **First 75 cars:** Bore, stroke and capacity 96.5 × 73mm., 4260cc. Maximum power 164bhp (net) at 4400rpm.; maximum torque 258lb.ft. at 2200rpm. **Later cars:** Bore, stroke and capacity 101.6 × 73mm., 4727cc. Maximum power 195bhp (net) at 4400rpm.; maximum torque 282lb.ft. at 2400rpm. Four speed manual gearbox in unit with engine. Hypoid bevel final drive.

Chassis: Front engine, rear drive. Separate tubular steel chassis frame, with plated reinforcement and crossmembers. Independent front suspension (pre-May 1965) by transverse leaf spring and wishbones, and subsequently by coil springs and wishbones. Steering (first 100 cars) by worm and sector, and on all later cars by rack and pinion. Independent rear suspension (pre-May 1965) by transverse leaf springs and wishbones, and subsequently by coil springs and wishbones. Four wheel disc brakes.

Bodywork: Light-alloy two-door two-seater open sports car style. Length 13ft. 2in.; width 5ft. 3in. (later 5ft. 8in.); height 4ft. 1in. Unladen weight 2315lb.

Performance: (4.7-litre engine). Maximum speed 138mph. 0-60mph 5.5sec. Standing ¼-mile 13.9sec. Typical fuel consumption 17mpg.

Note: From mid-1965, the 7-litre Shelby American Cobra also became available. Major differences were: Bore, stroke and capacity 104.9 × 101.1mm., 6989cc. Maximum power 345bhp (net) at 4600rpm.; maximum torque 462lb.ft. at 2800rpm.

Performance: Maximum speed 143mph. 0-60 4.8sec. Standing ¼-mile 12.9sec. Typical fuel consumption 12mpg.

AC 3000ME

Built: Thames Ditton, England, 1979 to date

The mid-engined 3000ME model from AC may go down in motoring history as the car with the longest gestation period of all time. First announced in time for the 1973 British motor show, its development suffered delay upon delay, and the very first production cars were not sold until the spring of 1979. Everything from new legislation, to other commercial and practical priorities, and a complete under-estimate of the time taken to prepare a new design for production, were responsible.

The heart of the 3000ME is Ford's British-built vee-6 three-litre engine, in wide use by Ford in 1973, but now only to be found in Ford Capris or light commercial vehicles. The structure itself, however, was not originally an AC design, but was developed from that of the one-off Diablo, evolved in 1972 by Peter Bohanna and Robin Stables. This car had used a transverse-engined Austin Maxi layout, but to get the performance they needed, AC decided to use the Ford engine, mated to special five-speed transmission developed by AC themselves, with gears manufactured by Hewland, of racing car fame.

In every way, it was as unlike the Cobras and Aces which it was to succeed as possible. It had a mid-engined layout, something quite unique to this concern, with a pressed and fabricated platform chassis (the Cobras and AC428s had used tubular frames), and with a glassfibre coupe bodyshell (all previous ACs had used coachbuilt shells and light alloy shells). It was, in other words, the first really modern design which AC had been preparing to sell for well over a generation.

Nothing inherent in the design of the car caused it to take more than five years to progress from concept to production. It could really be said that its original showing in

AC 3000 ME

1973 was decidedly premature, at a stage when other manufacturers would have had their car securely under wraps, but with the big and costly AC428 just going out of production, AC wanted the world of motoring to know that they were not abandoning the field altogether.

In many ways, the 3000ME was similar in layout to the Lancia Stratos, which was then being developed. It had the same stubby outlook, the same rugged and practical engineering layout, and the same mid-engined philosophy. The Stratos, however, was much more specialised, and AC were content to use mass-production Ford power to propel their new car. In Stratos or other mid-engined terms the 3000ME is almost conventional, with the engine mounted transversely across the chassis behind the two seats, and with a gearbox and final drive tucked behind and below the engine. There is some luggage space in front of the passenger compartment, and in the extreme rear, but internal accommodation is strictly for two people only. AC were originally talking about a production potential of 40 3000MEs a week, but *sales* of this nature will be difficult to achieve at the high price which now obtains. Only 30 cars were delivered in the first year of sales.

Specification

Engine and transmission: Six-cylinders, in 60-degree vee-formation, with pushrod-operated overhead-valve cylinder heads manufactured by Ford. Bore, stroke and capacity 93.66×72.4mm., 2994cc. Maximum power 138bhp (DIN) at 5000rpm.; maximum torque 173lb.ft. at 3000rpm. Five-speed manual gearbox in unit with engine and transaxle. Hypoid bevel final drive.
Chassis: Transverse mid-engine, rear drive. Separate pressed-steel platform chassis. Independent front suspension by coil springs and wishbones. Rack and pinion steering. Independent rear suspension by coil springs and wishbones. Four wheel disc brakes.
Bodywork: Glass-fibre bodyshell, in two-door two-seater notchback style. Length 13ft. 1in.; width 5ft. 5in.; height 3ft. 9in. Unladen weight 2040lb.
Performance: Maximum speed 120mph. 0-60mph 8.5sec. Standing ¼-mile 16.3sec. Typical fuel consumption 21mpg.

Alpine Renault A108/A110

Built: Dieppe, France, 1957 to 1977

In basic concept, the little rear-engined glass-fibre coupes built at Dieppe over a 20 year period, changed very little, but in detail there was a programme of almost continual improvement and modification. All the cars, however, relied on the famous Alpine backbone chassis, all used one or other of the Renault engines, and all − of their day − could be had as fierce, uncompromisingly sporting, little two-seaters. Only now that Alpine, like Lotus in Britain, have 'grown-up' and started to sell much more expensive cars, has the last car been built.

The first Alpines of all, designed by Jean Redele, appeared at the beginning of the 1950s, but relied on the chassis platform of the rear-engined Renault 4CV. The first 'backbone' Alpine, of the type discussed here, came along in 1957. It was based on a strong, tubular, backbone chassis, on to which were welded front and rear structural extensions and suspension pick-ups. As well as using Renault engines and transmissions, the cars also used Renault suspension components, allied (in later years) to special wheels and tyres. This meant that the Alpine's 'Achilles Heel' in regard to road holding was that the simple coil spring and swing axle rear suspension of Dauphine type was fitted, and this gave rise to the cars' characteristic tail-out oversteering attitude which a brave rally driver could use to such enormous effect.

The basic difference between A108 and A110 types was in the choice of engines. A108s relied on Renault Dauphine engines and transmissons (in other words, the smallest four-cylinder engine, evolved from that of the 4CV) while A110s were developed around the next-larger unit, first seen in R8s, in 956cc form, but developed and re-developed, and still an important part of the scene in modern Renaults.

A110s, called Berlinettes, eventually had engines of up to 1300cc, with or without the very special Gordini cylinder heads, according to their year of build, their purpose, or according to who was buying them, but all relied on the same distinctive low-slung fastback glass-fibre bodies. Although a convertible was listed for some years, the vast majority of all Alpine-Renaults were coupes. By 1965 the Berlinette, called a *Tour de France* in some versions, had the 1300cc (actually a 1255cc) engine, and was capable of more than 120mph.

Alpine Renault A110

From the mid-1960s, however, the new Renault R16, with its brand-new 1470cc four-cylinder engine and transmission, also began to bequeath its engines to the Alpine-Renault, and in this final form the car became an outright contender for rallying success. In 'works' competition hands, the already enlarged 1600cc production engines could be pushed out to 1.8-litres, and with around 180bhp they were formidable contenders. The chassis was developed so that the little car could be a winner on tarmac, or on rough events like Morocco. The final improvement, in 1973, included the double wishbone rear suspension of the new and bigger Alpine A310, which improved but did not transform the roadholding.

Production of the final, fastest, Berlinettes — the 1600SC (with carburettors) or the 1600SI (with fuel-injection) — ceased in 1975, by which time Alpine had really lost interest in the design, but for two more years an emasculated 1600SX, much detuned compared with the 1975 models, continued to be made. Up to 700 Alpines could be built in a good year, which kept the Dieppe factory very busy and profitable. Alpine is now a completely owned subsidiary of Renault, having been taken over in 1974 in the aftermath of the energy crisis of 1973, and a short-lived collapse in sales of such sporting cars.

Specification (A108 and A110)

Engine and transmission: Various modified Renault engines. A108 version with small Dauphine-type engine. A110 with R8/R12 types from 956 to 1255cc, R16 types to 1647cc. All have four cylinders, in-line, with pushrod-operated overhead valve cylinder heads. Most powerful version offers 1647cc 127bhp (DIN) Alpine 310 engine. Three-speed, four-speed, or (most often) five-speed manual gearbox in unit with engine and transaxle. Hypoid bevel final drive.

Chassis: Rear engine, rear drive. Separate chassis frame, with tubular backbone and outriggers. Independent front suspension by coil springs and wishbones. Rack and pinion steering. Rear suspension by coil springs and swing axles; from 1973 by coil springs and wishbones. Four wheel drum brakes, eventually replaced by four-wheel disc brakes.

Bodywork: Glass-fibre bodyshell, in two-door two-seater fastback coupe or convertible form. Length 12ft. 7.6in.; width 5ft. 1in.; height 3ft 8in. Unladen weight from 1200lb.

Performance: (1300 version, 1966). Maximum speed 123mph. 0-60mph 9.1sec. Standing ¼-mile 16.6sec. Typical fuel consumption 30mpg. **(1600S version, 1971).** Maximum speed 127mph. 0-60mph 6.3sec. Standing ¼-mile 15.0sec. Typical fuel consumption 28mpg.

Alpine-Renault A310

Built: Dieppe, France, 1971 to date

When it was launched in spring 1971, the rear-engined Alpine-Renault A310 was the first really new model introduced from the Dieppe concern since the A108 coupe of 1957. For all that, it relied very much on the same sort of formula as before, but packaged in a more appealing and modern style. Since the A108/A110 Berlinettes have now disappeared from the scene, the A310 is the only Alpine-Renault now in production.

Like the earlier cars, the A310 relied structurally on a steel backbone chassis frame with suspension outriggers, had all-independent suspension utilising many standard Renault parts, used (originally) a Renault 16 engine of 1605cc, suitably modified by Gordini, and was clothed in a rather rounded fastback 2 + 2 coupe shell constructed as usual of glass-fibre. Although it was rather larger than the A110 design it supplemented, it was clearly not as fast (it was bulkier and heavier), and the 2 + 2 seating was of questionable value. The nose was strikingly attractive, with its headlamps hidden behind perspex covers, Ferrari Daytona style.

The world of motoring was not to know that this was, in effect, only the interim design, but from the autumn of 1976 an additional model − the A310 V6 − was launched, where the basic structure and layout were mated to the 2.7-litre vee-6 engine already used in Peugeot, Volvo and Renault prestige saloons. This single overhead cam engine, matched to its own stronger transmission, created 150bhp at 6000rpm in spite of having very simple carburation, and endowed the car with a claimed maximum speed of more than 135mph. Shortly after this, and following the withdrawal of the A110 from production, the original four-cylinder A310 was also discontinued, and the vee-6 engined car now holds the limelight at Dieppe, effectively as Renault's prestige coupe. No other body variant has yet been seen.

The A310 vee-6 lays claim to be the fastest pure *rear*-engined car in the world apart from the Porsche 911 family.

Alpine Renault A310, 1605cc

Specification

Engine and transmission: Four-cylinders, in-line, with pushrod-operated overhead-valve cylinder head manufactured by Renault. Bore, stroke and capacity 78 × 84mm., 1605cc. Maximum power 127bhp (DIN) at 6250rpm.; maximum torque 108lb.ft. at 5000rpm. Five-speed manual gearbox in unit with engine and transaxle. Hypoid bevel final drive.

Chassis: Rear engine, rear drive. Separate chassis frame, with tubular backbone, and outriggers. Independent front suspension by coil springs and wishbones. Rack and pinion steering. Independent rear suspension by coil springs and wishbones. Front wheel disc brakes, and drum rears.

Bodywork: Glass-fibre bodyshell, in two-door 2 + 2 seating fastback coupe style. Length 13ft. 8.5in.; width 5ft. 3.8in.; height 3ft. 9.3in. Unladen weight 2075lb.

Performance: Maximum speed 131mph. 0-60mph 8.1sec. Standing ¼-mile 16.0sec. Typical fuel consumption 24mpg.

Note: From autumn 1976, the A310 also became available with a different engine: Six-cylinders, in 90-degree vee-formation, with single-overhead-camshaft cylinder heads, manufactured by Peugeot-Renault-Volvo. Bore, stroke and capacity 88 × 73mm., 2664cc. Maximum power 150bhp (DIN) at 6000rpm.; maximum torque 150lb.ft. at 3500rpm. Four-speed manual gearbox in unit with engine and transaxle. Hypoid bevel final drive. Unladen weight 2240lb.

Performance (Manufacturers' claims): Maximum speed 137mph. 0-60mph 7.5mph. Standing ¼-mile 15.4sec. Typical fuel consumption approx 25mpg.

ASA 1000 Coupe

Built: Milan, Italy, 1962-1967

For years the legend of a 'mini' Ferrari was just that — there was such a car, it was said, but no-one had seen it, and it never appeared in public. One thing seemed to be certain, that Ferrari had indeed built a tiny single-overhead camshaft four-cylinder engine, originally of 850cc, and eventually of just more than one-litre. It was not until 1961 that the project stopped being a legend, and came out into the open — on the Bertone stand at the Turin Motor Show.

For reasons known only to himself, Ferrari was very coy about this car, and on its first public appearance it carried no badges — although no attempt was made to hide its Ferrari ancestry. The chassis layout, and the detail of the little engine, were all absolutely typical of the Ferrari road cars of the day, and the nicely detailed two-seater coupe bodyshell, by Bertone (which was a surprise — as Ferrari was usually linked with Pininfarina/Scaglietti at the time), was at the same time practical, attractive, and bore a certain family resemblance to other Bertone coupes which were current, such as the Simca 1000 or Sport Prinz shapes.

Even in 1961, it was clear that Ferrari would not be manufacturing this delectable little machine, and that he was looking for a concern to take it over. By the autumn of 1962, a new company Autocostruzioni Societa per Azioni (ASA) had been formed by the de Nora electrochemical concern, and had taken over rights to make the car, which was accordingly renamed the ASA 1000.

ASA 1000 Coupe by Bertone, 1963

Production began at the beginning of 1963, and continued haltingly until 1967, but never achieved the numbers necessary for the little car to be an economic success; in 1964, for instance, only one car every week was delivered. Finally, after financial problems had intervened in 1966, ASA tried to retrieve the situation by announcing the Rollbar GT Spyder, which had a glass-fibre body and a *six*-cylinder 1.3-litre engine developed from that of the original ASA 1000, but it was a failure, and de Nora closed down their unsuccessful venture.

The ASA, like so many other excitingly-engineered cars of the period, was originally created for Ferrari by Bizzarrini, and was effectively a scaled-down 250GT. Its tubular chassis frame had coil spring independent front suspension and its live rear axle was located by radius arms and sprung on coil springs. The most important feature of the whole car, of course, was the little engine, which was effectively a four-cylinder bank developed from that of the Colombo vee-12 engine.

In the beginning, the prototype engines had dimensions of 65×64mm, and 850cc, but for production these dimensions were enlarged to 69×69mm., 1032cc. Although the detail design of valve gear, breathing, and combustion, was like that of the vee-12, it is worth recalling that these famous engines had a bore and stroke of 73×58.8mm, so there was no question of pistons or other moving parts being interchangeable. There was no gainsaying the power output of 84bhp, however, which was just as powerful, size for size, as the vee-12.

Without any doubt, the ASA 1000 was the world's fastest one-litre road car, which would undoubtedly have been more popular if only it could have been built in appropriate numbers and sold at a more reasonable price.

Specification

Engine and transmission: Four-cylinders, in-line, with single-overhead-camshaft cylinder head. Bore, stroke and capacity, 69×69mm, 1032cc. Maximum power 84bhp (DIN) at 6800rpm; maximum torque 66lb.ft. at 5500rpm. Four-speed gearbox and Laycock overdrive in unit with engine. Hypoid bevel final drive.

Chassis: Front engine, rear drive. Separate tubular chassis frame. Independent front suspension by coil springs and wishbones. Rack and pinion steering. Rear suspension of live axle by coil springs, radius arms and Watts linkage. Four-wheel disc brakes.

Bodywork: Light-alloy shells – designed by Bertone; fastback coupe built by Touring of Milan, and cabriolet by Corbetta, each with two seats.

Coupe: Length 12ft. 8.8in., width 5ft. 1in., height 3ft. 11.2in. Unladen weight 1830lb.

Cabriolet: Length 12ft. 8.8in., width 5ft. 1in., height 3ft. 11.2in. Unladen weight 1565lb.

Performance (Coupe): Maximum speed 115mph. 0-60mph 14.0sec. Standing ¼-mile 19.3 sec.

Bizzarrini GT Europa 1900

Built: Livorno, Italy, 1966-1969

Even though his 5.3-litre Strada 5300 was very fast, and enjoyed something of a reputation in Italy, Bizzarrini could not sell many of these enormously fast cars. He therefore tried (ultimately, it appears, without success) to broaden the base of his little company with a cheaper model. The GT Europa 1900 was the short-lived result.

In 1965/1966 Bizzarrini had been experimenting with a Fiat 1500-based prototype, but at the Turin Motor Show of 1966 this had been discarded in favour of another project, which became the Europa 1900. Shown very discreetly, with the minimum of details, and without naming the make of the engine, the Europa 1900 was obviously not yet ready to go into production, which followed in tiny numbers in 1967 and 1968.

Like the bigger Bizzarrini, it was based on a steel platform-style underpan, had all-independent suspension, Italian-style, by coil springs and wishbones, and four-wheel disc brakes. Styling of the fastback two-seater coupe was never specified, but was almost certainly by Bertone, as there was a strong family resemblance to the big Bizzarrini, and to the Iso Grifo for which Bizzarrini was also technically responsible.

The engine, so mysteriously not mentioned when the car was first shown, was a 1.9-litre Opel Rekord 'cam-in-head' unit, matched to that car's four-speed gearbox. Although this unit was quite unmodified (its claimed horsepower of 110bhp – gross – accords closely with that of the mass-production Opels of the day), the car was extremely light, and a maximum speed of about 130mph was claimed. The light weight was helped by the use of a glass-fibre bodyshell instead of the coachbuilt steel and light-alloy used by Bizzarrini on his larger model.

What Bizzarrini hoped to achieve from this model is not clear, as it was clearly more of a budding competition car than a road machine, yet it was endowed with an engine which was certainly not ideal for competition car use, *and* it would have to compete in the hotly-contested Porsche/Alfa Romeo category. It was all too much for the tiny Livorno concern, which closed its doors in 1969.

Specification

Engine and transmission: Four-cylinders, in-line, with cam-in-head operation of overhead-valve cylinder head, manufactured by Opel. Bore, stroke and capacity 93 × 69.8mm., 1897cc. Maximum power 110bhp (gross) at 5600rpm.; maximum torque 116lb.ft. at 3000rpm. Four-speed manual gearbox in unit with engine. Hypoid bevel final drive.

Chassis: Front engine, rear drive. Separate fabricated steel platform chassis, with coachwork attached on assembly. Independent front suspension by coil springs and wishbones. Recirculating ball steering. Independent rear suspension by coil springs and wishbones. Four wheel disc brakes.

Bodywork: Glass-fibre two-door two-seater fastback coupe body style. Length 12ft. 5.2in.; width 5ft. 3.8in.; height 3ft. 5in. Unladen weight 1500lb.

Performance (Manufacturers' claims): Maximum speed 128mph. Typical fuel consumption 32mpg.

Bizzarrini GT Europa 1900, 1966

Bond Equipe GT

Built: Preston, England, 1963-1970

Until the arrival in 1963 of the first Bond Equipe sporting coupe, every previous Bond had been a three-wheeler mini-car, so the leap in engineering and marketing intention was considerable. However, Bond did not make the mistake of several other specialist makers by trying to 'go it alone'; right from the start they carried out the programme in conjunction with Standard-Triumph, and enjoyed the support of the distributive and servicing network.

In every case – whether Bond Equipe GT, GT4S, or 2-litre GT, the basis of the design was a standard Triumph Herald or Vitesse chassis and mechanical components, which would normally disqualify the car from inclusion here. Bonds, however, were different in that their cars were built with the full knowledge and approval of the Triumph factory, and might almost be considered as supernumerary Triumphs. Even the doors, bulkheads and much of the glass was Triumph, but the rest of the body was by courtesy of Bond, in glass-fibre. All the cars, therefore, had whichever all-independent suspension, braking and mechanical installation as was appropriate to the Triumphs of the day.

The Equipe GT announced in 1963 utilised the 1147cc Spitfire engine, but the 4S which followed had somewhat more passenger space, due to a reshaped passenger compartment, and the upgraded 1296cc Spitfire engine.

The 2-litre GT of 1968-1970 used the 1998cc Triumph Vitesse 2-litre engine of 95bhp, and was capable of more than 100mph. It was also much more specialised in terms of body styling, and in the last season or so of production was also offered as a convertible.

The car sold well enough to keep Bond happy, but was eventually killed-off following a merger between Bond and Reliant. In spite of their originally-stated intentions, Reliant soon closed down Bond's Preston factories, concentrated on their own Scimitar GTE project, and the last four-wheeler Bond was made in 1970.

Bond Equipe GT4S, 1965

Bond Equipe 2-litre GT, 1969

Specification

Engine and transmission: Four-cylinders, in-line, with pushrod-operated overhead-valve cylinder head, made by Triumph. Bore, stroke and capacity 69.3 × 76mm, 1147cc. Maximum power 63bhp (net) at 5750rpm; maximum torque 67lb.ft. at 3500rpm. Four-speed gearbox in unit with engine. Hypoid bevel final drive.

Chassis: Front engine, rear drive. Separate pressed steel chassis frame with box-section members. Independent front suspension by coil springs, wishbones and anti-roll bar. Rack and pinion steering. Independent rear suspension by transverse leaf spring, swing axles and radius arms. Front-wheel disc brakes, and rear drums.

Bodywork: Composite pressed steel and glass-fibre bodywork, in close-coupled 4-seater coupe style. Length 13ft. 4in.; width 5ft. 0in.; height 4ft. 5in. Unladen weight 1835lb.

Performance: Maximum speed 82mph. 0-60mph 17.6sec. Standing ¼-mile 20.8sec. Typical fuel consumption 32mpg.

Note: For 1966 the car became the GT4S with 67bhp, and finally became the GT1300 in 1967 with an engine of 73.7 × 76mm, 1296cc, and 75bhp at 6000rpm.

A related car was the GT 2-litre, built 1967 to 1970, with 6-cylinder engine of 74.7 × 76mm, 1998cc. Maximum power was 95bhp at 5000rpm, later increased to 104bhp.

Performance: (GT4S) Maximum speed 91mph. 0-60mph 20.0sec. Standing ¼-mile 21.4sec. Typical fuel consumption 28mpg. **(2-litre):** Maximum speed 102mph. 0-60mph 10.7sec. Standing ¼-mile 18.6sec. Typical fuel consumption 24mpg.

Clan Crusader

Built: Washington New Town, England, 1971-1973

I can sum up the fortunes of the Crusader very briefly: it was one of the nicest, most integrated, neatly styled specialist cars to be made in the 1960s and 1970s. Unfortunately, it was almost inevitable that, as a 'kit' car, it should fall foul of the new British VAT laws of 1973, and be forced out of production.

Clan Crusader

Its basis was a complete glass-fibre monocoque which was stress-carrying in the way that only one other glass-fibre car has ever achieved – and that was the original Lotus Elite. It is by no means a coincidence that Paul Haussauer, founder and designer of Clan – the company and the car itself – was once a development engineer at Lotus in the 1960s.

The Clan's design philosophy was based on the use, *in toto*, of the Chrysler Imp Sport/Sunbeam Stiletto engine, transmission, front and rear suspensions and steering. The neat Clan glass-fibre coupe, with two seats and wedge-type styling, was therefore shaped around the rear-engined, light-alloy engine and transmission of the Imp/Stiletto.

The factory chosen was in Washington New Town, in the north-east of England, only a few miles from Newcastle, not the usual site for a car factory, but one which had various financial and personnel advantages for a small and developing concern. In spite of the glass-fibre construction, without the structural assistance of any steel or light alloy, the car met the latest EEC 30mph barrier crash tests with some ease, and considering its simple build, and the modest resources of the company itself, was a very refined and driveable little machine. Because it was small and light, it was adequately fast (100mph was just attainable with the standard engine), in spite of the use of an

47

875cc engine. The occasional Crusader, with engine enlarged to 998cc, and race tuned, was a formidable little Grand Touring car.

Like most tiny specialist cars, however, and in spite of its reasonable price, it only found a market because it was sold as a nearly-built-up 'kit' car, which meant that in Great Britain it was free of purchase tax. From the spring of 1973, however, when this country joined the Common Market, VAT was introduced, and this had to be charged on cars whether built-up or in kits. This hit Clan sales badly at once, and the final blow came later in the year when the company ran into severe financial difficulties and had to stop trading. Several hundred Crusaders had been built.

Specification

Engine and transmission: Four-cylinders, in-line, with single-overhead-camshaft cylinder head, installed at 45-degrees from vertical in car, built by Chrysler (UK). Bore, stroke and capacity 68 × 60.4mm, 875cc. Maximum power 51bhp (net) at 6100rpm; maximum torque 52lb.ft. at 4300rpm. Four-speed gearbox in unit with engine and hypoid bevel transaxle.

Chassis: Rear engine, rear drive. Monocoque construction, with glass-fibre shell locally reinforced with steel diaphragms and tubes. Independent front suspension by swing axles and coil springs. Rack and pinion steering. Independent rear suspension by semi-trailing wishbones and coil springs. Four-wheel drum brakes.

Bodywork: Glass-fibre shell, in unit with rest of shell, made by Clan, in two-seat close coupe form. Length 12ft. 6in.; width 4ft. 10.5in.; height 3ft. 7in. Unladen weight 1275lb.

Performance: Maximum speed 100mph. 0-60mph 12.5sec. Standing ¼-mile 18.8sec. Typical fuel consumption 40mpg.

Elva Courier

Built: Bexhill and Hastings, Croydon and Shenley, England, 1958-1968

The original Elvas of the mid-1950s, designed by Frank Nichols, were low-cost sports-racing cars, but the first two-seater road car finally appeared in 1958, at the height of interest in 'kit cars' with glass-fibre bodies. The name Elva, incidentally, evolved from the French exclamation *'Elle va!'*, which translates simply and accurately as 'She *goes!'*

The Courier was a very simple little design, as indeed it had to be if the tiny Sussex concern was to built it in any numbers. Its basis was a simple ladder-type tubular chassis frame, and the sporting bodyshell was constructed of glass-fibre mouldings. Front suspension was by Elva, and used Armstrong spring/damper units, while the rear suspension was at first by coil springs and radius arms, locating a BMC live axle, but was later to become all-independent, once again by coil springs and wishbones.

In almost every case, the engine and transmission was that of the MGA or MGB sports cars, though individual customers of these cars (which were supplied as kits) sometimes fitted units of their own preference.

Even by the end of 1961, by which time the MGA 1600 units had been in use for a couple of years, more than 700 Couriers had been delivered, but this building rate fell away as the 1960s progressed, and as no significant styling or – more important – refinement improvements were introduced. Frank Nichols eventually sold his rights to this car; Trojan had been making the car on his behalf for some time, and from 1964 they took over the company completely. For a time the car was built at Shenley, in North London, but returned to Croydon for its declining years, and the last example was delivered in 1968, after which all Elva production of road cars ceased.

Elva Courier

European Sports & GT Cars

Specification (1960s models)

Engine and transmission: Four-cylinders, in-line, with pushrod-operated overhead valve cylinder head, made by BMC (as normally fitted to MGA and MGB models). Engine sizes 1588cc, 1622cc or 1798cc (depending on engine in use by MG at the time). (1.8-litre version): Bore, stroke and capacity, 80.3 × 88.9mm., 1798cc. Maximum power 95bhp (net) at 5400rpm.; maximum torque 110lb.ft. at 3500rpm. Four-speed manual gearbox in unit with engine. Hypoid bevel final drive.

Chassis: Front engine, rear drive. Separate tubular steel chassis frame. Independent front suspension by coil springs and wishbones. Rack and pinion steering. Independent rear suspension by coil springs and wishbones. Front wheel disc brakes, rear drums.

Bodywork: Separate two-seater two-door open-sports bodyshell in glass-fibre. Length 12ft. 5.5in.; width 5ft. 0in.; height 3ft. 9.5in. Unladen weight (approx) 1430lb.

Performance: (Early car with 1489cc BMC engine) Maximum speed 97mph. 0-60mph 12.7sec. Standing ¼-mile 18.2sec. Typical fuel consumption 30mpg.

Note: The original Courier of 1958/1960 had a live rear axle, located by coil springs and radius arms, and 1489cc MGA engines were fitted.

Facel Vega Facellia

Built: Colombes, France, 1959-1963

Jean Daninos decided to follow up his limited, but prestigious, success with the big Chrysler-engined Facel Vega, by having a new, smaller, and altogether cheaper car designed. This decision, taken in 1957/1958, eventually ensured that the concern would stop building cars in 1964, for the new design was financially ruinous. Incidentally, although I have titled these cars Facellias, two further derivatives − the Facel III with a Volvo engine, and the short-lived Facel 6 with Austin-Healey power − all have to be covered in the same description.

The new design looked very similar to the other Facel Vegas, which was just what Daninos intended, and it had a very similar type of chassis and suspensions, but needed an entirely new engine which was to be the cause of all the subsequent trouble. The structure, therefore, was based on the use of a tubular chassis frame, to which a pressed-steel two-seater sports car body, with a hood or a hardtop, was welded on assembly at the Colombes factory.

The only source for a new engine, if it was not to be a proprietary unit, which Daninos did not want, had to be at Pont-a-Mousson, who already manufactured Facel's gearboxes. The new 1.6-litre unit, which had very modern engineering and detailing, including a twin-overhead camshaft cylinder head, would have been splendid if it only had been reliable. It was rated at 115bhp (gross), which maximum power was produced at no less than 6400rpm. The technical observer could not fail to be reminded of the MGA Twin-Cam unit, with which it was contemporary. There was one important difference, however − which was that MG was part of a very large industrial combine, was more capable of sorting out the teething troubles of its new design, and could afford more complete machine tooling with which to manufacture the components.

The Facellia was much too expensive to command a large market, and the engine also proved to be distressingly unreliable. Piston burning was one of its major problems, which was a surprise as it had been designed for Daninos by Carlo Marchetti, formerly of Talbot, and it took two years before this trait (which was caused by poor cylinder block cooling and a general lack of rigidity) could be eliminated. By then Facel were in desperate financial straits, and massive injections of capital from Pont-a-Mousson, Hispano-Suiza and Mobil-France in 1962 were not sufficient. Although the company had originally boasted about taking large orders for the Facellia, it is doubtful if more than 500 were ever built in this form.

In 1963, therefore, the Facellia was transformed into the Facel III, which had the same structure, chassis, and styling, but used the much-less exciting, but infinitely more reliable Volvo P1800 engine of 1.8-litres. Maximum power was down − to 90bhp at 5500rpm − but performance was still sufficiently interesting to make the cars on a par with the MGB and Triumph TR4.

No fewer than 1500 of the Volvo-engined cars were built, while the new regime, managed by Paul Badre, which was a subsidiary of Sud Aviation, cast around for new products. Facel designed a new all-aluminium engine which was reputedly powerful, but during 1964 they made a few modified Facel IIIs called Facel 6s with a 2.8-litre version of the rugged six-cylinder Austin-Healey 3000 engine instead of the boring Volvo unit.

By then, however, the sponsoring firm of SFERMA, which had been overlooking Facel Vega since bankruptcy was averted in 1963, decided not to carry on with a hopeless task, and the company was closed down.

Facel Vega Facellia, 1963

Specification

Engine and transmission: (Facellia) Four-cylinders, in-line, with twin-overhead-camshaft cylinder head, made by Pont-a-Mousson. Bore, stroke and capacity 82 × 78mm., 1647cc. Maximum power 115bhp (gross) at 6400rpm.; maximum torque not quoted. **(Facel III)** Four-cylinders, in-line, with pushrod-operated overhead-valve cylinder head, made by Volvo of Sweden. Bore, stroke and capacity 84.1 × 80mm., 1788cc. Maximum power 90bhp (net) at 5500rpm.; maximum torque 110lb.ft. at 3800rpm. **(Facel 6)** Six-cylinders, in-line, with pushrod-operated overhead-valve cylinder head, made by BMC (Austin-Healey) of Great Britain. Bore, stroke and capacity 82.5 × 88.9mm., 2851cc. Maximum power 150bhp (gross) at 5250rpm.; maximum torque not quoted. Four-speed manual gearbox in unit with engines; overdrives on Facel III and Facel 6. Hypoid bevel final drive.

Chassis: Front engine, rear drive. Separate tubular steel chassis frame, welded to body on final assembly. Independent front suspension by coil springs and wishbones. Cam and roller steering. Rear suspension of live axle by half elliptic leaf springs. Four wheel disc brakes (drum brakes were optional in 1960 and 1961).

Bodywork: Pressed-steel bodyshell, welded to chassis on assembly, in two-door two-seater open sports or hardtop style. Length 13ft. 7.5in.; width 5ft. 1.5in.; height 4ft. 2in. Unladen weight 2520lb.

Performance: (Facellia) Maximum speed 106mph. 0-60mph 11.9sec. Standing ¼-mile 19.2sec. Typical fuel consumption 27mpg.

Fairthorpe Zeta/Rockette/Electron series

Built: Gerrards Cross and Denham, England, 1958-1974

Air Vice-Marshall Donald Bennett commenced motor manufacture with the Atom coupe of the 1950s, which combined a tubular chassis and glass-fibre body with rear-mounted BSA motor cycle engines. This was a faster-than-usual mini-car, but lacked refinement. His second major effort was the Electron, which began life in 1958 with the famous Coventry-Climax light-alloy engine, but in later years was to be sold in many different forms. The Electron family was to be the mainstay of Fairthorpe's business until the 1970s, when its worth as a tax-free kit-car was finally destroyed by the introduction of Value Added Tax.

The basis of the design was a simple ladder-type tubular chassis frame, which could be made with the minimum of tooling, and this was topped with a two-seater glass-fibre sports bodyshell. Coil spring independent front suspension was always fitted (latterly with proprietary components from Triumph, as used on the Herald/Spitfire series), and on early cars this was matched by independent rear suspension, also by coil springs.

Although none of their Fairthorpes could ever be called pretty, they were at one and the same time light, remarkably rugged, fast for the engines chosen, and quite cheap. In the early 1960s production sometimes exceeded 20 cars a month, but by the end of the decade demand had tailed off to a mere fraction of this.

The attraction of the design to the well-known Air Vice-Marshall − known affectionately as 'Pathfinder' Bennett after his second world war exploits − was that it could speedily be adapted to a new market, or to accept new engines. The most popular version was the Electron Minor, which ran for more than ten years with one of the various Standard-Triumph small four cylinder engines, of between 948cc and 1296cc, but there was also the original Coventry-Climax engined Electron, the Zeta, with its six-cylinder Ford Zephyr engine, and the Rockette, which used a six-cylinder 1.6-litre Triumph Vitesse unit. In all these cases, the engine was matched to the appropriate gearbox and (at times) overdrive used by the engine in its more normal

Fairthorpe Zeta

mass-production habitat.

The Electron Minor progressed to EM3 in the mid 1960s with a Triumph Spitfire four-cylinder engine, and eventually became a Mk VI with a 1.3-litre version in the early 1970s. In all that time Fairthorpe never set up a dealer network, never sold complete cars, and never restyled their basic 1950s shape, except in minor detail.

Production ran out in favour of the TX series, which had been designed by the founder's son Torix Bennett, though only extremely limited numbers of these cars have ever been sold.

Fairthorpe Electron Minor III, 1965

Specification

Engine and transmission: Depending on model. **(Zeta)** Six-cylinders, in-line, with pushrod operated overhead valve cylinder head, built by Ford GB. Bore, stroke and capacity 82.5 × 79.5mm., 2553cc. Maximum power 137bhp (gross) at 5500rpm.; maximum torque 160lb.ft. at 3200rpm. **(Rockette)** Six-cylinders, in-line, with pushrod-operated overhead-valve cylinder head, built by Standard-Triumph. Bore, stroke and capacity 66.75 × 76mm., 1596cc. Maximum power 72bhp (net) at 5600rpm.; maximum torque 93lb.ft. at 2800rpm. **(Electron)** Four-cylinders, in-line, with single-overhead-camshaft cylinder head, built by Coventry-Climax. Bore, stroke and capacity 72.4 × 66.6mm., 1098cc. Maximum power 93bhp (gross) at 7000rpm.; maximum torque 71lb.ft. at 3000rpm. (1216cc engine also available). **(Electron Minor)** Four cylinders, in-line, with pushrod-operated overhead-valve cylinder head. Bore, stroke and capacity between 63 × 76mm., 948cc and 73.7 × 76mm., 1296cc. Power between 49bhp (net) at 4500rpm to 75bhp (net) at 6000rpm. Maximum torque between 49lb.ft. at 3000rpm and 75lb.ft. at 4000rpm. Four-speed manual gearbox and optional overdrive (on some models) in unit with engine. Hypoid bevel final drive.

Chassis: Front engine, rear drive. Separate steel tubular chassis frame. Independent front suspension by coil springs and wishbones. Rack and pinion steering. Rear suspension (earlier cars) independent by coil springs and trailing wishbones, (later cars) by live axle, coil springs and radius arms. Four wheel drum brakes (earlier cars), front wheel discs and drum rears (later cars).

Bodywork: Glass-fibre two-door two-seater open sports style. Length (slight differences over years) 15ft. 5in.; width 4ft. 10in.; height 3ft. 10in. Unladen weight (depending on engine) from 980lb to 1475lb.

Performance: **(Zeta)** Maximum speed 117mph. 0-60mph 7.9sec. Standing ¼-mile 15.8sec. Typical fuel consumption 21mpg. **(Rockette)** Maximum speed 99mph. 0-60mph 13.7sec. Standing ¼-mile 18.9sec. Typical fuel consumption 25mpg.

Fairthorpe TX series

Built: Denham, England, 1965 to date

Although the total production of all TX models cannot be much over 100 units, those produced with Torix Bennett's own specially-designed rear suspension are very noteworthy and 'different'. It was the rear suspension which made the TX project so interesting to the analysts who first saw it in 1965.

As the son of Air Vice-Marshal Bennett, Torix Bennett was able to draw on the resources of the little Fairthorpe concern to make chassis and new-style bodies for his cars. The chassis he chose was to be a simple multi-tubular device at first, though later a Triumph GT6 frame was modified instead. Almost from the start, however, with the GT6 frame in use, the TX models were offered either with the usual Triumph transverse leaf-spring arrangement, or with the TX set-up.

The secret of this TX layout was that chassis roll due to cornering forces actually enabled the rear wheels to take up slight negative camber qualities on inside and outside wheels. In other words, as the chassis leaned out and away from the corner, the wheels inclined slightly inwards, thus optimising the grip available from the tyres. Experience on prototypes (for no road-test cars were ever offered for the press to assess) showed that this system really worked, but at the expense of taking up a lot of space which might otherwise have been used for stowage of luggage, spare tyre, or fuel tank. This geometry was achieved with a combination of trailing links and transverse levers, both of which were connected to the rear wheel hubs. The problem, however, was not that this suspension might not work – which it most assuredly did – but that it showed up limitations in the front suspension (the perfectly adequate Triumph Spitfire assemblies) and that it was not all that much better on smooth roads than a well-located live-axle arrangement.

Various versions of the TX models – GT, S, and SS – have been sold, all based on the same glass-fibre fastback coupe style, and all fitted with one or other of Triumph's straight-six engines, with carburettors or fuel-injection. The most powerful – the SS – had a 2498cc engine with Lucas fuel-injection, which produced more than 150 (gross) horsepower. Prices have always been high, and the market very limited. The car has not been re-styled, nor noticeably developed, since the late 1960s when it was introduced.

Specification

Engine and transmission: Six-cylinders, in-line, with pushrod-operated overhead-valve cylinder head, built by Triumph. Bore, stroke and capacity **(GT and S)** 74.7 × 76mm., 1998cc. Maximum power (GT) 104bhp (net) at 5300rpm.; maximum torque 117lb.ft. at 3000rpm. Maximum power (S) 112bhp (net) at 5300rpm.; maximum torque 117lb.ft. at 3000rpm. Bore, stroke and capacity **(SS)** 74.7 × 95mm., 2498cc. Maximum power 132bhp (net) at 5450rpm.; maximum torque 153lb.ft. at 2000rpm. Four-speed manual gearbox (and overdrive, depending on model) in unit with engine. Hypoid bevel final drive.

Chassis: Front engine, rear drive. Separate steel tubular chassis frame. Independent front suspension by coil springs and wishbones. Rack and pinion steering. Independent rear suspension (1) by transverse leaf spring, lower wishbones and radius arms, or optionally (2) by coil springs, wishbones and TX control linkages. Front wheel disc brakes, rear drums.

Bodywork: Glass-fibre two-door two-seater fastback coupe style. Length 12ft. 2.5in.; width 5ft. 0in.; height 3ft. 10.5in. (GT) or 3ft. 8.5in.; (S and SS). Unladen weight 1795lb.

Performance (Manufacturers' claims) (TX-S): Maximum speed 115mph. Typical fuel consumption 26mpg.

Fairthorpe TX-GT

Gilbern GT

Built: Llantwit Fardre, Wales, 1960-1967

German-born Bernard Frieze studied engineering in his young days, and after working for a manufacturer of glass-fibre special bodies in the 1950s, decided that he could do the same thing on his own account. After building a special shell for Giles Smith of South Wales, the two got together to form the Gilbern business (GILes and BERNard is the source of the marque name), and began to design a new sporting coupe. They had to be content with their own chassis and bodywork, but had to buy — through retail sources — the power train and suspensions. The Gilbern GT was the result.

Gilbern GT

Frieze designed a multi-tube steel chassis frame, by no means a scientifically-designed space frame, but much more advanced than some of the simple ladder types used by his competitors. Almost all the mechanical fittings to this chassis were from BMC (or — more particularly — from MG and Austin-Healey models), and at first there was a choice of engines. Coil spring independent front suspension and the live rear axle were from the MGA/MGB models, as were the brakes and the steering gear.

At the beginning of the 1960s, three different engines — 948cc BMC 'A' Series engine with Shorrock supercharging, and an A-Series gearbox, 1588cc MGA engine and gearbox, or a 1098cc Coventry-Climax engine (as used in cars like the Lotuses of the period) and MGA gearbox. The Climax option was soon dropped, as it was both more expensive and less effective than the rugged MGA unit.

Only 11 cars were built in 1960, followed by 33 in 1961, and 52 in 1962, by which time the MG engine was standardised. For 1963, therefore, the enlarged 1798cc MGB engine and gearbox became normal to the Gilbern GT, and sales continued to expand – 85 cars in 1963, 123 in 1964, and no fewer than 157 in 1965. Even in 1966, when preparations were going ahead for a new model, the vee-6 engined Genie, to be announced, more than 100 of this chunky little car were being built.

The main attraction of the Gilbern GT, apart from its corrosion-proof glass-fibre body, which was entirely built by Gilbern at their little works, was that it could be bought in kit form, and according to British tax law this meant that purchase tax did not have to be charged on it. What actually happened was that the car was supplied with only its major components not already fitted, and most competent home mechanics were happy to deal with this. Even so, the Gilbern GT was not as refined nor as well-developed as the quantity-production cars like TR4s and MGBs with which it had to compete, and sales were always low.

The last GT was built at the beginning of 1967, as all space in the Llantwit Fardre factory was then taken over by the new Genie model.

Specification (With MGA 1600 engine)

Engine and transmission: Four-cylinders, in-line, with pushrod-operated overhead-valve cylinder head, manufactured by BMC (MG). Bore, stroke and capacity 75.4 × 88.9mm, 1588cc. Maximum power 80bhp (net) at 5600rpm; maximum torque 87lb.ft. at 3800rpm. Four-speed gearbox in unit with engine. Hypoid bevel final drive.
Chassis: Front engine, rear drive. Multi-tubular separate chassis frame. Independent front suspension by coil springs and wishbones. Rack and pinion steering. Rear suspension of live axle by coil springs, radius arms and Panhard rod. Front wheel disc brakes and rear drums.
Bodywork: Glass-fibre bodywork, in two-door close-coupled 4-seat fastback coupe style. Length 12ft. 6in.; width 5ft. 0in.; height 4ft. 2.5in. Unladen weight 1680lb.
Performance: Maximum speed 94mph. 0-60mph 13.8sec. Standing ¼-mile 19.0sec. Typical fuel consumption 35mpg.

Note: The GT was also available with the 948cc BMC engine, with the 1216cc Coventry-Climax engine, and later with the enlarged MG 1622cc or 1798cc engines. These were all fitted to the same basic chassis and structural layout.

Gilbern Genie and Invader

Built: Llantwit Fardre, Wales, 1966-1973

Following the steady, if unspectacular, success of their Gilbern GT, Bernard Frieze and Giles Smith decided to design and market a larger and more luxurious new model, using − as on their original car − mainly proprietary components. The result was the Gilbern Genie of 1966, which sold steadily until 1973 when the arrival of Value Added Tax on British cars (and an end to the concession to small concerns to sell 'kit cars' without charging tax on them) killed off the demand.

In general, the car was designed according to the same principles as the Gilbern GT had been. Proprietary (in this case MGB) independent front suspension and an MGB back axle were mounted to a strong three-dimensional multi-tubular chassis frame. A 3-litre Ford vee-6 engine of 2994cc was specified, along with the appropriate Zodiac four-speed gearbox, and the mechanical ensemble was clothed in a chunky but attractive four-seater two-door coupe bodyshell, made by Gilbern from glass-fibre. The style was unashamedly based on that of the Alfa Romeo Giulia Sprint GT of the day, with rather sharper crease lines, and was done without the benefit of wind-tunnel testing.

The first car was completed in a great hurry in time for showing at the 1966 Earls Court Motor Show, but production began almost at once, and deliveries began the

Gilbern Invader

following spring. Right from the start it was clear that the car's biggest failings were in road-holding, and in general refinement (both to be expected from a tiny concern in which one of the partners was also the chief engineer and development tester), and as the Genie was never cheap it was not at all surprising that buyers were hard to find.

The Genie became the Invader in 1969, with considerably more refinement and furnishing, and – most importantly – revised and improved suspension. For the 1970s, too, came a rather attractive small estate car (Scimitar GTE type) derivative on the same chassis, but even though both models had become Mark IIIs by 1973, Gilbern stopped trading at the end of that year, and the Invader was the last model made by that firm.

Specification

Engine and transmission: Six-cylinders, in 60-degree vee-formation, with pushrod-operated overhead-valve cylinder heads, manufactured by Ford. Bore, stroke and capacity 93.7×72.4mm, 2994cc. Maximum power 141bhp (net) at 4750rpm; maximum torque 181lb.ft. at 3000rpm. Four-speed gearbox in unit with engine. Hypoid bevel final drive.

Chassis: Front engine, rear drive. Multi-tubular separate chassis frame. Independent front suspension by coil springs and wishbones. Rack and pinion steering. Rear suspension of live axle by coil springs, radius arms and Panhard rod. Front wheel disc brakes and rear drums.

Bodywork: Glass-fibre bodywork, in two-door close-coupled four-seat notchback coupe style. Length 13ft. 3in.; width 5ft. 5in.; height 4ft. 4in. Unladen weight 1990lb.

Performance: Maximum speed 115mph. 0-60mph 10.7sec. Standing ¼-mile 17.8sec. Typical fuel consumption 21mpg.

Note: The Genie was eventually developed into the Invader, with only minor changes, and an estate-car body style was added to the range.

Ginetta G15

Built: Witham, England, 1967-1973

Although the Walklett family set up the Ginetta business in 1957, for some years they concentrated merely on building cars for use in British racing classes. Although these were built in significant numbers, and more than one of the sports cars could − in de-tuned form − have been suitable for road use, no true Ginetta road car was put on sale until 1967.

This road car was the G15 model, in which the powerpack was by courtesy of Rootes and the Sunbeam Stiletto model. Basis of the design was a tubular steel chassis frame, to the back of which was attached the entire Stiletto engine, transmission and rear suspension units, with invididually designed coil spring front suspension for the front wheels. The whole was clad by a shapely two-seater notchback coupe, fashioned at Witham in glass-fibre, and the styling would not have disgraced any small sports car produced by a much more ambitious and well-heeled manufacturer.

Even though the Stiletto's 875cc engine only produced 51bhp (DIN), this was enough to push the G15 along at speeds up to nearly 95mph. Fuel economy was usually well over 40mpg, and the roadholding (helped by the very light engine/transmission pack) was very sporting. One should not forget that the Stiletto's engine, first seen in single-carburettor form in the Hillman Imp saloon of 1963, had been designed as a fairly close copy of a Coventry-Climax racing unit (the FWMA 750cc engine), and was technically advanced, even if its reliability left something to be desired.

The G15, like many other small cars in Britain at the time, was sold in kit form, and it was this fact (the financial wrinkle that allowed it to be sold free of purchase tax) which eventually led to its downfall. When Value Added Tax was introduced in 1973 that concession was withdrawn, sales of G15 slumped, and the model was soon withdrawn from the market.

Ginetta G15

Specification

Engine and transmission: Four-cylinders, in-line, installed at 45-degrees to vertical, with single-overhead-camshaft cylinder head, built by Chrysler UK. Bore, stroke and capacity 68 × 60.4mm., 875cc. Maximum power 50bhp (DIN) at 5800rpm.; maximum torque 49lb.ft. at 4500rpm. Four-speed manual gearbox in unit with engine and transaxle. Spiral bevel final drive.

Chassis: Rear engine, rear drive. Separate steel tubular chassis frame. Independent front suspension by coil springs and wishbones. Rack and pinion steering. Independent rear suspension by coil springs and semi-trailing wishbones. Front wheel disc brakes, rear drums.

Bodywork: Glass-fibre, two-door, two-seater, hardtop coupe body style. Length 12ft. 0.5in.; width 4ft. 9in.; height 3ft. 8.5in. Unladen weight 1105lb.

Performance: Maximum speed 94mph. 0-60mph 12.9sec. Standing ¼-mile 18.8sec. Typical fuel consumption 41mpg.

Ginetta G21

Built: Sudbury and Witham, England, 1970 to date

Following the successful launch of the rear-engined G15, and the build-up of production of this small Essex-based concern, Ginetta next announced another entirely new road-car design, to be called the G21. Although it has always been built in much smaller quantities than the G15 (and − indeed − for a time production ceased altogether), it has proved to be a worthy if specialised product from Ginetta.

The G21, however, had a rather confused launch. In the beginning, it was revealed just in time for showing at Earls Court in 1970, with a choice of Ford 3-litre vee-6 or 1.6-litre four-cylinder engines, and with live axle rear suspension or the option of independent rear suspension for the vee-6 engined cars. Before the car went into production, however, the Ford four-cylinder engine had been abandoned, and in its place came the Rootes four-cylinder engine of 1725cc normally fitted to Sunbeam Rapiers and H120s. Further, the independent rear suspension appeared to have been dropped, even though road trials showed it to be a very satisfactory layout.

The basis of the G21's design was a simple square-section tubular frame, strengthened where appropriate with steel sheet and fabrications. Front suspension and steering came from the Triumph Vitesse, and the axle was from Ford, while the attractive fastback glass-fibre body style was by the Walkletts themselves.

Specification

Engine and transmission: Four-cylinders, in-line, with pushrod-operated overhead-valve cylinder head, built by Chrysler UK. Bore, stroke and capacity 81.5 × 82.55mm., 1725cc. Maximum power 85bhp (DIN) at 5200rpm.; maximum torque 107lb.ft. at 4000rpm. Four-speed manual gearbox and overdrive in unit with engine. Hypoid bevel final drive.

Chassis: Front engine, rear drive. Separate tubular steel chassis frame. Independent front suspension by coil springs and wishbones. Rack and pinion steering. Rear suspension of live axle by coil springs, radius arms and Panhard rod. Front wheel disc brakes, rear drums.

Bodywork: Two-door, 2 + 2 seater fastback style in glass-fibre. Length 13ft. 0.5in.; width 5ft. 3in.; height 3ft. 10in. Unladen weight 1740lb.

Note: Engine with 93bhp (DIN) at 5200rpm.; maximum torque of 106lb.ft. at 4000rpm, was also available.

Performance: (93bhp engine) Maximum speed 117mph. 0-60mph 9.2sec. Standing ¼-mile 17.0sec. Typical fuel consumption 28mpg.

Ginetta G21

Innocenti Coupe

Built: Milan, Italy, 1961-1970

Innocenti were already world-famous as makers of the Lambretta motor scooter in the 1950s, and it was not until 1960 that they branched out into car manufacture when they concluded a licence agreement with BMC to assemble the Pininfarina-styled Austin A40 saloon. The *Societa Generale per l'Industria Metallurgica e Meccanica* then followed this up with a very nice Ghia-styled version of the Sprite/Midget car, which made its bow at the Turin Show in November 1960.

Known at first as the Innocenti 950, it was the result of a complex commercial tie up involving a great deal of finance and factory space. Ghia styled the car, and in association with Fergat (who specialised in press tools and pressings), they formed *Officine Stampaggi Industriali*, which was more familiarly known as OSI. OSI's 200 000 square feet of factory, later to be taken over by Innocenti for their exclusive use, originally made the Innocenti 950 Spider and the entirely different Fiat 2100/2300 Coupes.

Mechanically, the Innocenti 950 was entirely familiar, for it used an unmodified Sprite/Midget floor pan, engine and transmission. Above the floorpan, the pressed-steel bodyshell was to the credit of OSI/Ghia, and was finished off and sold in Italy and in North America by Innocenti. The style was really very attractive, delicately shaped, and such a contrast to either the original frog-eye Sprite (the Midget had not even been announced in 1960, after all) or to the Mk II version of 1961, that BMC should be ashamed of never taking it up for their own use.

Since BMC supplied the assembled floor-pans, the Innocenti Coupe changed along with the Sprites and Midgets, which is to say that the engine was enlarged from 948cc to 1098cc (but never to 1275cc), that half-elliptic leaf springs replaced the original quarter-elliptic cantilever springs, and that disc brakes were fitted.

The smart and distinctive body style, however, was never completely reshaped, though the open car of the early 1960s gave way to the Innocenti C Coupe of 1967, in which OSI had added a smart and slightly angular steel hardtop to the original sports car shell, allied to a very generous provision of glass. It is worth noting, too, that the Innocenti cars had wind-up door glasses from the very beginning, whereas the BMC-built Sprites and Midgets did not inherit such refinements until 1964.

By the end of the 1960s Innocenti were becoming more and more involved with BMC, or British Leyland as it became in 1968, such that they were undertaking assembly of their own particular brand of Minis, and of the 1100/1300 models. The last of the C Coupes, therefore, was sold in 1970.

Innocenti Spider S

Specification

Engine, transmission and chassis: Mechanical basis was that of the equivalent Austin-Healey Sprite/MG Midget: a four-cylinder in-line engine with pushrod-operated overhead-valves, a four-speed manual gearbox in unit with it, and hypoid bevel final drive. A pressed-steel unit-construction underframe, coil spring independent front suspension, rack and pinion steering and live axle located by quarter-elliptic leaf springs or (from 1964) half-elliptic leaf springs, was that of the Midget/Sprite.

Bodywork: Pressed-steel two-door two-seater open sports style by Ghia, or closed coupe (by OSI). Length 11ft. 3in.; width 4ft. 9.9in.; height 3ft. 10.6in. Unladen weight (open sports) 1595lb. (coupe) 1700lb.

Performance: (1964 model, 1098cc) Maximum speed 85mph. 0-60mph 18.4sec. Standing ¼-mile 21.0sec. Typical fuel consumption 25mpg.

Jensen 541S

Built: West Bromwich, England, 1960-1963

Jensen, who had started building cars in small numbers in the 1930s, had sprung to prominence in the mid-1950s by putting their rakish 541 models into production. These had achieved fame by being fast, long-legged and reputedly durable, while being relatively exclusive and distinctively-styled. The brothers Jensen – Alan and Richard – still controlled the firm they had themselves started, and were still responsible for the shaping of their products. By the end of the 1950s, too, their factory was very busy building Austin-Healey 3000 bodies for BMC, and was preparing to build Volvo P1800s from bodies supplied by Pressed Steel.

The 541S was announced in 1960, logically enough replacing the 541R, and improving on it, though retaining the main elements of the tubular chassis and the glass-fibre bodyshell. The original 541 had appeared in 1953, and gone in to production during 1954. In every way it had been completely different from the Interceptor of the early 1950s, and was sufficiently tooled up to run for many years. Central to the design was a simple-to-build but complex chassis, which joined massive tubular frame members to pressed and fabricated steel panels, to make a self-supporting platform chassis. Powering it was a 4-litre Austin 6-cylinder engine and transmission, allied to Austin independent front suspension. The 541 had become the 541R with more power and – eventually – with disc brakes.

The 541S was a physically larger car than its ancestors, due to having a four-inch wider body. This was achieved, as could so easily be done, by cutting the body moulds down the middle and adding an extra four inch fillet from front to rear! The frame, also simple to modify, was changed in the same way, and a new rear axle was required to suit. At the same time the Jensens restyled the body somewhat, losing some of the quite distinctive features of the 541R, including that fascinating swivelling panel ahead

Jensen 541S, 1960

of the cooling radiator which was said to improve the aerodynamics when closed at high road speeds.

Austin 4-litre power outputs, after reaching a high point with the early 541R models, were now on the way down, and the 541S's output of about 130bhp was never officially revealed by Jensen, who did not wish to be seen to be 'progressing' backwards. The engine, incidentally, was that used in Austin's vast limousines, and also found a home in some of the BMC group's trucks.

The principal attraction of the 541S, apart from its increased interior space and revised fascia style, was that it was offered with optional automatic transmission. This option was no less than the Rolls-Royce four-speed system which that prestigious firm imported from General Motors, modified to their own purposes, and fitted to the 'Best Car in the World'. Although the 541S was nominally also available with the manual gearbox and overdrive specified for 541R models, very few of these were ever delivered. It was the beginning of the end for the manual-transmission Jensens.

Although the 541S was not a dramatically attractive car, it was adequate enough, and at a rate of no more than four or five cars a week it sold steadily. However, due to the less-powerful engine, and to the greater size and bulk of the re-styled body, the 541S was significantly slower than the car it had replaced, and potential customers began to complain loudly about this. Test cars achieved barely 110mph, whereas a 541R could beat 120mph with some ease.

Jensen therefore looked around for a more powerful engine. Austin could not supply one, so like Bristol (and others to follow) the West Bromwich concern looked to Detroit instead. The result was yet another much-modified car, the CV-8 of 1962, which became a Supercar in every way. 541S sales carried alongside the CV-8 for a time, but the last example was finished off in 1963.

Specification

Engine and transmission: Six-cylinders, in-line, with pushrod-operated overhead-valve cylinder head, built by Austin. Bore, stroke and capacity 87 × 111mm., 3993cc. Maximum power and maximum torque not revealed. Four-speed manual gearbox, optional overdrive, or four-speed Rolls-Royce/GM automatic transmission in unit with engine. Hypoid bevel final drive.

Chassis: Front engine, rear drive. Separate tubular and fabricated steel chassis frame. Independent front suspension by coil springs and wishbones. Rack and pinion steering. Rear suspension of live axle by half-elliptic leaf springs and Panhard rod. Four wheel disc brakes.

Bodywork: Glass-fibre two-door close-coupled four-seater fastback GT coupe style. Length 14ft. 10in.; width 5ft. 7in.; height 4ft. 6.4in. Unladen weight 3415lb.

Performance: (Automatic version) Maximum speed 109mph. 0-60mph 12.4sec. Standing ¼-mile 18.8sec. Typical fuel consumption 17mpg.

Lotus Seven & Super Seven

Built: Cheshunt, Hethel, Caterham, England, 1957 to date

The story of Colin Chapman's rise to eminence as a racing car and road car designer has been told many times, but it is worth recalling that his first cars were sold as 'kit cars' for assembly by the customer, and were intended for use in club racing, trials, or whatever was thought suitable. The early Lotus models used proprietary mechanical parts, complex multi-tubular chassis frames and light-alloy bodies. Although the Lotus Six of the mid-1950s was Chapman's first 'production model', it was the Seven which followed it, which really set the cash registers ringing. That, and the Elite announced in the same year, were the models which turned Lotus into serious car makers.

Because of the way Lotus operated, and because of the 'Meccano' method of construction and assembly which could be adopted with the Seven, it was often quite normal for a kit to be sold without engine and gearbox, and Lotus admit to many cases in which they did not know what engine would power a car when they sold it. As a consequence, in the lengthy period in which Sevens have been on sale, engines as diverse as side-valve Ford 100E units of 1172cc to 'Big Valve' twin-cam Lotus-Ford units race-tuned to give more than 160bhp have been fitted, with a great deal of variety in terms of A-Series BMC units, Coventry-Climax FWA engines, and any of the vast range of pushrod overhead valve Ford 'Kent' engines from 997cc to 1599cc.

All, however, had a scientifically-designed multi-tubular 'space-frame' chassis, where function and stressing came before convenience and access. All had coil spring independent front suspension, and all save one prototype had live rear axles accurately located by radius arms, and sprung on coil spring/damper units. There were no doors – merely cutaway sides – the wings were separate, the headlamps were proudly free-standing on each side of the nose, and it was virtually impossible to gain access to the seats if the hood was already erect.

Lotus Seven

The Lotus Seven's biggest advantages, however, were that it was very light, and that it handled superbly. In club racing, in sprints, and in most motoring activities where aerodynamics and creature comfort were not important, a Seven could be supreme.

To Lotus, however, the Seven eventually became an anachronism. They progressed to making smooth and refined road cars like the Elan Plus Two, and Seven did not line up with this new image. Even though they substantially revised the Seven for 1970, as the series IV, with revised front suspension and a glass-fibre bodyshell, they did not change its basic layout.

As the end of the 'kit car' era drew near with the arrival of VAT and the change in company policy, Lotus decided to drop the Seven Series IV. At this point, however, one of their main dealers, Caterham Car Sales, stepped in with an offer to take over manufacturing rights for the Seven, and began to build new supplies of the obsolete Series III model. This project is so successful that the 'Lotus' name has now been dropped, and the cars are simply known as 'Super Sevens'. Like the Morgans, these cars now seem to have a stable clientele who would be positively offended if the design was modernised.

It is an interesting truth that the cars are still so fast in 'standard' form that they have been declared ineligible for some forms of British club racing, and their manufacturing company make much of this in their publicity material. All in all, several thousands of these spidery but efficient little cars have been made, and sales continue into the 1980s.

Specification (Late 1970s Super Seven type)

Engine and transmission: Four-cylinders, in-line, with twin-overhead-camshaft cylinder head, Ford based, but manufactured by Lotus. Bore, stroke and capacity, 82.55×72.75mm, 1558cc. Maximum power 126bhp (DIN) at 6500rpm.; maximum torque 113lb.ft. at 5500rpm. Four-speed manual transmission in unit with engine. Hypoid bevel final drive.

Chassis: Front engine, rear drive. Multi-tubular steel 'space-frame', separate chassis. Independent front suspension by coil springs and wishbones. Rack and pinion steering. Suspension of rear live axle by coil springs, radius arms and Panhard rod. Front wheel disc brakes, rear drums.

Bodywork: Light-alloy body panels, in two-seat open sports car style, with no doors. Length 11ft. 0.5in.; width 5ft. 1.0in.; height 3ft. 1in. Unladen weight 1655lb.

Performance: Maximum speed 103mph. 0-60mph 7.1sec. Standing ¼-mile 15.5sec. Typical fuel consumption 19mpg.

Note: Super Sevens have also been sold with the 1599cc Ford pushrod ohv engine installed, and previous Sevens had a whole variety of engines, ranging from 948cc ohv BMC A-Series engines and 1172cc sv Ford 100E units to much more powerful units.
Performance (1340cc ohv Ford engine): Maximum speed 103mph. 0-60mph 7.6sec. Standing ¼-mile 15.8sec. Typical fuel consumption 25mpg.

Lotus Elite

Built: Cheshunt, England, 1959-1963

Although Colin Chapman had already established his reputation for designing successful racing cars by the mid-1950s, his first true road car, the Elite, was not actually put on sale until the end of that decade. As one would have expected from the technically adventurous Chapman, the first Elite was startingly 'different' in almost every way, and even though it was never a financial success it now has its own well-deserved legend.

The Elite was the first-ever car to use a complete monocoque of glass-fibre, with only a little local stiffening in steel. All previous cars with glass-fibre shells had used steel chassis frames in one form or another, but for the Elite Chapman was able to do away with this heavy item completely. However, the use of glass-fibre brought its own problems, most important being the difficulty with which sound and vibration could be suppressed. It is sad, but true, that the Elite is by no means the smooth and silky little coupe which it looks likely to be.

The two-seater coupe shell was built up in only three major sections – the floor, the structural centre section, and the one-piece outer skin – after which the moving panels such as doors and engine compartment lid were bolted into place. Power was provided by a four-cylinder Coventry-Climax unit with single overhead camshaft – the power and specification of this detuned racing unit was progressively pushed up from 71bhp at first to 100bhp, all from 1216cc – with a proprietary gearbox (BMC 'B' Series at first, and ZF on Series two cars).

Four wheel independent suspension and disc brakes were part of the very advanced (for 1957, when the car was announced) specification. Front suspension was by coil spring/damper units and double wishbones, allied to rack and pinion steering, while on the Series I cars rear suspension was an adaptation of the MacPherson strut layout, though in this case it was usually called the 'Chapman strut' system. On Series II cars, however, different lower wishbone geometry, allied to a fixed-length driveshaft, made its operation rather different.

The beautifully styled two-seater fixed-head coupe bodyshell was the work of Colin Chapman and his associates, and featured sharply angled windscreen and side glass. This, in fact, was always a problem, because the profile of the door skins and the side windows meant that the glass could not be wound down to encourage ventilation. Occupants either had to stew in an enclosed interior, or suffer draughts when the side windows were removed altogether.

The Elite's major selling points, after its styling, were its high performance allied to quite remarkable potential fuel economy, its light weight, and its roadholding, which was a complete class ahead of almost anything else sold for public road use. Although the prototype was first shown in the autumn of 1957, delivery of the first production cars did not begin until 1959, and once the Elan had been announced in 1962 the Elite's popularity was on the wane.

Quality and reliability problems, allied to a rather high price, meant that buyers were hard to find in later years. Even as late as 1964, however, Lotus considered re-launching the car with their own new Lotus-Ford engine in place of the now-obsolete Coventry-Climax engine, but nothing became of it. Only 988 were built.

Lotus Elite

In Team Lotus hands, and when used by several private owners, Elites could be formidable competitors on the race tracks, as their record in events like the Le Mans 24 Hour sports car race, at the Nurburgring, and all over Europe in less important events, proves.

Specification

Engine and transmission: Four-cylinders, in-line, with single overhead camshaft cylinder head, made by Coventry Climax. Bore, stroke and capacity 76.2 × 66.6mm, 1216cc. Maximum power (twin carburettor version) 83bhp (net) at 6250rpm; maximum torque 75lb.ft. at 4750rpm. Single carburettor version also available with 71bhp at 6100rpm; maximum torque 77lb.ft. at 3750rpm. Four-speed gearbox in unit with engine. Hypoid bevel final drive.

Chassis: Front engine, rear drive. Monocoque body chassis unit in glass-fibre, with local pressed and tubular steel strengthening. Independent front suspension by coil springs and wishbones. Rack and pinion steering. Independent rear suspension by coil springs, Chapman struts and fixed-length halfshafts (later models modified to have revised radius arm geometry). Four wheel disc brakes.

Bodywork: Glass-fibre bodywork, in unit with the glass fibre structure, in two-door two-seat coupe style. Length 12ft. 4in.; width 4ft. 11.25in.; height 3ft. 10.5in. Unladen weight 1455lb.

Performance: (Twin carburettor model) Maximum speed 118mph. 0-60mph 11.0sec. Standing ¼-mile 17.5sec. Typical fuel consumption 35mpg.

Note: In later years the engine was developed to produce up to 100bhp in production form.

Lotus Elan series

Built: Cheshunt and Hethel, England, 1962-1973

To replace his troublesome Elites, Colin Chapman chose to develop an entirely different type of road-going sports car for the 1960s. In some ways it was more complex, and in others rather more simple. It was an open car where the Elite had been a coupe, it had a separate chassis instead of a monocoque, and a Lotus engine instead of a bought-in item. It was also a great success. The Elan, more than any other car, brought respectability to Lotus as genuine production car manufacturers.

Central to the design thinking for the Elan was that it should have a simple steel chassis – simple to make, simple to repair, and simple to develop. Lotus's extensive design experience allowed this to be a sturdy backbone frame, with the engine and gearbox mounted in the front end, which was shaped somewhat like a tuning fork, and with the final drive and suspensions fixed to its rear. A feature, obvious when the glass-fibre body was removed, was that the MacPherson struts (combined springs and dampers) were mounted on high angle outriggers to the backbone, which looked weak but which were remarkably strong. There was a wide-based tubular lower wishbone, and the driveshafts were fitted with inner and outer rubber universal joints ('doughnuts' as they were soon affectionately known).

By now Lotus had become aligned with Ford in many ways, so it was no surprise to see that their own new engine was effectively the bottom end of the 1.5-litre Cortina unit, newly equipped with five-bearings, topped by a twin-cam light-alloy cylinder head and valve gear, which had been designed for Lotus by Harry Mundy of *The Autocar*, who had also been responsible for some of the Coventry-Climax racing engines of the 1950s. The gearbox and the differential gears were also by Ford.

Lotus Elan S4

When announced, this twin-cam engine actually shared dimensions with the Ford production unit (it was a 1499cc engine) but almost immediately after production began during 1963 the cylinder bore was increased, and the familiar (later, legendary) 1558cc capacity emerged.

Right from the start the Elan, which could be bought in kit form (as most were) or completely finished by Lotus, was a success, as it was fast, light, economical, and possessed of the most phenomenal roadholding and agility. If the lucky buyer could get reasonable insurance quotations, it could be a surprisingly economical car to run in all respects.

The Elan would be an important part of the scene at Lotus for ten years, during which it underwent many important development changes and improvements. However, the only significant body modification was that in the autumn of 1965 a stylish and very practical (if somewhat cramped) fixed-head coupe car was added. From then, until 1973, both types were produced.

In 1966 the nominal power output was increased from 105 to 115bhp, though subsequent experience suggested that both figures were somewhat 'gross', but the 'Big Valve' Sprint engines of 1971 onwards, with a very genuine 126bhp, were considerably more powerful.

S2 models were phased in late in 1964, S3 cars in 1965/1966, and S4 models in the spring of 1968. The Sprints were never officially S5s, though they superseded the S4s at the beginning of 1971.

The trim and equipment of the Elans was progressively improved over the years, and – most important – so was the quality and reliability of construction. Production was phased out in February 1973, due to several factors. Lotus were turning away from the kit-car concept, British Value Added Tax was about to render them unattractive to buyers, and the company was about to be re-tooled for the modern Elite-Eclat-Esprit models.

Specification (Elan 1600, 1963 model)

Engine and transmission: Four-cylinders, in-line, with twin-overhead-camshaft cylinder head, based on Ford design with Lotus cylinder head. Bore, stroke and capacity 82.55 × 72.75mm, 1588cc. Maximum power 105bhp (net) at 5500rpm; maximum torque 108lb.ft. at 4000rpm. Four-speed gearbox in unit with engine. Hypoid bevel final drive.

Chassis: Front engine, rear drive. Pressed steel backbone-type separate chassis frame. Independent front suspension by coil springs and wishbones. Rack and pinion steering. Independent rear suspension by coil springs, Chapman struts and lower wishbones. Four wheel disc brakes.

Bodywork: Glass-fibre bodywork, either in open-tourer or in fixed-head coupe, two-door two-seat style. Length 12ft. 1in.; width 4ft. 8in.; height 3ft. 9.5in. Unladen weight 1515lb.

Performance: Maximum speed 115mph. 0-60mph 8.7sec. Standing ¼-mile 16.4sec. Typical fuel consumption 30mpg.

Note: Special Equipment versions had 115bhp. Elan Sprint models introduced for 1971 had 126bhp (net) at 6500rpm; maximum torque 113lb.ft. at 5500rpm. Maximum speed 118mph. 0-60mph 7.0sec. Standing ¼-mile 15.0sec. Typical fuel consumption 26mpg.

Lotus Elan Plus 2 series

Built: Hethel, England, 1967-1974

The Elan Plus 2, announced in 1967, after the Lotus concern had moved into a new purpose-built factory at Hethel airfield, near Norfolk, was almost precisely what its model name might infer. It combined most of the engineering and all the qualities of the two-seater Lotus Elan in a bigger and more roomy glass-fibre bodyshell. Unlike the original Elan, however, the Plus 2 was never sold as a convertible; each and every Plus 2 was a slinky and rather cramped 2 + 2 coupe.

Lotus Elan Plus 2

The Plus 2 cars shared the engines, gearboxes and final drives of the smaller Elans, but had entirely different chassis and bodies. The layout of the steel backbone chassis was the same, but had to take account of the nine-inches longer wheelbase, and the greater wheel tracks, and there were suspension differences for the same reason. Like the two-seater cars, the Plus 2 models featured simple glass-fibre bodyshells, pop-up headlamps, and a surprisingly high standard of trim and equipment.

Like the two-seaters, too, Elan Plus 2s could be fast and remarkably sparing in their use of fuel, and they were sold in kit form or as completely built up models. Production began at the beginning of 1968, and continued until the end of 1974, by which time the much larger, more costly, and entirely different Elite had been phased in to production.

Mechanical improvements progressed hand-in-hand with the two-seater Elans. To look after the increased bulk and weight of the 'Plus 2' structure, the 'Special Equipment' engine was always standard at first. For 1971, the Plus 2, like the two-seater, received the 126bhp 'Big Valve' engine, and was renamed the Plus 2S 130. This was not the end of the road, however, for in the autumn of 1972 the car was also given the option of a five-speed gearbox with actual gears by courtesy of British Leyland. This box, if we did but know it, would also be an important item to be fitted to the next Lotus model, due in 1974. It was at about this time, too, that the 'kit car' derivative of the 2 + 2 Elan was withdrawn, as the company was moving very firmly up-market and wanted to keep a close tie on everything to do with production and testing of the finished product.

Like the much smaller two-seater car, the Plus 2 had outstanding roadholding, very supple suspension and an extremely flat ride. The engine, even in highly-tuned 'Big Valve' form, was flexible and reliable if properly serviced, and the whole car was remarkably simple and easy to maintain. It was only familiarity with its sleek good looks which made it any the less popular in 1974 than it had been in 1968.

Specification

Engine and transmission: Four-cylinders, in-line, with twin-overhead-camshaft cylinder head, based on Ford design with Lotus cylinder head. Bore, stroke and capacity 82.55 × 72.75mm, 1558cc. Maximum power 118bhp (net) at 6000rpm; maximum torque 108lb.ft. at 4000rpm. Four-speed gearbox in unit with engine. Hypoid bevel final drive.

Chassis: Front engine, rear drive. Pressed-steel backbone-type separate chassis frame. Independent front suspension by coil springs and wishbones. Rack and pinion steering. Independent rear suspension by coil springs, Chapman struts and lower wishbones. Four wheel disc brakes.

Bodywork: Glass-fibre bodywork, 2 + 2 seating in two-door coupe style. Length 14ft. 1in.; width 5ft. 6in.; height 3ft. 11in. Unladen weight 2085lb.

Performance: Maximum speed 118mph. 0-60mph 8.9sec. Standing ¼-mile 16.6sec. Typical fuel consumption 30mpg.

Note: Elan Plus 2S 130 models introduced for 1971 had boosted engines like Elan Sprint, and option of five-speed gearbox.

Performance: (Plus 2S 130/5) Maximum speed 120mph. 0-60mph 7.5sec. Standing ¼-mile 16.0sec. Typical fuel consumption 28mpg.

Lotus Europa series

Built: Hethel, England, 1967-1975

Although Colin Chapman took no time to bring his mid-engined single-seater racing cars to a high state of technical excellence, it was some years before he was ready to put such a layout on to the market as a road car. The problem, in the main, was that there was a lack of a suitable transaxle − gearbox and transmission − which could be matched with an engine acceptable to Lotus on performance and price. Not until the mid-1960s, when Lotus struck up a relationship with Renault, could anything be done about this.

The mid-engined Europa, announced at the end of 1966, was an interesting amalgam of Lotus engineering and Renault hardware. It was called the Europa quite simply because it was initially intended to be a car for sale only in Europe, and to emphasise the British-French links which brought about its design.

Central to the layout was the use of a Renault engine and transaxle, mounted in such a way that the engine was ahead of the line of the rear wheels, and the gearbox was behind that line. The engine was a tuned version of that fitted to the Renault 16 saloon car, and was matched to its transmission. This car, however, had front-engine/front-wheel-drive, and the engine is installed behind the line of the front wheels, so a moment's thought reveals that it was necessary not only to turn the combination through 180 degrees, but to modify the final drive gearing to suit (otherwise there would have been four reverse gears and one forward speed!)

Like the Elan which was in full production, the Europa had a pressed steel backbone chassis frame, with four-wheel independent suspension. The bodyshell was of glass-fibre, as usual for Lotus road cars, and because it had a mid-engine layout there was room only for two seats − one each slung on either side of the deep backbone frame.

On the first cars, the body-shell was actually bonded to the frame, but this feature was abandoned for the Series 2 Europa of 1968. Until 1969 the Europa was not available in Great Britain, but from the summer of that year it was put on sale, in kit form, or as a built-up example.

The Europa was always intended to be a relatively cheap Lotus, and − because of this − had a relatively simple mechanical specification. The problem was that customers were ungrateful, as they did not think the car had enough performance. In the autumn of 1971, therefore, Lotus reversed their policy for the car. After several thousand Renault-engined cars had been built, they dropped the power unit, and in its

Lotus Europa

place they fitted the well-known 1558cc Lotus-Ford engine, rated at 105bhp which was all the Renault 16-based gearbox could be expected to accept. This new model, the Europa Twin-Cam, also had modified rear body profiles, to improve three quarter rear visibility.

Only a year later, in October 1972, Lotus changed the Europa yet again, and the revised car, complete with the 'big valve' 126bhp engine, became the Europa Special. At first the Renault 12 Gordini's 5-speed gearbox (a development of the original box) was merely optional, but from the spring of 1974 it was standardised. By then, however, there was little future for the Europa, as it could no longer be sold in kit form in Britain, and with the continuing expansion of 'large Lotus' production it was finally and officially dropped in the autumn of 1975, to be replaced – of course – by the mid-engined Esprit.

Specification

Engine and transmission: Four-cylinders, in-line, with pushrod-operated overhead-valve cylinder head, built by Renault. Bore, stroke and capacity 76×81mm, 1470cc. Maximum power 78bhp (net) at 6000rpm; maximum torque 76lb.ft. at 4000rpm. Four-speed gearbox in unit with engine and transaxle. Hypoid bevel final drive.
Chassis: Mid-engine, rear drive. Pressed-steel backbone-type separate chassis frame (on early models, bonded to bodywork). Independent front suspension by coil springs and wishbones. Rack and pinion steering. Independent rear suspension by coil springs, fixed length driveshafts and radius arms. Front wheel disc brakes, rear drums.
Bodywork: Glass-fibre bodywork, in two-door two-seater fastback style. Length 13ft. 0.5in.; width 5ft. 4in.; height 3ft. 6in. Unladen weight 1350lb.
Performance: Maximum speed 120mph. 0-60mph 9.3sec. Standing ¼-mile 16.7sec. Typical fuel consumption 30mpg.

Note: From autumn 1970, the Europa became the Europa Twin-Cam, with the engine from the Elan (Ford-based Lotus engine with twin-overhead-camshaft cylinder head). From autumn 1972 the Europa Special was announced, with the engine from the Elan Sprint/Elan Plus 2S 130, and with optional 5-speed gearbox.
Performance: (Special) Maximum speed 121mph. 0-60mph 7.7sec. Standing ¼-mile 15.7sec. Typical fuel consumption 28mpg.

Lotus Europa Twin-Cam

Lotus Elite (1970s type) & Éclat

Built: Hethel, England, 1974 to date

It was Colin Chapman's determination to change the shape of his Lotus company, to turn it away from the business of making 'kit cars' with tiny bodies, and with space for only two people, and to start it making larger, faster and altogether more up-market products, which almost brought about its downfall. It was sheer bad luck, however, than Elan and Europa production ran out just after the post-Suez petrol-supply crisis hit the world at the end of 1973, and that the new Elite of 1974 took so long to get into its stride, and could never in any case be expected to sell in such large quantities.

The Elite of 1974, coded M50 at its formative stage, was the first of a new generation of Lotus road cars which now completely dominate the scene at Hethel, near Norfolk. Physically it was much larger than any previous Lotus (ignoring, of course, the Lotus-Cortina, which was really a modified Ford saloon car), had space for four passengers to travel in rather less than drawing room comfort, and it was powered by a new power unit which Lotus themselves had developed. This – the celebrated 16-valve four-cylinder unit used in every recent Lotus, in the Jensen-Healey of 1972-1976, and in the Talbot Sunbeam-Lotus – represented a major commitment in terms of time, resources, machine tools and investment.

The engine had originally been laid down in 1967/1968, as a 16-valve twin-cam conversion of the Vauxhall Victor unit which had just been revealed. In the course of development, however, Lotus developed their own light-alloy cylinder block and moving parts, so that it is now a unit entirely assembled and mainly machined by Lotus themselves. As it happens, the engine was ready before any of the cars for which it was intended, and was first seen in public in the Jensen-Healey of 1972. Although originally a two-litre unit, it has already been stretched to 2.2-litres for the Talbot Sunbeam-Lotus as an 'homologation special'.

Design of the new Lotus Elite, which has nothing in common with the original Elite of 1957 except the name, began in 1971. Like earlier Lotus road cars, it relied on a pressed and fabricated sheet-steel backbone chassis, had all-independent suspension, and used a glass-fibre bodyshell. The body style, however, by Lotus themselves, was neither a fastback coupe, nor a square-back sporting estate car, but something very

Lotus Elite

Lotus Eclat

dramatically and rakishly in between. It had two doors and a sharply-defined wedge motif, but the rear window/hatchback was almost all glass, and did not occupy all the back of the shell.

After a slow start, and after production began to build up, the Elite began to be made in several slightly-different varieties, not least with a still-powerful but detoxed engine for the North American market, with air-conditioning for those who wanted it, and even − sacrilege for a Lotus? − with Borg Warner automatic transmission.

From the autumn of 1975, too, the Eclat came along, which was effectively an Elite with a different fastback style of body behind the front doors, with less space in those rear seats (it was truly only a 2 + 2) and with a rather more simple mechanical specification and range of options.

Both models, and all the variations in specification, which were widened in the years which followed, continued side by side, and continue to be built as the 1980s begin. Along with the mid-engined Esprit, they represent specialist machines of which the British motor industry should be proud.

Specification

Engine and transmission: Four-cylinders, in-line, installed in chassis at 45 degrees to the vertical, with twin-camshaft cylinder head. Bore, stroke and capacity 95.25 × 69.24mm, 1973cc. Maximum power 160bhp (DIN) at 6500rpm; maximum torque 135lb.ft. at 5000rpm. Five-speed manual gearbox, or Borg Warner automatic transmission, in unit with engine. Hypoid bevel final drive.
Chassis: Front engine, rear drive. Pressed-steel backbone-type separate chassis frame. Independent front suspension by coil springs and wishbones. Rack and pinion steering. Independent rear suspension by coil springs, fixed length driveshafts, wishbone and radius arms. Front wheel disc brakes, and rear drums.
Bodywork: Glass-fibre bodywork, in three-door close-coupled four-seater sporting-estate style. Length 14ft. 7.5in.; width 5ft. 11.5in.; height 3ft. 11.5in. Unladen weight 2340lb.
Performance: Maximum speed 124mph. 0-60mph 7.8sec. Standing ¼-mile 16.4sec. Typical fuel consumption 25mpg.

Note: The Lotus Eclat has the same basic mechanical specification, but fast back two-door body style.
Performance: Maximum speed 129mph. 0-60mph 7.9sec. Standing ¼-mile 16.2sec. Typical fuel consumption 23mpg.

81

Lotus Esprit

Lotus Esprit

Built: Hethel, England, 1975 to date

At the end of 1975, Lotus completed a radical change in their model line-up when the Esprit was revealed. The well known Elans and Europas had been completely swept away, to be replaced by Elites, Eclats and the new Esprit. The mid-engined Esprit was effectively a replacement, though considerably more costly, for the Europa. There had been such a rush of new Lotus models, however, that deliveries of Esprits did not begin until the spring of 1976.

The car's coupe style is dramatic but, in many ways, typical of the Italian Supercar of the late 1970s. This is quite reasonable, for the car was shaped by Giugiaro's Ital Design studios in Italy, and was first seen as an 'ideas car' on that company's stand at a motor show. It is a wedge, constructed in this case from glass-fibre, by a special Lotus-developed method claimed to make the production process quicker and more predictable.

Like all modern Lotus road cars, the basis of the chassis is a pressed-steel backbone frame, which supports the mid-mounted engine and transaxle, the suspensions and all the principal mechanical components. Unlike other modern Lotus models, disc brakes are fitted to all wheels, those at the rear being mounted inboard.

The engine is the ubiquitous 16-valve 2-litre unit first seen in the Jensen-Healey of 1972, and now to be found on all Lotuses in production at the start of the 1980s, and is matched to the five-speed gearbox once used by Citroen in the Maserati-engined SM coupe. As this car had a front engine mounted behind the line of the rear wheels, the final drive arrangements have had to be changed to suit the new installation. Lotus, of course, are used to this sort of change, which was carried out on the Renault transmission used in the Europa.

Although Lotus originally claimed a maximum speed of up to 138mph, independent tests show that 130mph to 135mph is nearer the mark, but the chassis is certainly capable of dealing with much more than this.

Specification

Engine and transmission: Four-cylinders, in-line, installed in chassis at 45-degrees to the vertical, with twin-camshaft cylinder head. Bore, stroke and capacity 95.25 × 69.24mm, 1973cc. Maximum power 160bhp (DIN) at 6500rpm.; maximum torque 140lb.ft. at 4900rpm. Five-speed manual gearbox in unit with engine and transaxle. Hypoid bevel final drive.
Chassis: Mid-engine, rear drive. Pressed steel backbone-type separate chassis frame. Independent front suspension by coil springs and wishbones. Rack and pinion steering. Independent rear suspension by coil springs, fixed length driveshafts, wishbones and radius arms. Four-wheel disc brakes.
Bodywork: Glass-fibre bodywork, in two-door two-seat fastback style. Length 13ft. 9in.; width 6ft. 1in.; height 3ft. 7.75in. Unladen weight 2275lb.
Performance: Maximum speed 124mph. 0-60mph 8.4sec. Standing ¼-mile 16.3sec. Typical fuel consumption 26mpg. **(S2)** Maximum speed 135mph. 0-60mph 8.0sec. Standing ¼-mile 16.0sec. Typical fuel consumption 22mpg.

Marcos GT

Built: Bradford-on-Avon and Westbury, England, 1964-1971

At the end of the 1950s, Jem Marsh (the engineer) and Frank Costin (an aerodynamicist) developed a prototype GT car, inspired by modern aircraft and marine practice, which featured strange but effective aerodynamics and a chassis/body unit constructed mainly of marine plywood. In the next few years Marsh refined the idea further, and put a limited number of tiny Marcos cars on sale. His first true production car, however, was the Volvo P1800 engined machine of 1964, which was to form the mainstay of Marcos's output for the 1960s.

As originally conceived, the new car had a box-section chassis/lower body unit in marine plywood, which was at once corrosion proof and at the same time almost impossible to repair after an accident. The front mounted engine, transmission and front suspension were supported by a tubular steel subframe. The whole was clad in a remarkably sleek two-seater fastback coupe glass-fibre bodyshell, a shape so different from the monstrosities offered by the original Marcos concern that one found it difficult to accept that they were from the same house.

The first few cars, too, had a complex rear suspenion which had elements of independent and de Dion in it. This is to say that there was a de Dion tube which – as on the Rover 2000 – had a sliding joint, so that its only true function was to hold the rear wheels upright and parallel to each other, while Triumph 2000-type rear wishbones and springs looked after location and suspension.

The basic shape of Marcos was to remain in production for eight years, although there would be many changes under the skin. Like every other small independent concern, Marcos were quite incapable of financing their own engine designs and had to be reliant on supplies from large companies. The first cars in this series were built with the four-cylinder Volvo P1800 engine (as fitted to P1800/1800S models), but as the years progressed these were supplanted by a variety of British Ford engines – in-line fours, vee-fours and vee-sixes – the last giving the best performance of all.

However, it was fitment of the massive and heavy 3-litre Volvo six-cylinder engine which brought about the crisis in Marcos's affairs, for this engine was fitted (as an already proven and detoxed component) with an eye to expanding Marcos's sales in North America. It was a consequence of a move to a larger factory at Westbury to make space for this expansion, and of delivery of cars to the United States which could not be sold, which brought about the collapse of the concern during 1971.

Before then, however, there had been many significant chassis changes. The complex independent rear suspension was abandoned after a couple of years, in favour of a well-located live rear axle. There was also much criticism of the marine ply structure, not on the grounds of weakness, but because it could not be repaired even by experts, and did not meet USA Federal standards, and Marcos therefore converted the design to be based on a multi-tubular frame, built of square-section tubing. This weighed only 175lb, and was attached to the modified glass-fibre shell at no less than 47 points. It was obviously more able to withstand the rigours of USA crash testing, and was potentially more versatile. The same suspensions and choice of engines and transmissions were retained.

About 10 cars a week were built when production was going ahead at full blast, and a surprising number of these fine-looking cars have survived.

Specification

Engine and transmission: Choice of engines, from 1500cc four-cylinder Ford engine, to V4 and V6 Ford engines of two-litres and three-litres, and to the six-cylinder Volvo unit of 2979cc. Four-speed manual gearbox in unit with engine. Hypoid bevel final drive.
Chassis: Front engine, rear drive. Marine ply diaphragm-type chassis, bonded to glass-fibre bodyshell. Independent front suspension by coil springs and wishbones. Rack and pinion steering. Suspension of live rear axle by coil springs, radius arms and Panhard rod. (Early models had independent rear suspension by coil springs and semi-trailing arms). Front wheel disc brakes, rear drums. Later models had tubular steel chassis frames in place of marine ply structure.
Bodywork: Glass-fibre two-door two-seater fastback coupe style. Length 13ft. 3in.; width 5ft. 2.5in.; height 3ft. 5.5in. Unladen weight varied according to engine/transmission used; for example Marcos 1600 weighed 1660lb, 3-litre weighed 2000lb.
Performance: (1600) Maximum speed 109mph. 0-60mph 11.4sec. Standing ¼-mile 17.6sec. Typical fuel consumption 25mpg. **(1800)** Maximum speed 116mph. 0-60mph 8.2sec. Standing ¼-mile 16.3sec. Typical fuel consumption 30mpg. **(3-litre Volvo)** Maximum speed 120mph, 0-60mph 7.5sec. Standing ¼-mile 15.9sec. Typical fuel consumption 24mpg.

Marcos GT, 1800cc

Marcos Mantis

Built: Westbury, England, 1970-1971

Perhaps we shall never know if the individually-styled Marcos Mantis would have been a long term success, for production had only just got under way when the company had to go into liquidation due to financial problems already detailed. The Mantis, however, was a very controversial machine, having looks which might best be described as unique, and having a much more up-market specification than any previous Marcos.

The Mantis, in fact, did not look as its freelance stylist Dennis Adams had originally intended. Changes at the prototype stage, to suit both legal requirements, changes in mechanical specification, and because managing director Jem Marsh wanted them, made something of an ugly duckling of the car, which was nevertheless technically interesting.

The Mantis was, in every way, a larger car than the long-running and successful Marcos GT. Although it retained a glass-fibre bodyshell, there were four seats, with headroom rather than legroom being the limiting factor in rear seat accommodation. Because of the low height (3ft. 10in.) and the four-seater accommodation, the Mantis was unavoidably long at 15ft. 6.7in.

Like the later two-seater Marcos models, the Mantis had a multi-tubular chassis frame, which used square-section steel tubes, and the bodyshell, of glass-fibre, was formed from two large and complex mouldings – top half and bottom half. What made the styling look rather strange was that the front windscreen pillars were curved, and the windscreen was much more bowed than was considered normal at the time.

Mechanically, as is inevitable with cars built by small manufacturers, the Mantis was something of a mixture. At the prototype stage, apparently, there had been much discussion over the choice of engine. The lengthy six-cylinder Volvo unit, already offered in the two-seater, was discarded at an early stage, and it was almost decided to

Marcos Mantis

fit the Ford Capri 3-litre vee-6 instead. Indeed, the chassis was laid out for this unit. However, with future sales to the United States in mind, the six-cylinder Triumph TR6 engines were chosen instead, so that the powerful (150bhp) fuel-injected version could be fitted for most markets, and the detoxed engine (less powerful, and fitted with carburettors) could be used in cars built for Federal territories. This last minute change of plan explains why a Capri back axle was specified, although the gearbox was also from a TR6.

Independent front suspension was from the Triumph Vitesse, while rear suspension, incorporating combined coil spring/damper units, was specially developed by Marcos themselves.

The Mantis received what can only be called a mixed reception, almost entirely because of its looks. Less than 20 cars were built before Marcos went into liquidation, and the surviving cars are now collectors' pieces.

Specification

Engine and transmission: Six-cylinders, in-line, with pushrod-operated overhead-valve cylinder head, made by Triumph. Bore, stroke and capacity 74.7×95mm, 2498cc. Maximum power 150bhp (net) at 5700rpm.; maximum torque 158lb.ft. at 3000rpm. Four-speed manual gearbox and Laycock overdrive in unit with engine; optional Borg Warner 3-speed automatic transmission. Hypoid bevel final drive.
Chassis: Front engine, rear drive. Large-section multi-tubular steel separate chassis frame. Independent front suspension by coil springs and wishbones. Rack and pinion steering. Rear suspension of live axle by coil springs, radius arms and A-bracket. Front wheel disc brakes, rear drums.
Bodywork: Glass-fibre two-door close-coupled four-seater GT in fastback style. Length 15ft. 6.7in.; width 5ft. 11in.; height 3ft. 10in. Unladen weight 3200lb.
Performance: Not independently tested.

Matra Bonnet Djet

Built: Champigny-sur-Marne, France, 1962-1968

Rene Bonnet had joined forces with Deutsch in 1938 to build 'specials' based on Citroen *traction avant* components, but they formed their links with Panhard in 1948. The cars were called DB-Panhards until 1961, after which the partnership was dissolved, and Bonnet turned to the manufacture of cars carrying only his own name, and with Renault engines.

The transformation was complete – DB-Panhards had front engines with front-wheel-drive, whereas the new generation of Bonnets had mid-engines and rear-wheel-drive. Bonnet also carried out an active racing programme, and it was the twin attractions of racing and limited-production sports cars which led Matra (the French missile and armament giant concern) to take over the Bonnet company in 1964.

The car described here, therefore, really started life as a Bonnet Djet, and was transformed into a Matra-Bonnet immediately after the takeover, and forms the bridge between independent Bonnet production and the big-business approach of Matra. If Bonnet's own finances had been somewhat shaky at times, there was never any doubt about the resources behind the Matra concern.

Too many people look upon the Bonnet Djet as 'just another Alpine-Renault', which is quite wrong. The Bonnet was mid-engined – one of the very first road cars of this type – whereas the Alpine-Renault was a true rear-engined car. Both cars used the same derivatives of the Renault four-cylinder engines, and the matching transaxle, but the engine/gearbox assembly of the Bonnet was turned round through 180-degrees compared with its normal stance in the R8 on which it was based.

The chassis was a simple steel backbone tubular type, rather akin to that of the Alpine-Renault – but obviously designed and made by an entirely different concern, and was linked to all-independent suspension by coil springs and wishbones which was – theoretically at least – technically much superior to that of the rival French concern. The engine could be supplied in standard, or in tuned 'Gordini' form, and once the R8 Gordini had been announced, with its cleverly detailed hemispherical combustion chamber breathing this became a very popular option.

The body was a neat and instantly recognisable glass-fibre fastback two-seater, distinguished by a large 'goldfish-bowl' rear window which also covered the engine bay. For that reason, and because the glass-fibre shell was made to be light and streamlined, rather than sound-absorbing, the noise level inside the little cockpit can be imagined, and this explains why more Djets were sold with competition in mind rather than for road use.

Matra, however, had more grandiose plans for their newly-bought concern. On the one hand they wanted to extend their racing interests, but decided to do this at single-seater (F2 and eventually F1) and Le Mans level, while on the other hand they wanted to sponsor a much more refined road car. Accordingly, they decided to close down the original Bonnet factory, opened a new plant at Romorantin, and used it to produce the Ford-engined M530A, in 1967. Djet production carried on for a short time, but the last of these interesting and effective little cars was built in 1968.

Specification

Engine and transmission: Four-cylinders, in-line, with pushrod-operated overhead-valve cylinder head, built by Renault. Bore, stroke and capacity 70×72mm, 1108cc. Maximum power 72bhp (gross) at 5800rpm; maximum torque 56lb.ft. at 3200rpm. Four-speed manual gearbox in unit with engine and transaxle. Hypoid bevel final drive.

Chassis: Mid-engine, rear drive. Tubular backbone steel chassis frame. Independent front suspension by coil springs and wishbones. Rack and pinion steering. Independent rear suspension by double coil springs and wishbones. Four wheel disc brakes.

Bodywork: Glass-fibre bodywork in two-door two-seat fastback coupe style. Length 13ft. 10in.; width 4ft. 11in.; height 3ft. 11.2in. Unladen weight 1355lb.

Performance (Manufacturer's claims): Maximum speed 99mph. Typical fuel consumption 37mpg.

Note: Djet 5S model had 95bhp (gross) at 6500rpm.; maximum torque 72lb.ft. at 4000rpm.

From 1966, the most powerful model had the R8 Gordini 1300 engine. Bore, stroke and capacity 74.5×72mm.; 1255cc. Maximum power 103bhp (gross) at 6750rpm.; maximum torque 86lb.ft. at 5000rpm. Five-speed manual gearbox.

Matra Bonnet Djet 6

Matra M530A

Built: Romorantin, France, 1967-1973

After Matra had spent some little time making Rene Bonnet models under their own name, they were ready to start producing new models. At the Geneva Motor Show of 1967 they showed a design that was at one and the same time practical, relatively cheap to build, and certainly distinctive. This car, the Matra 530A, was to run for six years before being displaced by the stylish Bagheera of 1973.

The M530A had an angular body style which could not be confused with any other, and featured pop-up headlamps, 2 + 2 seating, a fixed-head style, and a roll-over hoop. As with other successful coupes of this type, the roof panel could be removed to give something approaching open-air motoring.

Its basis was a fabricated sheet-steel platform chassis, which also incorporated the inner body structure, including the roll-over hoop and screen surround; the whole was clothed in glass-fibre body panels. Power was by courtesy of Ford Germany, who provided not only the 1.7-litre vee-4 engine of the Ford Taunus 12M, but that car's transaxle. As the 12M was a front-wheel-drive car, with the engine ahead of the final drive, making a mid-engined Matra was only a matter of 'moving' the assembly back in space, and driving the rear wheels instead. The vee-4 engine, therefore, lived immediately behind the seats, and the gearbox itself was in the extreme tail. Not only was there space for luggage in the wide but shallow coffer between the front wheels,

Matra 530LX, front end styling

but there was a separate compartment behind the rear wheels, above the gearbox.

The M530A's basic problem was that it was neither fast enough nor pretty enough to attract a great deal of custom; in French terms it could best be described as *'Jolie laide'*. With a more glamorous style or a more powerful engine it would have been more of a match for its very adequate road behaviour.

Specification

Engine and transmission: Four-cylinders, in 60-degree-vee formation, with pushrod-operated overhead-valve cylinder heads, manufactured by Ford Germany. Bore, stroke and capacity 90×66.8mm, 1699cc. Maximum power 73bhp (DIN) at 4800rpm.; maximum torque 98lb.ft. at 2800rpm. Four-speed manual gearbox in unit with engine and transaxle. Hypoid bevel final drive.

Chassis: Mid-engine, rear drive. Unit construction steel hull, with glass-fibre skin panels. Independent front suspension by coil springs and wishbones. Rack and pinion steering. Independent rear suspension by coil springs and radius arms. Four-wheel disc brakes.

Bodywork: Glass-fibre skin panels on pressed steel hull in two-door, two-seat style. Length 13ft. 9in.; width 5ft. 1.4in.; height 4ft. 1in. Unladen weight 1930lb.

Performance: Maximum speed 95mph. 0-60mph 15.6sec. Standing ¼-mile 19.9sec. Typical fuel consumption 29mpg.

Matra 530LX, rear end styling

Matra-Simca Bagheera

Built: Romorantin, France, 1973 to date

Having changed the image of the ex-Bonnet concern, by making their own design of Ford-engined sports coupe, Matra then forged design and marketing links with Chrysler France (or Simca, if you were a traditionalist) in 1969. This was immediately obvious in the placarding of their racing sports cars, but in production terms nothing matured until 1973. The smart and individual Bagheera was the result.

Several car makers have now discovered that if they want to make a mid-engined car, it is often quite a straightforward matter (except for new gear linkage arrangements) to relocate the transverse front-engine/front-wheel-drive power pack of one model. Because of their links with Simca, Matra decided to utilise the Simca's 1100's power pack in this way, and the new car, called a Bagheera after that notable *Jungle Book* character, was the result.

The Bagheera, however, was not just any mid-engined coupe. It was quite unlike any of the others by having not two, but three seats in the passenger compartment. These were arranged in line-abreast layout, with the driver on the left having a normal seat, and with a pair of rather narrower seats to his right. It was smart, neat, practical if not all prospective occupants were husky men, but it completely eliminated any chance of providing a right-hand-drive version without a great deal more work than usual.

The basis of the design was a rather Italian-style chassis, made up of a multitude of tubes and with sheet and box-section metal stiffening in appropriate places. All round independent suspension was by torsion bars and wishbones, the components mainly coming from the Simca 1100 like the power train had done, and the whole was covered by a very nicely styled fastback coupe shell which had been styled by Matra themselves, and was fashioned in glass-fibre.

At first the car was marketed with a 1294cc engine, as used on the Simca 1100 Special, which produced an adequate but not startling 84bhp (DIN) at 6000rpm, and

Matra-Simca Bagheera

although this was enough to give the car a 100mph top speed it was obviously not enough to make the car prestigious enough against imported coupes, or against the venerable Alpine-Renaults. By 1977 the 1442cc version of the engine, as used in Simca 1308/Chrysler Alpine models (externally the same size, and matched up to the same transmission), which had 90bhp (DIN) at 5800rpm and produced a good deal more torque, was available, and from 1979 this became the only engine on offer.

In the meantime, the Bagheera had established itself thoroughly as a neat, practical, nimble and (which was very important in its home market) essentially French car, which had completed Matra's emergence as true car makers in their own right.

Specification (Original version)

Engine and transmission: Four-cylinders, in-line, with pushrod-operated overhead-valve cylinder head, mounted transversely across the car, manufactured by Chrysler-Simca. Bore, stroke and capacity 76.7 × 70mm, 1294cc. Maximum power 84bhp (DIN) at 6000rpm; maximum torque 78lb.ft. at 4400rpm. Four-speed manual gearbox in unit with engine and transaxle. Spur gear final drive.

Chassis: Mid-engine, rear drive. Multi-tubular separate chassis frame, with sheet and box section stiffeners. Independent front suspension by torsion bars and wishbones. Rack and pinion steering. Independent rear suspension by torsion bars and trailing arms. Four-wheel disc brakes.

Bodywork: Glass-fibre bodyshell, in two-door, three-abreast seating, in fastback coupe style. Length 13ft. 0.5in.; width 5ft. 8.3in.; height 3ft. 11.2in. Unladen weight 1950lb.

Performance: Maximum speed 101mph. 0-60mph. 12.3sec. Standing ¼-mile 18.7sec. Typical fuel consumption 32mpg.

Note: Latest models have 76.7 × 78mm engine, 1442cc. 84bhp (DIN) at 5600rpm; maximum torque 91lb.ft. at 3200rpm, or 90bhp (DIN) at 5800rpm; maximum torque 88lb.ft. at 3200rpm.

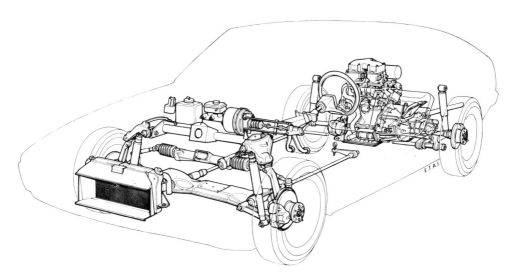

Matra-Simca Bagheera. Layout of major mechanical components

Morgan 4/4 family

Built: Malvern Link, England, 1955 to date

Every Morgan enthusiast knows why the 4/4 should be described as the oldest current sports car still being made — for in its basic layout and in its design philosophy it has roots in the original four-wheeler Morgan of 1936. The 4/4, however, disappeared in favour of the Plus 4 after the second world war, and was not born again until 1955, when the company perceived a gap in the market below the increasingly-costly and (by then) 100mph Plus 4.

In 1955, therefore, the basic Morgan was re-born. As with every other Morgan production car, it was based on the use of a simple ladder-type steel chassis frame with unique Z-section pressings, which was equipped with the ancient but still-effective pillar-type coil spring independent front suspension. The ride could charitably be described as hard, and was really shatteringly firm. The bodies — mainly two-seater sports shells, but with 2 + 2 and convertible variants, were all coachbuilt by Morgan themselves, using traditional methods, including ash frames and handformed steel skin panels.

Since 1955 there have been several different engines fitted. All, however, have been Ford-built, and have been current units in that vast concern's range. The original 4/4 used a 1172cc side-valve 100E unit (as fitted to Anglias and Prefects), but the 1961 4/4 was equipped with a 997cc overhead valve 105E unit (as fitted to the notch-rear window Anglias), which produced a mere 39bhp.

By 1963 the 4/4 had become the Series V, complete with 1498cc GT engine (and 78bhp) from the Cortina GT, although the earlier 1340cc Ford Classic engine remained available until 1965. At the beginning of 1968 the crossflow 1599cc Cortina GT engine became standard, and this engine has been retained ever since. All these engines, incidentally, are derivatives of the phenomenally successful Ford 'Kent' series which is still in production, and in each case they were matched with their own four-speed synchromesh Ford gearboxes. All-synchromesh gears were fitted from 1963, and no alternative — i.e. overdrive or automatic — has ever been offered.

Production of all Morgans has always been severely limited — not by demand, but by the choice of Peter Morgan, the company's owner and managing director — and never more than ten 4/4s a week have ever been made. The chassis design, however, has only changed in detail in the last 24 years, which means that the cars are still extremely simple and easy to repair. Small, with old-fashioned looks, and a positively prehistoric ride, the 4/4s represent PVT (post-vintage-thoroughbred) motoring from a car built today. Demand shows no sign of falling off and the model enters the 1980s in essentially unchanged form.

Specification

Engine and transmission: All engines based on same basic four-cylinders, in-line, with pushrod-operated overhead-valve cylinder head engine, built by Ford. 1961 engine was 80.97 × 48.41mm., 997cc. Maximum power 39bhp at 5000rpm.; maximum torque 53lb.ft. at 2700rpm. From 1967 the engine had been enlarged to 80.97 × 77.62mm., 1599cc. Maximum power 88bhp (net) at 5400rpm.; maximum torque 96lb.ft. at 3600rpm. Four-speed manual gearbox, Ford type, in unit with engine. Hypoid bevel final drive.

Chassis: Front engine, rear drive. Separate pressed-steel chassis frame with Z-section side members. Independent front suspension by coil springs and sliding pillars. Worm and peg steering. Suspension of rear live axle by half-elliptic leaf springs. Four-wheel drum brakes on early models; front wheel discs, rear drums from 1962.

Bodywork: Coachbuilt steel (or light-alloy on some versions) two-door two-seater or four-seater open or convertible sports body styles. Length 12ft. 0in.; width 4ft. 8in.; height 4ft. 3in. Unladen weight (early cars) 1475lb. (latest cars) 1625lb.

Performance (1340cc model): Maximum speed 92mph 0-60mph 10.5sec. Standing ¼-mile 18.1sec. Typical fuel consumption 29mpg. **(1599cc model)** Maximum speed 102mph. 0-60mph 9.8sec. Standing ¼-mile 17.2sec. Typical fuel consumption 31mpg.

Morgan 4/4, 1600cc

Morgan Plus 4

Built: Malvern Link, England, 1950-1968

Gradually and insidiously, the Morgan customers' demands grew and grew, so that the small-engined car announced in the late 1930s was no longer thought to be competitive by the end of the 1940s. It was to provide much more performance, and to restore the Morgan's competition-winning potential, that the Plus 4 came along in 1950.

Compared with the original 4/4, which was dropped, the Plus 4 had an entirely different engine – that of the Standard Vanguard – which was mounted separately from a proprietary Moss gearbox. After four years, however, Standard-Triumph's new 90bhp TR2 engine became available, and this turned the Plus 4 into something approaching a 100mph car, the first time that any Morgan had been capable of such dizzy speeds.

The 1960 Morgan Plus 4 was much like the car of 1954, except that certain smoothing out processes had been carried out to the frontal styling, which now included a reclined and rather bowed radiator grille, and that disc brakes had now been specified for the front suspension. Like the 4/4, the Plus 4 used a simple and sturdy ladder-type chassis frame, with Z-section side members, topped by one of several lightweight coachbuilt bodyshells – two-seater, so-called 4-seater, and a 2-seater drophead coupe.

In spite of the use of the old-fashioned Moss gearbox, which had a very 'slow' change, and almost negligible synchromesh, the Plus 4 was capable of really spirited performance. It was as light as a Triumph TR or MGA – the most serious rivals with which it had to compete in the 1950s and early 1960s – and although its ride was incredibly hard, its actual handling and 'chuckability' was quite unrivalled. On a rough road, therefore, a Morgan was not at all manageable, but on smooth surfaces it was a real joy to handle.

The car's specification kept abreast of whatever Triumph were using in the TRs. This meant that soon after Triumph went over to using 2138cc engines, they were made available for Morgan to use, and this gave another marginal though useful increase in

Morgan Plus 4

performance. By 1965, however, their performance was once again beginning to fall behind the competition, and the Super Sports derivative of the car, with Lawrencetune engine and light alloy body panels, was put on the market.

In response to taunts about their cars being decades behind the times, Morgan announced the Plus 4 Plus model in 1963, which rather incongruously combined the age old chassis and running gear with a bubble-topped glass-fibre two-seater coupe bodyshell. This, it must be admitted, was not attractive to many people, due to its controversial looks, and it was discontinued at the end of 1966 after no more than fifty cars had been built. The 'modernisation' experiment was never repeated.

In 1968, Morgan took another big step and finally discarded the wet-liner Standard-Triumph engine, which by then had also been dropped by the parent factory, and phased out the Plus 4 altogether after making a handful of cars every week from 1950 to 1968. It was replaced by the visually similar but much faster Plus 8.

Morgan Plus Four Plus

Specification

Engine and transmission: Four-cylinders, in-line, with pushrod-operated overhead-valve cylinder head, built by Standard-Triumph. Bore, stroke and capacity 83×92mm, 1991cc. Maximum power 100bhp (gross) at 5000rpm.; maximum torque 17lb.ft. at 3000rpm. (From 1962) Bore, stroke and capacity 86×92mm., 2138cc. Maximum power 100bhp (net) at 4600rpm.; maximum torque 128lb.ft. at 3350rpm. Four-speed manual gearbox separately mounted from engine. Hypoid bevel final drive.

Chassis: Front engine, rear drive. Separate pressed-steel Z-section chassis frame. Independent front suspension by coil springs and sliding pillars. Worm and peg steering. Rear suspension of live axle by half-elliptic leaf springs. Front wheel disc brakes, rear drums.

Bodywork: Coachbuilt steel (or light-alloy in some cases) two-door two-seater or four-seater open sports, convertible or hardtop body style. Length 12ft. 0in.; width 4ft. 8in.; height 4ft. 4in. Unladen weight 1915lb.

Performance: (Early 100bhp gross model) Maximum speed 96mph. 0-60mph 13.3sec. Standing ¼-mile 18.5sec. Typical fuel consumption 30mpg.

Note: the Plus Four Plus model was mechanically as the 2.2-litre Plus Four, but with glass-fibre two-door two-seater coupe body style. Length 12ft. 8in.; width 5ft. 1in.; height 4ft. 3in. Unladen weight 1820lb.

Morgan Plus 8

Built: Malvern Link, England, 1968 to date

With production of the four-cylinder Triumph TR engine running out in the summer of 1967, Morgan would clearly have to look around for alternative engine supplies to safeguard their future. After much experiment with other engines, and in spite of an offer from Triumph to supply early examples of the still-secret Stag vee-8 power unit, Morgan changed suppliers for the first time in nearly 20 years, and began taking supplies of vee-8 3528cc engines from Rover in Solihull. This engine, of course, was the one originally used by Buick in the United States between 1960 and 1963, which had then been taken over by Rover, and which had been in use in Rover cars since the autumn of 1967.

Thus it was that the Plus 8 emerged, in a very easy, logical and straightforward way. The separately-mounted Moss four-speed gearbox was retained – as old-fashioned as the engine was modern – along with the Z-section chassis frame members, and the craftsman-built two-seater sports bodyshell. Visually there were virtually no changes compared with the Plus 4, except that cast alloy roadwheels were fitted instead of the traditional wire spoked variety.

While retaining the traditional layout, the wheelbase was slightly increased, and the wheel tracks were significantly widened, which meant that the body contours were subtly but definitely changed. This, for Morgan, was great change indeed, and the Plus 8's performance also changed the car's image.

In place of an old-fashioned car which struggled to reach 100mph, here was a car with more than 150bhp which positively rushed up to more than 120mph, handled like a big go-kart, and exhilirated everyone who stepped in to it. By now, of course, there was no doubt that the performance had completely outstripped the ability of the chassis to handle it, even though the brakes and tyre specifications were amply good enough to maintain safety.

No matter. The waiting lists grew and grew, and it is now a fact that customers placing orders for new Morgans have to be prepared to wait at least five years before taking delivery. Never more than 15 cars a week were built by Morgan during the 1970s, and it is known that Peter Morgan has absolutely no desire to expand facilities to improve on this.

Morgan Plus 8

More than ten years after it was announced, the Plus 8 continues on sale, with only minor changes. Only the 2-seater sports bodywork was ever offered, usually panelled in steel, though a light-alloy version known as the Sports Lightweight was made available from the autumn of 1975. Engines have been improved in line with the standard item used by Rover – latest examples have a version of the more powerful unit fitted to the sleek modern Rover saloons.

The most important changes have been to the transmission. The original Moss gearbox was used until mid-1972, at which point it was discarded in favour of the four-speed all-synchromesh gearbox normally used in the Rover 3500S saloon car, mounted in unit with the engine. Although the Ford-engined cars had always had in-unit gearboxes, this was the very first time such a move had been for the most powerful cars. At the beginning of 1977, there was one further and very welcome change, when one Rover gearbox was dropped and another specified – this time the 5-speed new design recently adopted for the 'SD1' type of Rover. With that change, Morgan re-established links with the Triumph concern, for it was a box designed by their engineers and manufactured in their workshops.

In much the same form, and looking much as it did in 1960, the Morgan continues into the 1980s.

Specification

Engine and transmission: Eight-cylinders, in 90-degree-vee formation, with pushrod-operated overhead-valve cylinder heads, built by Rover. Bore, stroke and capacity 88.9×71.1mm., 3528cc. Original specification, maximum power 151bhp (net) at 5200rpm.; maximum torque 201lb.ft. at 2750rpm. Recent specification: 155bhp (DIN) at 5250rpm.; maximum torque 198lb.ft. at 2500rpm. Four-speed manual gearbox (separate from engine), four-speed manual gearbox or five-speed manual gearbox (both Rover units) in unit with engine. Hypoid bevel final drive.
Chassis: Front engine, rear drive. Separate pressed steel chassis frame, with Z-section side members. Independent front suspension by coil springs and sliding pillars. Worm and nut steering. Rear suspension of live axle by half-elliptic leaf springs. Front wheel disc brakes, rear drums.
Bodywork: Coachbuilt steel (or light-alloy on some versions) two-door two-seater open sports body style. Length 12ft. 3in.; width 4ft. 9.5in. at first, gradually increased by minor changes to 5ft. 2in.; height 4ft. 4in. Unladen weight 1875lb.
Performance: (1978 model) Maximum speed 123mph. 0-60mph 6.5sec. Standing ¼-mile 15.1sec. Typical fuel consumption 22mpg.

Panther J72

Built: Byfleet, England, 1972 to date

The whole secret of designing a replica of an older car is to make it how people *think* they remember the original – and perhaps that was one reason for the success of the original Panther J72. Designed originally by Robert Jankel as a one-off car for his own use, he was persuaded to put it into limited production in 1972. Since then it has been one of the most important and long-lasting models in the range of cars built at the ex-Cooper racing car factory at Byfleet, near the old Brooklands track.

The J72 is no more and no less than a liberal interpretation and style of the SS100 of the late 1930s, but with modern Jaguar engines and transmissions to give a great deal more performance and the advantage of easy availability of spare parts and maintenance. Designed as a starkly-equipped two-seater, it was about the same size as the original, but with the famous Jaguar XK engine installed (3.8-litre on the original cars, but almost immediately supplanted in favour of the 4.2-litre version), it was very fast indeed.

The chassis, designed to be assembled with the minimum of tooling and expertise, was a simple tubular affair, certainly as stiff as the original SS100's frame, and there were beam front and rear axles, both located properly by radius arms, Panhard rods and coil springs. The bodyshell was of the traditional type, with ash framing clothed in light-alloy handformed skin panels, and the whole was topped by a rudimentary hood.

Jankel put the car into production at a factory almost within sight of Brooklands, and drew on the coachbuilding skills of craftsmen who abounded in this area of south-west London (having once been employed by redundant concerns like Hooper). It was a great and lasting success in many export territories, where the love of looks and flashing performance was not tempered by the reaction of the jealous who thought such imitations to be vulgar and undesirable.

The J72 was soon joined by the J72 5.3, which was the same car fitted with Jaguar's magnificent vee-12 5.3-litre engine. This gave even more performance (up to 137mph was claimed by the factory – remarkable when the awful aerodynamics of that 1930s-style nose was considered), at the expense of a little more weight, and of two unsightly bulges in the bonnet panels.

In due course, demand from the wealthy customers suggested that strict adherence to the ride and handling standards of the 1930s was not really necessary, so from 1977 the front beam axle was discarded in favour of a modern coil spring and wishbone independent suspension. In spite of the fact that the customers, in general, were very wealthy, the gas-guzzling vee-12 engined J72 was dropped by then, as it was no longer in demand.

Robert Jankel has often been accused of having vulgar commercial habits – the use of the name 'Panther' for a Jaguar copy, and J72 (Jaguar – or Jankel? – of 1972) is often quoted against him. This cannot hide, however, the fact that the J72, which has a great deal of character and is instantly recognisable, has been a success, and that several hundred examples have been sold. It was, too, the springboard from which more ambitious Panther models could be launched.

Specification

Engine and transmission: Six-cylinders, in-line, with twin-overhead-camshaft cylinder head, Jaguar unit. Bore, stroke and capacity 92.05 × 106mm, 4235cc. Maximum power 190bhp (DIN) at 5000rpm; maximum torque 200lb.ft. at 2000rpm. Four-speed gearbox and overdrive in unit with engine. Optional Borg Warner automatic transmission. Hypoid bevel final drive.

Chassis: Front engine, rear drive. Separate chassis frame with tubular members. Front suspension of tubular axle beam by coil springs, radius arms and Panhard rod. From 1977, coil spring and wishbone independent front suspension was fitted. Recirculating ball steering. Rear suspension of live axle by coil springs, trailing arms and Panhard rod. Four-wheel disc brakes.

Bodywork: Coachbuilt bodyshell, of light-alloy panelling on wooden frame, by Panther, available only as open two-seater. Length 13ft. 4in.; width 5ft. 5.5in.; height 4ft. 5in. Unladen weight 2505lb.

Performance: Maximum speed 114mph. 0-60mph 6.4sec. Standing ¼-mile 15.3sec. Typical fuel consumption 15mpg.

Note: Optional Vee-12 version has following differences: Twelve-cylinders, in 60-degree vee-formation, with single-overhead-camshaft cylinder heads, Jaguar unit. Bore, stroke and capacity 90 × 70mm, 5343cc. Maximum power 266bhp (DIN) at 5750rpm; maximum torque 304lb.ft at 3500rpm. Overdrive not available. Unladen weight 2605lb.

Performance: Maximum speed (estimated) 137mph. Typical fuel consumption 12mpg.

Panther J72

Panther Lima

Built: Byfleet, England, 1976 to date

Although Robert Jankel's Panther Westwinds concern rapidly established itself, he did not allow his ambitions to rush ahead of his financial abilities and reserves. Thus it was not until 1976, four years after the launch of the original J72, that a truly 'down market' replicar was marketed. This was the Lima, physically the smallest Panther yet seen.

Panther Lima

It is worth recalling that many times in the early stages of Panther's development, Jankel swore that his cars would always have coachbuilt bodies, and that he would *never* stoop to the use of a glass-fibre body shell, however well constructed. The world of motoring was therefore very surprised to learn that this new model was to have — a glass-fibre body!

There was, however, a very good reason for this, for the Lima was destined to be produced in significantly larger quantities than any previous Panther, and than any previous 'replicar' for any other company. It came about as a result of a liaison between Panther and Vauxhall Motors. Although Panther customers had apparently been asking for something of this type for some time, and though Jankel dabbled with an MG TF type of style for a while, his chosen shape was completely anachronistic — still in the style of the 1930s with sweeping wings and a basically narrow shell, but with quite a rounded tail and a rather curvaceous nose. Unlike the J72, which was quite definitely an SS100 look-alike, the Lima was individual and instantly recognisable.

The 'chassis', though it was really a pressed-steel underpan, was from a Vauxhall Magnum saloon, and it is as well to remember that this was effectively the underpan of a Vauxhall Viva saloon with larger capacity engines and heavy duty transmission and suspensions fitted in the best GM 'product planning' manner. Thus, Magnum front

102

and rear suspension was also fitted, the 2279cc single-overhead camshaft engine (producing 108bhp DIN) and four-speed Vauxhall gearbox was also used, and the result was a nimble and cheap-to-build sports car which could be (and was) sold through the showrooms of selected Vauxhall dealers in Britain and overseas.

Panther themselves made the nicely-engineered glass-fibre bodyshell, though the doors were of pressed steel and looked uncommonly like those of the MG Midget.

Perhaps the Magnum's underpan was not torsionally rigid enough, for even from the start of production Panther found it necessary to strengthen the assembly with square-section longitudinal tubes under the floor. From the end of 1978, when a prototype was successfully homologated and entered in both the RAC and Monte Carlo rallies of that winter, Panther began to fit their own simple but strong and rugged multi-tubular design of frame, and traces of Vauxhall are now confined to the running gear and suspensions.

Not only the basic Lima, but models with engines tuned by the Dealer Team Vauxhall specialists Blydenstein, and turbocharged derivatives, are also offered. Like the much larger and more expensive J72 model, the Lima appeals to those who do not mind jibes about replicars and pseudo copies being aimed at them, and it seems to be a fact that many would-be Morgan customers, who cannot face a five-year wait for their cars, have turned to Panther for satisfaction.

Specification

Engine and transmission: Four-cylinders, in-line, with single-overhead-camshaft cylinder head, installed at 45-degrees to chassis. Manufactured by Vauxhall. Bore, stroke and capacity 97.5×76.2mm, 2279cc. Maximum power 108bhp (DIN) at 5000rpm; maximum torque 138lb.ft. at 3000rpm. Four-speed gearbox, or optional automatic transmission, in unit with engine. Hypoid bevel final drive.

Chassis: Front engine, rear drive. Initial version had pressed steel platform chassis floor pan; recent versions have separate tubular chassis frame. Independent front suspension by coil springs and wishbones. Rack and pinion steering. Rear suspension of live axle by coil springs, and radius arms. Front-wheel disc brakes, rear drums.

Bodywork: Glass-fibre bodyshell, by Panther, available only as an open two-seater. Length 12ft. 4in.; width 5ft. 4.2in.; height 4ft. 2in. Unladen weight 1900lb.

Performance: Maximum speed 98mph. 0-60mph 9.9sec. Standing ¼-mile 17.3sec. Typical fuel consumption 25mpg.

Reliant Sabre series

Built: Tamworth, England, 1961 to 1964

For many years, Reliant made only lightweight three-wheeler cars, very simply engineered to keep them below an arbitrary weight limit set by the British government for tax concessions to apply. It was not until they found the chance of making a sporting car – the Sabra – for Autocars of Israel, that they considered making a four-wheeler car for British and worldwide sale.

The original Reliant Sabre of 1961 was something of an ugly duckling, as it had been developed by a concern with very little experience of building four-wheeled cars, let alone fast sporting machines. To save time and – as they thought – to ease development, they hired Leslie Ballamy to design a chassis, and used a glass-fibre bodyshell of their own manufacture which had been designed by one of the 'special-building' concerns which abounded in Britain at the time. For an engine they chose Ford's plentiful, available, but essentially non-sporting 1.7-litre Consul four-cylinder units.

The chassis, of steel box section, was strong enough and adequately large to give sufficient passenger space for two occupants and their luggage, but its 'split axle' independent front suspension exhibited awful bump-steer and other side-effects which made high-speed handling an adventure. The looks of the body, too, which included a lengthy droop-snoot of a nose, excited much criticism.

The revised version, called SE2 (or Series 2) of autumn 1962 was a much better car. Firstly, Reliant had restyled the nose with a more conventional layout and a full-width grille, tried to improve the front suspension's performance, and made a Ford Zodiac 2553cc six-cylinder available as an option to the Consul engine. The body

Reliant Sabre Six

looked much more attractive than before, and when fitted with the optional fastback coupe top looked relatively sleek and up-to-date.

Reliant's confidence in their own abilities came in 1963, when a factory competition department was set up, and the rallying business was astonished when much-modified Sabre Sixes won their class in the Alpine Rally after the formidable opposition of a team of factory-entered Austin Healey 3000s had all dropped out. These Sabres, incidentally, were fitted with double wishbone front suspension of the TR4 type, which was a great and obvious improvement over that originally specified.

Thus equipped, a steady trickle of Sabres were sold in 1963 and 1964, the vast majority of them being the six-cylinder engined variety. More success, usually on the grounds of strength and reliability, rather than on sheer performance, came the way of the competition cars in 1964, and there is no doubt that a finely-tuned Sabre Six could be a very fast club racing car.

By the end of the summer of 1964, however, with no more than a couple of hundred Sabres sold (and the Sabra contract long since forgotten), Reliant had completely rethought their ideas on sports cars, and the Sabre was dropped in favour of the thoroughly modern Scimitar.

Specification

Engine and transmission: Six-cylinders, in-line, with pushrod-operated overhead-valve cylinder head, built by Ford. Bore, stroke and capacity 82.55 × 79.5mm., 2553cc. Maximum power 109bhp (net) at 4800rpm.; maximum torque 137lb.ft. at 2400rpm. Four-speed manual gearbox in unit with engine. Spiral bevel final drive.
Chassis: Front engine, rear drive. Separate pressed-steel chassis frame with box section side and crossmembers. Independent front suspension by swing axles and coil springs, later cars by coil springs and wishbones. Rack and pinion steering. Rear suspension of live axle by coil springs and Watts linkages. Front wheel disc brakes, rear drums.
Bodywork: Glass-fibre two-door two-seater bodyshell, in open sports or fastback coupe styles. Length 13ft. 2in.; width 5ft. 1in.; height 4ft. 2in. Unladen weight 1800lb.
Performance: Maximum speed 111mph. 0-60mph 12.2sec. Standing ¼-mile 18.3sec. Typical fuel consumption 23mpg.

Note: Four-cylinder engine also available, with same bore and stroke. 1703cc. Maximum power 90bhp (gross) at 5000rpm.; maximum torque 91lb.ft. at 2300rpm. Unladen weight 1750lb.
Performance: Maximum speed 90mph. 0-60mph 16.6sec. Standing ¼-mile 20.3sec. Typical fuel consumption 30mpg.

Reliant Scimitar series

Built: Tamworth, England, 1964-1970

If the Reliant Sabre was the first four-wheeler to be sold by the Tamworth firm, the Scimitar was their first truly successful model. Designed with an acute eye to the successes and failings of the Sabre, the Scimitar was the smart two-seater coupe which truly turned Reliant into a respected manufacturer of Grand Touring cars.

Apart from the use of its Triumph-derived wishbone front suspension, and that of the rear suspension axle location, the entire chassis layout was new. It was a solid and simple frame, with box section sidemembers, and a sturdy fabricated arrangement supporting the front suspension. The only controversial aspect of the rear suspension was that its twin longitudinal Watts linkage gave precise location, but were affixed to the axle so that an enormous anti-roll resistance was set up as the wheels began to move up or down.

The engine was the 2553cc six-cylinder Ford unit (the four-cylinder alternative had disappeared during the life of the Sabre), backed either by the Ford four-speed gearbox, or a much more expensive four-speed ZF gearbox which was soon dropped from the available specification.

There were absolutely no complaints about the body style on this occasion. Unlike the Sabre, the Scimitar had been styled by a reputable team of specialists — Ogle — who had evolved a distinctive two-door notchback fixed-head coupe style, which was smart and practical, with a great deal of extra space behind the seats.

Right from the start, the Scimitar was a success, and once the rear suspension location was revised in the autumn of 1965 to deal with the anti-roll stiffness criticism it became a very saleable car. As soon as Ford's range of vee-4 and vee-6 engines began to replace the straight-six units at the beginning of 1966, it was clear that the Scimitar must soon follow suit. From the autumn of 1966, therefore, the 2.6-litre engine was dropped, and the more powerful and more flexible 2994cc vee-6 unit, as used in Zodiacs, and later in Capris, took its place.

It was at the same time that disc wheels replaced the original wire spoked wheels, and when the ZF gearbox alternative was formally dropped.

From the summer of 1967 an alternative 2.5-litre Scimitar was put on sale (using the short-stroke 2495cc Ford vee-6 engine) but even though it was somewhat cheaper, it was never a success, and only 118 cars were built to this specification. The Scimitar GT, too, was overshadowed after the autumn of 1968 by the sleeker, smarter and altogether more versatile Scimitar GTE, described later, though production continued at a steady though diminishing rate until the autumn of 1970 when nearly 1000 of the 2.6-litre or 3-litre machines had been built. If space had not been required to expand production of GTEs, the car would undoubtedly have continued to sell for a while longer.

Specification (Original 2.6-litre version)

Engine and transmission: Six-cylinders, in-line, with pushrod-operated overhead valve cylinder head, built by Ford. Bore, stroke and capacity, 82.55 × 79.5mm., 2553cc. Maximum power 120bhp (net) at 5000rpm.; maximum torque 140lb.ft. at 2600rpm. Four-speed manual gearbox and optional overdrive or optional four-speed ZF gearbox in unit with engine. Spiral bevel final drive.

Chassis: Front engine, rear drive. Separate pressed-steel chassis frame, with box section side and crossmembers. Independent front suspension by coil springs and wishbones. Rack and pinion steering. Rear suspension of live axle (early cars) by coil springs and Watts linkages, (later cars) by coil springs, radius arms and Watts linkage. Front wheel disc brakes, rear drums.

Bodywork: Glass-fibre, two-door 2 + 2 seater bodyshell, in notchback coupe style. Length 14ft. 0in.; width 5ft. 1.5in.; height 4ft. 2.5in. Unladen weight 2200lb.

Performance: Maximum speed 116mph. 0-60mph 11.4 sec. Standing ¼-mile 18.0sec. Typical fuel consumption 22mpg.

Note: From autumn 1966, the Scimitar V6 was introduced, with the following important differences: Engine six-cylinders, in 60-degree vee-formation, built by Ford. Bore, stroke and capacity 93.7 × 72.4mm., 2994cc. Maximum power 136bhp (net) at 4750rpm.; maximum torque 192lb.ft. at 3000rpm. ZF gearbox not available. Unladen weight 2305lb.

Performance: Maximum speed 121mph. 0-60mph 10.0 sec. Standing ¼-mile 17.1sec. Typical fuel consumption 23mpg.

Note: A 2495cc, 93.66 × 60.35mm Ford engine with 112bhp (net) at 4750rpm was also available.

Reliant Scimitar

Reliant Scimitar GTE family

Built: Tamworth, England, 1968 to date

For their next new model, to supplant and eventually to replace the Scimitar GT, Reliant once again consulted Ogle, who – for a rather larger car – evolved a dramatic and versatile body style which has been the forerunner of so many others, including glamorous vehicles like the Lancia Beta HPEs and Ford Capris. The model's name – Scimitar GTE – gives a clue to its type, for the initials GTE stand for Grant Touring Estate, a title which describes the type perfectly.

Ogle, within the confines of a car barely over 14ft. long, produced a body style which was stylish, sporting, spacious, and extremely useful as a load carrier. They did this by carrying the roof line back to a squareback tail, in which the rear window was also an opening tailgate (top hinged), and by arranging for the close-coupled rear seats to be folded forward, estate car style, to allow a really useful loading area to be used behind the front seats if necessary. Like the evolution of the Mini in a different

context, here was a new concept in motor car packaging, which has been taken up by many distinguished imitators.

This style was made by Reliant themselves, in glass-fibre, and produced to a very high standard, with trim and fittings which have regularly been changed and updated over the last decade or so. As with the Scimitar, and so with the GTE, an entirely new chassis was perfected which had a longer wheelbase than that of the GT to make provision for occasional or 2 + 2 seating behind the front seats, and to allow for redisposition of spare wheel and fuel tank to allow the loading area to be wide and flat.

The new frame, like that of the Scimitar GT, was a simple tubular steel arrangement, with square and oblong section tubing, but was much more of a cruciform type with outrigged side members. The same basic front suspension members were used, though the track was considerably increased to match the increased bulk of the new car. The same type of rear suspension as the Scimitar GT was also retained, though this was, of course, allied to a widened rear axle.

The very satisfactory 3-litre Ford vee-6 engine was retained, as was that engine's matching gearbox, and although a 2.5-litre version was also offered on announcement,

Reliant Scimitar GTE

this does not seem to have been a significant part of Reliant's production plans. Overdrive was optional, as was Borg Warner automatic transmission. It was no sin to offer automatic on a car of this type, which was sure to be purchased by many other customers than the purely sporting types. On manual cars, incidentally, overdrive was standardised from mid-1971.

Several thousand of the original GTEs were made before, in the autumn of 1975, Reliant carried out yet another audacious and – assuredly – successful design change. Rather than have Ogle design yet another all-new bodyshell for them, they decided to make the GTE larger in most directions. The result was that the basic body moulds were, in effect, cut in half longitudinally and laterally, remade, and the 1976 and subsequent model year cars were four inches longer in the wheelbase, and three-inches wider. Superficially the later cars look like the originals, except that they are, obviously, somewhat larger, and they can be recognised by their larger sized outer pair of headlamps. All the extra length, included in the doors, was allocated to the rear seat area, which had always been somewhat marginal, though the extra width benefitted all occupants. Along with optional power-assisted steering, revised and improved instrumentation and better heating and equipment, the latest GTEs were much more 'softened' and more civilised cars.

Although Reliant had their share of financial problems in the 1970s (including a period in 1975 and 1976 when the cars were out of production as tooling changes were being made) the GTE continues in production at the beginning of the 1980s.

Specification

Engine and transmission: Six-cylinders, in 60-degree vee-formation, with pushrod-operated overhead-valve cylinder heads, built by Ford. Bore, stroke and capacity 93.66×72.4mm., 2994cc. Maximum power 138bhp (DIN) at 5000rpm.; maximum torque 174lb.ft. at 3000rpm. Four-speed manual gearbox with optional overdrive, or optional Borg Warner three-speed automatic transmission, in unit with engine. Hypoid bevel final drive.

Chassis: Front engine, rear drive. Separate pressed-steel cruciform-type chassis frame, with box section main and crossmembers. Independent front suspension by coil springs and wishbones. Rack and pinion steering. Rear suspension of live axle by coil springs, radius arms and Watts linkage. Front wheel disc brakes, rear drums.

Bodywork: Glass-fibre, two-door, 2 + 2 seater bodyshell, in hatchback coupe style. Length 14ft. 3in.; width 5ft. 4.5in.; height 4ft. 4in. Unladen weight 2440lb.

Performance: (1973 model) Maximum speed 121mph. 0-60mph 8.9sec. Standing ¼-mile 16.9sec. Typical fuel consumption 24mpg.

Note: From autumn 1975 the car was lengthened and widened, with the following important differences: Length 14ft. 6.5in.; width 5ft. 7.3in.; height 4ft. 4in. Unladen weight 2850lb.

Performance: Maximum speed 118mph. 0-60mph 9.4sec. Standing ¼-mile 17.2sec. Typical fuel consumption 23mpg.

Saab Sonett II

Built: Arlov, Sweden, 1966-1970

Although Saab had not entered the motor-manufacturing business until the late 1940s, they quickly built up their reputation by making very strong, rugged, handleable front-wheel-drive cars. Central to the design at first was a two-stroke engine — a two cylinder at first, but an in-line three-cylinder from the introduction of the 93 model. There were several sporting prototypes shown during the 1950s with the name of Sonett, but none went on sale. The company's rallying record became phenomenal after drivers like Erik Carlsson showed just how good a Saab could be.

The Sonett II was first seen in public in 1965, and went into relatively small scale production in 1966. Its actual model coding was Saab 97, which was never invoked in company publicity, and prototypes had been built in 1965 by two concerns — the Malmo Aircraft Industry (MFI) and the Swedish Railroad Works (ASJ). Both used the basis of a Saab 96 underpan, power train and suspensions, along with a glass-fibre fixed-head two-seater coupe bodyshell. After much study, the MFI design was chosen, while ASJ were asked to look after manufacturing. There was never likely to be a huge market for the Sonett II, especially as it was somewhat underpowered, with a 60bhp three-cylinder two-stroke 841cc engine, and in 1966 only the first 60 cars were made at Arlov, in South Sweden. Its slight lack of performance was nullified by the fine handling, helped by front wheel drive, but it was highly priced compared with the sporting Saab saloons.

A further 455 Sonett IIs were built in 1967, but by then there was news of a new Saab engine — the German-built 1.5-litre 60-degree four-stroke vee-4 — and the Sonett became the Sonett V4 for the 1968 season, with a humped bonnet moulding being necessary to clear the taller engine and its air cleaner. There is evidence to suggest that Saab dealers did not take this model very seriously, as it was often said that prospective purchasers were told to go to their dealers and ask for the the toy department!

Production at Arlov, many miles from the main Saab factory, continued at a slow rate until 1970, after which the model was replaced by the Sonett III.

Saab Sonett II

Specification (Sonett II)

Engine and transmission: Three-cylinders in-line, two-stroke operation. Bore, stroke and capacity 70 × 73mm., 841cc. Maximum power 60bhp (net) at 5200rpm.; maximum torque 69lb.ft. at 4000rpm. Four-speed manual gearbox in unit with engine and transaxle. Spiral bevel final drive.

Chassis: Front engine, front drive. Unit-construction pressed-steel platform chassis, based on Saab saloon car structure. Independent front suspension by coil springs and wishbones. Rack and pinion steering. Rear suspension of axle beam by coil springs and radius arms, and central locating bracket. Front wheel disc brakes, rear drums.

Bodywork: Glass-fibre two-door two-seater sports coupe in fastback style. Length 12ft. 4.4in.; width 4ft. 9in.; height 3ft. 9.7in. Unladen weight 1565lb.

Performance: No independent tests recorded.

Note: From Autumn 1967 the model became the Sonett V4, with the following important differences: Four-cylinders, in 60-degree vee-formation, with pushrod-operated overhead-valve cylinder heads, built by Ford Germany. Bore, stroke and capacity 90 × 58.86mm., 1498cc. Maximum power 65bhp (DIN) at 4700rpm.; maximum torque 85lb.ft. at 2500rpm. Length 12ft. 5in. Unladen weight 1700lb.

Performance (Manufacturer's claims): Maximum speed 100mph. 0-60mph 12.0sec. Typical fuel consumption 35mpg.

Saab Sonett III

Built: Arlov, Sweden, 1970-1974

By the end of the 1960s, the original Sonett production car was beginning to look rather dumpy and ordinary. Since the bodyshell was constructed from glass-fibre, and had moulds not too expensive to replace, it was decided to bring in an entirely new shape, and this was ready for 1970. Style suggestions for the revised car, still coded as a Saab 97, came from the Italian designer Sergio Coggiola, but many details were further developed and refined in Saab's own styling studio at Trollhattan.

Apart from its 'sharper' styling, particularly around the nose, the Sonett III also had a very practical opening rear hatch (luggage on the original car had had to be stowed through the doors after folding the seats). However, even though it was a better car in many respects, ASJ could still not make large numbers, and only 940 examples were built in 1970; this was in spite of the fact that the larger capacity (1.7-litre) Ford vee-4 engine was being fitted, with a power output of 75bhp, which guaranteed a top speed of more than 100mph.

Sales by 1972 were up to 2080 units, but this dropped to 1595 units in 1973. Most sales were to the United States, where the exhaust emission laws were hitting the output of the engine (and the car's performance) very hard. It was the onset of more, and yet more, USA regulations which caused Saab to abandon production of Sonetts in the autumn of 1974, when a grand total of 10 236 cars (Sonett II, V4 and III) had been built. No GT Saab (if one discounts the fabulous Turbo) has been built since then.

Specification

Engine and transmission: Four-cylinders, in 60-degree vee-formation, with pushrod-operated overhead-valve cylinder heads, built by Ford Germany. Bore, stroke and capacity 90×66.8mm., 1699cc. Maximum power 75bhp (DIN) at 5000rpm.; maximum torque 94lb.ft. at 2500rpm. Four-speed manual gearbox in unit with engine and final drive. Spiral bevel final drive.

Chassis: Front engine, front drive. Pressed-steel platform type chassis, based on underframe of Saab saloon model. Independent front suspension by coil springs and wishbones. Rack and pinion steering. Rear suspension of axle beam by coil springs, radius arms, and central locating bracket. Front wheel disc brakes, drum rears.

Bodywork: Glass-fibre two-door two-seater fastback sports coupe. Length 12ft. 10in.; width 4ft. 11in.; height 3ft. 10.9in. Unladen weight 1785lb.

Performance: Maximum speed 100mph. 0-60mph 14.4sec. Standing ¼-mile 19.0sec. Typical fuel consumption 29mpg.

Sbarro Replica BMW 328

Built: Gresey, Switzerland, 1974 to date

Although the Sbarro is undeniably a mere visual copy of the world-famous BMW 328 of the late 1930s, it uses many modern BMW mechanical components, and — depending on the choice of engine — can be a very fast car indeed. The Sbarro is to Switzerland like the Panther is to Britain. Production is limited, prices are expensive, but the demand is undoubtedly sufficient to keep the little concern busy.

The body style itself, an open-top two-seater, is almost uncannily like the BMW 328 in every detail of shape, but to suit modern economic building requirements it is in glass-fibre. Under the skin, however, everything is different.

As with so many modern cars built in small numbers, there is a simple tubular chassis frame, reinforced suitably with sheet-steel fabricated panels to add rigidity and torsional stiffness. Independent front suspension was by coil springs and wishbones, while the independent rear suspension used elements of the BMW 2002 'chassis' on which much of the rest of the car was based.

The original Sbarro had a 1990cc four-cylinder BMW 2002 engine, but in the next few years the car was to be sold with the 1.6-litre version of this unit, and with the 2.0-litre and 2.3-litre versions of the very latest BMW 'small' six-cylinder unit, as used in the new 320 and 323 models.

Sbarro BMW 328 Replica

Specification

Engine and transmission: Choice of BMW engines from 1.6-litres (4-cylinder) to 2.3-litres (6-cylinder). Four-cylinder or 6-cylinder, in-line, with single overhead camshaft cylinder heads. 4-speed or 5-speed gearboxes in unit with engine. Hypoid bevel final drive.

Chassis: Front engine, rear drive. Tubular chassis frame. Independent front suspension with coil springs and wishbones. Rack and pinion steering. Independent rear suspension by coil springs and semi-trailing links. Four-wheel disc brakes.

Bodywork: Glass-fibre coachwork in traditional BMW 328 style of 1930s, in two-seater open sports form. Length 12ft. 1.6in.; width 5ft. 1.4in.; height 3ft. 9.2in. Unladen weight (depending on engine) from 1765lb.

Trident series

Built: Woodbridge or Ipswich, England, 1965-1974

Although Tridents were eventually made as a separate marque, they were originally styled by Trevor Fiore with a view to being adopted by TVR. Indeed, prototypes of the TVR Trident were shown at Geneva in 1965, but as that company was on the way to one of its periodically recurring financial crises the design never went into production.

The layout was therefore sold to W.J. Last, a TVR dealer in Woodbridge, Suffolk, not without various misunderstandings. Development continued, and it took ages for serious production to begin in 1969. By this time the two-door fastback style had been tooled-up for glass-fibre manufacture, and had been mated to one of two chassis, depending on which power train was chosen.

The original cars used an Austin-Healey 3000 chassis and suspension, even though this model became redundant at the end of 1967, with a 4.7-litre AC Cobra-type unit for the Clipper. A British-built Ford 3-litre vee-6 unit, and Triumph TR6 chassis with independent rear suspension were used for the Venturer.

Also available in the early 1970s were the Tycoon (TR6 chassis and 2.5-litre TR6 engine) or the Clipper II with a vast Chrysler 5.6-litre engine.

The company did not survive the combined economical and social effects of the Suez War and energy crisis of 1973/1974.

Trident Venturer V6

Specification (Venturer model)

Engine and transmission: Six-cylinders, in 60-degree vee-formation, with pushrod-operated overhead-valve cylinder heads, manufactured by Ford. Bore, stroke and capacity 93.7 × 72.4mm, 2994cc. Maximum power 138bhp (DIN) at 5000rpm.; maximum torque 174lb.ft. at 3000rpm. Four-speed manual gearbox (with optional overdrive), or optional Borg Warner automatic transmission, in unit with engine. Hypoid bevel final drive.

Chassis: Front engine, rear drive. Separate pressed-steel chassis frame with box section sidemembers. Independent front suspension by coil springs and wishbones. Rack and pinion steering. Independent rear suspension by coil springs and semi-trailing wishbones. Front wheel disc brakes, rear drums.

Bodywork: Glass-fibre two-door 2 + 2 seater in fastback coupe style. Length 13ft. 9in.; width 5ft. 8in.; height 4ft. 1.7in.

Note: This car was also sold as the Tycoon, with six-cylinder in-line 2498cc Triumph engine. Bore, stroke and capacity 74.7 × 95mm, 2498cc. Maximum power 152bhp (gross) at 5500rpm.; maximum torque 158lb.ft. at 3000rpm.

Other derivatives included the Clipper I and Clipper II models, with the Austin-Healey 3000 chassis in place of the Triumph TR6 chassis, which meant that a live rear axle and half-elliptic leaf springs were specified.

TVR Grantura Mk 2

Built: Blackpool, England, 1960-1962

Before the definitive Mk 3 Grantura was introduced in 1962, TVR were building a series of Mk 2 Granturas, whose chassis design was developed from that of the original TVR of the late 1950s. This was not as refined and developed a chassis as that of the Mk 3, and featured all independent suspension by trailing arms and transverse torsion bars, whose components were actually those of the VW Beetle.

There was virtually the same choice of engines, and the bodystyle was the same, with that distinctive glassfibre fastback style.

Specification (Mk 2 and Mk 2A)

Engine and transmission: Choice of four-cylinder in-line engines, by Ford, BMC, or Coventry-Climax. Most cars sold with one or other of MGA engines. **1588cc unit:** Bore, stroke and capacity 75.39 × 88.9mm., 1588cc. Maximum power 80bhp (net) at 5600rpm.; maximum torque 87lb.ft. at 3800rpm. **1622cc unit (from mid-1961):** Bore, stroke and capacity 76.2 × 88.9mm., 1622cc. Maximum power 86bhp (net) at 5500rpm.; maximum torque 97lb.ft. at 4000rpm. Four speed manual gearbox in unit with engine. Hypoid bevel final drive.

Chassis: Front engine, rear drive. Separate multi-tubular steel chassis frame. Independent front suspension by trailing arms and transverse torsion bars. Worm and sector steering. Independent rear suspension by trailing arms and transverse torsion bars. Front and rear wheel drum brakes; front wheel disc brakes from spring 1961 production.

Bodywork: Glassfibre bodyshell, in two-door two-seater fastback coupe style, by TVR. Length 11ft. 6in.; width 5ft. 4in.; height 4ft. 0in. Unladen weight (MG engine) 1570lb.

Performance: With Coventry-Climax engine, as for Mk 3.

TVR Grantura MkIII

Built: Blackpool, England, 1962-1967

Although there had been earlier models of TVR, production had been very limited, and the Mark III Grantura with its redesigned tubular chassis of 1962 really heralded the start of serious production by this small Blackpool concern. As with so many other small British sports car manufacturing companies, the basic design centred around a tubular chassis, used proprietary engines, transmissions and other components, and topped the whole with individually-styled glass-fibre bodies.

The TVR, like many other cars of the day, was sold in kit form, and was only sold as a two-seater hardtop coupe, with a style distinguished by a low 'shovel' nose, and by a short sloping fastback tail. The chassis featured independent suspension on original cars by VW Beetle-style trailing links and transverse torsion bars, later by coil springs and wishbones from the announcement of the Mk III.

TVR, incidentally, was a name brought about as a contraction of TreVoR Wilkinson, who set up the struggling little company in the 1950s, but who had left the

concern by the middle of the 1960s.

Because the TVR was a kit car, it was sold with a range of optional engines – Ford, MGA/MGB and Coventry-Climax FWA being the most common. Towards the middle of the 1960s, however, use of the expensive Coventry-Climax engine died away, and the majority of late-model Granturas were fitted with the 1.8-litre MGB engine with 95bhp. This guaranteed the cars a 100mph maximum speed, and as they were also light the fuel economy was surprisingly good.

TVRs, however, were functional rather than refined sporting cars, and it is a fact that features like sound-deadening, water-sealing and anti-vibration engineering did not figure prominently in the specification.

TVR had a troubled financial history, and there were no fewer than four different companies making the car during the first six years of the 1960s. With the arrival of the Lilley family – father and son – however, and the formation of TVR Engineering Ltd. in 1965, welcome stability was assured, and the TVR Vixen, a successor to the Grantura, was the result.

TVR Grantura, 1962

Specification

Engine and transmission: Variety of four-cylinder engines offered, to customer choice, including Ford, MGA/MGB and Coventry-Climax ohc unit. Four-speed manual gearbox usually matched to the engine (i.e. BMC with BMC engine, Ford with Ford unit, German ZF unit supplied with Coventry-Climax engines), and mounted in unit with engine. Hypoid bevel final drive.

Chassis: Front engine, rear drive. Separate multi-tubular chassis frame. Independent front suspension by coil springs and wishbones. Rack and pinion steering. Independent rear suspension by coil springs and wishbones. Four wheel drum brakes (early cars), front wheel discs and rear drums (later cars).

Bodywork: Glass-fibre two-door two-seater fastback coupe body style. Length 15ft. 6in.; width 5ft. 4in.; height 4ft. 0in. Unladen weight, depending on engine specified, from 1540lb.

Performance: (Coventry Climax 1098cc version, with 83bhp) Maximum speed 101mph. 0-60mph 10.8sec. Standing ¼-mile 18.3sec. Typical fuel consumption 28mpg.

TVR Vixen series

Built: Blackpool, England 1967-1973

With TVR, as with other specialist models, it is often difficult to know when one model range really goes out of production, as demand for the occasional example can usually be satisfied. Thus the Vixen, which grew out of the Grantura in 1967 after a considerable overlap, was effectively replaced by the 'M' bodied cars in 1972, but was still around for a while after that.

Vixens used essentially the same chassis (multi-tubular), all-independent suspension (by wishbones and coil springs at the front), and glass-fibre coupe bodyshell as the previous TVR Grantura. The new management, which had taken over in 1965, and had been working for some time to improve quality, service back-up, and the cars' reliability, looked on the Vixen as an entirely fresh approach to the building of such a specialist model.

Visually, you tell the Vixens by the sharply cut-off styling at the tail, which (though continuing in the sloping back window of the Grantura) now lacked the swept extreme tail in favour of a Kamm-like style. Vixens, too, gave rise to Tuscans, which are described later.

Almost all Vixens were supplied as kits, and the two engines fitted to them were Ford Cortina GT units (1599cc crossflow, with a twin-choke Weber carburettor) or MGB units (1798cc, with twin SU carburettors), each engine being matched to its own appropriate gearbox. Although the MGB unit was marginally more powerful, it was also rather heavier, and the effective road performance was the same no matter which engine was fitted.

Original Vixens of 1967 gave way to Series II Vixens in the autumn of 1968, where the principal change was that the body was bolted to the chassis rather than moulded to it on assembly. Series III Vixens followed at the end of 1970, without major changes,

TVR Vixen

and the last Series IV cars were built in 1972 and 1973. It is also worth noting that in 1971 and 1972 there was a short run of TVR 1300s, which were effectively Vixens with Triumph Spitfire 1296cc engines and gearboxes, but these were not a success as they were somewhat underpowered, and that chassis/engine choice was not repeated for the M-type models. The last Vixens – the Series IV models – used the much-changed M-Type chassis and suspensions, which – while of the same basic type – were much improved in detail and function.

The main feature of the TVR Vixen, apart from its looks, was that it was wide, with a short wheelbase, which meant that it could be a very handleable car in experienced hands. It was also a much more refined car than its predecessors, and began to sell to people other than out-and-out sporting enthusiasts. This evolutionary process was to be carried forward even further with the M-Type cars of 1972.

Specification

Engine and transmission: Four-cylinders, in-line, with pushrod-operated overhead-valve cylinder head, built by Ford. (Other engines, including MGB 1.8-litre units, also supplied). Bore, stroke and capacity 80.97 × 77.62mm., 1599cc. Maximum power 88bhp (net) at 5400rpm.; maximum torque 96lb.ft. at 3600rpm. Four-speed manual gearbox in unit with engine. Hypoid bevel final drive.

Chassis: Front engine, rear drive. Separate multi-tubular steel chassis frame. Independent front suspension by coil springs and wishbones. Rack and pinion steering. Independent rear suspension by coil springs and wishbones. Front wheel disc brakes, rear drums.

Bodywork: Glass-fibre two-door two-seater fastback coupe body style. Length 12ft. 1in.; width 5ft. 4in.; height 4ft. 0in. Unladen weight (depending on engine) 1680lb.

Performance: Maximum speed 106mph. 0-60mph 11.0sec. Standing ¼-mile 18.1sec. Typical fuel consumption 27mpg.

TVR Tuscan V6 and Griffith

Built: Blackpool, England, 1964-1971

Chronologically, the Griffith came first, being a very high-powered derivative of the Grantura, and the Tuscan followed several years later, as a faster, more powerful and up-market version of the Vixen. The two cars were connected philosophically due to the concept of putting big vee-layout Ford engines into a chassis originally designed only to cope with more modest four-cylinder engines.

Griffith 200s were built at Blackpool, and shipped to the United States, where big 4.7-litre Ford vee-8 engines and appropriate engines were installed by Griffith Motors Inc., and the result was a car of shattering (in the wrong hands, quite frightening) performance. These cars, naturally enough, were marketed solely in North America, though one or two isolated examples came back to this country where they were raced with considerable success and panache.

The Tuscan V6 of 1969, however, was the more civilised, the more believable way, to go about this up-engining process, and indeed formed the basis of the current highly-successful TVR models. The V6 engine in question was the easily-available British Ford vee-6 2994cc unit which among other things found a home in Ford's own Capris and Zodiacs, and in the Reliant Scimitar GTE. It is interesting to recall that it was the interruption in vee-6 engine supplies due to a lengthy strike at Ford which caused TVR to develop an alternative derivative of this car with the Triumph 2.5-litre six-cylinder engine, which was already de-toxed and suitable for fitment to cars to be sold in North America.

TVR Tuscan V6

For a short time, Tuscan V8 models were made, which were really more civilised versions of the original Griffith, and these were superseded by the V6 model of 1969. The V6 was dropped in favour of the new M-model in 1972, not because it was a failure, but because the new model took over its marketing slot, and capitalised on the earlier success.

Specification

Engine and transmission: Six-cylinders, in 60-degree vee-formation, with pushrod-operated overhead-valve cylinder heads, built by Ford. Bore, stroke and capacity 93.66 × 72.4mm., 2994cc. Maximum power 128bhp (DIN) at 4750rpm, later models 138bhp (DIN) at 5000rpm. Maximum torque 173lb.ft. at 3000rpm. Four-speed manual gearbox in unit with engine. Hypoid bevel final drive.

Chassis: Front engine, rear drive. Separate multi-tubular steel chassis frame. Independent front suspension by coil springs and wishbones. Rack and pinion steering. Independent rear suspension by coil springs and wishbones. Front wheel disc brakes, rear drums.

Bodywork: Glass-fibre two-door two-seater fastback coupe body style. Length 12ft. 1in.; width 5ft. 4in.; height 4ft. 0in. Unladen weight 2000lb.

Performance: Maximum speed 125mph. 0-60mph 8.3sec. Standing ¼-mile 16.2sec. Typical fuel consumption 26mpg.

Note: For sale in the United States, the TVR Griffith was effectively a Tuscan with a Ford USA vee-8 engine. Bore, stroke and capacity 101.6 × 73mm., 4727cc. Maximum power 271bhp (gross) at 7000rpm.

Performance: Maximum speed 155mph. 0-60mph 5.7sec. Standing ¼-mile 14.1sec. Typical fuel consumption 17mpg.

TVR 3000M and M-Type family

Built: Blackpool, England, 1972 to 1979

The Lilley family took several years to swing the TVR concern completely back to complete financial stability, and it was not until the early 1970s that they were able to consider introducing radically new models. The new family, the M-models ('M' stands for Martin Lilley, by the way) being the result.

There was nothing startlingly different about the new cars, which started from the basis of the well-known glass-fibre bodyshell in two-door two-seater fastback coupe form. Under the skin, however, there was a brand-new multi-tubular steel chassis, which was effectively a backbone chassis as the four principal tubes surrounded the engine and transmission. This supported the bolt-on glass-fibre body, had four-wheel independent suspension by coil springs and wishbones, and could accept a great variety of different engines.

The body was extensively modified, with a longer and sleeker nose, and with a lengthened and more shapely tail, all to match the increased wheelbase, longer doors, and more spacious cabin of the passenger compartment. Although kit-cars were initially supplied, it was always the Lilleys' intention to get out of this market sector, which they duly did in 1973. All modern TVRs are now completely assembled and tested at the Blackpool works.

The Ford vee-6 2994cc engine has always dominated the production lines, along with (for United States sale only) the six-cylinder Triumph 2498cc unit normally found in the TR6. For a short time in 1972 and 1973, and again in low numbers in 1976 and

TVR 3000M Convertible

1977, there was a 1600M, which used the Cortina GT 1599cc unit of the old Vixen SIV.

As TVR have gone from strength to strength, so have they also been able to offer the body derivatives which might have come years earlier. From the autumn of 1976 the Taimar model was made available, in which a big hatchback window was the feature of the tail of the car, and from 1978 a convertible model was also put on sale. All were based on the same basic chassis and body, and all continued to be built until the end of 1979. By now the TVR company's image had changed completely, and the cars were being sold to a much more demanding and sophisticated clientele. Almost as Lotus began to find new markets with their Elans, so did TVR with their factory-assembled M-models, which feature an impressive amount of equipment, and are much quieter, silkier and more delicate to drive than TVRs of ten years ago.

Specification

Engine and transmission: Six-cylinders, in 60-degree vee-formation, with pushrod-operated overhead-valve cylinder heads, built by Ford. Bore, stroke and capacity 93.66 × 72.4mm., 2994cc. Maximum power 142bhp (DIN) at 5300rpm.; maximum torque 172lb.ft. at 3000rpm. Four-speed manual gearbox in unit with engine. Hypoid bevel final drive.

Chassis: Front engine, rear drive. Separate multi-tubular steel chassis frame. Independent front suspension by coil springs and wishbones. Rack and pinion steering. Independent rear suspension by coil springs and wishbones. Front wheel disc brakes, rear drums.

Bodywork: Glass-fibre two-door two-seater fastback coupe body style. Length 13ft. 2in.; width 5ft. 4in.; height 3ft. 11in. Unladen weight 2240lb.

Performance: Maximum speed 121mph. 0-60mph 7.7sec. Standing ¼-mile 16.0sec. Typical fuel consumption 24mpg.

Note: Also sold was the 1600M, with Ford-built four-cylinder in-line engine. Bore, stroke and capacity 80.97 × 77.62mm., 1599cc. Maximum power 84bhp (DIN) at 5500rpm.; maximum torque 92lb.ft. at 3500rpm. Unladen weight 1975lb.

Performance: Maximum speed 105mph. 0-60mph 10.4sec. Standing ¼-mile 17.6sec. Typical fuel consumption 28mpg.

Note: Also sold was the 2500M, with Triumph-built six-cylinder in-line engine. Bore, stroke and capacity 74.7 × 95mm., 2498cc. Maximum power 105bhp (DIN) at 4900rpm.; maximum torque 117lb.ft. at 3000rpm.

Performance: Maximum speed 109mph. 0-60mph 9.3sec. Standing ¼-mile 17.3sec. Typical fuel consumption 29mpg.

Note: Taimar model is basically as 'M' models, but with opening hatchback. 3000 Taimar weighs 2260lb., has same performance as 3000M. Convertible model is also available.

TVR Turbo

Built: Blackpool, England, 1975 to 1979

The most astonishing TVR of all, if one ignores the essentially competition-car Griffith 200 type, was the Turbo. Like all good turbo-charged cars, it could be driven as a docile road machine, or as a very fast road burner indeed. Although the Turbocharged engine is rather special, it was offered in any one of the three different TVR bodies – coupe, Taimar coupe, or convertible, all of which shared the same chassis and suspension layout.

The Turbocharged engine installation, starting from the use of a Ford vee-6 2994cc engine as its basis, was developed by Broadspeed in the midlands, and all production engines were supplied from that concern. Even though there was considerably more bulk to such a unit (the charger and the manifolding take up a lot of space, unavoidably), it all fits neatly into the roomy engine bay of the TVR. The performance gains were quite remarkable, and the TVR Turbo only just fails to squeeze into the Supercar category due to its own humble origins and to the way the performance standards have risen in the 1970s.

TVR Turbo

Specification

Engine and transmission: Six-cylinders, in 60-degree vee-formation, with pushrod-operated overhead-valve cylinder heads, built by Ford, and turbo-charged by Broadspeed. Bore, stroke and capacity 93.66 × 72.4mm., 2994cc. Maximum power 230bhp (DIN) at 5500rpm.; maximum torque 273lb.ft. at 3500rpm. Four-speed manual gearbox in unit with engine. Hypoid bevel final drive.

Chassis: Front engine, rear drive. Separate multi-tubular steel chassis frame. Independent front suspension by coil springs and wishbones. Rack and pinion steering. Independent rear suspension by coil springs and wishbones. Front wheel disc brakes, rear drums.

Bodywork: Glass-fibre bodyshell, in two-door two-seater fastback coupe or convertible body styles, or fastback hatchback style. Length 13ft. 2in.; width 5ft. 4in.; height 3ft. 11in. Unladen weight (coupes) 2300lb. (convertible) 2435lb.

Performance: Maximum speed 139mph. 0-60mph 5.8sec. Standing ¼-mile 14.5sec. Typical fuel consumption 19mpg.

Warwick GT

Built: Colnbrook, England, 1960-1962

Although the numbers of Warwick GT cars built between 1960 and 1962 would not have justified its inclusion on its own account in this book, these cars were really little more than slightly-improved Peerless GT cars, which were built in rather higher numbers between 1957 and 1960. At the highest rate of production, more than five cars a week could be delivered, and there seemed to be enough customers for what was really a special coupe derivative of TR3 ideals.

The Peerless/Warwick enterprise was of a car designed by Bernie Rodger, who later went on to become involved in the Gordon Keeble project. It had a multi-tubular chassis frame, using small-section steel tubes, with de Dion rear suspension, and Triumph TR3 engines and transmissions, along with TR3 front suspension. By the standards of the day it was a low-slung close-coupled 2 + 2 sports coupe, and the bodies were built from glass-fibre, and with a bonnet and front wings which swung forward as a complete unit giving access to the engine bay and front end. Even though the car was somewhat bulkier than the TR3, it was very little heavier, so the performance was on a par with that famous sports car.

Not enough customers could, however, be found for the Peerless to be profitable in its Slough factory, and that business was closed down. Bernie Rodger then re-established it on a smaller scale a few miles away at Colnbrook, near London's Heathrow airport. However, like many other cars of this type, the Warwick GT's performance and road behaviour were far ahead of its refinement and creature comforts, with the result that customers, or potential customers, were often disappointed by the high noise levels and general lack of refinement in the design.

Even though a few cars were built as Warwick-Buicks, powered by the light-alloy 3.5-litre Buick vee-8 engines, it was not enough, and the business closed down at the end of 1962.

Specification

Engine and transmission: Four-cylinders, in-line, with pushrod-operated overhead-valve cylinder head, built by Triumph. Bore, stroke and capacity 83 × 92mm, 1991cc. 100bhp (net) at 5000rpm; maximum torque 118lb.ft. at 3000rpm. Four-speed gearbox and optional Laycock overdrive in unit with engine. Hypoid bevel final drive.

Chassis: Front engine, rear drive. Multi-tubular chassis frame. Independent front suspension by coil springs and wishbones. Cam and peg steering. Rear suspension de Dion, with half-elliptic leaf springs. Front-wheel disc brakes, and rear drums.

Bodywork: Glass-fibre, two-door coupe style, with 2 + 2 seating. Length 13ft. 6in.; width 5ft. 3in.; height 4ft. 4in. Unladen weight 2240lb.

Performance: Maximum speed 103mph. 0-60mph 12.8sec. Standing ¼-mile 18.6sec. Typical fuel consumption 26mpg.

Warwick GT

Chapter Four

Quantity production types

To sell a new sporting model in large numbers, manufacturers have always had to tailor their designs very carefully. To attract their customers, the cars had to be as fast, as excitingly styled, and as special as possible in every way. But it had to be available at the right price, which meant that it had to be simple to build, and many of its components had to be shared with a real mass-production touring car. In the 1960s and 1970s, when production and tooling costs went through the roof, it was a miracle that such cars continued to be developed.

Quantity-production manufacturers, in fact, have the most difficult job of any group covered in this book. Within reason, most specialist concerns can be excused for cutting a few corners in the specification and manufacture of their cars. Most of them, indeed, take advantage of this. The 'homologation specials' which are covered in a later section are rarely more than halfway complete models in the engineering sense, as their customers are expected to spend a great deal of money on making them fully competitive. Makers of Supercars, on the hand, know that they can virtually ask their own price for superlative performance and styling, so the expensive handwork needed to achieve this is accepted without compromise.

Economically, of course, the majority of all Grand Touring and sports car customers fall into this group, and – paradoxically enough – it has always seemed that they are not willing to equate a bargain selling price with a very ordinary specification. Models without number have gained a poor reputation because their costs and their performance have been pared down so far that their attraction has also disappeared. Some cars – like British Leyland's MGB – have been produced for so many years to squeeze the last drop of profit out of them that they fall completely behind the times and become the object of some ridicule.

What do I mean by "quantity production"? That is difficult to define, but on the other hand it is easy enough to identify models which qualify. BMW, Jensen, Mercedes-Benz and Porsche all provide perfect examples. The M1, Interceptor/FF, 300SL and 928 models are – or were – real Supercars. BMW 3-litre coupes, Jensen-Healeys, Bagheeras, 230SLs, and 924s are all quantity-production machines by any definition. In some cases, as at Jensen, for example, Supercars and quantity production models took shape side by side on parallel assembly tracks.

Nevertheless, providing a competent but simple design, and applying careful costing techniques, has not always ensured lasting success. Both Jensen and Glas, for instance, suffered financial catastrophe which killed off their sporting cars. Changes of ownership and policy killed off the Daimler SP250. Neither Opel, nor Chrysler UK, were sufficiently committed to sports car motoring to persist with successors to the Opel GT and Alpine models.

It needs real commitment, and an enormous build up of sheer experience and know-how, to gain a long-lasting reputation for making quantity-production sports cars. In Great Britain MG (with Austin-Healey, for many years) and Triumph have achieved this status, as have all three major Italian concerns – Alfa-Romeo, Fiat and Lancia. There will always, it seems, be sporting BMWs (even if at a considerable price), luscious Mercedes-Benz coupes, and a seemingly endless supply of new Porsches. It is a sad reflection on the times, and the economic conditions for motoring, that the only true quantity-production sporting marque to be established in the last ten years has been Ford, with the Capris. Apart from them, whose failure would have been unthinkable, only Matra-Simca looked likely to bring a new name to this sector of the market in the 1970s.

It is in this section that I have often had to make harsh decisions about cars which have had to be turned down. As I pointed out in the introduction, it has been my decision to include Capris because their structure is entirely special, and their purpose unmistakeable, and I have ignored many cars because they were no more and no less than modified versions of bread-and-butter touring cars.

Not that this process is simple, or foolproof. No-one surely, would want to see Alfa-Romeo Giulia Sprint GTs or Spiders thrown out because they have so much in common with the Giulia saloons? Or to banish the NSU Sport Prinz just because its family car derivative was a rather cheap and nasty mini-car? On the other hand, I have had to split my thoughts on Renault coupes down the middle. I could not begin to enthuse over the basic 15s and 17s, in that they struck me as no more than rebodied 12s, but I thought the 17TS/Gordini model special enough to be included.

From 1961 to date, therefore, I have chosen to list twenty-one different marques, and of these just nine go forward into the 1980s. In terms of numbers built, and different models put on the market, Fiat, Ford, MG, Porsche and Triumph are the leaders. If prestige and reputation are thought to be more important, then my palm goes to BMW, Mercedes-Benz and Porsche. Of the twelve marques which did not survive, perhaps the saddest loss was that of Austin-Healey. Both the Sprites and the 'big' Healeys had a great deal of character. Both made a great deal of money for BMC, and for British Leyland, and both were eliminated in nothing more than an ill-judged act of rationalisation. I was sorry to see that the VW-Porsche failed to prove that a mid-engined layout could be both practical and saleable, but I blame the styling as much as the layout for that. And in spite of its very controversial looks, I was sorry that the Daimler SP250 could not survive to give that fine and under-appreciated vee-8 engine a chance in further models. I have little doubt, incidentally, that the nine survivors will all continue to prosper in the 1980s, but I think it highly unlikely that any new competitors will appear.

The trend in mechanical layout and specification has followed that of mass production quite closely, which was inevitable when one considers the origins of many of these cars' major components. Between front-wheel-drive, mid-engine and rear-engine there is as much disparity here as in any other section covered by the book, but this is not due to brave designing. In almost every case it is because the mass-production cars were so equipped. In half the cases, something other than the classic front-engine/rear-drive layout has featured, though I have to say that most of the really big sales (such as Ford, MG and Triumph) were achieved in this manner.

Front-wheel-drive, in spite of the benefits in handling and stability which it often confers, has only been adopted by four marques -- Alfa-Romeo, Lancia, Panhard and Renault -- and it was always done because suitable engine and transmission power packs were already in use by the firms in question. No quantity-production sporting car has been put on the market where the conversion to front-wheel-drive was done especially for that model; the potential cost, complication, and aggravation always ruled it out.

Most interesting, however, is the short and necessarily brief survey of the mid-engined cars put on sale in this period, for in spite of the fashionable nature of the layout only three separate models -- the Fiat X1/9, the Lancia Monte Carlo (Scorpion in the United States) and the VW-Porsche 914 family -- made it to the showrooms. All had their engines mounted behind the seats but ahead of the line of the rear wheels, all drove the rear wheels, and all have been delivered in considerable quantities.

So much is not in dispute. But what is fascinating is that in every case the engine and transmission pack was converted to this use from another configuration. In the case of the VW-Porsches, these were taken from the layout of other *rear*-engined VW or Porsche models, turned round through 180-degrees, and given modified final-drive gearing arrangements to ensure that they were not equipped with four or five reverse gears and only a single forward gear! In the two Fiat-inspired cases, both were derived from assemblies already in use for front-wheel-drive cars; in effect, all that was necessary was for the packs to be moved back several feet in the wheelbase, be asked to drive the rear instead of the front wheels, and to be given new rear suspension such that the wheels could no longer be steered.

In the case of the X1/9 this maneouvre was enormously successful, but the Lancia Monte Carlo solution had to be withdrawn, temporarily, until 1980.

For the record, the power packs came from Fiat 128/Fiat Ritmo (Strada), Lancia Beta and VW411/Porsche 911 models respectively.

Rear-engined cars, from Fiat, NSU, Porsche and Simca, for instance, all relied exclusively on rear-drive packs developed from rear-engined touring cars. It is significant, surely, taking account of modern standards required of car's handling and weight distribution (and, surely, safety regulations have something to do with this?) that no quantity-produced rear-engined car of this type and class is still on sale; the last survivor was the Fiat 850 Coupe/Spider range, which was eventually ousted by the mid-engined X1/9.

Unit cost and high initial investment weigh against anything very exciting being chosen for engines in this group. Water-cooled four-cylinder and six-cylinder in-lines abound, but there is also a good selection of different vee-configuration units, ranging, from German Ford vee-4s (used in Capris and in the Matra 530A) to the big vee-8s found in MGB V8s, Sunbeam Tigers, Triumph TR8s and the expensive Mercedes-Benz coupes. Given half a chance, if their financial problems had disappeared, Glas would have joined in. Air-cooled engines featured in NSU, Porsche and VW-Porsche models.

In one instance, and then only in a single model, a Wankel rotary engine was used. This type, a single-rotor engine of 500cc nominal capacity, was installed in the rear of the NSU Wankel Spider, as a testbed for the NSU concern's future plans, and it was linked with an open version of the Sport Prinz's body. But the engine was neither as smooth, nor anything like as reliable, as had been hoped, so it was shortlived and unsuccessful.

A few of this group of cars was offered with the alternative of automatic transmission. However, unless the model involved was relatively expensive, fast and plushy in the first place, it was rarely a popular option. In the case of cars like the MGB, the customers soon showed that they were not interested, and the option was withdrawn. A halfway stage, using torque converters but with the gear stick retained, found a home in cars like the Porsches and VW-Porsches. Five-speed manual gearboxes are now becoming the norm, even in small cars like the latest Fiat X1/9s, and many models have been sold with the option of an electrically-operated overdrive unit.

Predictably, in view of the rate of production to be achieved by these cars, virtually all of them were designed to have pressed-steel bodies, and most of them also featured chassisless unit-construction structures. Triumph's Spitfire actually goes on into the 1980s with a separate box-section chassis frame, and is therefore unique. Before that the other anachronistic survivor was another Triumph – the TR6, of which the last example was made in the summer of 1976. Both these Triumph frames, incidentally, were first seen in 1962 and 1965 respectively, and in true quantity-production firms no new models have been given separate frames since that time.

Most manufacturers either build their own pressed-steel bodyshells, or buy them in from large concerns like Pressed Steel (who are now part of British Leyland, but who were independent until the mid-1960s, and who – logically enough – now supply MG and Jaguar with bodies for their sports cars). In Italy, concerns like Pininfarina are in great demand to do much of the assembly of cars like the Lancia Monte Carlo, while Bertone build the Fiat X1/9, and in Germany Karmann have often given similar support to BMW.

Of all the cars I list, however, just one – the Daimler SP250 – had a glass-fibre bodyshell, which must suggest that production quantities achieved were verging on the 'Specialist' category. As I have already pointed out, in regard to specialist manufacturers, the problem with using glass-fibre is that it takes a good deal of time for a new shell to 'cure', and there are practical limitations on factory space to the number of bodies which can be in build at any one time.

At the beginning of the period, careful cost control often ruled out much-needed refinements like all-independent suspension, but modern customers are now sophisticated enough to demand this feature – and they usually get it. The X1/9 and the Lancia Monte Carlo, designed by the same team, the Porsche 924, and the latest 6-series BMWs all feature all-independent suspension. Cars ruthlessly designed down to a price range (like Ford's Capris), or full-bloodedly aimed at the North American market (where such things are not considered essential) can get away with front engines and live rear axles. The TR7/TR8 family is a perfect example – and note that it came along as a replacement for the all-independent TR6, and is made alongside the all-independent Spitfire.

Open coachwork seems to be on the decline, in spite of the recent launch of a convertible Triumph TR7. Brought about by two factors – by unfavourable North American safety legislation, and by the fact that really *fast* open cars can be unpleasant to drive – it has led either to the stylish closed coupe (the Capri, for all its ubiquity, is a very popular example), or to cars sold with a single removable roof panel (Fiat X1/9, Porsche Targas – or even the TR4/4A/5 family of the 1960s). The steel sliding sunroof has made something of a comeback, though in small cars the aperture provided is really only a gesture. Cars *designed* as open machines are now dying out, though it seems that the latest interpretation of North American legislation may encourage a reversal of the trend. Even so, it is a fact that in many cases, where a straight choice is given between open or coupe derivatives (like the Alfa Giulia GT and Lancia Beta families, for instance) the closed car is much more popular.

Much mention has been made of the North American market, because it is a fact of life that most of the world's sporting cars are sold in that continent, and a good proportion of them go to sun-drenched California. It is fair to say that without the buoyancy of this huge market, true convertibles like the MGB and the Fiat 124 Sport Spider would have died out long ago, as would the MG Midget (finally dropped in 1979) and the Triumph Spitfire (due to be dropped in 1980). Cynics have suggested that if the Japanese troubled to sell convertibles instead of fine modern coupes like the Toyota Celicas and Datsun 'Z' family, then the Europeans would be in dire trouble; in view of the impact they made on the coupe market sector, I have no cause to dispute this.

A final word about seating arrangements, and about mid-engined cars in particular, is appropriate. To an enthusiast, a true sports car has only two seats, and no provision for more, which means that a mid-engined car (which − almost by definition − cannot accommodate more even if the sales staff would like it) should be ideal. But it seems to be true that some mid-engined designs, the VW-Porsche in particular, suffered because of this very failing.

Two-plus-two, or close-coupled four-seater layouts, on the other hand, are very popular indeed where front-engined cars are concerned. Even though the biggest sellers of all − TR7, MGB, and Fiat 124 Sport Spider − are almost pure two-seaters, the Porsche 924, the Lancia Fulvia Coupes, and particularly the Ford Capri and BMW coupes all managed to squeeze space for four people inside a stylish body shape.

In spite of every possible economic vicissitude, however, the quantity-production sporting car seems sure to survive into the 21st century, and it looks as if there will always be plenty of red-blooded customers queueing up to buy.

Alfa Romeo Giulietta Sprints & Spiders

Built: Milan, Italy, 1954-1963

Following the successful launch of the 1900 model in 1950, which began to build up the volume of production at Alfa Romeo to levels never seen before, the company next turned its mind to an entirely new project which they hoped would transform them into a truly large concern. That project was the Giulietta design, and it has proved to be quite remarkably successful. Out of the Giulietta came the Giulia, followed by the 1750 and 2000 ranges, and the derivatives of the original Giulietta engine are still made in their thousands for all manner of modern Alfas being built at the end of the 1970s.

Every component of the Giulietta design was new – engine, transmission, axle, suspensions, body and styling, so no part of the layout had to be compromised by existing equipment. Even so, much of the design had philosophical links with the famous cars of the 1930s and 1940s, and those links were usually plain even to a casual glance.

Strangely enough it was the sporting coupe derivative of the basic design which was revealed first, in 1954, with the four-door saloon following a year later in 1955. The mechanical layout of this car, however, has been a classic in its own lifetime. Most important of all was a brand-new twin-overhead-camshaft engine, with bore and stroke of 74×75mm., a swept volume of 1290cc, and a power output in original Sprint form of 80bhp at 6300rpm; the Sprint Veloce tune which followed in 1956 increased this figure to 90bhp at 6500rpm. The fine engine had a rigid five-bearing crankshaft, slip-fit wet cylinder-liners, and camshaft drive by duplex chain. Matching it was a new all-synchromesh four-speed gearbox, and the hypoid bevel rear axle was accurately located on coil springs, radius arms and a centrally-positioned A-bracket. Front suspension was by coil springs and wishbones.

Alfa Romeo Giulietta Sprint

Alfa Romeo Giulietta Spider

While the mass-production saloon was a neat little four-door design by Alfa-Romeo themselves, the fastback Sprint coupe was a mouth-wateringly beautiful style by Bertone, with 2 + 2 seating accommodation. From the distinctive nose, with its delicately shaped grille arrangement, to the swept tail and sloping rear window, there was not a line or a contour out of place, and not for nothing was this car often dubbed the most beautiful coupe in the world. It was, however, just the first of several renderings on this excellent little chassis.

Within a year of the announcement of Bertone's coupe, Pininfarina had produced a cheekily attractive two-seater open Spider derivative of the design, with the same chassis and tunes of engine, but with a body style which Touring so obviously used as a guide when shaping the 2000 Spider of 1958. Its wheelbase was 13cm (5.1in.) shorter than that of the saloons and Sprints, but Pininfarina was quite capable of making this change from production floorpans when assembling the bodies in his own factory.

Although these were the two high production derivatives of the basic design – 25 239 of the Sprints and 17 207 of the Spiders were made – two other specialised cars were also built. Bertone produced the Giulietta SS or Sprint Speciale, which was an entirely different and elongated shape of coupe, which had been extensively wind-tunnel tested, and which – combined with a 100bhp version of the engine – allowed maximum speeds of around 125mph to be reached (on 1.3-litres!); 1459 of these cars were built between 1960 and 1962. Zagato, however, went one better, by combining the short chassis and 100bhp engine with a short, stubby, but undeniably effective little two-seater coupe which proved itself to be a rally winner by anyone's standards. Only 200 of these excellent machines were built from 1960 onwards, but these are the cars which spearheaded Alfa's rallying victories in the early 1960s. Both these cars, incidentally, had five-speed gearboxes, while other Giuliettas had four-speed boxes.

When the Giulia range was announced in 1962, complete with the 1570cc version of the original engine, Sprint, Spider and SS models carried on a Giulias for a time, but no 1.6-litre Sprint Zagatos were built.

137

Specification (Sprint and Spider)

Engine and transmission: Four-cylinders, in-line, with twin-overhead-camshaft cylinder head. Bore, stroke and capacity 74×75mm, 1290cc. Maximum power 80bhp (net) at 6000rpm.; maximum torque 72lb.ft. at 3500rpm. Four-speed manual gearbox in unit with engine. Hypoid bevel final drive.

Chassis: Front engine, rear drive. Pressed-steel unit construction bodyshell and structure. Independent front suspension by coil springs and wishbones. Worm and sector steering. Suspension of rear live axle by coil springs, radius arms and A-bracket. Four wheel drum brakes.

Bodywork: Pressed-steel bodyshell, styled by Bertone. **Sprint:** Length 12ft. 7.5in.; width 5ft. 0.5in.; height 4ft. 4in. Unladen weight 1935lb. **Spider** (by Pininfarina): Length 12ft. 7.5in.; width 5ft. 2.25in.; height 4ft. 1.25in. Unladen weight 1860lb.

Note: Veloce engine gave 90bhp (net) at 6000rpm.; maximum torque 80lb.ft. at 4500rpm.

Performance (Sprint Coupe): Maximum speed 103mph. 0-60mph 13.2sec. Standing ¼-mile 19.2sec. Typical fuel consumption 38mpg. **(Spider Veloce):** Maximum speed 113mph. 0-60mph 11.0sec. Standing ¼-mile 17.1sec. Typical fuel consumption 31mpg.

Note: Giulietta Sprint Speciale (by Bertone and by Zagato) were also available, with 100bhp net at 6000rpm.; maximum torque 83lb.ft. at 4500rpm. Overdrive was fitted to the gearbox.

Performance (Sprint Zagato): Maximum speed 122mph. 0-60mph 11.2sec. Standing ¼-mile 17.8sec. Typical fuel consumption 27mpg.

Alfa Romeo Giulietta SS

Alfa Romeo 2000 & 2600 family

Built: Milan, Italy, 1958-1968

Following the devastation caused by Allied bombing during the second world war, it took years for Alfa Romeo to return to normal conditions. The first truly postwar model was the 1900, with its twin overhead camshaft (82.55×88mm) 1884cc engine. Various successful coupe, sprint and cabriolet versions of this, the first-ever unit-construction Alfa Romeo, were made. In 1958, however, this car was replaced by the new 2000 series, which had a slightly enlarged version of that twin-cam engine.

By now the large-engined (relatively speaking) Alfa Romeos were not the backbone of production, as they were completely outnumbered by the Giulietta and later by the Giulia models. However, smart and stylish Spider and Sprint bodies were developed, which were to carry on until the entire model range was discontinued in 1968. The Spider had a $2+2$ seating package and a style by Carrozzeria Touring of Milan, and was announced in 1958; it was built on a shortened version of the 2000's pressed-steel floorpan. The 2000 Sprint, by Bertone, was also built on a shortened wheelbase, and was revealed in 1960.

After 3443 of the Spiders and just 700 of the Sprint coupes had been produced, the 2000 range was made obsolete in 1962 by the announcement of the 2600 models, all of which used the same basic chassis, suspensions and body styles. The new six-cylinder engines (83×79.6mm, 2584cc) were similar in layout and design philosophy to the redundant 'fours', but quite different in detail, for they had wet-liner cylinder barrels, and of course they were considerably more powerful. The more highly-tuned versions

Alfa Romeo 2000 Spider

fitted to Sprints and Spiders produced no less than 145bhp at 5900rpm, which endowed the cars with a maximum speed of nearly 120mph.

Although the styling of the two quantity-production 2600s was the same as that of the 2000s, there was no similar parallel with the last derivative of all to appear – the 2600SZ. Sharing the same short-wheelbase chassis and suspensions of the Sprint and Spider models, the SZ had a dramatic and purposeful 2 + 2 coupe style by Zagato, which featured rectangular headlamps, a flowing profile, and a prominent and distinctive rendering of the classic Alfa radiator shape. Although it was no more powerful than the more mundane (if only by comparison) sporting 2600s, it had a higher performance due to its sleeker shape and lighter weight. Its maximum speed was quoted at 210kph – just over 130mph – and it looked capable of all of that. Like many similar Zagato styles, however, it was designed more for effect and performance than for refinement, and that extra performance had to be paid for in terms of less space and rather more noise.

The SZ, announced in 1965, was also marketed until 1968, when all the 2600s were dropped in favour of the new 1750 saloons and their derivatives.

Specification

Engine and transmission: (2000) Four-cylinders, in-line, with twin-overhead-camshaft cylinder head. Bore, stroke and capacity 84.5×88mm, 1975cc. Maximum power 115bhp (net) at 5700rpm.; maximum torque 112lb.ft. at 3500rpm. Five-speed manual gearbox in unit with engine. **(2600)** Six-cylinders, in-line, with twin-overhead-camshaft cylinder head. Bore, stroke and capacity 83×79.6mm., 2584cc. Maximum power 130bhp (net) at 5900rpm.; maximum torque 139lb.ft. at 4000rpm. Five-speed gearbox in unit with engine. Hypoid bevel final drive.

Chassis: Front engine, rear drive. Unit-construction pressed-steel body/chassis assembly. Independent front suspension by coil springs and wishbones. Worm and sector steering. Suspension of rear live axle by coil springs, radius arms and A-bracket. Front wheel disc brakes (2600), but four wheel drum brakes (2000).

Bodywork: Pressed steel two-door four-seater closed coupe Sprint by Bertone, or two-door four-seater open tourer Spider by Touring.

Sprint: Length 14ft. 4in.; width 5ft. 7in.; height 4ft. 4in. **Spider:** Length 14ft. 9in.; width 5ft. 5in.; height 4ft. 4in. Unladen weight from 2600lb (2000 Spider) to 2820lb. (2600 Sprint).

Performance (2000 Spider): Maximum speed 111mph. 0-60mph 14.2sec. Standing ¼-mile 19.5sec. Typical fuel consumption 15mpg. **(2600 Sprint):** Maximum speed 117mph. 0-60mph 11.7 sec. Standing ¼-mile 18.0sec. Typical fuel consumption 19mpg.

Alfa Romeo Giulia series

Built: Milan, Italy, 1962-1979

Cars built under the sporting Giulia banner fall into two distinct categories − those which were really Giuliettas in style but fitted with larger engines, and those which were truly Giulias. The Giulietta-based cars were built between 1962 and 1964, having the new 1570cc engines giving 92bhp at 6200rpm; 7083 of the Sprint Coupes and rather more of the Spiders and Sprint Speciales were constructed.

Alfa Romeo Giulia Sprint GT

Each of these cars, however, was only an interim, almost an expedient, to keep the sporting Alfas before the eyes of the public while new models were being prepared. These, headed by the Giulia Sprint GT of 1963, have dominated the scene at Milan for many years since then.

The myriad complications, engine sizes, tuning specifications, and sub-variations of each can best be summed up as inspired Italian product planning, or − to put it more crudely − mechanical meccano. It is possible that no other series of cars have been built and sold in such bewildering variety unless we consider cars like Ford's Capris, or the various North American designs which made variety their main selling point.

It is easiest to start by considering the body styles. First, most graceful, and most popular in terms of the huge numbers sold, was the Sprint GT coupe style. Like that of the original Giulietta, this was a Bertone shape, although it managed to provide a close-coupled four-seater arrangement under a rather more bulky but still extraordinarily graceful fastback shape. Its wheelbase, at 7ft. 10.5in., was 6.3-inches less than that of the Giulia saloon underpan on which it was based, and its clean lines were undoubtedly those of a true Italian master.

Complementary to it, from 1966, was the Pininfarina-styled open Spider, which had an even shorter wheelbase − by another four-inches − offered only two seats, and had a strange but distinctive 'flattened cigar' shape with − at first − a long tail. This had elements of Pininfarina's contemporary Ferrari designs around its nose, but was not nearly as graceful as the bulkier but practical Bertone Sprints. At first the spider had no name, but after a magazine contest in Italy it became known as the "Duetto."

As year followed year, Alfa Romeo chopped and changed their engine line-up, expanded them, rationalised them, made some versions more powerful, and occasionally produced limited numbers of lightweight specially-tuned versions with sporting competition and 'homologation' in mind. It is enough to state that all cars had derivatives of the twin overhead camshaft Giulia/Giulietta engines, all had five-speed manual gearboxes, live rear axles, and coil spring suspension all round.

Engines varied from the relatively tame 1290cc unit found in the 1300 versions of both Sprint and Spider, through two different quantity-production 1570cc engines, a 1779cc engine produced at the same time as that engine was available for the 1750 saloon, and finally a 1962cc engine whose bore and stroke (84 × 88.5mm) were the maximum which could be wrung from the original dimensions of the four-cylinder cylinder block.

The most special cars − both Sprint Coupes − were the 1300GTA Junior and the 1600GTA, in which the 'A' stood for Aluminium bodywork, in which twin-plug cylinder heads were specified, and in which the potential power was such as to make the cars suitable for racing and rallying all over the world.

There were no major styling revisions to the Sprint coupe bodyshell over the years, except for the adoption of four headlamps in due course, and other related details; the last of these cars − the GT 1600 Juniors − were built in 1977. The major change to the Duetto, or spider, came in 1969 with the adoption of the 1779cc engine, when the tail was chopped shorter, to the minor detriment of the stowage space, but making it easy to avoid damage in close parking situations.

In addition to the two mass-production bodies by Bertone and Pininfarina, there was a limited-production lightweight "Junior Z" body by Zagato, which was distinctive and attractive, with only two seats under a steeply angled roof, and built on the shortest (Spider) wheelbase. This was only ever offered in 1300 and 1600 form.

Production of all these cars began to run down when the new Alfetta range was introduced progressively from 1972, and the last types of all − the Spiders − were soon to be rendered obsolete as this book went to press.

Specification

Engine and transmission: Four-cylinders, in-line, with twin-overhead-camshaft cylinder head. Engines varying from 74 × 75mm, 1290cc to 84 × 88.5mm., 1962cc, from 103bhp (gross) at 6000rpm and maximum torque of 101lb.ft. at 3200rpm, to 131bhp (DIN) at 5500rpm.; maximum torque 134lb.ft. at 3500rpm. Five-speed manual gearbox in unit with engine. Hypoid bevel final drive.

Chassis: Front engine, rear drive. Pressed-steel unit construction bodyshell, and structure. Independent front suspension by coil springs and wishbones. Recirculating ball steering. Rear suspension of live axle by coil springs, radius arms and A-bracket. Four-wheel disc brakes.

Alfa Romeo Giulia Spider (Duetto)

Bodywork: Pressed-steel bodyshell, in two-door 2 + 2 seater fastback coupe style by Bertone. (For a time a convertible, the Giulia GTC, was also available). Length 13ft. 5in.; width 5ft. 2in.; height 4ft. 4in. Unladen weight from 2180lb. (1300) to 2290lb. (2000).

Performance: (2000 GTV version) Maximum speed 120mph., 0-60mph 9.2sec. Standing ¼-mile 16.4sec. Typical fuel consumption 23mpg. **(1600 GTV)** Maximum speed 113mph. 0-60mph 11.1 sec. Standing ¼-mile 17.7sec. Typical fuel consumption 25mpg. **(1300 Junior)** Maximum speed 102mph. 0-60mph 13.2sec. Standing ¼-mile 19.1sec. Typical fuel consumption 27mpg.

Note: Giulia Sprint Spider, also known as Duetto, had Giulia Sprint GT mechanical specification, but following dimensions:

Bodywork: Pressed steel unit construction two-door, two-seat open sports car style by Pininfarina. Length (original) 13ft. 11.5in., (later cars) 13ft. 6.2in.; width 5ft. 4in.; height 4ft. 3in. Unladen weight (depending on engine fitted) approximately 2295lb.

Performance (1600 Duetto): Maximum speed 113mph. 0-60mph 11.3sec. Standing ¼-mile 18.5sec. Typical fuel consumption 29mpg. **(1750):** Maximum speed 114mph. 0-60mph 9.9sec. Standing ¼-mile 17.5sec. Typical fuel consumption 30mpg. **(2000)** Maximum speed 116mph. 0-60mph 9.8sec. Standing ¼-mile 17.1sec. Typical fuel consumption 27mpg.

Alfa Romeo Alfetta Coupes and Sprints

Built: Milan, Italy, 1974 to date

Following the launch of the Giulietta model of 1954, Alfa Romeo settled down to a lengthy period of concentration on the development of that basic theme; Giulia, 1750 and 2000 were all updated derivatives of the same basic layout. It was not until 1972 that a radically new mechanical layout – the Alfetta saloon – was revealed, and the coupe versions of this new design followed in 1974.

The Alfetta broke new ground in several technical respects, though it retained the same basic Alfa Romeo four-cylinder twin-overhead-camshaft engine which had been in use since the mid-1950s. The style of the new car (by the Alfa Romeo design office) was smart and up-to-date, but it completely hid the innovations under the skin.

Most important of all was that the Alfetta had its all-new five-speed gearbox in unit with the final drive unit, all of which was bolted to the pressed-steel body underframe. The engine was front-mounted, as usual, and was connected to the transmission by a two-piece propeller shaft. Wishbone and torsion bar independent front suspension was conventional enough, but at the rear there was de Dion suspension by coil springs, semi-trailing radius arms, and a Watts linkage. At first only the 1779cc engine was offered, but as the old Giulia and 2000 models were phased out the other sizes – 1570cc or 1962cc – were also offered.

Alfa Romeo Alfetta GTV2000

The Alfetta coupes were launched in 1974, and effectively replaced the old, but still elegant, Giulia Sprint coupes. Not only was the mechanical layout a break with tradition, but the coupe's bodystyle – by Giugiaro (who later formed Ital Design) instead of Alfa's traditional supplier, Bertone – was also new. In the entire mechanical/style/body combination, only the name of Alfetta – which harked back to those splendidly successful supercharged racing cars of the late 1930s and 1940s – was traditional.

Compared with the redundant Giulia Sprint coupes, the Alfettas were rather bulkier, much more spacious, and altogether more practical; they were also rather more aerodynamically efficient, which showed up in improved top speed and potentially lower fuel consumption. In the modern trend, too, the tails had transverse spoilers to trim the lift characteristics, and there was a combined lift-up rear window and hatchback loading door. It was not immediately obvious that the coupes were actually built on a shortened Alfetta saloon wheelbase (the reduction was 11cm, or 4.3in.), as all the steel-panelling with the exception of the underpan was entirely new.

Once the Alfetta saloon had blossomed into a three-engine-size range, it was to be expected that the coupes would follow suit. During 1976, along with some minor style changes and more obvious identification, the 1.6-litre and 2.0-litre Alfetta coupes were announced, while at the same time the original 1.8-litre-engined car was dropped – such a logical rationalisation being very strange for Alfa Romeo, who are renowned for the way they juggle their available resources of engines and bodyshells!

As the coupes are really very stylish close-coupled four-seater cars, instead of personal two-seaters, they have become very popular, the lines are very attractive and the styling is not at all stereotyped. The 2.0-litre car has a maximum speed of nearly 120mph, with acceleration to match.

Specification

Engine and transmission: Four-cylinders, in-line, with twin-overhead-camshaft cylinder head. Bore, stroke and capacity 78×82mm, 1570cc, 80×88.5mm, 1779cc or latterly 84×88.5mm, 1962cc. For 1962cc version, maximum power 130bhp (DIN) at 5300rpm.; maximum torque 130lb.ft. at 4000rpm. Five-speed manual gearbox in unit with final drive.

Chassis: Front engine, rear transmission/rear drive. Pressed-steel unit construction body/chassis unit. Independent front suspension by torsion bars and wishbones. Rack and pinion steering. De Dion rear suspension by coil springs, radius arms and Watts linkage. Four wheel disc brakes.

Bodywork: Pressed-steel bodywork in three-door close-coupled four-seater fastback coupe style. Length 13ft. 7.5in.; width 5ft. 5.5in.; height 4ft. 4.5in. Unladen weight from 2295lb. (1600) to 2380lb. (2000 model).

Performance: (2000) Maximum speed 118mph. 0-60mph 8.9sec. Standing ¼-mile 16.9sec. Typical fuel consumption 25mpg.

Alfa Romeo Alfasud Sprint

Built: Naples, Italy, 1976 to date

So radically new was the little Alfasud model of 1971 that for some time Alfa Romeo tried to encourage the press to consider the cars as entirely different marques – Alfasuds, not Alfa Romeos. A completely new factory, near Naples, was built to make these cars, and the launch was a little premature, for deliveries did not begin until 1972. Absenteeism, strikes, and Alfa's many financial problems meant that the various more specialised versions of the Alfasud did not reach the public as soon as hoped. The very smart little Alfasud Sprint, which had been rumoured (and even photographed) in the continental press from 1973, was not announced until 1976.

The Alfasud, though designed and developed in Milan, had absolutely no mechanical links with any other Alfas. It was the first-ever front-wheel-drive Alfa Romeo car, the first to have a flat-four engine configuration, and the first to be built away from the North of Italy. Policy decisions pointing to a new 'small' Alfa had apparently been taken back in the 1950s, but were not followed up for many years due to the restricted facilities in the Milan factories.

Much rumoured, and much 'leaked' before announcement, the Alfasud was therefore not as unexpected as it might have been. Although there were snide remarks about its resemblance to the Citroen GS model, there seems to have been no contact between the French and Italian concerns. Like the GS, however, the Alfasud had a pressed-steel unit-construction fastback bodyshell, front-wheel-drive, and a flat-four single-overhead-camshaft engine mounted ahead of the final drive with a gearbox behind it, close to the driving compartment.

Alfa Romeo Alfasud Sprint, 1978

One of the persistent complaints about the Alfasud was that it had a tiny engine. This, at first, was 1186cc, but with a bore and stroke of 80×59mm there was obviously room for the stroke to be lengthened and capacity increased. The 'ti' model introduced shortly afterwards, provided more performance without increasing that size.

When the Sprint was launched in 1976, it was seen to be a very smart fastback coupe, very obviously and proudly shaped like that of its 'Big Brother' the Alfetta GT. This was reasonable, as the style was by Giugiaro, and had been completed at about the same time as the bigger car. Like the Alfetta GT, this new coupe was based on the floorpan of the equivalent saloon, but in this case the unmodified, unshortened Alfasud floorpan was used, along with that car's suspensions.

At last, (and years overdue, the analyses all repeated), a bigger version of the engine was used. The stroke had been lengthened to 64mm, the swept volume to 1286cc, and the maximum power to 76bhp (DIN) at 6000rpm; it was also allied to the five-speed gearbox first used in the Alfasud ti saloon.

Once in the market with their smart little 2+2 coupe (which really replaced, in the hearts of enthusiasts if not in direct mechanical terms, the Giulietta and 1.3-litre Giulias of the 1950s to 1970s), Alfa Romeo then decided to make it even faster. The 1.5-litre version of the engine (84×67.2mm., 1490cc) followed in 1978, and is now standard on the model, and available on some other Alfasud touring cars as well.

Like the Alfetta GTs, the Alfasud Sprints were smart and practical little cars, with excellent handling (aided by the front-wheel-drive), 2+2 seating, and a useful hatchback feature. It is, incidentally, equally as heavy, if not slightly more bulky, than the equivalent two-door Alfasud saloon, much of the increase over a normally light coupe being due to the extensive use of sound-deadening treatment.

The Alfasud Sprints, like the Alfetta GTs, will obviously be important models in the Alfa Romeo range throughout the 1980s.

Specification

Engine and transmission: Four-cylinders, in horizontally-opposed layout, with single-overhead-camshaft cylinder heads. Bore, stroke and capacity 84×67.2mm., 1490cc. Maximum power 84bhp (DIN) at 5800rpm.; maximum torque 89lb.ft. at 3500rpm. 1976-1978 models had a 1286cc engine, with bore and stroke of 80×64mm. Maximum power 76bhp (DIN) at 6000rpm.; maximum torque 88lb.ft. at 3500rpm. Five-speed manual gearbox in unit with engine and transaxle. Hypoid bevel final drive.
Chassis: Front engine, front drive. Unit-construction pressed-steel body-chassis unit. Independent front suspension by coil springs and MacPherson struts. Rack and pinion steering. Suspension of rear axle beam by coil springs, Watts linkages and Panhard rod. Four wheel disc brakes.
Bodywork: Pressed-steel bodywork in three-door, closed-coupled four-seater fastback coupe body style. Length 13ft. 2.3in.; width 5ft. 3.4in.; height 4ft. 3.4in. Unladen weight 2040lb.
Performance (1.5 litre Sprint): Maximum speed 103mph. 0-60mph 11.2sec. Standing ¼-mile 18.6sec. Typical fuel consumption 27.6mpg.

Austin-Healey 3000 series

Built: Abingdon, England, 1959 to 1967

Donald Healey's '100' model, first shown in 1952, was immediately adopted by BMC, renamed the Austin-Healey 100, and put into production at Longbridge. After four-years the design was reworked, the wheelbase being slightly lengthened and the new six-cylinder BMC 'C' Series engine fitted. This was the Austin-Healey 100/6. Final assembly was soon moved to the MG factory at Abingdon, and the 3000 model emerged in the summer of 1959 when the enlarged 2912cc engine began to be fitted. With no more than minor styling changes (the final car was still an obvious derivative of the original 1952 '100'), the series was built until the end of 1967. Out of a grand total of 73 728 'Big Healeys' of all types, 42 925 were 3000s.

Austin-Healey 3000 MkIII

The original model had been designed by Donald Healey's son Geoffrey, effectively taking part in a BMC 'design competition' for a new sports car which would use a large proportion of standard-production BMC parts, including complete engine, gearbox and back axle. However, although previous Healey sports cars had all been assembled in Warwick, the numbers envisaged for the new model meant that it would have to be tooled up for quantity production; Jensen, therefore, built the bodyshells, and the cars were shipped to a BMC factory for final assembly.

If the basic layout had a serious fault, it was that the ground clearance was rather limited, and though this made it low and sleek to look at, it also made the car rather vulnerable to under-chassis damage on rough ground. There was no solution to this, although improvements in rear wheel movement and somewhat better ground clearance was achieved when the 'phase 2' 3000 Mk III was introduced during 1964; 16 322 of these definitive cars were built.

The car's low build, however, did not stop it becoming a successful rally car. As prepared by the BMC Competitions Department at Abingdon, the 'works' cars were enormously strong and rugged. Progressive development of the cars eventually endowed them with light-alloy cylinder heads (and a light-alloy block on one or two cars), three twin-choke Weber carburettors, and more than 200bhp from the 3-litre engine.

The original 3000 was available as a two-seater or as a very occasional 2 + 2 seater (the extra seats being squeezed into the same basic bodyshell), and was sold with a folding hood, or with a detachable glass-fibre hardtop. It became the Mk II in 1961, with more power and a triple-SU carburettor installation, but only a year later even more power and a twin-SU system were adopted. More important was that wind-up door windows and a fully convertible hood were fitted. The last major change, introduced in the spring of 1964, was that there was another sizeable increase in power (to the final figure of 148bhp), along with a fascia re-style, and it was in this form that the 3000 carried on until 1967. It was eventually dropped for a variety of reasons − it was time for a completely new model, which BMC wanted to tackle themselves, a 3-litre competitor from MG (MGC) had just been introduced, and in North America (which was the most important market for these cars) the latest safety regulations were weighing very heavily on its viability.

The 'Big Healey', as it was always affectionately known, was a real he-man's car. It was heavy, rugged, by no means refined, and was − in many ways − a throwback to the thoroughbred cars of the pre-war era. It was a marvellously responsive car to those who like to be the master of their machines, but it must also be admitted that it could feel like, and act like, a real pig to others. Nevethess, surviving examples are now in great demand.

Specification (1961 Mk I model)

Engine and transmission: Six-cylinders, in-line, with pushrod-operated overhead-valve cylinder head. Bore, stroke and capacity 83.34 × 88.9mm., 2912cc. Maximum power 124bhp (net) at 4600rpm.; maximum torque 167lb.ft. at 2700rpm. Four-speed manual gearbox with optional overdrive in unit with engine. Hypoid bevel final drive.

Chassis: Front engine, rear drive. Separate design of pressed-steel chassis frame, with box section members (body welded to this on assembly). Independent front suspension by coil springs and wishbones. Cam and peg steering. Rear suspension of live axle by half-elliptic leaf springs. Front wheel disc brakes, rear drums.

Bodywork: Pressed-steel bodyshell, welded to chassis frame on assembly, in two-door two-seater (some cars 2 + 2 seating) open sports car style, with optional hardtop. Length 13ft. 1.5in.; width 5ft. 0in.; height 4ft. 0.75in. Unladen weight 2465lb.

Performance: Maximum speed 114mph. 0-60mph 11.4sec. Standing ¼-mile 17.9sec. Typical fuel consumption 22mpg.

Note: The model was progressively modified, to Mk II with more power, to the 'Convertible' with foldaway hood, and finally to the Mk III, with 148bhp (net) at 5250rpm.; maximum torque 165lb.ft. at 3500rpm.

Performance (Mk III):Maximum speed 121mph. 0-60mph 9.8sec. Standing ¼-mile 17.2sec. Typical fuel consumption 22mpg.

BMW 700 Coupe

Built: Munich, Germany, 1959-1966

BMW had a difficult time re-establishing themselves as volume producers of motor cars after the second world war, principally because their Eisenach factory was now behind the Iron Curtain in East Germany, and the hardware and tooling for building their late-1930s cars was beyond them. Their 500-series cars were large, heavy and luxurious, did not sell in huge quantities (BMW, indeed, were not at all equipped to make them in such numbers), and were not therefore profitable.

It was to reverse this process that the factory began making small cars, first the tiny Isetta 'bubblecar', then the strange 600 model with its front-opening door (inherited from the Isetta), and finally − in 1959 − the 700 series.

The 700, announced first as a coupe with close-coupled four-seater accommodation, was an entirely new chassis, though the air-cooled flat-twin engine was an enlarged and developed version of that already being made for the 600. In many ways it was the last desperate throw by BMW to gain volume (and respectability) before they achieved Bavarian government finance and managed to put the outstanding 1500/1600/1800/2000 range of saloons on to the market at the beginning of the 1960s.

The 700 Coupe had a neat and simply styled notchback coupe style, in pressed-steel, built as a monocoque on a unit-construction 'chassis'. Four-wheel independent suspension was a feature, and although the car looked as if it might have a conventionally-mounted engine in the nose, the flat twin unit was actually positioned in the tail, behind the line of the rear wheels. In spite of a weight distribution which put no less than 63-per-cent of weight over the rear wheels, the handling was surprisingly civilised, and when the engines were tuned to their limit the cars could be surprisingly effective in their class on the race circuits.

No significant changes were made to the design over the years, and it was withdrawn in 1966 when the successful large BMWs came to dominate the scene at Munich.

BMW 700 Coupe

Specification

Engine and transmission: Two-cylinders, air-cooled and horizontally-opposed, with pushrod-operated overhead-valve cylinder heads. Bore, stroke and capacity 78×73mm., 697cc. Maximum power 30bhp (DIN) at 5000rpm.; maximum torque 37lb.ft. at 3400rpm. Note: a tuned version with 40bhp (DIN) at 5700rpm.; maximum torque 38lb.ft. at 4000rpm, was also available. Four-speed manual gearbox in unit with engine and transaxle. Spiral bevel final drive.

Chassis: Rear engine, rear drive. Unit construction pressed-steel body chassis unit. Independent front suspension by coil springs and trailing arms. Rack and pinion steering. Independent rear suspension by coil springs and trailing wishbones. Four wheel drum brakes.

Bodywork: Pressed-steel two-door four-seater notchback coupe style. Length 11ft. 7.3in.; width 4ft. 10.3in.; height 4ft. 1.2in. Unladen weight 1325lb.

Performance: (40bhp version) Maximum speed 78mph. 0-60mph 23.4sec. Standing ¼-mile 22.8sec. Typical fuel consumption 37mpg.

BMW 2000CS and 2800CS Coupes

Built: Munich, Germany, 1965-1971

Following the limited-production but prestigiously important 507 and 3200CS Coupes, BMW followed up with a car derived from the four-cylinder touring car which was completely reviving their fortunes in the 1960s. The new car, announced in 1965, was to go on in more and more modified form until it was replaced by an entirely new design ten-years later.

The original coupes, effectively the 2000CS and 2800CS models, were based on the engineering of the 1600/2000 underpan, suspensions and general layout, but were equipped with a rather flashy and distinctive two-door four-seater coupe bodyshell by Karmann, who had well-forged links with the Munich concern.

That is to say that MacPherson strut front suspension and semi-trailing link coil spring rear suspension was specified, that one or other of the overhead-camshaft engines was specified, and that – depending on the actual model variant – automatic transmission was also available.

In engineering terms, the 2000CS (C = Coupe, S = Sport, incidentally) was the most 'pure', as the engine installation was precisely as intended for the pressed-steel underpan. That underpan, however, had been conceived in the 1950s for the original 1500, which grew up to become the 1600, 1800 and finally the 2000, so that when the new six-cylinder 2.8-litre 2800 engine was shoehorned into place in the autumn of 1968, to replace the 2000CS model, it required a considerable amount of cutting and carving by Karmann to make a competent engineering job of it.

However, along with a considerable re-style, this new model was a great success, with a maximum speed of more than 120mph. Customers were not to know that as far as BMW were concerned it was only an interim solution, as the fully-matured 3.0CS cars would follow in 1971. They were the definitive Karmann-styled coupes which helped complete BMW's sporting image in the 1970s.

BMW 2000 CA/CS, 1965

BMW 2800CS, 1968

Specification (2000CS and 2800CS Coupes)

Engine and transmission: Four-cylinders, in-line, with single-overhead-camshaft cylinder head. Bore, stroke and capacity 89 × 80mm., 1990cc. Maximum power 120bhp (DIN) at 5600rpm.; maximum torque 123lb.ft. at 3500rpm. Four-speed manual transmission in unit with engine. Hypoid bevel final drive. Automatic transmission available with 100bhp (DIN) at 5500rpm.; maximum torque 115lb.ft. at 3000rpm.

Chassis: Front engine, rear drive. Unit-construction, pressed-steel body-chassis unit. Independent front suspension by coil springs, MacPherson struts and wishbones. Worm and sector steering. Independent rear suspension by coil springs and semi-trailing wishbones. Front wheel disc brakes, rear drums.

Bodywork: Pressed-steel two-door 2 + 2 notchback coupe bodystyle by Karmann. Length 14ft. 10in.; width 5ft. 6.2in.; height 4ft. 6.2in. Unladen weight 2535lb.

Performance: (2000CS) Maximum speed 110mph. 0-60mph 10.4sec. Standing ¼-mile 17.9sec. Typical fuel consumption 22mpg.

Note: 2800CS Coupe, which replaced 2000CS, had six-cylinders, bore, stroke and capacity of 86 × 80mm., 2788cc.; maximum power of 170bhp (DIN) at 6000rpm. Maximum torque 173lb.ft. at 6000rpm. Power assisted steering. Length 15ft. 3.4in. Unladen weight 2845lb.

BMW 3-Litre Coupes

Built: Munich, Germany, 1971-1975

With the six-cylinder derivative of the original overhead-camshaft four-cylinder engine already on the market, BMW set out on a policy of widening their product range. Without ever admitting it, they set out to offer as many models for as many people as did Mercedes-Benz with their petrol-engined cars, and by the end of the 1970s they had succeeded admirably. The refinement and improvement of their fine six-cylinder engine was one reason, and the establishment of a splendid sporting image in motor sport was another. It was the more extreme derivatives of their 3-litre Coupes which enabled them to do this.

Compared with the interim 2800CS Coupes which these new cars replaced, the chassis was extensively reworked by Karmann. The underpan, effectively, became special to the coupes, and included the suspension hardware and settings from the large 3-litre saloons.

For the enthusiasts, however, most of the interest was in the way the engine power, or its potential power, was pushed progressively up and up. The original 3.0CS had the 2985cc engine with carburettors and 180bhp, but within a year, for 1972, the 3.0CSi had been announced, in which the Bosch fuel-injection was allied to 200bhp. This was the car which promised well as a racing 'saloon' in Group 2, but BMW had plans to do even better. In the autumn of 1972 they launched the exciting 3.0CSL (where the 'L' was short for Light, in whatever language you were using), which was effectively the 3.0CSi with many light-alloy skin panels, sparse trim, and a very slightly overbored engine to make the capacity 3003cc and put the 'new' model into the over 3-litre category.

BMW 3.0CSL

The secret of the 3.0CSL, therefore, was not that it was much lighter than before (which, indeed, it was) but that its engine could now be enlarged as far as the strength of the cylinder block and crankcase would allow. BMW had realised that their great rivals — Ford, with the German-built Capris — were stuck with a vee-6 engine which could not be enlarged beyond 3-litres at the time (though they discovered a way, by using another vee-6 engine, a couple of years later), and wanted to gain a displacement advantage over them. The result was that, before BMW stopped supporting the cars in European Group 2 competition, engines of up to 3.5-litres had been developed, with exotic 24-valve cylinder heads, and more than 400bhp. All of which made the cars into exciting racing projectiles, and helped pave the way for the engines now used in the mid-engined M1 cars put into production in 1979.

From 1972 all 3.0-litre coupe development was concentrated on the CSL, while the less exclusive models continued unchanged. CSLs were built in two guises — in the original ultralight specification, in which much refinement had been lost with the weight, or in a more plushly-trimmed version which retained some of the lightweight panelling. For competition use, from the autumn of 1973 (exactly at the time the Suez-inspired petrol supply crisis erupted), the CSL was given an optional kit of aerodynamic fittings including a front air dam, front wing strakes, and a massively obvious rear aerofoil, and cars fitted with these items (which were undoubtedly very effective) were immediately dubbed 'Batmobiles.'

CSLs with various engine capacities of more than 3-litres were listed — including 3.3-litre units shared with those developed for the current BMW limousine — though all were more-or-less based on the same six-cylinder unit first seen in public in 1968.

When the 3.0-litre cars were withdrawn in favour of an entirely new bodyshell for 1976, enthusiasts searched in vain for a new generation of 'Batmobile'. It is a car which will go down in history as one of the most extraordinary (and effective) aerodynamic developments ever seen in motorsport.

BMW 3.0CSi

Specification (3.0CS and CSi Coupes)

Engine and transmission: Six-cylinders, in-line, with single-overhead-camshaft cylinder head. Bore, stroke and capacity 89×80mm., 2985cc. Maximum power 180bhp (DIN) at 6000rpm.; maximum torque 188lb.ft. at 3700rpm. Four-speed manual gearbox (CS) or three-speed Borg Warner automatic (CSa) in unit with engine. Hypoid bevel final drive. CSi version, with fuel injection, produced: Maximum power 200bhp (DIN) at 5500rpm.; maximum torque 200lb.ft. at 4300rpm.

Chassis: Front engine, rear drive. Unit-construction, pressed-steel body-chassis unit. Independent front suspension by coil springs, MacPherson struts and wishbones. Power-assisted worm and sector steering. Independent rear suspension by coil springs and semi-trailing wishbones. Four wheel disc brakes.

Bodywork: Pressed-steel two-door 2 + 2, notchback coupe bodystyle, by Karmann. Length 15ft.3.4in.; width 5ft.6.4in.; height 4ft. 5.6in. Unladen weight 3030lb.

Performance: (3.0CS) Maximum speed 131mph. 0-60mph 8.0sec. Standing ¼-mile 16.2sec. Typical fuel consumption 24mpg. **(3.0CSi)** Maximum speed 139mph. 0-60mph 7.5sec. Standing ¼-mile 15.4sec. Typical fuel consumption 21mpg.

Note: The 3.0CSL was a limited-production model intended for competition use. Important differences were: **(Early cars)** 89.25×80mm., 3003cc. Automatic transmission not available. Unladen weight 2600lb. **(Later cars)** 89.25×84mm., 3153cc. Maximum power 206bhp (DIN) at 5600rpm.; maximum torque 211lb.ft. at 4200rpm. Unladen weight 2775lb.

Performance: (3003cc version) Maximum speed 133mph. 0-60mph 7.3sec. Standing ¼-mile 15.7sec. Typical fuel consumption 18mpg.

BMW 3200CS Coupe

Built: Munich, Germany, 1962-1965

BMW took time to re-start private car production after the second world war, and produced their new family of big saloons, starting from the base of the 501 model, in 1952. These cars used a cheap-to-tool multi-tubular chassis frame, with heavy pressed-steel and coachbuilt bodies. The 501 had the familiar 1971cc six-cylinder from pre-war days, but the 502 which followed in 1954 featured a brand-new pushrod vee-8 engine of 2580cc. A year later the larger version of this engine – a 3.2-litre derivative – appeared, and the two sporty BMWs of the 1950s – the 503 and the sensational 507 – followed in 1956.

After the 503/507 models disappeared in 1959 there was a three-year gap (while BMW fought for economic survival, and concentrated on making small cars) before one final derivation of the original 501 design was launched. This was the 3200CS coupe, which was also an interesting precursor to the hugely-successful 2000CS which followed it.

The long-wheelbase tubular chassis was used, with its all-torsion-bar suspension, its expensive but precise bevel-gear steering, and with the 160bhp 3168cc vee-8 engine installed. To match this fine, if costly, engineering, BMW contracted the Italian styling house of Bertone to produce a sleek and purposeful two-door coupe body which could seat four people in reasonable comfort. Naturally, because of the time at which the styling was done, there was a superficial resemblance to the Iso Rivolta shape, and the two cars were, indeed, broadly the same size. At the front however, the 3200CS carried a family-style of grille and air-intake shape, and could not have been mistaken for anything else.

Production began in the spring of 1962 (though the prototype was shown at the 1961 Frankfurt Motor Show), and ended during 1965. Just 603 of these interesting cars were built, the last of all the vee-8 BMWs.

BMW 3200CS

Specification

Engine and transmission: Eight-cylinders, in 90-degree vee-formation, with pushrod-operated overhead-valve gear. Bore, stroke and capacity 82×75mm., 3168cc. Maximum power 160bhp (DIN) at 5600rpm; maximum torque not revealed. Four-speed manual transmission in unit with engine. Hypoid bevel final drive.

Chassis: Front engine, rear drive. Separate multi-tubular chassis frame with separate pressed-steel bodywork. Independent front suspension by longitudinal torsion bars and wishbones. Bevel-gear steering. Rigid rear axle, and suspension by longitudinal torsion bars and links, and A-bracket. Front wheel disc brakes, and rear drums.

Bodywork: Coachbuilt steel two-door notchback four-seater coupe body style, by Bertone. Length 15ft. 10.2in.; width 5ft. 7.7in.; height 4ft. 9.5in. Unladen weight 3310lb.

Performance (Manufacturer's claims): Maximum speed 124mph. Typical fuel consumption 21mpg.

BMW 6-Series Coupes

Built: Munich, Germany, 1976 to date.

To replace their popular and long-running 3-litre coupes, which — in racing form — had done so much for their image in the 1970s, BMW chose to produce a bigger, 'softer', and more refined car without any pretensions to possible use in motorsport. Whereas the earlier cars had 'grown up' from the original BMW 2000, the new cars were, in every significant way, related to a new generation of large six-cylinder saloons.

Collectively known as the '6-Series' cars, the first in a steadily growing family was seen at the Geneva Motor Show of March 1976. As with previous specialised BMWs, the unit-construction bodyshells were built and finished off by Karmann, the specialist body builders, although styling had been completed by BMW themselves. In a way, the new cars were less individual in their looks, though undeniably more roomy, well-equipped, very fast and — most importantly — were well-engineered to look after the demands of the North American market.

Compared with the obsolete coupes, the new cars broke no new technical ground, for they relied on the same well-developed single-cam six-cylinder engines, in carburettor-equipped or fuel-injected guise. At first there was a 2985cc engine and 3210cc engine, but after only a short time an even fiercer 3453cc unit (using the same bottom end as that of the twin-cam M1 model) was also added — and the latter model almost qualifies as a Supercar with a maximum speed of 140mph and acceleration to match.

There is a choice of transmissions: four-speed or five-speed manual, or ZF three-speed automatic boxes, depending on the model ordered. Naturally four-wheel disc brakes and four-wheel independent suspension is standardised, along with power-assisted steering.

Like the Mercedes-Benz coupes with which these modern BMWs obviously compete in world markets, the cars are efficient and reliable first, fast and lively second, and sporting last of all. Nevertheless, there are many well-to-do customers who will want nothing else.

Specification

Engine and transmission: Six-cylinders, in-line, with single-overhead camshaft cylinder head. Three different engine variants as follows: **630CS:** Bore, stroke and capacity 89 × 80mm., 2985cc. Maximum power 185bhp (DIN) at 5800rpm.; maximum torque 188lb.ft. at 3500rpm. **633CSi:** Bore, stroke and capacity 89 × 86mm., 3210cc. Maximum power 200bhp (DIN) at 5500rpm.; maximum torque 210lb.ft. at 4250rpm. **635CSi:** Bore, stroke and capacity 93.4 × 84mm., 3453cc. Maximum power 218bhp (DIN) at 5200rpm.; maximum torque 224lb.ft. at 4000rpm. four-speed manual, five-speed manual, or three-speed ZF automatic gearbox (depending on model, or market) in unit with engine. Hypoid bevel final drive.

Chassis: Front engine, rear drive. Unit-construction pressed-steel body-chassis unit. Independent front suspension by coil springs, MacPherson struts and wishbones. Power-assisted worm and roller steering. Independent rear suspension by coil springs and semi-trailing wishbones. Four wheel disc brakes.

Bodywork: Pressed-steel two-door close-coupled four-seater notchback coupe style (built by Karmann). Length 15ft. 7.2in.; width 5ft. 9in.; height 4ft. 6.5in. Unladen weight (depending on engine and specification) from 3200lb. to 3310lb.

Performance: (633CSi) Maximum speed 131mph. 0-60mph 8.1sec. Standing ¼-mile 14.9sec. Typical fuel consumption 23mpg. **(635CSi)** Maximum speed 140mph. 0-60mph 8.5sec. Standing ¼-mile 16.2sec. Typical fuel consumption 19mpg.

BMW 633CSi

Daimler SP250

Built: Coventry, England, 1959 to 1964

Daimler's short-lived SP250 sports car represented a complete change in design policy for the long-established Coventry concern. Before this, their only sporting connections had been through special roadster and high-performance saloon derivates of normal touring cars. The decision to build a two-seater sports car came about after a change of management, and because the new Managing Director, Edward Turner, was a brilliant designer of motor cycle engines.

The new car, which was originally called the 'Dart', until Dodge complained that they had a trade mark of that model name, had a chassis and suspension layout which was unashamedly and admittedly copied from that of the Triumph TR3A, as was the gearbox. The engine, however, was a 90-degree vee-8 of 2548cc, whose valve gear owed much to Turner's previous experience with Triumph motor cycle units, and should not be confused with a larger 4.5-litre vee-8 engine which he also designed, and which was used in the Majestic Major and large Daimler limousines of the early 1960s.

It was possible to have the chassis made by an industry component supplier, and Daimler machined their own engines and transmissions, but for the quantities envisaged the body supply presented a problem. It was therefore decided to use glass-

Daimler SP250

fibre (the bodies were manufactured by Daimler themselves); the styling, to say the least, was controversial, and it is a fact that prototypes were at once more simple and (to many eyes) more attractive than the production cars.

Announced in the spring of 1959, the car went into production as the SP250 in the autumn. It was immediately apparent that the body was lacking in stiffness and refinement, and the 'B' and 'C' specification improvements introduced in the next few years were aimed at correcting these problems; on the original cars, for instance, it was not unknown for the doors to fly open when the car was being driven hard over rough surfaces.

For all that, the SP250 began to make itself a reputation for high-performance and excellent fuel economy, and filled a gap between the TR3A and Jaguar XK150/E-Type market. Like the TR3A on which the chassis was based, the ride was hard, and basic, almost in the 'vintage' style, but the engine soon had an excellent reputation, and – with overdrive not available – its refinement became the more obvious. The SP250 was one of the few open sports cars built at the time with the option of automatic transmission.

If Daimler had continued to be owned by the BSA group, the SP250 might have had a long-term future (a successor, with a less idiosyncratic body style had already been built); however, Sir William Lyons's Jaguar concern took control of Daimler in 1960, and eventually killed it off as it did not accord with Sir William's standards of looks or of refinement. The engine, by the way, found a home in Jaguar's Mk II bodyshell, to give birth to the Daimler V8-250 saloon, which was built until the end of the 1960s.

Following integration into the Jaguar group (and, from 1966, into British Motor Holdings), policy decisions meant that no more sporting Daimlers were produced.

Specification

Engine and transmission: Eight-cylinders, in 90-degree vee-formation, with pushrod-operated overhead-valve cylinder heads. Bore, stroke and capacity 76.2 × 69.85mm, 2548cc. Maximum power 140bhp (net) at 5800rpm; maximum torque 155lb.ft. at 3600rpm. Four-speed gearbox or optional Borg Warner automatic transmission in unit with engine. Hypoid bevel final drive.

Chassis: Front engine, rear drive. Separate chassis frame with box-section side members. Independent front suspension by coil springs and wishbones. Cam and lever steering. Rear suspension of live axle by half-elliptic leaf springs. Four-wheel disc brakes.

Bodywork: Glass-fibre bodyshell by Daimler, available as sports 2 + 2 seater. Length 13ft. 4.5in.; width 5ft. 0.5in.; height 4ft. 2.25in. Unladen weight 2220lb.

Performance: Maximum speed 121mph. 0-60mph 10.2sec. Standing ¼-mile 17.8sec. Typical fuel consumption 30mpg.

Fiat 1200 to 1600S Coupes

Built: Turin, Italy, 1959-1966

By the end of the 1950s, Fiat, who were (and still are) Italy's largest manufacturer of cars, were expanding their model range in all directions. In the 1950s they had been marketing a rather plain sports car which Pininfarina had been building much against their better judgement, but from 1959 a much more satisfactory arrangement, in design *and* manufacturing terms, was concluded. A new model, smart and up to the minute, was styled by Pininfarina and was sold with new engines.

The new model was first seen at the Geneva motor show of 1959, with a particularly trim open bodyshell. Known as the 1200 Spider, it used a classic front-engine/rear-drive/live-rear-axle layout, and had the uprated engine of the Fiat 1200 Gran Luce, which had pushrod ohv. That was only the start, however, for later in the year the same basic unit-construction model became available with a twin-overhead-camshaft engine of 1491cc, which was a product of co-operation between Fiat and Osca (which was a Modena company owned by the Maserati brothers). Osca designed the engine, which was made by Fiat at the Mirafiori works; Osca, incidentally, bought back the engine for their own use, and for selling in very limited numbers in their own special cars. Although the cylinder block was in cast-iron, a light-alloy cylinder head was featured, and the widely-splayed valves were arranged Jaguar-fashion to give very efficient breathing.

Nevertheless, the engine was never to be offered in any other Fiat model, and the basic pressed-steel bodyshell was never adapted to other uses, nor gave rise to other models. At first production was never at more than 50 units a day, and as far as Fiat were concerned this was always a limited-production model.

Production carried on with minor but worthwhile changes, including the specification of four-wheel Dunlop disc brakes on twin-cam models from 1962, although the smaller-engined 1221cc model retained its drum brakes to the end of production in 1963.

Perhaps the Fiat 1500 Cabriolet – to give the twin-cam model its full title – was never a roaring success in its native Italy because it was badged as a 'Fiat', instead of something more exotic. It had to face formidable competition in the same price and engine size bracket from the very stylish Alfa-Romeo Giulia models, where snob appeal far outweighed the practicalities of buying a Fiat model. To rescue some of the car's reputation (and even though the original car was good for about 106mph in top speed), the size of the twin-cam engine was increased to 1568cc in 1963 (by increasing the cylinder bore), the maximum power was increased to 100bhp and the car became the 1600S. At the same time a new pushrod 1500 model, with the engine of the Fiat 1500 saloon, was introduced, and these two models carried on in production until 1966. A five-speed gearbox became available in 1965 on the 1600S twin-cam model.

Production ran out in the summer of 1966, as Fiat prepared for the introduction of the commercially important Fiat 124 Sports Coupes and Spiders. The engine, as designed by Osca, was then discontinued, though the five-speed gearbox carried on in the new sporting 124 models.

Specification

Engine and transmission: Four-cylinders, in-line. 1200 and 1500 units with pushrod-operated overhead-valve cylinder heads. 1500 and 1600 units with twin-overhead-camshaft cylinder heads. Four different engines fitted during life of the car: **1200:** Bore, stroke and capacity 72×75mm., 1221cc. Maximum power 63bhp (gross) at 5300rpm.; maximum torque 61lb.ft. at 3000rpm. **1500 with overhead valves:** Bore, stroke and capacity 77×79.5mm., 1481cc. Maximum power 80bhp (gross) at 5200rpm.; maximum torque 87lb.ft. at 3200rpm. **1500 with twin overhead camshafts:** Bore, stroke and capacity 78×78mm., 1491cc. Maximum power 80bhp (net) at 6000rpm.; maximum torque 77lb.ft. at 4000rpm. **1600 with twin overhead camshafts:** Bore, stroke and capacity 80×78mm., 1568cc. Maximum power 100bhp (gross) at 6000rpm.; maximum torque 98lb.ft. at 4000rpm. Four-speed or five-speed manual gearbox in unit with engine. Hypoid bevel final drive.

Chassis: Front engine, rear drive. Unit-construction pressed-steel body/chassis unit. Independent front suspension by coil springs and wishbones. Worm and roller steering. Rear suspension of live axle by half-elliptic leaf springs. Four wheel disc brakes on 1600S model. Four wheel drum brakes on other models.

Bodywork: Pressed-steel monocoque two-door two-seater open sports or hardtop coupe styles by Pininfarina. Length 13ft. 2.7in.; width 4ft. 11.9in.; height 4ft. 3.25in. Unladen weight, depending on engine and specification, from 1985lb. to 2185lb.

Performance (1200): Maximum speed 90mph. 0-60mph 19.1sec. Standing ¼-mile 21.0sec. Typical fuel consumption 36mpg. **(1500 S twin-cam):** Maximum speed 105mph. 0-60mph 10.6sec. Standing ¼-mile 18.5sec. Typical fuel consumption 30mpg.

Fiat 1600S Cabriolet

Fiat 850 Spider and Coupe

Built: Turin, Italy, 1965-1974

Like many other successful sporting models built in the last half-century, Fiat's 850 Spider and Coupe cars were closely based on a more humble saloon car. In their case the 'building block' was the boxy Fiat 850 saloon which made its bow in 1964, and the sporting models followed at the Geneva Show of 1965.

As with many of their sporting cars, Fiat entrusted the styling of the coupe to their own engineers, but the Spider was designed by Bertone. Both, however, used the same pressed-steel floor pan and suspensions, which meant that suitable high-speed handling had to be assured from a 'chassis' where the cast-iron engine was mounted to the rear of the line of the back wheels, in unit with the final drive and the new four-speed all-synchromesh gearbox.

In accommodation, the Fiat-designed coupe was a smart though thoroughly practical close-coupled four-seater car, while the Bertone spider was a sleek little two-seater open car, with cowled in headlamps, and the choice of a fold-down hood or a detachable hardtop. Because either of the two cars could be sold at attractively low prices, they sold in large quantities and kept that popularity for a number of years. Although the handling was something which had to be learned by the new owners, the rear-engine oversteering characteristics were tamed by Fiat development staff, so that these were enjoyable little road cars. Carlo Abarth's tuning workshops produced some extraordinary hybrids by slotting in derivatives of his own twim-cam engines in place of the humble little pushrod Fiat units, but these were strictly for racing and do not truly count as road cars.

When Fiat decided on a general upgrading of performance for their small sports cars, they enlarged the engine to its practical limit of 903cc (with a slight increase in stroke from 63.5mm to 68mm), and the cars, complete with styling revisions including exposed headlamps for the Spider, made their debut at the Geneva Show of March 1968.

Both cars then carried on until the end of 1971, when the coupe was withdrawn in favour of the 128 Coupe (which was a less specialised type of car, evolved from the front-wheel-drive 128), but even though the mid-engined X1/9 was announced in 1972 the very popular Bertone-bodied Spider carried on for another couple of years, mainly for sale in markets where an open topped sports car was still popular. It was the last of Fiat's *rear*-engined cars.

Specification

Engine and transmission: Four-cylinders, in-line, with pushrod-operated overhead-valve cylinder head. **(Early cars)** Bore, stroke and capacity 65×63.5mm., 843cc. Maximum power 54bhp (gross) at 6400rpm.; maximum torque 45lb.ft. at 4000rpm. **(Later cars)** Bore, stroke and capacity 65×68mm., 903cc. Maximum power 52bhp (net) at 6500rpm; maximum torque 48lb.ft. at 4000rpm. Four-speed manual gearbox in unit with engine and transaxle.

Chassis: Rear engine, rear drive. Unit-construction pressed-steel body/chassis units. Independent front suspension by transverse leaf spring and wishbones. Worm and roller steering. Independent rear suspension by coil springs and semi-trailing wishbones. Front wheel disc brakes, rear drums.

Bodywork: Pressed-steel monocoque bodies in two styles, two-door two-seater open Spider (with optional hardtop) by Bertone, and two-door close-coupled four-seater fastback coupe by Fiat. **(Spider)** Length 12ft. 4.9in.; width 4ft. 11in.; height 4ft. 0in. Unladen weight 1620lb. **(Coupe)** Length 11ft. 10in.; width 4ft. 11in.; height 4ft. 3.2in. Unladen weight 1610lb.

Performance: (843cc engine) Maximum speed 87mph. 0-60mph 18.2sec. Standing ¼-mile 21.0sec. Typical fuel consumption 33mpg. **(903cc engine)** Maximum speed 91mph. 0-60mph 15.6sec. Standing ¼-mile 20.4sec. Typical fuel consumption 35mpg.

Fiat 850, 850 Coupe and 850 Spider

Fiat 124 Sport and Spider series

Built: Turin, Italy, 1966 to date

Designed originally to replace the relatively unsuccessful Osca-engined Fiat 1600S cabriolet models, but to sell in much higher quantities, the 124 Sport and Spider cars developed into some of the most long-running and most successful cars ever sold by Fiat. Although the 124 Sports Coupe model – the closed four-seater car – was finally discontinued in 1975, the open car, continually updated and modified, is still made for sale exclusively in North America.

Fiat 124 Sport Coupe

The Fiat 124, new in concept if not in basic layout, was the first of a new wave of Fiat models which began to appear in 1966. The 124 was a conventional four-door four/five-seater saloon car with a new design of pushrod overhead-valve engine, but what no-one realised was that this engine was merely the first of dozens of versions which would be appearing in the next ten years.

At the Turin Show, in November of 1966, both the Sport Coupe and the Spider cars were shown, and both were graced with twin-overhead-camshaft engines converted from the original pushrod layout. This was the first of the Fiat-designed twin-cams of modern times, which have been refined, improved, enlarged and further developed ever since then. At first, in 124 Sport/Spider form, the capacity was 1438cc, with a bore and stroke of 80×71.5mm, but the latest engines have a capacity of 1995cc, with a bore and stroke of 84×90mm.

As the development of the engines defines the progress made by the models themselves, it is worth noting that the first enlargement, to 1608cc, came for the Fiat 125 of 1967, but was later adopted (in 1969) for the sporting 124s. Then, for the 132 saloon of 1972, the engine was thoroughly and completely re-designed, with a longer cylinder block and revised cylinder centres, so that 1756cc was possible from 84×79.2mm. At the same time, the '1600' version became 1592cc (80×79.2mm).

Still more changes were to follow, influenced by the development of new engines (pushrod and overhead camshaft) for the 131 saloons. In 1973 this model had a new combination of dimensions (1585cc 84×71.5mm) which were never applied to the 124 models. Finally, at first only on the 131 Abarth 'homologation special' in 1976, but from 1977 on a growing number of other Fiat models, the 1995cc (84×90mm) long-stroke version, thought to be the final stretch of a wonderfully versatile design, was made available.

As far as the 124 models were concerned, the 1608cc engines became available, with some style changes, in 1969, and the 1756cc engined cars with even more styling improvements followed in 1972; as the 1.8-litre version came in, so was the original 1.4-litre engine dropped. These cars – the coupe by Fiat themselves, and the open sports Spider by Pininfarina – were extremely successful, as they were a tasteful combination of mass-production economics, fine styling, and good road behaviour. Both were heavily dependent on the 124 saloons for their existence – as they shared that car's underpan and suspensions (that of the Spider, as so often in Italy, having a shortened floorpan and only two seats) – but even after the 124 was dropped in favour of the 131 Mirafiori they both carried on for a time.

The last of the closed four-seater coupes was built in 1975, and has never been replaced by a 131-based car. The open Spider, in the manner of the MG MGB, carries on with strong sales in North America, where its open-air attractions seem to outweigh its dated styling and rather restricted performance. The restrictions of North American exhaust emissions regulations mean that the 1995cc engine produces only 87bhp at 5100rpm, whereas the original unfettered 1438cc engine produced 90bhp at 6500rpm. Such, in North American terms, is progress...

Fiat 124 Sport Spider

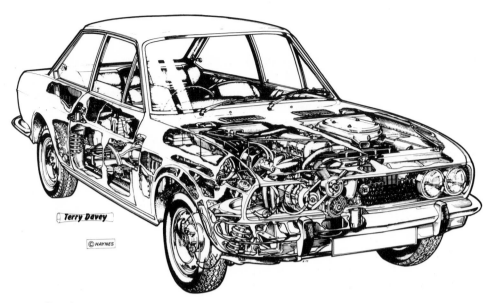

Terry Davey

© HAYNES

Specification

Engine and transmission: Four-cylinders, in-line, with twin-overhead-camshaft cylinder heads. Four different engines fitted during the model's life: **1400:** Bore, stroke and capacity 80×71.5mm., 1438cc. Maximum power 90bhp (DIN) at 6500rpm.; maximum torque 80lb.ft. at 4000rpm. **1600:** Bore, stroke and capacity 80×80mm., 1608cc. Maximum power 110bhp (DIN) at 6400rpm.; maximum torque 101lb.ft. at 3800rpm. **1600 (later model):** Bore, stroke and capacity 80×79.2mm., 1592cc. Maximum power 108bhp (DIN) at 6000rpm.; maximum torque 101lb.ft. at 4200rpm. **1800:** Bore, stroke and capacity 84×79.2mm., 1756cc. Maximum power 118bhp (DIN) at 6000rpm.; maximum torque 113lb.ft. at 4000rpm. **2000:** (North America only): Bore, stroke and capacity 84×90mm., 1995cc. Maximum power 87bhp (DIN) at 5100rpm.; maximum torque 104lb.ft. at 3000rpm. Four-speed or five-speed manual gearbox or GM automatic (2000 model for North America) transmission in unit with engine. Hypoid bevel final drive.

Chassis: Front engine, rear drive. Pressed-steel unit-construction body/chassis unit. Independent front suspension by coil springs and wishbones. Worm and roller steering. Rear suspension of live axle by coil springs, radius arms and a Panhard rod. Four wheel disc brakes.

Bodywork: Pressed-steel monocoque bodies in two styles, two-door two-seater open Spider by Pininfarina, and two-door, close-coupled four-seater notchback coupe by Fiat. **(Spider)** Length 13ft. 0.3in.; width 5ft. 3.4in.; height 4ft. 1.2in. Unladen weight 2085lb. **(Coupe)** Length 13ft. 6in.; width 5ft. 5.8in.; height 4ft. 4.7in. Unladen weight 2195lb.

Performance (124 Coupe 1438cc): Maximum speed 102mph. 0-60mph 12.6sec. Standing ¼-mile 18.8sec. Typical fuel consumption 24mpg. **(1800 Coupe):** Maximum speed 107mph. 0-60mph 10.5sec. Standing ¼-mile 17.4sec. Typical fuel consumption 24mpg. **(2000 Spider, USA market version):** Maximum speed 102mph. 0-60mph 10.6sec. Standing ¼-mile 18.1sec. Typical fuel consumption 26mpg.

Fiat Dino series

Built: Turin and Maranello, Italy, 1967-1973

Although the mass-production sporting possibilities for Fiat in the late 1960s lay with the 124 models, the glamour and the excitement was most certainly with the very special Dinos. Introduced at the same time – late 1966 – they combined Fiat chassis engineering, specialist coachbuilt styling, and the use of Ferrari-based vee-6 engines. Those engines, incidentally, were not merely there because the name sounded good, but because Ferrari needed to sell considerable numbers to secure homologation approval for the use of the engine in their Formula 2 cars of 1967.

The heart of the cars, therefore, was this vee-6 engine, which had Ferrari's own rather specialised 65-degree angle between cylinder banks. In both forms used – 1987cc at first, 2418cc from 1970 – it was the same basic engine as that used in Ferrari's own Dinos, and this has caused a great deal of confusion over the years. The 'Dino' title properly belongs to the vee-6 engine itself, though models powered by that engine have usually been given the same title. The front-engined Fiat Dinos should not, therefore, be confused by the transverse mid-engined Ferrari Dinos, from which they were otherwise completely different.

The original 2-litre engine had a light-alloy cylinder block, and for Fiat was tuned to give 160bhp (DIN) at 7200rpm. In this form it was linked to a Fiat five-speed manual gearbox and a heavy-duty live rear axle.

Two body styles, both based on the same special pressed-steel underpan, were available. The open two-seater was by Pininfarina, on a wheelbase of 7ft. 4.8in, and was announced first. The sleeker, fastback four-seater coupe style by Bertone on a much longer 8ft. 4.4in. wheelbase was a more versatile, if not as exciting, model, and was announced at the 1967 Geneva Motor Show. Both cars shared the same

Fiat Dino Coupe

suspensions — coil spring and wishbone independent at the front, and with the live axle supported by single leaf springs and radius arms (forward facing).

Sales began in 1967 and though adequate enough for Ferrari to secure approval for use of the engine in his racing cars, were not enough for Fiat. The problem was that the combination of price and complex engine specification often overcame the car's animal appeal, and there was no doubt that performance wasnot as sparkling as hoped. At the Turin Show of 1969, therefore, considerably revised Dinos were shown, although the smart styling of these cars was retained.

The engine was completely revised, with the Fiat 130's cast-iron block being used, with increased cylinder dimensions (92.5×60mm., 2418cc instead of 86×57mm., 1987cc), and a great deal more power and torque. Of equal importance was the adoption of a ZF five-speed gearbox and the use of independent rear suspension by coil springs and semi-trailing arms in place of the crude half-elliptic leaf spring set up of the original cars. Bigger brakes, fatter tyres and many other details all went in to making a much more desirable car, which in coupe form had a maximum speed of at least 130mph.

Even so, the Dinos were never more than Fiat prestige models, and so had little attention in terms of production space, marketing and development attention. By this time, too, Fiat had farmed out the assembly of all Dinos to the expanded Ferrari plant at Maranello (in which they were now commercial partners), and it was in this rarified atmosphere that the last of the Fiat Dinos was built in 1973. No other similarly exciting Fiat has replaced the Dino, though the super-sophisticated 131 Abarth saloon qualifies in some respects.

Fiat Dino Spider

Specification

Engine and transmission: Six-cylinders, in 65-degree vee-formation, with twin-overhead-camshaft cylinder heads. **(Early models)** Bore, stroke and capacity 86 × 57mm., 1987cc. Maximum power 160bhp (DIN) at 7200rpm.; maximum torque 127lb.ft. at 6000rpm. **(Later models)** Bore, stroke and capacity 92.5 × 60mm., 2418cc. Maximum power 180bhp (DIN) at 6600rpm; maximum torque 159lb.ft. at 4600rpm. Five-speed manual gearbox in unit with engine. Hypoid bevel final drive.

Chassis: Front engine, rear drive. Unit-construction pressed steel body/chassis unit. Independent front suspension by coil springs and wishbones. Worm and roller steering. **(Early cars)** Suspension of rear live axle by half-elliptic leaf springs, radius arms and Panhard rod. **(Later 2.4-litre cars)** Independent rear suspension by coil springs and MacPherson struts. Four wheel disc brakes.

Bodywork: Two different pressed-steel styles on same basic steel underpan (and different wheelbases). Two-door two-seater open spider style by Pininfarina; Length 13ft. 5.7in.; width 5ft. 7.3in.; height 4ft. 1in. Unladen weight 2600lb. Two-door close-coupled four-seater fastback coupe by Bertone; Length 14ft. 9.7in.; width 5ft. 7.3in.; height 4ft. 3.9in. Unladen weight 2825lb.

Performance (2.0-litre Spider): Maximum speed 127mph. 0-60mph 8.1sec. Standing ¼-mile 16.0sec. Typical fuel consumption 20mpg. **(2.4-litre Coupe):** Maximum speed 130mph. 0-60mph 8.7sec. Standing ¼-mile 16.1sec. Typical fuel consumption 20mpg.

Fiat X1/9

Built: Turin, Italy, 1972 to date

It is not going too far to suggest that Fiat's X1/9 sports coupe, styled so crisply and elegantly by Bertone, immediately made all other small sporting cars look out of date. Even several years later, when it has earned the nickname of being a 'mini Ferrari', it is still the standard by which all other sports cars with small engines should be judged.

Throughout the 1960s, Fiat did not market an outstanding coupe or sports car with a small engine, though their links with Ferrari (which gave birth to the Dinos) showed that they were both capable and committed, if the time could be spared. The X1/9 came along in the end to replace the long-runing 850s. Strangely enough, however, Fiat were not at the time considering a car of Fiat X1/9 type, but were persuaded to tackle the concept after Bertone had shown them really startling concept sketches and mock-ups which had been conceived as an engineering exercise.

The X1/9 − a Fiat project number which was never changed when the car came to be put on sale − uses an entirely special pressed-steel monocoque, with the engine mounted behind the seats and ahead of the line of the rear wheels, with two-seater accommodation, a stylish but fixed roll-hoop which doubles as a part of the roof, and has a removable roof panel which instantly converts into a type of 'Targa' convertible when the weather conditions permit.

The secret of the design is that the engine, transversely mounted in unit with its own transmission and final drive, is basically that of a related front-wheel-drive Fiat touring car. The original X1/9, therefore, used the powerpack from the Fiat 128 Rally (with 1290cc single overhead cam engine), while the latest X1/9 1500 uses the power pack from the Fiat Ritmo (or Strada in certain markets), in which case it is also graced with the undeniable advantage of a five-speed gearbox.

Fiat X1/9 1500

For packaging and structural reasons, MacPherson strut independent suspension is used at front and rear; this is an elegant solution to the problem found on several other Fiat models, and gives a combination of supple springing and great refinement.

Even though the X1/9 has now been on the market for several years, its potential has by no means been exhausted. Larger versions (in engine size and in accommodation) will undoubtedly be built in the 1980s, and its layout will probably be the continuing standard for rivals to attempt to beat.

Incidentally, an engineering comparison with the layout of the Lancia Monte Carlo is instructive, as this model (originally to be badged as a 'Fiat') was designed by the same team at about the same time.

Specification

Engine and transmission: Four-cylinders, in-line, mounted transversely across chassis, with single-overhead-camshaft cylinder head. **(1300 version)** Bore, stroke and capacity 86×55.5mm., 1290cc. Maximum power 75bhp (DIN) at 6000rpm.; maximum torque 72lb.ft. at 3400rpm. Four-speed manual gearbox in unit with engine and final drive. **(1500 version)** Bore, stroke and capacity 86.4×63.9mm., 1499cc. Maximum power 85bhp (DIN) at 6000rpm.; maximum torque 87lb.ft at 3200rpm. Five-speed manual gearbox in unit with engine and transaxle. Spur gear final drive.

Chassis: Mid-engine, rear drive. Unit construction pressed-steel body/chassis unit. Independent front suspension by coil springs and MacPherson struts. Rack and pinion steering. Independent rear suspension by coil springs, MacPherson struts and wishbones. Four wheel disc brakes.

Bodywork: Pressed-steel two-door two-seater mid-engined notchback coupe style, with removable roof, by Bertone. Length 12ft. 7in.; width 5ft. 2in.; height 3ft. 10in. Unladen weight (1300 version) 1940lb.; (1500 version) 2025lb.

Performance (1300) Maximum speed 99mph. 0-60mph 12.7sec. Standing ¼-mile 18.8sec. Typical fuel consumption 34mpg. **(1500)** Maximum speed 106mph. 0-60mph 11.0sec. Standing ¼-mile 17.8sec. Typical fuel consumption 29mpg.

Ford Capri series

Built: Liverpool, England, and Cologne, West Germany, 1969 to date

Ford of North America caused a major sensation, and precipitated a marketing revolution throughout the world, when they launched their Ford Mustang in 1964. It was no less interesting to the world of motoring in Europe when they repeated the approach by launching the Ford Capri in 1969. Dubbed by many the 'European Mustang', the Capri had much in common in thinking, if absolutely nothing in terms of engineering and the use of components.

The Capri philosophy, adopted from that of the Mustang, was that a single pressed-steel coupe monocoque, providing space — almost — for four people, should be sold in a myriad versions, with a number of engine options backed by seemingly endless trim and equipment packages, and extra equipment.

Thus, the first Capri, launched in January of 1969, was to be made by both Ford of Europe concerns — in Britain and in West Germany — and was to be sold with a choice of engines from the humble 1.3-litre pushrod unit normally found in Escorts, to the massive 3.0-litre vee-6 engine normally fitted to Zodiacs and even to light commercial vehicles. Between these two units was an often confusing mixture of overhead valve and overhead camshaft 'fours', vee-4s and vee-6s built in Britain, and vee-4s and vee-6s of an entirely different pedigree built in Germany. In many cases, these engines were sold in more than one state of tune, so it is enough to state that engine sizes of 1.3, 1.6, 1.7, 2.0, 2.3, 2.6 and 3.0-litres have all been seen in quantity-production Capris, not forgetting a very special 3.1-litre Capri 3100 made for a few months at the end of 1973 with motor sport in mind.

The basis of the Capri was a pressed-steel two-door close-coupled four-seater body, a roomy engine bay to accommodate all the engines already mentioned, MacPherson strut front suspension, and simple half-elliptic leaf spring suspension of a variety of live rear axles. Transmission choice, too, was confusing, for there were at least four different manual gearboxes, and an automatic gearbox option on most

Ford Capri MkI

Ford Capri III S, 1978

models which was originally served by Borg Warner, but eventually taken over by Ford's own automatic, made in Bordeaux. Already, in ten years, there have been three generations of Capri. The original car ran for more than five years, before being replaced by a much more versatile and practical hatchback model, in which the floorpan and some inner engine bay panels were the same as before, but which otherwise qualified as a completely new style. The hatchback body had been influenced by the Reliant Scimitar GTE/Volvo 1800ES styles, and proved to be exactly what the sporting/GT market wanted. In 1978 the third generation was revealed, really only a face-lifted Mk 2 car, but with many important detail improvements, particularly to the aerodynamics, where the faster 'S' models received a tail spoiler, and where all models inherited a chin spoiler first blooded only on Mk 2 'S' cars.

The huge sales achieved by this car prove that a model does not need to be incredibly expensive to fulfil many sporting roles. A Capri can be as useful as a small family saloon (indeed, many 1.3-litre models are bought as a stylish alternative to some boring hatchback), and the really quick versions can be as fast across country as many more sleek and expensive GTs.

In the early 1970s, Ford used the Capri for racing with considerable success. The German competition department developed their RS2600S and own vee-6 engines (with the aid of Britain's Harry Weslake), such that the final 2.9-litre cars produced considerably more than 300bhp. For 1974, on the basic design of the 3.1-litre RS3100, they had a most fearsome 3.4-litre four-camshaft Cosworth derivative of the engine which produced more than 400bhp. Great things were expected of this design, which proved itself capable of beating all comers in touring car races, but the after-effects of the fuel crisis put a stop to the programme, and the cars were not raced again.

Numerically, if not in prestige terms, the Capri is probably the most popular GT machine in Europe.

Specification

Engine and transmission: Various engines, between 1298cc four-cylinder with 52bhp (DIN) at 5000rpm, and 3093cc vee-6 cylinder with 148bhp (DIN) at 5500rpm. Straight four, vee-4, and vee-6 engine configurations. All with overhead valves, except 'Pinto' units, which have a single overhead camshaft layout. Four-speed manual gearboxes, in unit with engine. Optional automatic transmission (Borg Warner or – later models – Ford) on most models, but not on 1.3-litre cars, or on RS2600 and RS3100 models. Hypoid bevel final drive.

Chassis: Front engine, rear drive. Unit-construction, pressed-steel body/chassis assembly. Independent front suspension by coil springs and MacPherson struts. Rack and pinion steering (power assisted on some 3.0-litre cars). Suspension of rear live axle by half-elliptic leaf springs (and radius arms, 1969-1972). Front wheel disc brakes, rear drums.

Bodywork: Pressed-steel two-door close-coupled four-seater coupe (with hatchback on Mk 2 and third series cars). Mk I (1969-1974) Length 13ft. 11.8in.; width 5ft. 4.8in.; height 4ft. 2.7in. Unladen weight from 1940lb. (1.3-litre car) to 2380lb. (3.0-litre car). Mk 2 and third series (1974 to date) Length 14ft. 2.9in.; width 5ft. 6.9in.; height 4ft. 3.1in. Unladen weight from 2225lb. (1.3-litre car) to 2580lb. (3.0-litre car).

Performance: (Examples only) **(1.3-litre Mk 2)** Maximum speed 86mph. 0-60mph 18.8sec. Standing ¼-mile 21.0sec. Typical fuel consumption 32mpg. **(1.6-litre Mk 1 GT)** Maximum speed 96mph. 0-60mph 13.4sec. Standing ¼-mile 18.8sec. Typical fuel consumption 25mpg. **(2.0-litre Mk 2)** Maximum speed 106mph. 0-60mph 10.4sec. Standing ¼-mile 17.9sec. Typical fuel consumption 26mpg **(3.0-litre Mk 3)** Maximum speed 117mph. 0-60mph 8.6sec. Standing ¼-mile 16.6sec. Typical fuel consumption 21mpg.

Glas 1300GT and 1700GT

Built: Dingolfing, Germany, 1963-1967

With hindsight, it can be argued that Glas always tried to make too many models in the 1960s, especially when it is noted that their average annual output was no more than 30 000 cars a year – less than 1.5-percent of the West German market. This, however, never deterred their engineers or the family-controlled management. The interesting Glas 1300 model, announced in 1963, was a case in point.

Glas chose the Frankfurt Motor Show of 1963 to launch a new range of cars with a brand-new single-cam four-cylinder engine as the centrepiece. This unit, to be built in various sizes, was distinguished by the use of a cogged-belt camshaft-drive – the very first such application in a European car. Along with the new family cars, Glas also showed a new coupe derivative, with fastback bodies to be made in Italy, with styling by Frua.

The engine was either 1289cc or 1682cc (the larger engine having a slightly enlarged bore and a considerably longer stroke), and drove through a four-speed all-synchromesh gearbox to a 'live' rear axle. Apart from the differences in engine size and power output – 75bhp compared with 100bhp, both extremely creditable figures – the two models, dubbed 1300GT and 1700GT, were virtually identical, and both featured disc front brakes, which were still not universal fittings on smaller cars of the day.

Production began, somewhat haltingly, during 1964, and was always limited by two factors – by Frua's inability to make more than five bodies a day, and by Glas's rudimentary tooling failing to produce the engines in any quantity. The 1300GT engine block and cylinder head was later used to good effect for the 2600GT V8 to be produced in 1965, but by this time the Glas company was in financial trouble. Takeover by BMW occurred in 1966, and shortly after this the entire range of Glas GT cars was dropped.

Glas 1300GT

Specification

Engine and transmission: Four-cylinders, in-line, with single-overhead-camshaft cylinder head. **(1300GT)** Bore, stroke and capacity 75×73mm., 1289cc. Maximum power 75bhp (DIN) at 5500rpm.; maximum torque 80lb.ft. at 3500rpm. Four-speed manual gearbox in unit with engine. Hypoid bevel final drive. **(1700 GT)** Bore, stroke and capacity 78×88mm., 1682cc. Maximum power 100bhp (DIN) at 5500rpm.; maximum torque 108lb.ft. at 3000rpm. Four or five-speed manual gearbox in unit with engine. Hypoid bevel final drive.

Chassis: Front engine, rear drive. Pressed-steel unit-construction body-chassis unit. Independent front suspension by coil springs and wishbones. Worm and sector steering. Rear suspension of live axle by half-elliptic leaf springs and Panhard rod. Disc front brakes, rear drums.

Bodywork: Monocoque pressed-steel two-door 2+2 seater, in fastback coupe or cabriolet style, by Frua. Length 13ft. 5.4in.; width 5ft. 1in.; height 4ft. 2.3in. Unladen weight (Coupe) 1830lb., (Cabriolet) 1875lb.

Performance (1300GT, 85bhp); Maximum speed 98mph. 0-60mph 12.5sec. Standing ¼-mile 18.9sec. Typical fuel consumption 35mpg. **(1700GT)** Maximum speed 112mph. 0-60mph 11.2sec. Standing ¼-mile 18.2sec. Typical fuel consumption 27mpg.

Note: Later 1300 models were fitted with an 85bhp engine.

Following BMW's takeover of Glas, the 1700GT was redeveloped by BMW engineers, given a BMW grille on an otherwise unchanged body style, and fitted with BMW engine, transmission and rear suspension. It was not a success – 1255 were sold in 1967 and 1968. Specification differences were as follows: Four cylinder BMW engine. Bore, stroke and capacity 84×71mm., 1573cc. Maximum power 105bhp (DIN) at 6000rpm. Maximum torque 97lb.ft. at 4500rpm. Independent rear suspension by coil springs and semi-trailing wishbones. Unladen weight (coupe) 2115lb.

Performance (Manufacturer's claim): Maximum speed 118mph. 0-60mph (approx) 10.8sec. Typical fuel consumption 28mpg.

Glas 2600 V8 and 3000 V8 Coupe

Built: Dingolfing, Germany, 1965-1968

In spite of the fact that Glas's production rate was rather restricted, the company was never short of ambition, and in 1965 they decided to go all out for a company flagship, to be introduced as a fast and pretty coupe. Although the car was duly announced in the autumn, it did not go into production until after the BMW takeover, and only 71 cars were to be built in all.

Glas 2600 V8

The 2600, which used a pressed-steel platform chassis frame like that of the smaller-engined Glas coupes, had a Frua-designed two-door fastback body built by Maggiora in Turin, with a close-coupled four-seater arrangement. The style looked remarkably like that of current Maserati models, which is hardly surprising as Frua were also responsible for some of those, and it seems that there were some common components to the cars in question.

The most interesting aspect of the short-lived design was the 2576cc vee-8 engine, which had a single overhead camshaft to each cylinder head, driven by cogged belts from the crankshaft. Effectively, this unit comprised two Glas 1300GT cylinder blocks and heads mated to a common crankcase, and − unlike many previously unsuccessful 'Meccano' jobs of this nature − appears to have worked well and produced a great deal of power.

De Dion rear suspension and self-levelling Boge dampers were features, as was the power-assisted steering, and the disc brakes fitted to all four wheels. There was a very rigid driveline, with enclosed propeller shaft, and with rear disc brakes mounted inboard, on each side of the final drive casing.

It was unfortunate that Glas descended into financial trouble almost as soon as this exciting-looking new model had been announced, and they had to be taken over by BMW of Munich (geographically this made a great deal of sense). BMW built a small series of these 2600 V8 and 3000 V8 models in 1967 and 1968 from components and bodyshells already available, after which the model was dropped, and the factory sold off to Audi.

Specification

Engine and transmission: Eight-cylinders, in 90-degree vee-formation, with single-overhead-camshaft cylinder heads. **(2600):** Bore, stroke and capacity 75 × 73mm., 2576cc. Maximum power 140bhp (DIN) at 5600rpm.; maximum torque 152lb.ft. at 3000rpm. **(3000):** Bore, stroke and capacity 78 × 78mm., 2982cc. Maximum power 160bhp (DIN) at 5100rpm.; maximum torque 173lb.ft. at 3400rpm. Four-speed manual gearbox in unit with engine. Hypoid bevel final drive.

Chassis: Front engine, rear drive. Pressed-steel platform chassis frame. Independent front suspension by coil springs and wishbones. Power-assisted recirculating ball steering. De Dion rear suspension by leaf springs, Panhard rod, and self-levelling Boge struts. Four wheel disc brakes.

Bodywork: Coachbuilt steel and light-alloy two-door close-coupled four-seater fastback coupe style by Frua. Length 15ft. 2in.; width 5ft. 9in.; height 4ft. 7in. Unladen weight 2485lb.

Performance (2600 V8) (Manufacturer's claims): Maximum speed 124mph. 0-60mph approx 10.5sec. Typical fuel consumption approx 20mpg. **(3000 V8):** Maximum speed 125mph. 0-60mph 9.0sec. Typical fuel consumption 18mpg.

Jensen-Healey and Jensen GT

Built: West Bromwich, England, 1972-1976

The Jensen-Healey of 1972 was the direct result of the takeover of Jensen by Kjell Qvale of North America in 1970, and was the reason for that takeover, for Qvale made the move in concert with Britain's Donald Healey, who had a new design of sports car up his sleeve. Even so, the new car, which was dimensionally similar to an MGB or a TR6, never sold in the numbers envisaged at first, and Jensen had to stop trading in 1976. No attempt to revive the firm was successful.

The Jensen-Healey started life as a pure Healey project. Once British Leyland made it clear that they were to stop producing Austin-Healeys, and that their consultancy agreement with the Healey concern was to be terminated, Kjell Qvale (who, as a Californian motor trader, had been responsible for selling a great many of the fabulous old 3000s, Sprites and MGs) asked Donald Healey to start designing a new car which would not use British Leyland components. At first this car concentrated on using Vauxhall components, and was really no less than a sports car with Viva GT power train and suspensions.

Jensen-Healey

Jensen GT

Before the project could progress much further, however, somewhere had to be found to build it in quantity. As Jensen had built the bodies for the Austin-Healey 3000 for many years, and as they had recently stopped making these and the Sunbeam Tigers, they were in need of a new 'volume production' car to keep their factories busy. The new 'Healey', therefore, became the 'Jensen-Healey' following takeover, and was ready for launch in the spring of 1972.

Before then, however, the Vauxhall engine had to be rejected as it was by no means powerful enough when USA exhaust emission regulations were met. In its place, after cursory studies of BMW and Ford engines had been carried out, came the then-new 2-litre Lotus engine, which was dimensionally almost identical with the Vauxhall unit, had a 16-valve cylinder head, and was potentially very powerful even when fully 'detoxed'. When matched, at first, to a Chrysler (Rapier H120) gearbox and overdrive, a very satisfactory power train developed. At announcement, therefore, the only Vauxhall components which remained were front and rear suspensions and steering gear, for the entire pressed-steel body chassis unit was to be built by Jensen themselves. The least outstanding feature of the car was the rather anaemic styling of the open two-seater car, which was an amalgam of several attempts to find a distinctive line, and it was this which contributed to the car's slow acceptance by the buying public.

Sales began in the early summer of 1972, and apart from reliability problems with the Lotus twin-cam engine (which had not then even been fitted to a Lotus production car) the car seemed to be a success. Small cosmetic changes were made in 1973, but in

1974 a major transmission change occured, when the Chrysler gearbox was abandoned, along with its overdrive, in favour of a newly-developed five-speed Getrag box which has now been adopted on other European cars including the Vauxhall Chevette 2300HS.

In 1975, however, the emphasis changed direction, with the launch of the rather different Jensen GT, which was effectively a Reliant Scimitar GTE approach to clothing this basic chassis. In many ways the 'GT' was rather more upmarket than the original Jensen-Healey had been, being more lavishly trimmed and more refined, but its styling still excited controversy as it was rather long and slim, and the new '2 + 2' seating was very marginal for all except small children.

When Jensen Motors stopped trading in 1976, the Jensen-Healey/GT strain disappeared and was not revived by new management.

Specification

Engine and transmission: Four-cylinders, in-line, but installed in chassis at 45-degree inclination, with twin-overhead-camshaft cylinder head. Bore, stroke and capacity 95.2 × 69.3mm., 1973cc built by Lotus. Maximum power 140bhp (DIN) at 6500rpm.; maximum torque 130lb.ft. at 5000rpm. Four-speed manual gearbox with overdrive, or five-speed manual Getrag gearbox in unit with engine. Hypoid bevel final drive.

Chassis: Front engine, rear drive. Pressed-steel unit-construction body-chassis unit. Independent front suspension by coil springs and wishbones. Rack and pinion steering. Rear suspension of live axle by coil springs and radius arms. Front wheel disc brakes, rear drums.

Bodywork: Pressed-steel two-door two-seater open sports car (Jensen-Healey) or 2 + 2 hatchback sporting estate style (Jensen GT). Length 13ft. 10in.; width 5ft. 3.2in.; height 3ft. 11.5in. (Jensen-Healey) or 4ft. 0.5in. (Jensen GT). Unladen weight (Jensen-Healey) 2340lb., (Jensen GT) 2400lb.

Performance: (Jensen-Healey) Maximum speed 119mph. 0-60mph 7.8sec. Standing ¼-mile 16.2sec. Typical fuel consumption 24mpg. **(Jensen GT)** Maximum speed 119mph. 0-60mph 8.7sec. Standing ¼-mile 16.7sec. Typical fuel consumption 21.5mpg.

Lancia Appia sporting series

Built: Turin, Italy, 1953-1964

In its mechanical layout, Lancia's little Appia was one of the last 'traditional' models from that family-owned Turin concern, which is to say that it was one of the last to have a front-mounted engine in narrow vee-layout, driving the back wheels.

The Appia was launched in 1953, with its 1089cc engine, to replace the Ardea, which had in fact been a pre-world war two design. The Appia's engine was tiny in most respects, with a 10-degree angle between the pairs of cylinders (a casual glance into the engine bay revealed an engine which looked as if it was just a short and squat in line unit — the block was only 9.5-inches long), and the whole design was distinctly Lancia.

Apart from the engine itself, the rest of the layout was conventional enough, and Lancia would have retorted that to them the engine layout was perfectly normal as well. Independent coil spring suspension was Lancia-style, in sliding pillars linked by what looked like a normal axle beam, while the rear axle was located on half-elliptic leaf springs. The original Appia was a four-door saloon car, with integral construction, and liberal use of light-alloy door and other skin panels.

During the 1950s, several companies, with Lancia's explicit approval, built coupes and spiders on this base, the most numerous probably being from Vignale, Pininfarina and Zagato. Only the Zagato car had completely light-alloy coachwork, while the others used a framework of pressed-steel on the pressed-steel underpan, but with alloy skins. By Lancia standards, these good looking but not very fast little sporting cars were a success. In 1963 the all-new Fulvia was announced, which spelled imminent extinction for the Appia, and the last of the sporting models followed a short time after that.

Specification

Engine and transmission: Four-cylinders, in 10-degree vee-formation, with pushrod-operated overhead-valve cylinder head. Bore, stroke and capacity 68×75mm., 1089cc. Maximum power 53bhp (DIN) at 5200rpm.; maximum torque 64lb.ft. at 3500rpm. **(Zagato model, 1961 on):** 60bhp (DIN) at 5400rpm. Maximum torque 63lb.ft. at 4250rpm. Four-speed manual gearbox in unit with engine. Hypoid bevel final drive.
Chassis: Front engine, rear drive. Pressed-steel unit-construction body-chassis unit. Independent front suspension by coil springs and vertical sliding pillars. Worm and sector steering. Rear suspension of live axle by half-elliptic leaf springs. Four wheel drum brakes.
Bodywork: Several types, of two-door 2 + 2 seater fastback coupe/cabriolet styles, by Viotti/Pininfarina Vignale and Zagato. Zagato with light alloy coachwork, others with pressed-steel coachwork. (Zagato) Length 13ft. 1in.; width 4ft. 8.3in.; height 4ft. 0.4in. Unladen weight 1740lb. (Pininfarina coupe) Length 13ft. 6.6in.; width 4ft. 10.7in.; height 4ft. 3.6in. Unladen weight 2040lb.

Lancia Appia Coupe

Lancia Flaminia sporting cars

Built: Turin, Italy, 1956-1969

The Flaminia model of 1956, which had already been previewed by the Pininfarina-styled Florida show car of a year earlier, represented something of a complete change for the old-established Turinese concern. For one thing it was an altogether larger car than the Aurelia it was to replace, and for another it was *the* first Lancia for many many years to abandon the sliding-pillar coil spring independent front suspension. Although it was never to be a large seller, the Flaminia and its often graceful sporting descendants was to be part of the Lancia scene until the end of the 1960s.

Lancia Flaminia Coupe

The chassis featured a platform-style chassis and floor, with a massive subframe bolted-up to support the front suspension and engine. The engine itself was a 60-degree vee-6, an obvious derivative of that used on the outdated Aurelia, and in its original form was of 80×81.5mm., 2458cc., and the four-speed manual transmission was in unit with the final drive unit, allied to de Dion rear suspension, all as so well-known and well-liked on the Aurelia model.

Although the four-door pillarless saloon style was attractive in itself, the specialised and short chassis derivatives evolved by three coachbuilders – Touring, Zagato and Pininfarina, all with Lancia's approval – were even more beautiful. The Zagato car, like others he was to do for Lancia in future years for the Fulvia and Flavia models, had a long slinky fastback shape, with faired-in headlamps, while the Pininfarina car was much more squared-up and formal, after the fashion dictated by that eminent styling house at the time, with vestigial tail fins along the top of the rear wings. The Pininfarina car, being built on a longer version of the Flaminia saloon's wheelbase (the Zagato was rather drastically shortened) had more space, and four adequate seats. The Touring model had a rather more anonymous style, and was built on the shortened-wheelbase like the Zagato model.

All the sporting Flaminias made their entry at the 1958 Turin Show, and were given four-wheel disc brakes from 1959. To keep their performance up to standard against the burgeoning competition, Lancia managed one last stretch of the vee-6 engine (which had already been enlarged several times in the past − to 2775cc, with a bore and stroke of 85×81.5mm, and made this engine available on all models − saloons and the sporting types − from 1963. For the next few years, while Lancia concentrated more and more on their small Fulvia and Flavia models, the Flaminias soldiered on, but their design and their rather ponderous and stately behaviour was more of the 1950s than the 1960s.

The last of the cars, which had been built only to special order for some time, was completed in 1969, by which time Lancia were in serious financial trouble, and shortly afterwards the entire company was sold to Fiat.

Lancia Flaminia Zagato

Specification

Engine and transmission: Six-cylinders, in 60-degree vee-formation, with pushrod-operated overhead-valve cylinder heads. Bore, stroke and capacity 80 × 81.5mm., 2458cc. Maximum power **(Coupe)** 119bhp (net) at 5100rpm.; maximum torque 137lb.ft. at 3500rpm. Maximum power **(Zagato Sport)** 140bhp (net) at 5600rpm.; maximum torque 150lb.ft. at 3600rpm. From 1963, cars were sold with 2775cc engines, with 85 × 81.5mm bore and stroke. Maximum power 150bhp (net) at 5400rpm.; maximum torque 165lb.ft. at 3500rpm. Four-speed manual gearbox in unit with hypoid bevel final drive.

Chassis: Front engine, rear drive. Pressed-steel platform-type chassis, with subframe for front suspension and engine. Independent front suspension by coil springs and wishbones. Recirculating ball steering. Rear suspension by de Dion, with half-elliptic leaf springs and Panhard rod. Four wheel drum brakes, (early cars), four wheel disc brakes on later models.

Bodywork: Two main types: two-door close-coupled four-seater notchback coupe (Pininfarina) or cabriolet (Touring), and two-door two-seater light-alloy fastback coupe by Zagato. (Pininfarina coupe) Length 15ft. 4.5in.; width 5ft. 8.5in.; height 4ft. 7.9in. Unladen weight 3265lb. (Zagato coupe) Length 14ft. 9in.; width 5ft. 4.1in.; height 4ft. 3.4in. Unladen weight 2670lb.

Performance (Pininfarina coupe, 2.5-litre model): Maximum speed 106mph. 0-60mph 13.6sec. Standing ¼-mile 19.1sec. Typical fuel consumption 22mpg. **(Zagato coupe, 2.5-litre model):** Maximum speed 110mph. 0-60mph 13.2sec. Standing ¼-mile 19.0sec. Typical fuel consumption 23mpg. **(Pininfarina coupe, 2.8-litre 1965 model):** Maximum speed 112mph. 0-60mph 12.7sec. Standing ¼-mile 18.7sec. Typical fuel consumption 18mpg.

Lancia Flavia and 2000 sporting cars

Built: Turin, Italy, 1960-1975

When the Flavia was announced by Lancia in 1960, it caused something of a sensation, for it represented a complete breakaway from the last of Lancia's noble traditions. Designed by Prof. Fessia, whose earlier work had included the first of Fiat's Topolino's, the Flavia featured front-wheel drive and a flat-four cylinder engine layout. It was the first front-wheel-drive car ever to be built in Italy, antedating anything Fiat had in mind by three or four-years, and there was absolutely no carryover of parts from any previous Lancia models. In fact there had been a huge gap in the model line-up for years, with the little Appia at one extreme, and the large and prestigious Flaminia at the other end of the spectrum.

Lancia Flavia Coupe 1800 by Pininfarina

The Flavia saloon itself was a stubby and none-too-attractive four-door saloon car, but it was not long before the inevitable Pininfarina, Zagato and Vignale sporting cars came along. Right from the start the Flavia was a suitable subject for this sort of treatment, for it had a very tuneable engine, good handling due to its front-wheel-drive, and a compact mechanical layout. Front wheel driveshafts were surrounded by a wishbone suspension linkage, but suspension and the transverse leaf spring which provided the springing medium was all mounted on a massive pressed and fabricated subframe which also supported the engine. Rear suspension of the 'dead' axle beam was simply by half-elliptic leaf springs.

The flat-four engine was water cooled, with pushrod operation of the inclined overhead valves, but was balanced as a true 'boxer' with individual crankpins. Drive

191

was over the final drive to the manual gearbox, then back to the spiral bevel line drive. Original saloons had a rather horrid steering column gearchange, but sporting models were not saleable without a floor change.

As was becoming conventional with Lancia's marketing plans, Pininfarina sold the more formal close-coupled four-seater coupe sporting car, while Zagato was responsible for a really way-out looking 2 + 2 coupe, in which the body construction was at the same time lighter, more complex, more wind-cheating – and more expensive.

In its original form, the flat-four engine was a 1.5-litre unit, but 1.8-litre versions became available in 1963, and the final 2.0-litre was offered from the spring of 1969. This 1990cc engine was introduced at the same time as a restyled Pininfarina coupe bodyshell, and was never applied to the lightweight Zagato model, which was discontinued at the same time. The 'new' Pininfarina shell had a smoother and more integrated nose, without the separate Lancia grille, but with a full-width grille incorporating four headlamps.

Not only did the new engine produce a very creditable 131bhp (gross) at 5400rpm., but a more highly tuned version with Kugelfischer fuel-injection was also available, and this produced 140bhp (gross) at 5600rpm. This was enough for the car to be marketed as the company's 'flagship' in the early 1970s (after the Fiat takeover, and while the Italian giant was content for this sort of indulgence to continue), although sales were not at a high level.

The last of these long-running models, by then named a Lancia 2000 Coupe HF, was sold in 1975, and was replaced by the more modern, but also front-wheel-drive, Lancia Beta Coupe.

Lancia 2000 Coupe

Specification

Engine and transmission: Four-cylinders, horizontally-opposed, with pushrod-operated overhead-valve cylinder heads. Three engine sizes (depending on model and year produced); from bore, stroke and capacity of 82×71mm., 1500cc to 89×80mm., 1990cc. Maximum power 90bhp (net) at 5800rpm. to 140bhp (gross) at 5600rpm. Maximum torque 85lb.ft. at 4500rpm to 142lb.ft. at 4000rpm. Four-speed manual gearbox in unit with engine and transaxle. Hypoid bevel final drive.

Chassis: Front engine, front drive. Pressed-steel unit-construction body-chassis unit. Independent front suspension by transverse leaf spring and wishbones. Worm and roller steering (power assisted on some models). Rear suspension of axle beam by half-elliptic leaf springs and Panhard rod.

Bodywork: Two-style: two-door close-coupled four-seater fastback coupe by Pininfarina in pressed-steel, or two-door two-seater fastback coupe with light-alloy bodyshell by Zagato (plus convertible version of Pininfarina car, by Vignale). **(Pininfarina)** Length 14ft. 8.5in.; width 5ft. 3.4in.; height 4ft. 5in. Unladen weight (depending on engine and year built) approx 2550lb. **(Zagato)** Length 14ft. 7.6in.; width 5ft. 4.4in.; height 4ft. 4.7in. Unladen weight 2340lb.

Performance: (Flavia Farina Coupe 1.8) Maximum speed 107mph. 0-60mph 13.2sec. Standing ¼-mile 19.1sec. Typical fuel consumption 24mpg. **(Flavia Zagato 1.8-litre)** Maximum speed 113mph. 0-60mph. 11.9sec. Standing ¼-mile 18.3sec. Typical fuel consumption 21mpg.

Lancia Fulvia Coupe and Zagato

Built: Turin, Italy, 1965-1976

Without doubt, the Fulvia Coupe was one of the most elegant, popular, and successful the privately-owned Lancia firm ever produced. In terms of numbers built it will one day be overtaken by the Beta coupes and Spiders, but these are larger and (because of their links with the HPE and other types) more versatile. In every way the little Fulvias were personalised and quite unmistakeable machines.

The Fulvia range, as was usual Lancia, was first announced as a four-door saloon car, and only branched out into sporting derivatives at a later date. Also, as usual, there were two specific types of coupe – a close-coupled four-seater (or, more realistically, a 2 + 2) coupe, this time styled and completely manufactured by Lancia themselves, and a wickedly sleek two-seater fastback with light-alloy panelling by Zagato. No open car was ever produced for sale, though special racing Fulvias were sometimes made with this layout.

The Fulvia, like the Flavia and the Flaminia before it, was yet another very new layout from this firm which, in truth, should not have been able to afford to spend so much time, effort and capital on tooling up for new engines, transmissions and bodies. As with the Flavia, the Fulvia was designed under the direction of Professor Fessia, and had front-wheel-drive. Like the Flavia, transverse leaf spring front suspension was used, as was half-elliptic spring location of the rear 'dead' axle beam. However, although the engine was a narrow-angle vee-4, it was entirely different from that of the Appia. The angle between pairs of cylinders was 13-degrees, but the whole engine was

Lancia Fulvia Coupe

much larger, to allow – if only we had realised it – for considerable future stretching of capacity. Not only this, but the engine layout featured two overhead camshafts, with an ingenious valve gear arrangement which allowed one exhaust camshaft to look after both sets of valves, and the same layout for the inlet side of things.

The transmission casing and final drive layout was that of the larger Flavia, which allowed considerable scope for power increases over the years. To take care of the stopping power, four large Dunlop disc brakes, like those of the Flavia, were specified.

The chunky and distinctive Lancia-styled coupe was to remain in production for 11-years, and was still selling steadily and successfully when dropped in 1976, as part of the Fiat-owned concern's rationalisation plan; in Lancia's scheme of things, if not in the heart of the enthusiast, it has now been replaced by the Lancia Beta Coupe, which is a much larger and bulkier model altogether.

The more specialised Zagato coupe was built from 1966 to 1973, and shared the same mechanical components as the factory-built coupe, including the same shortened (7ft. 7in.) wheelbase version of the saloon car's bodyshell. Although this car had only two seats, it was nicely trimmed, and had a lot of useful luggage accommodation.

The story of these cars' development was one of progressive engine improvements, and the link with Lancia's sporting ambitions. Firstly, in 1967, the original 1216cc was enlarged to 1298cc, but from the end of 1968 an alternative – the '1600HF' – came along with no less than 1584cc. Lancia, determined to develop a winning rally car, had launched the Fulvia Coupe HF in January 1966. 'HF' denoted High Fidelity, which was what Lancia's Jolly Club owners gave to their marque, and it signified a lightweight bodyshell with the very minimum of trim, and the addition of other competition fittings. HFs became 1300s as soon as the engine was available, but really came to maturity in the 1600HF Lusso, where the most powerful engine, the five-speed gearbox of the Flavia, and the lightweight panelling of the rally cars were all brought together.

As often happens, the HFs, and particularly the 1600HF Lusso of 1968, were meant to be competition cars only, but the public queued up to buy them, and they were made in considerable numbers. It was only after the Stratos appeared, and after Beta Coupe built up, that 1600HF sales were closed down, and the last production cars of all were called Coupe S3s, with the 90bhp (DIN) 1298cc engines.

Specification

Engine and transmission: Four-cylinders, in 13-degree vee-formation, with two overhead-camshafts between two cylinder heads. Bore, stroke and capacity from 76×67mm., 1216cc to 82×75mm., 1584cc. Maximum power from 80bhp (DIN) at 6000rpm, to 115bhp (DIN) at 6200rpm.; maximum torque from 77lb.ft. at 4000rpm to 112lb.ft. at 4500rpm. Four-speed or five-speed manual gearbox in unit with engine and transaxle. Hypoid bevel final drive.

Chassis: Front engine, front drive. Pressed-steel unit-construction body-chassis unit. Independent front suspension by transverse leaf spring and wishbones. Worm and roller steering. Rear suspension of axle beam by half-elliptic leaf springs and Panhard rod. Four wheel disc brakes.

Lancia Fulvia Zagato

Bodywork: Two types: Pressed steel (with light alloy panels on HF Lusso models) two-door, 2 + 2 seater notchback coupe style, or two-door 2 + 2 seater fastback coupe style by Zagato. **(Coupe)** Length 13ft. 0.5in.; width 5ft. 4in.; height 4ft. 3in. Unladen weight, depending on model, from 1975lb to 2110lb. **(Zagato)** Length 13ft. 5in.; width 5ft. 1.8in.; height 3ft. 11.2in. Unladen weight 2060lb.
Performance: (Fulvia Coupe 1.2-litre) Maximum speed 100mph. 0-60mph 15.8sec. Standing ¼-mile 20.0sec. Typical fuel consumption 33mpg. **(Zagato 1.3-litre)** Maximum speed 109mph. 0-60mph 13.0sec. Standing ¼-mile 19.1sec. Typical fuel consumption 34mpg. **(1600HF Lusso)** Maximum speed 106mph. 0-60mph 9.9sec. Standing ¼-mile 17.6sec. Typical fuel consumption 24mpg.

Lancia Beta Coupes & HPE

Built: Turin, Italy, 1973 to date

By the end of the 1960s, Lancia were in deep financial trouble, so it was no great surprise when Fiat took them over in the autumn of 1969. The price for the entire company was a mere one-million Lira (about £670 at the time), which sounds unbelievable, until one remembers that Fiat also took over responsibility for the Lancia company's huge debts, said to be in excess of £67 millions! Fiat were certainly interested in bringing about major improvements at Lancia, but there would be no new models until 1972. The Beta range announced then has since become the backbone of the revived company's product range.

Although the Beta was clearly influenced by Fiat – it had, for instance, a range of Lancia-modified Fiat twin-cam engines of the type used in the 124 Sport coupe and Spider models – it was to follow the usual Lancia trends. The four-door (or, really, the five-door, for this car had a hatchback) touring car came first in the autumn of 1972, and all the sporting derivatives followed in the next couple of years. By the clever juggling of engines, wheelbases, body panels, and a combination of all these, a most impressive range of new cars evolved from a single basic design.

Central to the concept was a transversely-mounted front-engine, front-wheel-drive layout, with the Fiat twin-cam engine to the right side of the car's centreline driving to a new five-speed gearbox on the left, and with the final drive tucked in behind the assembly. All round independent suspension by MacPherson struts was a feature, as was the use of four-wheel disc brakes. The car was nostalgically named 'Beta', which is

Lancia Beta Coupe

Lancia Beta Spider

not the first letter in the Greek alphabet, but was the second ever Lancia production car's name in 1909, this car, therefore, was meant to be a rebirth in every way.

The saloon car, with its choice of 1.4, 1.6 and 1.8-litre engines, was rather plain, if not actually ugly. The sporting cars which followed, however, were very striking, and soon became very popular. First, from the summer of 1973, came the Beta Coupe, which combined entirely fresh styling and sheet metal with a shortened version of the Beta's floor pan, 2 + 2 seating accommodation, and a choice of (at first) 1.6 and 1.8-litre engines.

In the spring of 1975, however, came an even more elegant combination − the HPE, where those initials stood for High Performance Estate car. This combined the full-length saloon car floorpan, the complete Coupe nose, screen and front door pressings, and a strikingly sleek sporting estate type of rear style, in Reliant Scimitar GTE layout. At the end of the year, too, the engine range was further rationalised and expanded. In place of the original choice of sizes, 1.3, 1.6 and 2.0-litre engines were on offer, and the Coupes and HPEs naturally were most popular with the long-stroke 1995cc engines installed.

In terms of economics and product planning, many of Lancia's and Fiat's most popular models now made use of one or other of the engines in this range. The Beta sporting derivatives soon established a fine name for good roadholding, high performance, and great practicality, and with only minor cosmetic attention in 1979 go on uninterrupted into the 1980s.

Specification

Engine and transmission: Four-cylinders, in-line, transversely mounted, with twin-overhead-camshaft cylinder head. Depending on year built, and model, engines from 76×71.5mm., 1297cc to 84×90mm., 1995cc are fitted. Maximum power from 82bhp (DIN) at 5800rpm to 119bhp (DIN) at 5500rpm.; maximum torque from 80lb.ft. at 3300rpm to 129lb.ft. at 2800rpm. Five-speed manual gearbox in unit with engine and transaxle. Spur gear final drive.

Chassis: Front engine, front drive. Pressed-steel unit-construction body-chassis unit. Independent front suspension by coil springs and MacPherson struts. Rack and pinion steering. Independent rear suspension by coil springs, MacPherson struts and lower wishbones. Four wheel disc brakes.

Bodywork: Pressed-steel bodywork (Beta Coupe) two-door close-coupled four seater notchback coupe, (Spider) two-door close-coupled four-seater Cabriolet, (HPE) three-door 'high performance estate' four-seater. Length (Coupe) 13ft. 1.2in., (Spider) 13ft. 3in., (HPE) 14ft. 0.7in., width 5ft. 4.8in.; height (Coupe) 4ft. 2.4in., (Spider) 4ft. 1.2in., (HPE) 4ft. 3.5in. Unladen weights, depending on model, from 2160lb. to 2335lb.

Performance: (Beta Coupe 1600) Maximum speed 113mph. 0-60mph 10.4sec. Standing ¼-mile 17.3sec. Typical fuel consumption 26mpg. **(HPE 2000)** Maximum speed 116mph. 0-60mph 10.6sec. Standing ¼-mile 17.7sec. Typical fuel consumption 22mpg.

Lancia Monte Carlo

Built: Turin, Italy, 1975-1978

In 1973 and 1974, a great deal of rumour circulated regarding Fiat's plans to add a larger type of mid-engined sports car to their range, to complement the new Fiat X1/9. Prototypes usually referred to as X1/20s, often in race- or rally-modified form, were seen in 1974, including a car shown by Abarth at the Turin Motor Show. It was therefore a shock to see that a productionised version, shown at the 1975 Geneva Motor Show, was badged as a Lancia!

The new car, badged as a 'Monte Carlo' to mark the great successes notched up in recent years by Lancia in the Monte Carlo Rally, was styled by Pininfarina (who also made the body structures); even though it carried the same family lines as the X1/9, it should be noted that this small car was by Bertone. It had obviously been a late decision to badge the car as a Lancia, as the cars carried Fiat chassis number sequences throughout their lives.

Although called, if given its complete title, a Beta Monte Carlo, this striking mid-engined sports coupe was really an entirely special layout with a number of important Beta components. The body/chassis unit, of course, was by Pininfarina. A modified version of the 1995cc Fiat/Lancia twin-cam four-cylinder engine was used in a complete transversely-mounted Beta power pack, but effectively moved back from the nose to a position behind the seats. All-round MacPherson strut suspension was similar to that of the Beta front-engined cars, but different in terms of wishbones and links.

The Monte Carlo was primarily intended for sale to the United States, and this was undoubtedly one important reason why it was withdrawn (temporarily, in fact) from production in 1978 and 1979. The style used integrated '5mph' bumpers, and the entire structure was meant to look after North American safety and emission laws. The problem, however, was that whereas European Monte Carlos had engines developing a very creditable 120bhp at 6000rpm, the North American version (badged, incidentally, as a Scorpion) only boasted 84bhp at 5800rpm.

Lancia Beta Monte Carlo

To look after the 'fresh air fiends', Monte Carlos were built with the feature of a removable roof panel (as was the Fiat X1/9), and in spite of the stubby layout and compact styling there was a good deal of luggage space ahead of the driving compartment.

Although the new car's weight distribution was surprisingly well balanced, with 41-percent of weight over the front wheels, there was no doubt that roadholding and grip was something of a problem. Early tests turned up a tendency to brake locking and wayward behaviour at the front. This, combined with the strictly two-seater accommodation (a bane of almost every mid-engined car on the market) and the lack of performance in the commercially-important North American versions, led to the Monte Carlo being withdrawn from production in 1978. An improved version was re-introduced at the beginning of 1980.

The factory competition department has now campaigned a turbocharged racing Monte Carlo with some success, and it obviously has an important place in the corporate future.

Specification

Engine and transmission: Four-cylinders, in-line, transversely mounted, with twin-overhead-camshaft cylinder head. Bore, stroke and capacity 84×90mm., 1995cc. Maximum power 120bhp (DIN) at 6000rpm.; maximum torque 126lb.ft. at 3400rpm. Five-speed manual gearbox in unit with engine and transaxle. Spur gear final drive.
Chassis: Mid-engine, rear drive. Unit-construction pressed-steel body-chassis unit. Independent front suspension by coil springs and MacPherson struts. Rack and pinion steering. Independent rear suspensions by coil springs, MacPherson struts and lower wishbones. Four wheel disc brakes.
Bodywork: Pressed-steel two-door, two-seater fastback coupe style by Pininfarina. Length 12ft. 6.1in.; width 5ft. 5.8in.; height 3ft. 10.6in. Unladen weight 2290lb.
Performance: Maximum speed 119mph. 0-60mph 9.8sec. Standing ¼-mile 16.0sec. Typical fuel consumption 28mpg.

MG Midget & Austin-Healey Sprite family

Built: Abingdon, England, 1961 to 1979

Although the first-ever MG Midget had been built in 1928, the Midget of 1961 was not originally an MG design. The basis of the design was the Austin-Healey Sprite, built at Abingdon from 1958, and which was to continue in production alongside the Midget until 1971.

The Sprite had been conceived by the prolific Healey family in 1956, in response to BMC's request for a small and inexpensive two-seater sports car to add to the MGA and Austin-Healey 100/6 ranges. In its first Austin-Healey form, its unit-construction bodyshell had no external access to the luggage compartment, and a cheeky frontal style including protruding 'frog-eye' headlamps.

From June 1961, however, the range was redesigned and widened. There were to be Austin-Healey Sprite and MG Midget versions, mechanically and bodily identical, except for minor cosmetic differences to indicate the MG version. The restyled car had more conventional lines, with wing-positioned headlamps, and with a boot compartment with lid. All versions were strict two-seaters, though optional hardtops were available to the open sports body.

Progressive mechanical improvements were introduced in line with changes made on other BMC cars. The engine was enlarged to the new long-stroke 1098cc size in autumn 1962 at the same time as that engine was introduced for the front-wheel-drive Morris 1100, and in the autumn of 1966 the 'productionised' 1275cc unit took its place. Although these engines all have different bores and strokes, they are all based on the amazingly versatile BMC 'A Series' unit, whose origins are in the Austin A30 of 1951. From the autumn of 1974, six-years after the formation of British Leyland, a Triumph

MG Midget MkI

Austin-Healey Sprite III, 1964

Spitfire 1500 engine and gearbox was adopted, to commonise the specification with that of the Spitfire, and because the ageing A-Series engine could no longer keep abreast of North American exhaust emission requirements.

The only significant change to the chassis layout came in the spring of 1964 when the rear suspension was redesigned. Half-elliptic leaf springs were adopted, in place of the cantilever quarter-elliptics and radius arms fitted on Sprites and Midgets up to that point. Front wheel disc brakes, too, had been standardised when the 1098cc engine was introduced.

Apart from the fitment of controversial '5mph' bumpers, which are bulky, black, and in soft plastic, in autumn 1974, there have been no major styling changes to the exterior, though regular attention to the interior, and the fascia, has been made.

Midgets and Sprites sold in very large numbers indeed − more than 200 000 Midgets, and nearly 130 000 Sprites − but eventually began to fall out of favour in their most important market, which was North America. Production was phased out towards the end of 1979, and British Leyland's only surviving small sports car is the Triumph Spitfire. Each and every one had a cheeky, bright, character, and − in every way − behaved as a traditional sports car should.

Specification (Original 1961 model)

Engine and transmission: Four-cylinders, in-line, with pushrod-operated overhead-valve cylinder head. Bore, stroke and capacity 62.9×76.2mm., 948cc. Maximum power 46.5bhp (net) at 5500rpm.; maximum torque 53lb.ft. at 2750rpm. Four-speed manual gearbox in unit with engine. Hypoid bevel final drive.

Chassis: Front engine, rear drive. Unit construction pressed-steel body/chassis unit. Independent front suspension by coil springs and wishbones. Rack and pinion steering. Rear suspension of live rear axle by cantilever quarter-elliptic leaf springs and radius arms. Four-wheel drum brakes.

Bodywork: Pressed-steel bodyshell, in two-door two-seater open sports style, with optional hardtop. Length 11ft. 4.25in.; width 4ft. 5in.; height 4ft. 1.75in. Unladen weight 1565lb.

Performance: Maximum speed 85mph. 0-60mph 19.8sec. Standing ¼-mile 21.8sec. Typical fuel consumption 37mpg.

Note: From autumn 1962 the engine size was increased to 64.6×83.7mm, 1098cc, and front wheel disc brakes were standardised. From March 1964 rear suspension was by half-elliptic leaf springs with no radius arms. From October 1966 the engine size was increased to 70.6×81.3mm, 1275cc. From autumn 1974 the engine was changed to a Triumph Spitfire unit, 73.7×87.5mm, 1493cc.; Maximum power 65bhp (DIN) at 5500rpm.; maximum torque 77lb.ft. at 3000rpm. Unladen weight 1720lb.

Performance of final version: Maximum speed 101mph. 0-60mph 12.3sec. Standing ¼-mile 18.5sec. Typical fuel consumption 30mpg.

Note: The Austin-Healey Sprite (renamed Austin Sprite in 1971) was mechanically identical to the Midget in every way, and the two cars were built on the same production line.

MG MGA 1600 Mk II

Built: Abingdon, England, 1961 and 1962

The MGA was in production from 1955 to 1962, but the only model which falls within the scope of this book is the 1600 Mk II, which was the last type to be launched, and was only in production for rather more than one year. 8719 examples were built before the model range was phased out in favour of the MGB.

The MGA had originally been designed in the early 1950s (its body style evolved from that of a special MG TD which raced at Le Mans), and a trio of prototypes raced successfully at Le Mans in 1955, before the car was put on sale later that year. As the first new MG produced after the merger of Nuffield and Austin, it was the first to use 'corporate' mechanical parts. The engine, gearbox and axle were all derived from those of the Austin A50.

A feature was the enormously strong box-section chassis frame (too strong, many said – certainly it was heavy), and the very smart body style. Although sold as an open sports car at first, a rather exclusive bubble-top fixed-head coupe with wind-up door windows was also available from 1956, and this choice carried on until the end of production in 1962.

The original engine size was 1489cc, but this became 1588cc in 1959, and – for the final Mk II – 1622cc. The increase, in each case, was achieved by enlarging the cylinder bore, though much more detail work than that was involved. It is worth noting that a twin-overhead camshaft derivative of the 1588cc engine (the Twin Cam) was also built between 1958 and 1960, and that this was matched to a special chassis including

MGA 1600 MkII

four-wheel disc brakes and centre lock disc wheels.

MGA 1600 MkIIs were sold as open or coupe models, and a limited number of 'de Luxe' cars were built — the label indicating that the special Twin Cam chassis, brakes and suspensions had been combined with the normal pushrod overhead valve engine.

More than 101 000 MGAs of all types were built, and this was mostly due to their great popularity in the United States. Not only was the MGA a very attractive car, visually, but it had adequate performance, was rugged, and had quite impeccable road manners. It is a remarkable tribute to the MGB to say that it improved on this in almost every respect.

Specification (MGA 1600 Mk II)

Engine and transmission: Four-cylinders, in-line, with pushrod-operated overhead-valve cylinder head. Bore, stroke and capacity, 76.2×88.9mm, 1622cc. Maximum power 86bhp (net) at 5500rpm.; maximum torque 97lb.ft. at 4000rpm. Four-speed manual gearbox in unit with engine. Hypoid bevel final drive.

Chassis: Front engine, rear drive. Separate pressed steel chassis frame, with box section members. Independent front suspension by coil springs and wishbones. Rack and pinion steering. Rear suspension of live axle by half elliptic leaf springs. Front wheel disc brakes, rear drums.

Bodywork: Pressed-steel body-shell, in two-door two-seater open tourer or fixed head coupe style. Length 13ft. 0in.; width 4ft. 9.25in.; height 4ft. 2in. Unladen weight 1985lb.

Performance Maximum speed 101mph. 0-60mph 13.7sec. Standing ¼-mile 19.1sec. Typical fuel consumption 27mpg.

MG MGB four-cylinder family

Built: Abingdon, England, 1962 to date

With the single exception of the Datsun 240Z range, the MGB is numerically the most successful sporting car built anywhere in the world. Although it was announced in September 1962, and has never been restyled, it is still a very popular car (especially in North America), and more than half a million have now been delivered. Although from time to time MG thought about making a completely new design to replace it, its continuing success (more than 50 000 a year have been sold at times) has made this unnecessary.

Whereas the MGA – which the MGB was to replace – had a massive separate chassis frame, the MGB was designed as a unit-construction shell, following the same philosophy as that adopted for the much smaller Sprite/Midget. Although the original car was an open two-seater, within three-years a very graceful fastback hatchback coupe (called the MGB GT) had been prepared, and the two derivatives have been in production ever since.

Like many previous MGs, the MGB relied on BMC for its major mechanical components. The engine, gearbox and back axle were all closely related to those fitted to mass-production Austin/Morris touring cars. In the 17-years that the car has been in

MGB Roadster, 1962

MGB Roadster, 1975

production, the only significant styling change has been the adoption of the massive black plastic bumpers at front and rear, which many MG devotees do not like, but which allow the car to comply with the latest North American safety regulations. Right through the car's life, the BMC 'B Series' engine had been used, in 1798cc guise, and this is a final development of that used by the MGAs built from 1955 to 1962.

The original gearbox had no synchromesh on first gear, but from the autumn of 1967 a new all-synchromesh gearbox, basically common with that fitted to the then-new Austin 3-litre and to the MGC, was adopted. At the same time Borg Warner automatic transmission became optional, but a lack of demand caused it to be dropped in the mid-1970s. The back axle, too, was changed from the introduction of the MGB GT, and was also common with that used on more powerful MGB derivatives.

Although there have been regular cosmetic changes to the interior of the car, to the badging, and to other detail, the MGBs built at the moment are very similar to those originally designed, which says much for the merit of the original design, and for the conservative taste of the customers. By now, of course, MGBs have been left behind in the performance race, and their main appeal to North American buyers is as convertibles (which have become very rare in that market in recent years). Exhaust emission limitations have taken dreadful toll of the power output, and the later MGBs were certainly no faster than the original MGAs of the 1950s.

All, however, combine elegant good looks with supple roadholding and civilised accommodation, and the fastback GT is still an impressively practical way of combining carrying capacity with a sporting package. Predictably enough, the vast majority of all MGBs built have been sold in North America.

Specification

Engine and transmission: Four-cylinders, in-line, with pushrod-operated overhead-valve cylinder head. Bore, stroke and capacity 80.26 × 88.9mm., 1798cc. Maximum power 95bhp (net) at 5400rpm.; maximum torque 110lb.ft. at 3000rpm.; subsequently recalibrated to 84bhp (DIN) at 5250rpm.; maximum torque 104lb.ft. at 2500rpm. Four-speed manual gearbox with optional overdrive (standard from 1975) or optional Borg Warner three-speed automatic transmission (1967-1973) in unit with engine. Hypoid bevel final drive.

Chassis: Front engine, rear drive. Unit-construction pressed-steel body/chassis unit. Independent front suspension by coil springs and wishbones. Rack and pinion steering. Rear suspension of live rear axle by half-elliptic leaf springs. Front wheel disc brakes, rear drums.

Bodywork: Pressed-steel bodyshell in unit with structure, in two-door two-seater tourer or three-door two-seater fastback coupe. Length 12ft. 9.3in.; width 4ft. 11.7in.; height 4ft. 1.4in. Unladen weight 2030lb. (From autumn 1974, with 'soft' nose/tail bumpers, length increased to 13ft. 2.25in.; height 4ft. 2.9in.).

Performance: Maximum speed 103mph. 0-60mph 12.2sec. Standing ¼-mile 18.7sec. Typical fuel consumption 25mpg.

MGB Cutaway

MG MGC

Built: Abingdon, England, 1967 to 1969

By the time the original 4-cylinder MGB had successfully been launched, the Austin-Healey 3000s which were also assembled at Abingdon were beginning to look old-fashioned. BMC, the masters of MG, therefore decided that a more powerful version of the MGB should be developed to replace it, and to extend the MGB range. The 3-litre MGC of which more than 9000 examples were to be built in less than two years, was the result.

Although the two cars look nearly identical at a casual glance, they were fundamentally different underneath. A lengthy Austin six-cylinder engine (which was not at all the same unit as that used in the Austin-Healey) provided the power, but to accommodate its bulk a new type of front suspension, by wishbones and longitudinal torsion bars, had to be designed. This, together with the new all-synchromesh gearbox, and larger wheels, made the new car, dubbed MGC, a very different animal.

It is now well-documented history that in MG terms the MGC was not a success, as

MGC Roadster

its handling, balance, and general response, was not what the public apparently wanted. There is an enthusiastic faction, still, which claims that the MGC's purpose was, and is, misunderstood, and that it does the job it set out to do very competently. It is true, however, that compared with the MGB the car was nose-heavy, prone to understeer, and did not have a very free-revving engine.

Visually, and in its cockpit appointments, the MGC was very similar to the MGB, and only the bonnet bulges and the larger wheels give the game away. Like MGBs of the period, there were two body styles – open sports and fastback hatchback GT; a buyer could have manual transmission, an optional overdrive, or automatic transmission.

Production was discontinued in 1969, a year after the formation of British Leyland, and there is evidence to suggest that the MGC (by then a much-improved car) might have continued if BMC had kept their independence. Philosophically, the MGC was succeeded by the MGB V8, after a four-year gap.

Specification

Engine and transmission: Six-cylinders, in-line, with pushrod-operated overhead-valve cylinder head. Bore, stroke and capacity 83.34 × 88.9mm., 2912cc. Maximum power 145bhp (net) at 5250rpm.; maximum torque 170lb.ft. at 3400rpm. Four-speed manual gearbox, optional overdrive, or optional three-speed Borg Warner automatic transmission in unit with engine. Hypoid bevel final drive.

Chassis: Front engine, rear drive. Unit construction pressed steel body/chassis unit. Independent front suspension by torsion bars and wishbones. Rack and pinion steering. Rear suspension of live axle by half-elliptic leaf springs. Front wheel disc brakes, rear drums.

Bodywork: Pressed-steel bodyshell in unit with structure, in two-door two-seater tourer or three-door two-seater fastback GT coupe. Length 12ft. 9.2in.; width 5ft. 0in.; height 4ft. 2.25in. Unladen weight **(Tourer):** 2460lb **(GT):** 2610lb.

Performance: Maximum speed 120mph. 0-60mph 10.0sec. Standing ¼-mile 17.7sec. Typical fuel consumption 19mpg.

MG MGB GT V8

Built: Abingdon, England, 1973 to 1976

After the six-cylinder MGC had been dropped, only the very successful four-cylinder MGB was in production at Abingdon for some time. However, a demand for more powerful versions appeared to exist. Now that Rover were a constituent firm in British Leyland, of which MG was a part, their light-alloy 3.5-litre vee-8 looked attractive both in engineering and marketing terms. In a programme pushed through with some urgency, therefore, MG produced the MGB GT V8, which was really a marriage between the existing car and the big Rover engine.

It is important to make it clear that the MGB GT V8 was not derived from the MGC, as that car's torsion bar suspension and bodyshell was not used. In fact the Rover engine was only a few pounds heavier than the four-cylinder engine it displaced, so no more than minor suspension changes were needed for it. Yet another set of gear ratios were derived, and for marketing reasons only the closed GT type of body was offered.

Like the MGC, however, the GT V8 had a very short life. It was announced in 1973 and was withdrawn in 1976, after a mere 2591 examples had been built. Various explanations have been made for this, the most compelling being that Rover could never supply enough engines to satisfy the demand, but the real and basic problem appears to have been that the car looked visually like the four-cylinder car, and it carried a relatively high price.

MGB GT V8

Even so, it combined the elegance and practicality of the MGB GT with refined and silky engine behaviour, and was really very fast by most standards. It is a car which will undoubtedly become a collector's item in years to come.

Since 1976, MG have made no further attempt to market a high-powered version of their long-running MGB.

Specification

Engine and transmission: Eight-cylinders, in 90-degree vee-formation, with pushrod-operated overhead-valve cylinder heads, built by Rover. Bore, stroke and capacity 88.9×71.1mm., 3528cc. 137bhp (DIN) at 5000rpm.; maximum torque 193lb.ft. at 2900rpm. Four-speed manual gearbox and overdrive in unit with engine. Hypoid bevel final drive.

Chassis: Front engine, rear drive. Unit construction pressed steel body/chassis unit. Independent front suspension by coil springs and wishbones. Rack and pinion steering. Suspension of rear live axle by half-elliptic leaf springs. Front wheel disc brakes, rear drums.

Bodywork: Pressed-steel bodyshell, in three-door two-seater fastback GT coupe style. Length 12ft. 10.7in. (13ft. 2.25in. from autumn 1974); width 5ft. 0in.; height 4ft. 2in. (4ft. 3in. from autumn 1974). Unladen weight 2390lb.

Performance: Maximum speed 124mph. 0-60mph 8.6sec. Standing ¼-mile 16.4sec. Typical fuel consumption 25mpg.

MGB GT V8 engine compartment

Mercedes-Benz 190SL

Built: Stuttgart, Germany, 1954 to 1962

Although this car is really a product of the 1950s, it was produced at Sindelfingen, near Stuttgart, until the end of 1962. Throughout this time, Mercedes-Benz had two entirely different types of sports car on sale – the 300SL, which was in every way a Supercar, and the 190SL, which was much less adventurous, technically, and rather more of a 'Touring' sports machine.

After the end of the second world war, it was some time before Mercedes-Benz could rebuild their factories, and their sales, to allow postwar designs to evolve. The 300SL had already been raced in prototype form, and a production car was no great surprise, but the launch of the 190SL was unexpected.

However, in entirely logical ways, its engineering was closely based on that of the 180/220 saloon cars which were the first of the truly postwar models. The floorpan of the unit-construction bodyshell was derived from that of the 180, as were the suspension units and many other details. Swing axle rear suspension was a feature, but as the performance of the car was relatively restricted this did not excite much adverse comment from road testers or customers.

Remarkably, in the nine-years during which it was on the market, the 190SL received little obvious attention, either from stylists or engineers, though it was improved in detail.

Mercedes-Benz 190SL

Specification

Engine and transmission: Four-cylinders, in-line, with single-overhead camshaft cylinder head. Bore, stroke and capacity 85×83.6mm, 1897cc. Maximum power 105bhp (gross) at 5800rpm.; maximum torque 114lb.ft. at 3800rpm. Four-speed manual gearbox in unit with engine. Hypoid bevel final drive.

Chassis: Front engine, rear drive. Pressed-steel unit construction shell. Independent front suspension by coil springs and wishbones. Recirculating ball steering. Independent rear suspension by coil springs and swing axles. Four wheel drum brakes.

Bodywork: Pressed-steel, two-door two-seater shell (in unit with chassis), in open sports or hardtop style. Length 14ft. 0.8in.; width 5ft. 8.5in.; height 4ft. 4in. Unladen weight 2515lb.

Performance: Maximum speed 107mph. 0-60mph. 13.3sec. Standing ¼-mile 17.8sec. Typical fuel consumption 24mpg.

Mercedes-Benz 230SL/250SL/280SL family

Built: Stuttgart, Germany, 1963 to 1971

By the beginning of the 1960s, Mercedes-Benz had expanded mightily. They turned attention to their sporting models, realised that the 190SL was beginning to look somewhat old-fashioned, and decided that the 300SL was far too complex and specialised to sell much longer in any number. In 1963, therefore, they replaced both the old models with a single new design — the 230SL.

Mercedes-Benz 230SL

If for no other reason, the 230SL will always be remembered for its unique 'pagoda-roof' hardtop body style. This, Mercedes-Benz point out with truth, was not adopted to lower the roof line, but to make the side vision and glass area bigger than would otherwise have been possible. One must note, however, that the car was sold either as an open tourer, with folding hood, or with this massive but detachable hardtop.

Like the 190SL before it, the 230SL was closely based on touring car engineering; in this case, much of the chassis was derived from the well-known and popular 220SE saloon, along with the enlarged engine, and the choice of manual or automatic transmissions. Unlike the 190SL, however, the new car had the later type of low-pivot swing-axle rear suspension, which made cornering behaviour 'on the limit' more predictable. By comparison with the 190SL, the new car was much sleeker, more stylish, better equipped and considerably faster. By comparison with the 300SL it was rather slower, but mechanically more simple and considerably more easy to service and maintain.

It was a success at once, and in the gruelling Liège-Rome-Liège marathon rally later in the year a factory-entered example was driven to a conclusive victory by Eugen Bohringer. This served to prove both performance and strength. The styling, meantime, rapidly gained acceptance, and the car was soon selling well all over the world. In that the 230SL was more of a mature man's sports car than earlier cars had been, it is not surprising that many examples were built with automatic transmission. This, incidentally, was Mercedes-Benz's own design, combining a simple fluid-flywheel with a four-speed epicyclic gearbox.

During the life of the car, however, it began to be overhauled in performance terms by its competitors, particularly in the United States. Fortunately, larger derivatives of the engine were already available, and there was no great problem in adapting them to the 230SL's chassis. Even so, it was very puzzling that the factory should adopt what we know now as the 'interim' engine of 2496cc (thus producing the 250SL) for just one year, and follow this by fitting the 2778cc engine (and thus making the basic design into the 280SL), which carried on for three more seasons.

As the years passed, however, Mercedes-Benz cars in general had become larger, plushier, and more costly, so it was no surprise when the 280SL was replaced, in 1971, by altogether larger cars with even greater performance.

Specification (Original 230SL model)

Engine and transmission: Six-cylinders, in-line, with single-overhead-camshaft cylinder head. Bore, stroke and capacity 82×72.8mm, 2308cc. Maximum power 170bhp (gross) at 5600rpm.; maximum torque 159lb.ft. at 4500rpm. Four-speed manual gearbox or optional Mercedes-Benz four-speed automatic gearbox in unit with engine. Hypoid bevel final drive.

Chassis: Front engine, rear drive. Pressed-steel unit construction body/chassis unit. Independent front suspension by coil springs and wishbones. Recirculating ball, with optional power assistance. Independent rear suspension with coil springs and low-pivot swing axles. Front wheel disc brakes, rear drums.

Bodywork: Pressed-steel, two-door two-seater in open sports, convertible, or hardtop style with 'Pagoda' roof. Length 14ft. 1.5in.; width 5ft. 9.2in.; height 4ft. 3.5in. Unladen weight from 2855lb.

Performance (230SL): Maximum speed 120mph. 0-60mph 10.7sec. Standing ¼-mile 17.5sec. Typical fuel consumption 26mpg. **(280SL):** Maximum speed 114mph. 0-60mph 9.9sec. Standing ¼-mile 17.1sec. Typical fuel consumption 23mpg.

Mercedes-Benz 350SL/450SLC family

Built: Stuttgart, Germany, 1971 to 1979

As the Mercedes-Benz combine moved towards the 1970s, it was making more and more cars, of higher and higher performance, and was selling to a very sophisticated class of customer. When a successor to the well-established 230SL/280SL model was needed, therefore, it was decided to build an altogether more complex, versatile and faster range of cars.

The first of these cars appeared in 1971, but most of the range had been launched within a couple of years. Like the superseded 280SLs, these cars shared their chassis and power train engineering with a Mercedes-Benz touring car, in this case the S-Class saloons and coupes, though with a special floorpan and entirely special styling and body superstructure. The 'smaller' of the two Mercedes-Benz vee-8 engines was specified in each case, though both sizes − 3.5 or 4.5-litre − rapidly became available.

Unlike the old 280SL, this was meant to be a complete range of cars. Not only was there a choice of fuel-injected vee-8 engine size, but there would be two wheelbases. The short-wheelbase cars, known as 350SLs and 450SLs, could be built as convertibles, or with removable hardtops, while the longer-wheelbase models (longer by 14 inches) would only be sold with permanently attached coupe roofs. These were the 350SLC/450SLC models, which were also distinguished by having close-coupled four-seater passenger accommodation.

Without the fuel crisis (and the hoist in petrol prices which followed) of 1973, it is doubtful if the range would have been further enlarged. As a direct result of this, however, came the 2.8-litre twin-cam six-cylinder versions (280SL) which used engines also 'borrowed' from another Mercedes-Benz saloon car.

More exciting for the enthusiast, however, was the rather special and very powerful version of the 450SLC, which was the 5.0-litre derivative. This used a

Mercedes-Benz 450SLC

Mercedes-Benz 350SL

developed version of the vee-8 engine, enlarged to 5025cc, notable for its use of a light-alloy cylinder block (the other engines have a cast-iron block), and disposing of no less than 240bhp at 5000rpm. In the context of this book, the 450SLC 5.0 is probably a Supercar, but performance figures for this exciting car are not yet available.

In every way these cars are massive, typically Teutonic, very reliable, and not at all as ponderous as their bare specification might suggest. 450SLCs, after all, dominated the 1978 Round South America marathon, while cars fitted with the latest engines failed only narrowly to win the East African Safari rally and won the Bandama rally in 1979.

There is no doubt, however, that they are extremely complex, and cannot be maintained by the average owner. But it is some years since a Mercedes car was sold to an 'average' buyer, so the factory do not mind this. They are interested only in building the best possible car, and – for its purpose – the 350SL/450SLC family approaches this concept fairly well.

219

Specification (350SL)

Engine and transmission: Eight-cylinders, in 90-degree vee-formation, with single-overhead-camshaft cylinder heads. Bore, stroke and capacity 92 × 65.8mm, 3499cc. Maximum power 200bhp (DIN) at 5800rpm.; maximum torque 211lb.ft. at 4000rpm. Four-speed or five-speed manual gearbox or Mercedes-Benz three-speed automatic transmission in unit with engine. Hypoid bevel final drive.

Chassis: Front engine, rear drive. Pressed-steel unit construction body/chassis unit. Independent front suspension by coil springs and wishbones. Power assisted recirculating ball steering. Independent rear suspension by coil springs and semi-trailing wishbones. Four wheel disc brakes.

Bodywork: Pressed-steel, two-door 2 + 2-seater, in open sports, convertible or hardtop style. Length 14ft. 4.1in.; width 5ft. 10.5in.; height 4ft. 5in. Unladen weight from 3400lb.

Performance (350SL): (Four-speed manual) Maximum speed 126mph. 0-60mph 9.3sec. Standing ¼-mile 17.0sec. Typical fuel consumption 15mpg. **(350SLC)** Maximum speed 124mph. 0-60mph 10.9sec. Standing ¼-mile 18.4sec. Typical fuel consumption 20mpg.

Note: This basic car was also sold with a six-cylinder twin-overhead-camshaft engine (86 × 78.8mm, 2746cc. Maximum power 185bhp (DIN) at 5800rpm; maximum torque 177lb.ft. at 4500rpm), or with the 4.5-litre engine of the 450SLC.

Specification (450SLC)

Engine and transmission: Eight-cylinders, in 90-degree vee-formation, with single-overhead-camshaft cylinder heads. Bore, stroke and capacity 92 × 85mm, 4520cc. Maximum power 217bhp (DIN) at 5000rpm.; maximum torque 265lb.ft. at 3250rpm. Four-speed, five-speed or Mercedes-Benz three-speed automatic transmission in unit with engine. Hypoid bevel final drive.

Chassis: Front engine, rear drive. Pressed-steel unit-construction body/chassis unit. Independent front suspension by coil springs and wishbones. Power-assisted recirculating ball steering. Independent rear suspension by coil springs and semi-trailing wishbones. Four wheel disc brakes.

Bodywork: Pressed-steel, two-door close-coupled four-seater, in coupe body style. Length 15ft. 7in.; width 5ft. 10.5in.; height 4ft. 4.4in. Unladen weight 3595lb.

Performance: (Automatic version) Maximum speed 136mph. 0-60mph 9.0sec. Standing ¼-mile 16.9sec. Typical fuel consumption 15.5mpg.

Note: This basic car was also sold with the same 2.8-litre six-cylinder and 3.5-litre vee-8 engines as are offered for the 350SL. In addition there was the 450SLC 5.0, with bore, stroke and capacity of 97 × 85mm, 5025cc. Maximum power 240bhp (DIN) at 5000rpm.; maximum torque 296lb.ft. at 3200rpm.

NSU Sport Prinz

Built: Neckarsulm, Germany, 1960-1968

It is not going too far to suggest that the little NSU Sport Prinz was really a sheep in wolf's clothing, as its very stylish fastback Bertone coupe body concealed nothing more dramatic and effective than a two-cylinder 598cc engine. For all that, it was still quite a notable little car, which found its own limited but steady market.

The Prinz itself was NSU's own mincar design of the 1950s and, in the manner of the day, had a rear-engine layout. The Prinz, however, had its parallel twin-cylinder water-cooled engine mounted transversely behind the line of the final drive. The original car was an ugly little beast, and the Prinz IV of 1961 (with Corvair-like styling) came along *after* the Bertone coupe was finished. It was therefore quite remarkable that Bertone even took the trouble to make this silk purse out of what was undoubtedly a sow's ear at first.

The car's engineering was in steel, based on the pressed-steel floorpan of the saloon, and included four-wheel independent suspension. Front wheel disc brakes were added to the specification from 1965. Although not commercially important itself, it was significant because Bertone developed a spider version, and this was given the single-cylinder NSU Wankel engine to become the world's first Wankel-engined car to be sold commercially.

NSU Sport Prinz

Specification

Engine and transmission: Two-cylinders, in-line, with single-overhead-camshaft cylinder head. Bore, stroke and capacity 76×66mm, 598cc. Maximum power 30bhp (DIN) at 5500rpm; maximum torque 33lb.ft. at 3250rpm. Four-speed gearbox in unit with engine and transaxle.

Chassis: Rear engine, rear drive. Unit-construction bodyshell, styled by Bertone. Independent front suspension by coil springs and wishbones. Rack and pinion steering. Independent rear suspension by coil springs, swing axles, and supplementary air suspension units. Front wheel disc brakes (from 1965), rear drums.

Bodywork: Pressed-steel coupe unit-construction bodyshell, with 2 + 2 seating. Length 11ft. 8.1in.; width 5ft. 0in.; height 4ft. 0.6in. Unladen weight 1225lb.

Performance: Maximum speed 75mph. 0-60mph 27.7sec. Standing ¼-mile 23.5sec. Typical fuel consumption 42mpg.

NSU Wankel Spider

Built: Neckarsulm, Germany, 1963 to 1966

Felix Wankel persuaded NSU to be the very first car manufacturers to take up his revolutionary (in more ways than one!) new engine design. Before NSU decided to commit the Wankel layout for fullscale production in twin-rotor form (in the Ro80 saloon), they thought it prudent to make a limited number of single rotor engines. By mating this with the small NSU chassis, they would gain experience and public acceptance at the same time.

It was decided to make the short-run car into a sports machine, so the Wankel engine was installed in the rear of a Bertone-styled open Spider derivative of the Sport Prinz, and the rest of the chassis was virtually unchanged. Although this was a true rear engined car (that is to say that the engine was behind the line of the rear wheels) the handling was perfectly acceptable, even though there was considerably more performance than that available in the Sport Prinz coupe.

Customers soon found that the single-rotor engine was by no means as free of vibration as the early publicity had implied, even though it revved very freely, and they later discovered all the snags of being 'guinea-pigs' for the factory. Wankel engine reliability in those days was by no means acceptable, and many engines needed to be changed after less than a year's life after rotor seals wore out, or chambers cracked under thermal stresses.

NSU Spider (Wankel)

Although the nominal capacity of the single-rotor unit was 500cc, the fact that there were effectively twice as many firing impulses per revolution as compared with a piston engine meant that the Wankel Spider was always thought of as a 1-litre sports car. By these standards, and in comparison with cars like the MG Midget and Triumph Spitfire, its performance was competitive without being in any way remarkable.

Like the Sport Prinz, however, the Spider was distinguished with fine Italian-inspired styling, and all-independent suspension. With greater reliability it might have become a firm favourite. However, NSU were content with the exposure and the experience gained, and withdrew the model as they prepared to produce large numbers of the Ro80 saloon cars. No other Wankel-engined NSU (or NSU-badged VW – the merger took place in spring 1969) has ever been built since then.

Specification

Engine and transmission: Single rotor Wankel engine, nominal capacity 1000cc, actual capacity of chambers 500cc. Maximum power 50bhp (DIN) at 6000rpm; maximum torque 52lb.ft. at 2500rpm. Four-speed gearbox in unit with engine and transaxle. Spiral bevel final drive.

Chassis: Rear engine, rear drive. Unit-construction bodyshell, styled by Bertone. Independent front suspension by coil springs and wishbones. Rack and pinion steering. Independent rear suspension by coil springs and semi-trailing arms. Front wheel disc brakes, rear drums.

Bodywork: Pressed-steel open sports two-seater bodyshell. Length 11ft. 11in.; width 5ft. 0in.; height 4ft. 1.6in. Unladen weight 1545lb.

Performance: Maximum speed 92mph. 0-60mph 16.7sec. Standing ¼-mile 20.5sec. Typical fuel consumption 31mpg.

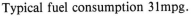

Opel GT

Built: Russelsheim, Germany, 1968 to 1973

Like other famous cars which evolved only from a pretty idea, the Opel GT was the direct descendant of a 'show special' or 'dream car', first displayed by Opel at the Frankfurt Motor Show of 1965. At the time they publicly stated that they had no intention of making the cars in quantity, and that in view of the demand (which they thought would be limited) it would have been uneconomic to do so. Less than three years later, the philosophical somersault was complete. The Opel GT went into production, and Opel had got round the problem of bodyshell production by contracting this out to Brissoneau and Lotz of France.

The shell was built up from steel pressings, and was based on the floorpan of the Kadett saloon, along with its suspensions, and the choice of engines already found in that car. There were two versions − 1100 and 1900 − of which the 1897cc engined 1900 was the most popular. The GT was a great departure for Opel who, although in

Opel GT, 1100cc

the course of thoroughly modernising their image, were still thought to make a series of boring, stodgy, if reliable, cars in the true General Motors tradition. The GT, therefore, was a very engaging first step towards the new more sporting image, which carried on in the 1970s with cars like the Manta and the smart Rekord and Commodore Coupes.

The GT was only ever sold as a strict two-seater fixed-head coupe car, and it is instructive to compare its overall shape with that of the long-running Corvette, which had also been introduced to the public as a 'dream car', the Mako Shark. Although there are some superficial detail resemblances to the Lotus Elan (such as the pop-up, or rather swivel-up, headlamps), this seems to be no more than coincidence. British and Commonwealth customers were always unhappy to know that no right-hand-drive version was ever made.

It was the first and last two-seater Opel to be made in the postwar period, and Opel show no signs of getting back into that market.

Specification

Engine and transmission: Four-cylinders, in-line, with camshaft-in-head valve gear layout. Bore, stroke and capacity 93 × 69.8mm, 1897cc. Maximum power 90bhp (DIN) at 5100rpm; maximum torque 108lb.ft. at 2500rpm. Four-speed gearbox or optional GM automatic transmission, in unit with engine. Hypoid bevel final drive.

Chassis: Front engine, rear drive. Unit-construction bodyshell, of steel-pressings, by Brissoneau & Lotz of France. Independent front suspension by wishbones and transverse leaf spring. Rack and pinion steering. Rear suspension of live axle by coil springs, radius arms and Panhard rod. Front wheel disc brakes, rear drums.

Bodywork: Pressed-steel bodyshell, available only as two-door two-seater coupe body style. Length 13ft. 6in.; width 5ft. 2in.; height 4ft. 0.2in. Unladen weight 2110lb.

Performance: (1900) Maximum speed 115mph. 0-60mph 12.0sec. Standing ¼-mile 18.6sec. Typical fuel consumption 30mpg.

Note: Optional 1100cc version had bore, stroke and capacity of 75 × 61mm, 1078cc. Maximum power 60bhp (DIN) at 5200rpm; maximum torque 61lb.ft. at 3800rpm. Automatic transmission not available. Unladen weight 1865lb.

Panhard 24CT

Built: Paris, France, 1964-1967

Panhard was one of the longest-established of all the world's car makers, and certainly one of its most famous for years, but by the 1950s it had lost most of its 'image'. Financial trouble led to Citroen taking an interest in 1955, and a complete takeover followed in 1965. In the meantime, however, Citroen had influenced the design of a new car with typically idiosynchratic styling. This was the 24CT, announced in 1964, which was in fact to be the last Panhard model of all.

Although the styling was certainly distinctive (as Citroen's own DS19 had been in 1955), it concealed some familiar engineering. The basis of the design was the floorpan, engine and transmission of the now obsolete PL17 Panhards, of which the engine and transmission dated back to the 1940s and the original postwar Gregoire design which set Panhard on its feet after the hostilities were over. The flat-twin engine was air-cooled, and lay ahead of the final drive, and a feature was that the valve springs, most unusually, were torsion bars, not the more usual coils.

The 24CT was the faster sporting coupe — its makers claimed 100mph maximum

Panhard 24CT

speed from the 50bhp car, however 90mph was nearer the mark — there was also a 24C which had more space, but was considerably less powerful.

Like the Panhard Tigre before it (which had, after all, won a Monte Carlo Rally whose rules had been especially written to make that possible) the 24CT had good performance for its weight and engine size, and had its adherents, but Citroen (who were not too financially well off themselves) soon despaired of turning this shaky firm into a profit maker. In 1967 the last Panhard was built, and the factory space was integrated into the Citroen facilities.

Specification

Engine and transmission: Two-cylinders, horizontally-opposed, with pushrod-operated overhead-valve cylinder heads. Air-cooled. Bore, stroke and capacity 84.85 × 75mm, 848cc. Maximum power 50bhp (DIN) at 5800rpm; maximum torque 56lb.ft. at 3500rpm. Four-speed gearbox in unit with engine and transaxle. Spiral bevel final drive.

Chassis: Front engine, front drive. Unit-construction bodyshell, of steel-pressings. Independent front suspension by transverse leaf springs. Rack and pinion steering. Rear suspension of dead axle by torsion bars and radius arms. Four-wheel drum brakes.

Bodywork: Pressed-steel bodyshell, available as two-door 2+2 coupe style only. Length 14ft. 0in.; width 5ft. 3.8in.; height 4ft. 0in. Unladen weight 1850lb.

Performance: Maximum speed 89mph. 0-60mph 22.3sec. Standing ¼-mile 22.5sec. Typical fuel consumption 35mpg.

Porsche 356 family

Built: Stuttgart, Germany, 1949 to 1965

Although Dr. Ferdinand Porsche had been world-famous for many years, he did not make cars badged with his own name until the late 1940s. These were originally assembled in Austria, but almost immediately production was centred in Stuttgart, where the company's facilities have remained ever since.

That original design, based so closely on the VW Beetle, remained on sale until the mid 1960s, though in detail its layout became more and more specialised, less and less VW, as the years passed. By the beginning of the 1960s, with the firm's designers concentrating on a new design (the 912/911 family) the 356 range had settled down. There were four basic variants of the aircooled rear-engined design – the 60bhp, 75bhp and 90bhp overhead-valve engined cars, and the very special twin-cam Carrera 2 car, with its race-proved and completely different flat-four engine.

Even though the cheapest and least powerful version could achieve more than 100mph, all except the Carrera models had to make do with drum brakes (the later Carreras had four-wheel discs), and all had simple swing axle suspension, which was refined and refined, but which nevertheless lead to dramatic oversteering handling characteristics when the cars were driven over their natural limits.

Porsche 356

Even so, customers flocked to buy these Porsches, not only because they were stylish and effective, but because they were now known to be extremely reliable and long-lived, and because they had a great deal of that particular 'Porsche' character which means so much to that sort of buyer. It has often been said that the 356 design as a whole was a great triumph of development over design, which is perhaps unkind but demonstrably true. To use the VW Beetle's basic chassis layout, with trailing link front suspension and high-pivot swing axle rear suspension, was to invite road-holding problems, and only the most diehard Porsche enthusiasts would say that these had been overcome by the time the model had been dropped.

This, of course, made Porsche motoring completely distinctive, for no other manufacturer was producing the same sort of car; and certainly not with an air-cooled engine mounted in the rear, combined with a wind-cheating shape. A characteristic, of the engine was that it was essentially a low-revving unit, and because the car was high-geared to suit this, the result was that it could be both quiet, and relatively economical.

It was because of this unique combination of very saleable qualities that Porsche had a great dilemma with the launch of the 911 family in 1963, and why they had to produce the Type 912 as a half-way house between the two very different machines.

Specification

Engine and transmission: Four-cylinders, air-cooled, horizontally opposed, with pushrod-operated overhead-valve cylinder heads. Bore, stroke and capacity 82.5 × 74mm., 1582cc. (1600 model) Maximum power 60bhp (net) at 4500rpm.; maximum torque 82lb.ft. at 2800rpm. (1600S model) 75bhp (net) at 5000rpm.; maximum torque 88lb.ft. at 3700rpm. (Super 90 model) 90bhp (net) at 5500rpm.; maximum torque 99lb.ft. at 4300rpm. Four-speed manual gearbox in unit with engine and transaxle. Spiral bevel final drive.

Chassis: Rear engine, rear drive. Pressed-steel platform type chassis, with body welded to it on assembly. Independent front suspension by torsion bars and trailing arms. Worm and peg steering. Independent rear suspension by transverse torsion bars, swing axles and radius arms. Four wheel drum brakes.

Bodywork: Pressed-steel two-door, two-seater in fastback coupe or cabriolet style. Length 13ft. 2in.; width 5ft. 5in.; height 4ft. 4in. Unladen weight (depending on engine) from 2060lb.

Performance: (60bhp model) Maximum speed 102mph. 0-60mph 14.1sec. Standing ¼-mile 19.1sec. Typical fuel consumption 33mpg. **(90bhp model)** Maximum speed 111mph. 0-60mph 11.5sec. Standing ¼-mile 18.3sec. Typical fuel consumption 26mpg.

Note: The Carrera 2 model was basically the same car, with the following important differences. Twin-overhead-camshaft cylinder heads. Bore, stroke and capacity 92 × 74mm., 1966cc. Maximum power 130bhp (DIN) at 6200rpm.; maximum torque 119lb.ft. at 4600rpm. Four-wheel disc brakes. Unladen weight 2230lb.

Porsche 912

Built: Stuttgart, Germany, 1965 to 1969 (Reintroduced for USA, 1976/1977)

When Porsche put the flat-6 911 series into full scale production in 1964, they realised that they were moving up to an entirely different market sector from that covered by the old 356 series, which was about to be phased out. As an interim 'gap-bridging' model, therefore, they produced the 912 type, which was effectively the 911 coupe with the old 1582cc pushrod overhead-valve 356 engine, coupled to rather less complete equipment and a considerably lower price. The performance, however, was still very competitive – road-test cars could achieve nearly 120mph.

The 912's development was carried out in parallel with that of the 911, which is to say that wheel rim widths were increased at the same time, and that the wheelbase was increased in the autumn of 1968. Four-speed or five-speed gearboxes were both available, though Sportomatic transmission was not made available as it would have taken away too much of the car's performance.

To rationalise the range, and to allow more of the prestigious 911s to be made, the 912 was phased out in the summer of 1969. However, there was an intriguing but short-lived sequel, for in 1976 and 1977 Porsche re-introduced a 912 (the 912E) for United States sales only. This car had the old four-cylinder engine, but in 2-litre VW-Porsche form with fuel-injection. Its place has now been completely taken over by 924 derivatives.

Porsche 912

Specification

Engine and transmission: Four-cylinders, aircooled, horizontally-opposed, with pushrod-operated overhead-valve cylinder heads. Bore, stroke and capacity 82.5 × 74mm., 1582cc. Maximum power 90bhp (net) at 5800rpm.; maximum torque 90lb.ft. at 3600rpm. Four-speed or five-speed manual gearbox in unit with transaxle. Spiral bevel final drive.

Chassis: Rear engine, rear drive. Unit-construction, pressed-steel body-chassis unit. Independent front suspension by torsion bars and wishbones. Rack and pinion steering. Independent rear suspension by transverse torsion bars and semi-trailing wishbones. Four wheel disc brakes.

Bodywork: Pressed-steel body in two-door 2 + 2 seater fastback coupe style. Length 13ft. 8in.; width 5ft. 3.5in.; height 4ft. 4in. Unladen weight 2135lb.

Performance (912): Maximum speed 119mph. 0-60mph 11.9sec. Standing ¼-mile 18.2sec. Typical fuel consumption 25mpg. **(2-litre 912E):** Maximum speed 115mph. 0-60mph 11.3sec. Standing ¼-mile 18.2sec. Typical fuel consumption 29mpg.

Porsche 924 family

Built: Neckarsulm, Germany, 1975 to date

Ever since the firm had been founded in the 1940s, Porsche had built nothing but rear-engined cars with aircooled horizontally-opposed engines. It therefore came as a terrible shock to many people when the 924 was announced with a watercooled engine, of in-line layout, mounted at the front and driving the rear wheels!

The 924, in fact, originally started life as a VW-Audi project, designed on their behalf by Porsche, but at a fairly late stage changed to becoming a pure Porsche, but was to be built at the ex-NSU factory at Neckarsulm which VW had owned since 1969. Indeed, the 928 Supercar which followed it was actually schemed out earlier, but had to be postponed to make way for this commercially important machine.

As a VW-Audi project, it was laid out to make as much use as possible of that group's components, which explains the 2-litre Audi engine, VW Golf front suspension and VW Beetle-derived rear suspension, along with K70 brakes and many other smaller but still vital components. Although the body is a conventional-looking 2 + 2 seater hatchback in pressed-steel, it hides a combined transaxle (final drive and gearbox) at the rear, which is in effect a repositioned component from the front-wheel-drive Audi 100. Engine and transaxle are connected by a rigid steel tube, in Alfetta fashion, and the result is a very well-balanced structure which works well.

The family has already expanded to include a splendid turbocharged version, and different models have four-speed, five-speed or automatic transmissions.

By comparison with the long-running Porsche 911 family, the 924s are almost diametrically different, but they point the way to Porsche's long-term future. Styling, as one would expect from Porsche, is at once simple and distinctive, and there is a really marked similarity to the entirely Porsche-built 928, which nevertheless has a completely different bodyshell. The 924 is selling in larger quantities than any previous Porsche, and is really the spiritual successor to the mid-engined VW-Porsches, which were also conceived, developed, and manufactured in the same cooperative venture.

Porsche 924

Porsche 924 'Celebration'

The 924, too, is something of a throwback to the old Porsche 356 style, where the engineering was rather simple, but the execution rather special, and where a completely new (lower) level of prices has been achieved. There seems to be no doubt that it will continue to sell for many years to come, and that − like the 911 family − its variants will continue to appear, in more and more types. Eventually, a convertible version should not be ruled out.

Specification

Engine and transmission: Four-cylinders, in-line, with single-overhead-camshaft cylinder head. Bore, stroke and capacity 86.5 × 84.4mm., 1984cc. **(Standard model)** Maximum power 125bhp (DIN) at 5800rpm.; maximum torque 121lb.ft. at 3500rpm. **(Turbo model)** Maximum power 170bhp (DIN) at 5500rpm.; maximum torque 181lb.ft. at 3500rpm. Four-speed or five-speed manual gearbox, or three-speed automatic gearbox (depending on model) in unit with hypoid bevel final drive.
Chassis: Front engine, rear drive. Unit-construction, pressed-steel body-chassis unit. Independent front suspension by coil springs and MacPherson struts. Rack and pinion steering. Independent rear suspension by torsion bars and semi-trailing wishbones. Front wheel disc brakes and rear drums on normal models, four wheel disc brakes on Turbo models.
Bodywork: Pressed-steel body on two-door 2 + 2 fastback coupe style. (Standard model) Length 13ft. 8.2in.; (Turbo) 13ft. 9.3in.; width 5ft. 5.2in.; height 4ft. 1.6in. Unladen weight, depending on model, 2380lb. to 2600lb.
Performance: (Standard model) Maximum speed 126mph. 0-60mph 9.5sec. Standing ¼-mile 17.2sec. Typical fuel consumption 23mpg. **(Turbo)** Maximum speed 142mph. **0-60mph 6.9sec. Standing ¼-mile 15.0sec. Typical fuel consumption 22mpg.**

Renault 17TS & Gordini

Built: Paris, France, 1971-1976

The Renault 15/17 range, still in production in truncated form at the end of the 1970s, was a classic case of an ordinary car turned into something really special at the top of its range. Whereas the Renault 15s were little more than special-bodied Renault 12s, the 17TS/Gordini cars were altogether more exciting.

The range was announced in the autumn of 1971, when it was seen to be yet another clever combination of existing Renault components, all hidden away under a coupe shape. The basis of the design was the mundane front-wheel-drive Renault 12's floorpan, engine/transmission layout and suspensions. In this instance, therefore, the four-cylinder engines were ahead of the line of the front wheels, while the transmission was behind, and close to the toeboard.

The bodies, styled by Renault themselves, allowed four passengers to be carried, had a fastback style, and a large lift-up hatchback/tailgate. There were two slightly different styles, to distinguish the mundane from the more exciting models. The 15TL models, initially called 'saloons' by Renault in any case, had more simple detailing of the sides and windows, while the 17s had abbreviated quarter windows with stylised grilles behind them. 15s had 1289cc engines, 15TS and 17TL models were mechanically identical with 90bhp 1565cc engines modified from the Renault 16. These two engines, incidentally, are of entirely different types and construction.

It was the 17TS model which caused most comment, for not only did it have fuel-injection for its 1565cc engine, and 108bhp at 6000rpm, but it also had a five-speed manual gearbox and four-wheel disc brakes to complete a very interesting package.

Renault 17 Gordini

However, in spite of its obvious merits, Renault saw no use for this model in competitions, and preferred to have its engine and transmission used in the rear-engined Alpine-Renaults instead.

It was interesting to note that the gearbox was already a Renault production item, in the 12 Gordini, and comprised the Renault 16's four-speed box with the extra gear in a light alloy casing on the end of the case.

To try to give this top-of-the-line model a bit more marketing appeal, Renault changed its name from 17TS to 17 Gordini (after the renowned French tuner who was now working with Renault) in 1974, by which time the engine had already been increased in size to 1605cc (by a minor bore increase) without any noticeable effect on the power output or performance. This was of more sporting significance for Renault-Alpine models which shared the engine, for it meant that the unit could be enlarged to its practical limit of 1.8-litres without infringing any regulations, as it fell into the *over* 1600cc class in series-production form.

In the spring of 1976, however, Renault restyled, rationalised, and reduced their 15/17 range, and the Gordini version disappeared. The most powerful version then inherited the 1647cc engine of the Renault 16TX, along with the five-speed gearbox once fitted to Gordinis.

Specification

Engine and transmission: Four-cylinders, in-line, with pushrod-operated overhead-valve cylinder head, and fuel-injection. **(1971-1973 model)** Bore, stroke and capacity 77×84mm., 1565cc. Maximum power 108bhp (DIN) at 6000rpm.; maximum torque 98lb.ft. at 5500rpm. **(1973 to 1976, including all 1974-1976 Gordinis)** Bore, stroke and capacity 78×84mm., 1605cc. Maximum power 108bhp (DIN) at 6000rpm.; maximum torque 100lb.ft. at 5500rpm. Five-speed manual gearbox in unit with engine and transaxle. Hypoid bevel final drive.
Chassis: Front engine, front drive. Unit-construction, pressed-steel body-chassis unit. Independent front suspension by coil springs and wishbones. Rack and pinion steering. Rear suspension of axle beam by coil springs and radius arms. Four wheel disc brakes.
Bodywork: Pressed-steel, two-door close-coupled four-seater in fastback coupe style with hatchback. Length 14ft. 0in.; width 5ft. 4.2in.; height 4ft. 3.6in. Unladen weight 2325lb.
Performance: (Gordini) Maximum speed 111mph. 0-60mph 9.8sec. Standing ¼-mile 17.4sec. Typical fuel consumption 27mpg.

Simca 1000 & 1200 Coupe

Built: Paris, France, 1962-1971

For many years Simca had built perfectly conventional cars, with the classic front engine/rear drive layout, so it was a great surprise to see that their new Simca 1000 small car of 1961 had its cast-iron four-cylinder engine placed at the rear, behind the line of the rear wheels. It was a well-engineered little car, if endowed with rather strange handling, due to the heavy rearward weight bias, and was already beginning to sell well when Bertone caused a sensation with his sleek new coupe version of the car, at the Geneva Show of 1962.

The Bertone-styled car, which incidentally was rather like the shape of the NSU Sport Prinz which had preceded it in 1960, and remarkably similar to the tiny Ferrari prototype which the same designer had completed in 1961, was not ready to go into production until the end of the year. Although it had been promised to have a 55bhp engine – a considerable boost for the 944cc engine compared with the standard product, all production cars were delivered with the standard 40bhp output engine, and performance was somewhat disappointing. Even though four-wheel-disc brakes were specified, like the similar Bertone-inspired NSU this was a sheep in wolf's clothing, and sales were somewhat slow.

Without any larger version of the engine to fall back on, Simca were rather powerless to do much about the performance deficiency, and it was not until 1967 that they could give the model a boost. But when the '1000' became the '1200' much more

Simca 1200S Coupe

than an engine change was involved. Many features intended for future Simca-mass production cars were introduced, including the use of an entirely new cylinder block casting, a larger cylinder bore, and a resulting capacity of 1204cc; with two large twin-choke Solex carburettors the power output was up to 80bhp (DIN) at 6000rpm — double that of the original milk-and-water car. To kerb this power the water radiator was moved up to the nose of the car, which resulted in the inclusion of those distinctive mesh air outlet grilles in the bonnet panel.

Suspension changes to match included a redesigned transverse leaf spring front end, and double-jointed rear driveshafts with more precise location and control of the steering geometry. It was obvious that Simca meant to transform the car's image altogether, for the standard specification included strident air horns, and a restyled nose including extra lamps, along with the use of Michelin's latest XAS radial-ply tyres.

The 1200 Coupe, however, was indeed a much more expensive car, and due to the fact that Bertone could only build a certain number of bodies at a fairly high price this could not be reduced. Production went on to the end of 1970, and it is believed that the last of several thousand cars was sold in 1971. Simca (or, rather, Chrysler-France, as they had become) never built another coupe model of their own, and the Matra-Simca Bagheera is really the stable descendant of this model.

Specification (1000 Coupe and 1200 Coupe)

Engine and transmission: Four-cylinders, in-line, with pushrod-operated overhead-valve cylinder head. **(1000)** Bore, stroke and capacity 68 × 65mm., 944cc. Maximum power 40bhp (DIN) at 5400rpm.; maximum torque 47lb.ft. at 3400rpm. **(1200S)** Bore, stroke and capacity 74 × 70mm., 1204cc. Maximum power 80bhp (DIN) at 6000rpm.; maximum torque 76lb.ft. at 4500rpm. Four-speed manual gearbox in unit with engine and transaxle. Hypoid bevel final drive.

Chassis: Rear engine, rear drive. Unit-construction pressed-steel underpan, based on Simca 1000 design. Independent front suspension by transverse leaf spring and wishbones. Worm and sector steering. Independent rear suspension by coil springs, and semi-trailing links. Four-wheel disc brakes.

Bodywork: Two-door, 2+2 seater fastback coupe body style by Bertone. Length 12ft. 10.5in.; width 5ft. 0in.; height 4ft. 1.4in. Unladen weight (1000) 1755lb., (1200S) 1965lb.

Performance: (1200) Maximum speed 107mph. Standing ¼-mile 18.0sec.

Sunbeam Alpine series

Built: Coventry, England, 1959 to 1968

Rootes' first Alpine was a two-seater open sports version of the Sunbeam-Talbot 90 saloon, which was built from 1953 to 1955, after which there was a three-year gap without any such sporting machine in the Rootes line-up. The Alpine sports car which arrived in 1959 was an entirely different type of design.

Although the Alpine was a very smart and fashionable open two-seater, its 'chassis' was based on nothing more exciting than the Hillman Husky utility estate car! To be precise, one basic design made up the Minx/Husky/Rapier/Alpine family of 1955 onwards. The Husky was a short-wheelbase derivative of the Minx/Rapier layout, and it was on this base that the Alpine style evolved. The superstructure, however, was entirely special, and the power train was always the same as that fitted to the current Sunbeam Rapier coupe. The Minx-based engine had an aluminium cylinder head, and Laycock overdrive was always optional. An all-synchromesh gearbox was fitted from the autumn of 1964.

At first, the Alpine (developed on Rootes' behalf, incidentally, by Armstrong-Siddeley, also in Coventry) was distinguished by its prominent fins, but these were cropped for Series IV, which arrived at the beginning of 1964. There was always an optional hardtop version, and from the launch of the Series III for 1963 this was a very stylish, fully-trimmed and sharply-styled device. Automatic transmission was available for a time, but this took the edge off what was already no more than average performance.

The Alpine's problem was that it was quite bulky and heavy compared with both its main competitors – the Triumph TRs and the MGA/MGB series – and not nearly as powerful. Even so, with engines suitably modified and power-tuned, cars prepared by the factory performed with distinction at Le Mans in the 24-Hours race. Harrington, British coachbuilders, also produced a smart fastback derivative with factory approval (one of the Le Mans cars was equipped with this bodystyle), which is now more fashionable among 'classic car' enthusiasts.

Once Rootes' new owners, Chrysler, began to influence the destiny of future models, it became clear that the Alpine's days were numbered. It is said that it was never a profitable project, which made it easy for Chrysler to drop it from the line-up, thus making sure that the range of models was even less interesting than before. From 1964, however, the Alpine had given rise to the exciting Tiger sports car, which is covered in the next analysis. The last Alpine was built at the beginning of 1968, and the name was revived for 1970 on a very down-market version of the four-seater Rapier coupe.

Sunbeam Alpine, 1959

Specification

Engine and transmission: Four-cylinders, in-line, with pushrod-operated overhead-valve cylinder head. Engines evolved from 81.5 × 76.2mm., 1592cc to 81.5 × 82.55mm., 1725cc after 1965. Maximum power (1725cc version) 92bhp (net) at 5500rpm.; maximum torque 110lb.ft. at 3700rpm. Four-speed manual gearbox and optional overdrive, or three-speed Borg Warner automatic transmission (some models only), in unit with engine. Hypoid bevel final drive.

Chassis: Front engine, rear drive. Unit-construction pressed-steel body/chassis unit. Independent front suspension by coil springs and wishbones. Recirculating ball steering. Rear suspension of live axle by half-elliptic leaf springs. Front wheel disc brakes, rear drums.

Bodywork: Pressed-steel two-door two-seater body style, as open sports car or with hardtop. Length 13ft. 0in.; width 5ft. 0.5in.; height 4ft. 3.5in. Unladen weight (open sports) 2190lb. (GT) 2235lb.

Performance: (Series II 1961 model) Maximum speed 97mph. 0-60mph 14.8sec. Standing ¼-mile 19.7sec. Typical fuel consumption 23mpg. **(Series V, 1725cc)** Maximum speed 98mph. 0-60mph 13.6sec. Standing ¼-mile 19.1sec. Typical fuel consumption 26mpg.

Sunbeam Tiger

Built: West Bromwich (Jensen), England, 1964 to 1967

Almost as soon as the AC Cobra had made its shatteringly exciting debut in the United States, Rootes executives in that country got together with the Shelby company to carry out the same transformation on the Sunbeam Alpine. However, although Shelby built the first prototype, all subsequent work was done by Rootes in England, and the cars were marketed through normal Rootes channels.

The basic Sunbeam Alpine structure and style was retained, but a completely new power train was inserted − 4.2-litre vee-8 Ford engine, new gearbox and final drive units − all supplied by, or after advice by, Ford of Detroit. Rack and pinion steering and Panhard rod location of the rear suspension were also features.

To do this required a considerable amount of modification to the basic Alpine body/chassis unit, and rather than commit themselves to extensive and costly new tooling, Rootes decided to subcontract the entire conversion and assembly process to Jensen Motors of West Bromwich. For Jensen, this meant that not only were they building their own cars, but that they were heavily committed to both BMC (with the 'Big' Healey) and to Rootes. The new car, appropriately enough in view of its road behaviour, was dubbed a 'Tiger', and was announced early in 1964.

Although its handling and traction were somewhat uncontrolled and extrovert, especially if radial-ply tyres were not fitted, and if the rather restricted engine output was increased, the Tiger was a fast, relatively cheap (by North American standards), and attractive car. In spite of the fact that it looked virtually the same as the much less

Sunbeam Tiger 4.2-litre MkI

spirited Alpine (the only external difference was in the badging and other minor decoration) it found a ready sale. Deliveries were confined to the United States market at first, but the Tiger became available in Europe a year later.

The Tiger showed promise as a competition car, but the Rootes factory's own entry in the Le Mans 24 Hour race was something of a disaster, as both cars retired with engine blow-ups early in the event. In works rally form, however, Tigers were much more successful, and a company more committed to competitions than Rootes might have made an overall winner out of it.

At the beginning of 1967 the Tiger gave birth to the Tiger II, which was a fiercer version, fitted with the more powerful 4.7-litre Ford vee-8 engine; only a handful of these were ever sold in Europe. By now, however, corporate problems were at hand. Chrysler had now taken a large interest in the Rootes combine, and it soon became clear that they did not approve of the fitment of a rival's engine to one of the Rootes models. As soon as contractual commitments would allow, therefore, production was phased out. Plans to reintroduce the car with a Chrysler vee-8 engine fitted came to nothing, as those engines were substantially larger (too large, in fact, to be fitted) and heavier, so that a viable solution could not be found.

In the two-seater sports car field, it was Rootes's last, and most interesting effort. Nothing as exciting and blood-stirring has been seen from the company, before or since.

Specification

Engine and transmission: Eight-cylinders, in 90-degree vee-formation, with pushrod-operated overhead-valve cylinder heads, built by Ford USA. Bore, stroke and capacity 96.5 × 73mm., 4261cc. Maximum power 164bhp (gross) at 4400rpm.; maximum torque 258lb.ft. at 2200rpm. Four-speed manual gearbox in unit with engine. Hypoid bevel final drive.

Chassis: Front engine, rear drive. Unit-construction pressed-steel body/chassis unit. Independent front suspension by coil springs and wishbones. Rack and pinion steering. Rear suspension of live axle by half-elliptic leaf springs and Panhard rod. Front wheel disc brakes, rear drums.

Bodywork: Pressed-steel two-door two-seater bodystyle, as open sports car or with hardtop. Length 13ft. 0in.; width 5ft. 0.5in.; height 4ft. 3.5in. Unladen weight (open sports) 2525lb.

Performance: Maximum speed 117mph 0-60mph 9.5sec. Standing ¼-mile 17.0sec. Typical fuel consumption 19mpg.

Note: In 1967 a short run of Tiger II models were built with the following important differences: 101.6 × 72.9mm., 4727cc. 203bhp (gross) at 4400rpm.; maximum torque 282lb.ft. at 2400rpm.
Performance: Maximum speed 122mph. 0-60mph 7.5sec. Standing ¼-mile 16.0sec. Typical fuel consumption 24mpg.

Triumph Spitfire MkI, 1962

Triumph Spitfire series

Built: Coventry, England, 1962 to date

Along with the MGB, now built by the same industrial group, Triumph's Spitfire is one of the longest-running of all sports cars. Unlike the MGB, however, it has received much more in the way of change and improvement over the years. It started life in the early 1960s as a sporting derivative of the Triumph Herald touring car; since the end of 1973, however, when the related GT6 (see later) was dropped, it has been an obvious anachronistic model in the Triumph range.

The original two-seater sports car derivation from the Herald was designed by Michelotti, without any specific encouragement from Triumph, but when management saw the result they took it over for themselves. Although the production car used modified Herald engine, transmission and suspension parts, its backbone chassis frame was unique. The bodyshell, too, was not based on any other, and featured a big combined bonnet and front wings section which gave unrivalled access to the engine bay and front suspension.

Intended to be a 'little sister' to the TR series, it was an immediate and lasting success. Like the Sprite/Midget cars from Abingdon, with which it has always been in direct competition, it was meant to appeal to people who lusted after the faster car, but who could not afford it. Even in its original 1147cc form, its performance was interesting without being outstanding, but the roadholding was marred by the use of

243

simple high-pivot swing axle independent rear suspension, which could not easily be tamed.

Even so, the factory did so, and between 1964 and 1966 embarked on a successful racing and rally programme. The race cars were entered for Le Mans and Sebring, taking good class wins often against more special opposition; they had streamline fastback hardtops developed from the GT6 shape, and at Le Mans could lap in excess of 100mph.

Over the years the engine size was increased, and the power crept up with it. Although the original 1500 version of 1975 had been made necessary to provide enough power in exhaust-emission-strangled North America, in European form it endowed the car with a 100mph maximum; the same engine was adopted by the MG Midget from late 1974. Unlike the Midget, however, the Spitfire remains in production as the 1980s open, as it is still a very strong seller in North America, where true convertibles are much appreciated. Production will end in 1980.

Superficially the latest car looks much like the original of 1962, but in fact a complete reskinning operation, with many subtle changes (including one obvious one — the squared off tail), was introduced for the Mark IV at the end of 1970. At the same time, minor but important changes to the rear suspension meant that the handling was much improved.

By comparison with the Sprite/Midget family (with which cars it was always in conflict), the Spitfires were and are not quite as sporty, or easy to handle, but they have always been considered visually more attractive, and have always been considerably more roomy. By offering such popular options as overdrive, and smart detachable hardtops, they have appealed to equally as many people, if not to the same type of people. More than 300 000 Spitfires of all types have now been made.

Specification (original model)

Engine and transmission: Four-cylinders, in-line, with pushrod-operated overhead-valve cylinder head. Bore, stroke and capacity 69.3 × 76mm, 1147cc. Maximum power 63bhp (net) at 5750rpm.; maximum torque 67lb.ft. at 3500rpm. Four-speed manual gearbox with optional overdrive in unit with the engine. Hypoid bevel final drive.

Chassis: Front engine, rear drive. Separate pressed-steel backbone type of frame, with box section members. Independent front suspension by coil springs and wishbones. Rack and pinion steering. Independent rear suspension by swing axles and transverse leaf spring. Disc front brakes and drum rears.

Bodywork: Pressed-steel bodyshell, in two-door, two-seat open sports style, with optional hardtop. Length 12ft. 1in.; width 4ft. 9in.; height 3ft. 11.5in. Unladen weight 1570lb.

Performance: Maximum speed 92mph. 0-60mph 17.3sec. Standing ¼-mile 20.9sec. Typical fuel consumption 33mpg.

Note: In 1967 the engine was enlarged to 1296cc, and from 1975 it was enlarged to 73.7 × 87.5mm, 1493cc. Maximum power 71bhp (DIN) at 5500rpm.; maximum torque 82lb.ft. at 3000rpm.

Performance (1967 Mk 3): Maximum speed 100mph. 0-60mph 13.6sec. Standing ¼-mile 19.3sec. Typical fuel consumption 29mpg. **(1500):** Maximum speed 100mph. 0-60mph 13.2sec. Standing ¼-mile 19.1sec. Typical fuel consumption 32mpg.

Triumph Spitfire 1500

Triumph GT6 MkIII

Triumph GT6 series

Built: Coventry, England, 1966 to 1973

The separate chassis philosophy pursued by Triumph at the beginning of the 1960s allowed many model permutations to be produced without vast expense in press tools. As the six-cylinder Vitesse touring car had evolved from the Herald, therefore it was straightforward enough for a similar transformation to be applied to the little Spitfire sports car. The GT6, however, which appeared in 1966, was only ever sold as a fastback hatchback derivative, while the body it used was never made available on the Spitfire.

The 2-litre six-cylinder engine was merely that of the Triumph 2000, slightly modified, and was fitted concurrently to the related 2-litre Vitesse models. Because it was lengthy, and because the extra length could only be accommodated in the nose of the attractive shape, the original weight distribution of the Spitfire was upset; this, together with the uncouth habits of the swing-axle rear suspension, meant that the first GT6s had very suspect and unlikeable handling.

It was to improve this, and turn the car into something more akin to the 'mini-E-Type' it had once been dubbed, that a new and more sophisticated rear suspension was designed. This, made available on Mark IIs from the end of 1968, used Grand Prix type reversed bottom wishbone linkage with the existing transverse leaf spring, along with rubber 'doughnuts' in the drive shafts to allow the whole thing to work properly. Thus equipped, the car was endowed with completely transformed roadholding, and was now an interesting, if tiny, two-seater 2-litre coupe.

If the onset of North American safety and exhaust emission legislation had not meant a mountain of work for Triumph's sports-car-orientated planners, the GT6 might be with us still, but the company were faced with dropping something to keep their workload within reasonable limits. Even though the GT6, by then, had been further upgraded to a Mark III, and the rear suspension of the pivotting-spring (Spitfire) type had been fitted without complaint from the customers, it was phased out at the end of 1973.

Specification (Original model)

Engine and transmission: Six-cylinders, in-line, with pushrod-operated overhead-valve cylinder head. Bore, stroke and capacity, 74.7 × 76mm., 1998cc. Maximum power 95bhp (net) at 5000rpm.; maximum torque 117lb.ft. at 3000rpm. Four-speed manual gearbox and optional overdrive in unit with the engine. Hypoid bevel final drive.

Chassis: Front engine, rear drive. Separate pressed-steel backbone type of frame, with box-section members. Independent front suspension by coil springs and wishbones. Rack and pinion steering. Independent rear suspension by swing axles and transverse leaf spring (1968 to 1972 by transverse leaf spring and lower wishbones). Disc front brakes and drum rears.

Bodywork: Pressed-steel bodyshell, in two-door two-seater fastback coupe style. Length 12ft. 1in.; width 4ft. 9in.; height 3ft. 11in. Unladen weight 1905lb.

Performance: Maximum speed 106mph. 0-60mph 12.0sec. Standing ¼-mile 18.5sec. Typical fuel consumption 24mpg.

Note: Engine power was increased in 1968: Maximum power 104bhp (net) at 5300rpm.; maximum torque 117lb.ft. at 3000rpm.

Performance: (Mk III) Maximum speed 112mph. 0-60mph 10.1sec. Standing ¼-mile 17.4sec. Typical fuel consumption 28mpg.

Triumph TR3A family

Built: Coventry, England, 1953 to 1962

The famous TR2/TR3/TR3A family of 2-litre Triumph sports cars really belong to the 1950s, but a substantial number were built in the 1960s, even after the modernised TR4 cars were launched. One must recall that the TR2 had evolved from a very simple chassis, body and power train supply, had been refined and improved, and had finally equalled the MGA's popularity in world markets.

By the beginning of the 1960s, the TR3A was already at its most popular, being lightweight, having an unburstable engine, creditable fuel economy, and reliability to its credit. Front disc brakes were standard (the first such fitting on a series-built sports car), overdrive was optional, and a more torquey 2.2-litre engine was available for the asking. The body equipment, however, needed modernisation, which is what the TR4 was designed to satisfy.

There is evidence to suggest that TR3As were over-produced in 1960, for production slumped badly in 1961, even before the TR4 arrived. Even so, after that launch, a series of more than 3000 TR3Bs, visually and mechanically almost identical to late-model TR3As, were built, mostly with the larger engine, and with the new all-synchromesh TR4 gearbox. The last TR3B was built in the autumn of 1962, and sold in the United States early in 1963. Well over 80 000 'classic' TRs were built.

Triumph TR3A

Specification

Engine and transmission: Four-cylinders, in-line, with pushrod-operated overhead-valve cylinder head. Bore, stroke and capacity, 83 × 92mm, 1991cc. Maximum power 100bhp (gross) at 5000rpm.; maximum torque 117lb.ft. at 3000rpm. Four-speed manual gearbox, with optional overdrive, in unit with engine. Hypoid bevel final drive. (Optional TR4-type 2138cc engine).
Chassis: Front engine, rear drive. Pressed-steel separate chassis frame, with box-section member. Independent front suspension by coil springs and wishbones. Cam and lever steering. Suspension of rear live axle by half-elliptic leaf springs. Front wheel disc brakes, rear drums.
Bodywork: Pressed-steel bodyshell, in two-door two-seat open sports car style, with optional hardtop. Length 12ft. 7in.; width 4ft. 7.5in.; height 4ft. 2in. Unladen weight 2050lb.
Performance: Maximum speed 102mph. 0-60mph 12.5sec. Standing ¼-mile 18.7sec. Typical fuel consumption 28mpg.

Triumph TR4, TR5, TR6 series

Built: Coventry, England, 1961 to 1976

Although the last of the Triumph TR6s, built in the summer of 1976, was almost completely different in every way from the first TR4 of 1961, the evolution of one car from the other had been a gradual but easily-traceable business, and all have to be considered together. Each car, in its own way, was an updated version of the TR2 which Triumph had launched in 1953. However, by the time the last car was built, sports car fashions had changed enormously. While the TR2 had been thought to be up-to-date and modern in its approach, the TR6 was considered as one of the 'last of the dinosaurs', having taken over that mantle from the late and much-loved Austin Healey 3000.

The TR4 of 1961 was essentially a rebodied TR3A/TR3B. The chassis, apart from wider wheel tracks and rack-and-pinion steering, was the same, as was the wet-liner engine, and the back axle. Only the all-synchromesh gearbox, quite an innovation, was mechanically new. The bodyshell, styled by Michelotti, was distinguished by having face-level ventilation and what was in effect an optional 'Targa' hardtop, years before both were re-invented by Ford and Porsche respectively. It was smart, and its wind-up windows gave salooncar comfort when the hardtop was specified.

The roadholding, not helped by hard springs and limited wheel movement, was criticised from many quarters, so for the next model − the TR4A of 1965 − a brand new chassis with semi-trailing link independent rear suspension (like that of the Triumph 2000) was fitted. For North America, where such things were neither considered necessary nor appreciated at the time, a live axle was retained as an option.

The new chassis was the first of three major changes, and would be retained until the end. The next, however, was to install more power, and this was done in 1967, when a much-modified 2000 six-cylinder unit was enlarged to 2498cc with a longer stroke, given Lucas fuel-injection, and could boast of 150 gross bhp. The performance of the TR − now called a TR5 − was transformed, and a 120mph maximum speed was possible. The live axle alternative for the United States disappeared, but to meet that country's new exhaust emission laws a carburettor version of the engine with much less power was marketed; this was the TR250.

Only 15-months later, the TR5 gave way to the TR6, which had a substantially redesigned bodyshell, both styled and tooled by Karmann of Germany. This was the third and last major transformation in the series, and the TR6 was to continue in production for more than seven-years, becoming the most numerous (so far) of all the Triumph TR sports cars.

Although it was the fuel-injected cars which had the glamour and gave the most performance, the vast majority of all TR6s were sold in North America and had less powerful engines with carburettors. It was for that market that the rugged old TR6 was continued for a further two seasons after the all-new TR7 had been launched; sales in Europe had ceased at least a year earlier.

Triumph TR4

Specification (TR4)

Engine and transmission: Four cylinders, in-line, with pushrod-operated overhead-valve cylinder head. Bore, stroke and capacity 86×92mm, 2138cc. Maximum power 100bhp (net) at 4600rpm.; maximum torque 127lb.ft. at 3350rpm. (Optional 1991cc engine with 83mm bore). Four-speed manual gearbox with optional overdrive in unit with engine. Hypoid bevel final drive.

Chassis: Front engine, rear drive. Separate box section pressed steel chassis frame. Independent front suspension by coil springs and wishbones. Rack and pinion steering. Suspension of rear live axle by half-elliptic leaf springs. Front wheel disc brakes, rear drums.

Bodywork: Pressed steel bodyshell, in two-door, two-seater style, in open sports or hardtop coupe versions. Length 12ft. 9.6in.; width 4ft. 9.5in.; height 4ft. 2in. Unladen weight 2130lb.

Performance: Maximum speed 102mph. 0-60mph 10.9sec. Standing ¼-mile 17.8sec. Typical fuel consumption 26mpg.

251

Note: In 1965 the TR4A replaced the TR4, with independent rear suspension by coil springs and semi-trailing wishbones; cars for the USA market retained the live axle as an option.

Performance: Maximum speed 109mph. 0-60mph 11.4sec. Standing ¼-mile 18.5sec. Typical fuel consumption 30mpg.

Specification (TR5)

Engine and transmission: Six-cylinders, in-line, with pushrod-operated overhead-valve cylinder head. Bore, stroke and capacity 74.7×95mm, 2498cc. Maximum power 150bhp (net) at 5500rpm.; maximum torque 164lb.ft. at 3500rpm. Four-speed manual gearbox with optional overdrive in unit with the engine. Hypoid bevel final drive.

Chassis: Front engine, rear drive. Pressed-steel separate chassis frame. Independent front suspension by coil springs and wishbones. Rack and pinion steering. Independent rear suspension by coil springs and semi-trailing wishbones. Front wheel disc brakes, rear drums.

Bodywork: Pressed-steel bodyshell, in two-door two-seat style, in open sports or hardtop coupe versions. Length 12ft. 9.6in.; width 4ft. 10in.; height 4ft. 2in. Unladen weight 2270lb.

Performance: Maximum speed 120mph. 0-60mph 8.8sec. Standing ¼-mile 16.8sec. Typical fuel consumption 24mpg.

Note: The TR250 was a 105bhp version of the TR5. The TR6 was announced in 1969: Length 13ft. 3in. Unladen weight 2475lb.

Performance (TR250): Maximum speed 107mph. 0-60mph 10.6sec. Standing ¼-mile 17.8sec. Typical fuel consumption 30mpg. **(TR6):** 119mph. 0-60mph 8.2sec. Standing ¼-mile 16.3sec. Typical fuel consumption 22mpg.

Triumph TR6

Triumph TR7 family

Built: Liverpool, England, 1965 to 1978 & Coventry, England, 1978 to 1980

To succeed their long-running TR4/5/6 sports car series, Triumph chose a completely new mechanical approach. They chose to design a much simpler car around a unit-construction bodyshell, and they clad it in a very controversial wedge-style shape, initially with a small-windowed notchback hardtop style. A new factory built in the outskirts of Liverpool was chosen to build and assemble this new car, which was to be the first of a burgeoning family of models.

Sales, however, though creditable, were not up to the required standards, the factory was always under-utilised, and after a long crippling strike over the winter of 1977-1978 it was decided to close it down completely, and transfer production to Coventry. After several months when no TR7s were built, final assembly recommenced in Coventry. The long-awaited convertible version has been on sale since the summer of 1979, and other derivatives will surely follow.

The unit-construction shell was Triumph's first such layout for a sports car (Spitfire, GT6 and TR6 had all had separate chassis, though the GT Stag had also had a unit-construction layout), and compared with earlier Triumphs it was distinguished by not having independent rear suspension. The MacPherson strut front suspension was shared with a new saloon car design (which was subsequently cancelled before production commenced), while the engine, gearbox and back axle were all Triumph Dolomite units.

The controversial styling (by the Austin office at Longbridge) was a talking point, but undoubtedly led to poor driver visibility, and there is a distinct lack of space inside the cockpit. The tragedy of this, indeed the tragedy of British Leyland, is that the full flowering of the original design may never appear; in the pipeline before industrial trouble hit the project was a sleek and attractive long-wheelbase 2+2 hatchback version of the car, where the frontal styling looked much more integrated and suitable.

Compared with the obsolete TR6, the TR7 was not as fast, but was considerably cheaper, lighter, and more economical to run. It also had much more supple, predictable roadholding and handling, a higher-revving engine, and was simpler to maintain. Its styling was apparently perfectly acceptable in North American markets, where the majority of cars are sold, and now that the convertible version is available it should appeal to even more customers. Indeed, it is an interesting point that Britain's other popular convertible in North America in this class is the MGB, which must suffer by comparison of its styling and unchanged looks after such a lengthy period.

Like all successful cars of modern times, the TR7 range is well product planned. At first there were four-speed or five-speed gearboxes (though the four-speed box has now been dropped), along with the alternative of automatic transmission.

Triumph TR7

Specification

Engine and transmission: Four-cylinders, in-line, installed in the bodyshell at an angle of 45-degrees, with single-overhead-camshaft cylinder head. Bore, stroke and capacity, 90.3 × 78mm, 1998cc. Maximum power 105bhp (DIN) at 5500rpm.; maximum torque 119lb.ft. at 3500rpm. Four-speed manual, five-speed manual or Borg Warner three-speed automatic transmission in unit with engine. Hypoid bevel final drive.

Chassis: Front engine, rear drive. Unit construction pressed-steel body/chassis unit, sold as a fixed head coupe or (since 1979) as a convertible. Independent front suspension by coil springs, MacPherson struts and wishbones. Rack and pinion steering. Rear suspension of live axle by coil springs and radius arms. Front wheel disc brakes, rear drums.

Bodywork: Pressed-steel bodyshell, in two door two seat coupe or convertible body styles. Length 13ft. 4.1in.; width 5ft. 6.2in.; height 4ft. 1.9in. Unladen weight 2205lb.

Performance: Maximum speed 109mph. 0-60mph 9.1sec. Standing ¼-mile 17.0sec. Typical fuel consumption 29mpg.

Volvo 1800 family

Built: West Bromwich, England, 1960 to 1964
& Gothenburg, Sweden, 1964 to 1973

When Volvo, previously known only for building stodgy, reliable and very safe saloon and estate cars, decided to enter the sports coupe market, they did it through a third party. A new bodyshell would be tooled up and manufactured by Pressed Steel in Britain, while final assembly would be entrusted to Jensen of West Bromwich, in England.

The new car went into production in 1960, with power train and all chassis components, based on the 122 touring car series, supplied from Sweden. This coupe two-seater was distinguished by a high waistline, and low seating, which made visibility less than ideal. However, the early model made its name by being chosen as 'The Saint's' car in the TV series which was popular all over the world, and in which Roger Moore starred. Though the Volvo engine was never a high-revving unit, overdrive was a feature of the transmission, and the car was soon known as a long-legged and civilised sports coupe.

Cars built by Jensen were known as P1800s, but from 1964 final assembly was moved back to Sweden, where the quality and specification of the car was improved, the power output increased, and the name changed to 1800S. It may be no more than coincidence that as P1800 production left Jensen, that Sunbeam Tiger production moved in. It was said, too, that Volvo had not been happy with the standard of the cars built by Jensen.

The car's basic chassis was not altered in the next decade, but the car was progressively improved. The engine was enlarged to a full two-litres in 1968, and from 1969 it was equipped with Bosch fuel-injection (producing 125bhp gross), at which point it was re-christened the 1800E. The final improvement, visually obvious and interesting in marketing terms, was that the bodyshell was restyled, so that the final version, to be called 1800ES, was a tiny sports hatchback, with large opening rear window/hatch. This followed the success of Reliant's Scimitar GTE, and pre-dated cars like the enormously popular Ford Capri IIs and Series III models.

Production ran out in 1973, however, as Volvo began to concentrate more and more on vast, heavy, and very boring safety-conscious saloon cars again, and no sporting Volvo has been built since then. In every way, therefore, the 1800 coupe series has been the most sporting, and interesting, yet to emerge from the Swedish concern.

Volvo 1800ES

Specification (Original version)

Engine and transmission: Four-cylinders, in-line, with pushrod-operated overhead-valve cylinder head. Bore, stroke and capacity 84.2 × 80mm, 1778cc. Maximum power 96bhp (DIN) at 5800rpm.; maximum torque 103lb.ft. at 3800rpm. Four-speed gearbox and Laycock overdrive in unit with engine. Hypoid bevel final drive.

Chassis: Front engine, rear drive. Unit construction pressed-steel structure, made by Pressed Steel (England) and completed by Jensen (England). Independent front suspension by coil springs and wishbones. Worm and sector steering. Rear suspension of live axle by coil springs, radius arms and Panhard rod. Front wheel disc brakes, rear drums.

Bodywork: Pressed-steel unit-construction two-seater coupe shell. Length 14ft. 5.2in.; width 5ft. 6in.; height 4ft. 2.4in. Unladen weight 2360lb.

Performance: Maximum speed 107mph. 0-60mph 11.9sec. Standing ¼-mile 18.6sec. Typical fuel consumption 26mpg.

Note: For 1969 the engine size was increased to 88.9 × 80mm, 1986cc. Maximum power 105bhp (DIN) at 5500rpm.; maximum torque 119lb.ft. at 3500rpm. From autumn 1969 Bosch fuel-injection was adopted, and the new rating was 120bhp (DIN) at 6000rpm; maximum torque 123lb.ft. at 3500rpm. The model became known as 1800E. From autumn 1971 the body was restyled as a sporting hatchback, and had optional automatic transmission. Unladen weight 2625lb.

Performance (1800E): Maximum speed 115mph. 0-60mph 10.1sec. Standing ¼-mile 17.5sec. Typical fuel consumption 26mpg. **(1800ES Hatchback):** Maximum speed 111mph. 0-60mph 9.7sec. Standing ¼-mile 17.1sec. Typical fuel consumption 23mpg.

VW-Porsche 914 series

Built: Osnabruck, Germany, 1969 to 1975

Ever since Dr. Ferdinand Porsche designed a new 'Peoples' Car' in the 1930s, which was eventually to become the VW Beetle, he had retained links with that concern. His original Porsche sports car was based on a Beetle platform chassis, suspensions and power train. In 1969, therefore, it was no surprise to learn that a new sports car, with a mid-engined layout, had been designed and was to be called a VW-Porsche.

In the mid and late 1960s, motoring fashion swung towards mid-engines, which could give better roadholding characteristics than a rear-engined car, but which unfortunately meant that passenger space would be lost. The 914 project was no better than most. It was a strict two-seater, which was in itself a step back from the generous 2 + 2 accommodation of the Porsche's 911 series, and was made doubly controversial by its very sharp-edged body styling.

On announcement in 1969, there were two versions – the pure 914 having a VW 411 engine and transmission reversed in the chassis (and 80bhp), while the 914/6 had a 2-litre flat-six Porsche 911T engine (and 110bhp). Accommodation for luggage was cleverly arranged – there were front *and* rear stowage compartments, and the engines were effectively hidden from view under swivelling panels. Karmann of West Germany, who produced the bodies, also built the complete car on Porsche's behalf. VW carried the credit for the marque's name, and there was a special marketing organisation to sell and distribute the car.

Enthusiasts, however, always looked on this model as a down-market Porsche, which was unfortunate, as the 914/6 was very little cheaper than the least expensive 911, and was thought by many to have less attractive equipment and behavioural features. The 914/6, in fact, was not a success, and was withdrawn after only three years. The VW-engined 914, however, was progressively improved, and 1973 model year cars saw the introduction of the full 2-litre flat-four VW engine of 1971cc. This engine, with 100bhp and fuel-injection, effectively took the place of both original models, but it did little to increase the popularity of the car.

Although the roadholding was good, and the engineering competently carried out, the VW-Porsche never developed the 'image' of a proper Porsche, and was not much sought after by VW customers. There is no doubt, too, that the strict two-seater layout was less practical than that offered by other Porsches, and that the styling was not to everyone's taste. Sales were never as high as VW or Porsche would have liked, and when the next collaborative exercise (the 924) got under way, the companies were glad to drop the 914.

Specification (Original version four-cylinder)

Engine and transmission: Air-cooled four-cylinder, horizontally-opposed, with pushrod-operated overhead-valve cylinder heads. Bore, stroke and capacity 90 × 66mm, 1679cc, built by VW. Maximum power 80bhp (DIN) at 4900rpm; maximum torque 98lb.ft. at 2700rpm. Five-speed gearbox in unit with engine and transaxle. Spiral bevel final drive.

Chassis: Mid-engine, rear drive. Unit-construction pressed-steel structure, made by Karmann. Independent front suspension by torsion bars and MacPherson struts. Rack and pinion steering. Independent rear suspension by coil springs and semi-trailing arms. Four-wheel disc brakes.

Bodywork: Pressed-steel unit construction two-seater sports car shell, built only as a coupe with removable roof panel. Length 13ft. 2in.; width 5ft. 5in.; height 3ft. 11.5in. Unladen weight 1900lb.

Performance: Maximum speed 102mph. 0-60mph 14.8sec. Standing ¼-mile 19.9sec. Typical fuel consumption 25mpg.

Note: From autumn 1972, 2-litre version became available: Bore, stroke and capacity 94 × 71mm, 1971cc. Maximum power 100bhp (DIN) at 5000rpm; maximum torque 116lb.ft. at 3500rpm.

Performance: Maximum speed 119mph. 0-60mph 10.3sec. Standing ¼-mile 17.8sec. Typical fuel consumption 31mpg.

Note: The 914/6 version had following important differences: Air-cooled six-cylinder engine. Bore, stroke and capacity 80 × 66mm, 1991cc. Maximum power 110bhp (DIN) at 5800rpm; maximum torque 116lb.ft. at 4200rpm. Unladen weight 2070lb.

Performance: Maximum speed 125mph. 0-60mph 8.3sec. Standing ¼-mile 16.2sec. Typical fuel consumption 23mpg.

VW-Porsche 914-6

Chapter Five

GTs, Homologation specials & motor sporting machines

Before the 1960s, the 'Homologation Special' category did not exist. It is true that for many years previously, cars had often been built specifically for use in competition – usually in rallying rather than racing – but the rules had usually allowed them to be built in tiny numbers. In the years under study, however, starting with cars like the Mini-Cooper S and the Lotus-Cortina in Britain, and progressing to the Renault 8 Gordini and the NSU Prinz TTS in Europe, cars we might once have thought to be GT models began to be sold with their motor sporting potential at the top of the list of features. Numerically, therefore, they are the most important group in this section of the book.

As I pointed out in my introduction, motor industry publicists have very successfully managed to devalue the meaning of the 'Grand Touring' label, which they have applied to all manner of only slightly modified family saloons. By refusing to consider these, and by separating the 'homologation specials' according to their purpose in life, it is easy to see that the line-up of true GTs which is rather more than a species of tarted-up quantity-production car is very exclusive indeed.

However, as happens too often when we are considering this type of motoring the 'gut feeling' for the sort of cars which should be included, rather than the consideration of a theoretical specification, is most important. Some GTs, of course, are so formidably fast that they are really Supercars, and will be considered later. This explains, for instance, the relative absence of Bristols, and the complete lack of Ferraris and Maseratis with the exception of the 275LM. Cars like the 6.9-litre Mercedes-Benz and 5.3-litre Jaguar saloons are extremely fast touring cars which would surely have qualified if only their manufacturers had made any attempt to market them as Grand Touring machines instead of merely as a wealthy man's touring car. No doubt I should really have included the Rolls-Royce Camargue here as a GT car, but it is so outstanding in every way except that of straight-line performance that I have defined it as a Supercar. Whatever my choice, I doubt if Rolls-Royce will be very worried....

Some 'homologation specials' are more practical road cars than others. While, within reason, you might buy and habitually use an Escort RS1800 as a road car (even though the vast majority of these cars become out and out competition machines), no one in his right mind would buy a Ferrari 275LM unless he intended to use it as a circuit racing car. An even better example is that of the Lancia Stratos; in spite of the fact that some examples have been seen in normal road use, I would guess that Lancia never expected their mid-engined Stratos to be a day-to-day machine. I hesitated for some time over the status of the BMW M1, complete with mid-engine and avowed Group 5 racing ambitions, but decided that in spite of all this it qualified as a road car, and a Supercar at that. The Aston Martin DB4GT Zagato, however, with a bodyshell so flimsy and so delicate that it cannot be practical for road use, qualifies perfectly for inclusion here.

It goes without saying, I hope, that almost every car sold as a *basic* competition machine is not usually as fast or as highly-tuned as the car which might finally appear on the track, so the specification and the performance figures quoted below all apply to the basic machine as catalogued by the makers. A good example here is that of the Ford Escort RS1800, catalogued for two years with 115bhp and an 1845cc engine, and possessed of a top speed of 111mph. Race or rally cars have engines enlarged to 1998cc, which usually produce between 260 and 280bhp at between 8500 and 9000rpm, and – if suitably geared – would certainly be capable of speeds of more than 150mph or even 160mph. Usually, however, in rallying guise, they are geared for no more than 120mph, and benefit from flashing acceleration.

In terms of specification, it is interesting to note that most true Grand Touring Cars have had, and many still retain, classic front-engine, rear-drive layouts in the majority of cases. Splendid cars like the Citroen SM have front engines linked to front-wheel-drive, not because of any packaging advantages (the SM, indeed, is particularly profligate in its use of space, and gives a disgracefully small amount of passenger space in relation to its 16-foot overall length) but because of the long-standing Citroen front-drive tradition. Mid-engined or rear-engined Grand Tourers – as such – do not exist, and this is quite simply due to their lack of passenger space. One of the few GT definitions which I would always make is that cars which qualify should provide adequate four-seater accommodation; it is a sad fact that no manufacturer, not even Porsche, has yet managed to provide this in a car which is adequately fast, and which is also possessed of good stability and roadholding.

On the other hand, there is now a definite tendency for modern 'homologation specials' to take the form of mid-engined machines, which almost automatically makes them less attractive as cars for exhilirating road use. Whereas the Fiats and Fords of the mid-1970s which won rallies and races were competition cars based on the bare bones of front-engined mass-production bodyshells, there is every sign that the trend has been reversed. In the 1980s, for sure, more and more mid-engined competition cars will be evolved, and Renault, with their turbocharged R5, have already shown their hand.

AC Greyhound

Built: Thames Ditton, England, 1959 to 1963

It would be quite right to suggest that the 2 + 2 AC Greyhound is related to the Ace sports cars, but quite wrong to infer that its chassis engineering was based on that of the Ace. The two cars, in fact, were completely different. Engines and transmissions, however, were like those used in the Ace and Aceca cars, which is only reasonable when the limited resources of the Thames Ditton company were considered.

The Greyhound made its debut in 1959, but was not ready for production until 1960 or 1961. It took the Aceca philosophy of closed sports car motoring one stage further, with a rather similar fastback body style, but it was considerably more bulky, heavier, more costly, and had what could be claimed as close-coupled four-seater accommodation. It could be ordered either with the venerable, but technically interesting, light-alloy AC six-cylinder engine, or with the much more modern long-stroke Bristol six-cylinder engine – both of which were of two-litres capacity.

Its chassis was often described, wrongly, as being of 'spaceframe' type, which is inaccurate. Main structural loads were carried by a tubular ladder-type chassis, on to which door sills and all the main body supports were formed in Superleggera fashion (though this concern was not credited with the layout). Its suspension was more advanced than that fitted to the two-seater Ace/Aceca, with coil spring and wishbone i.f.s., and with semi-trailing coil spring independent rear suspension. Rack and pinion steering was also specified.

One reason for the Greyhound taking ages to get into production was that it took time to develop the handling and roadholding to an acceptable standard – a problem made more difficult because the chassis was none too stiff, and because the semi-

AC Greyhound

trailing rear suspension was something quite new to AC themselves. When it eventually reached production, sales were difficult to achieve because the car was extremely expensive of its type, quite a lot more costly than its two-seater relatives, and because it did not reach the high standards of equipment and refinement that a Grand Touring car of this type needed.

AC, therefore, were happy to concentrate on two-seater production, and once they had geared up to producing the required number of body/chassis units for Carroll Shelby to complete as AC Cobras, they were happy to drop the Greyhound altogether. Cobra production began at the end of 1962, and the last Greyhound was built at about the same time. No AC with more than two seats has been built since then.

Specification

Engine and transmission: Six-cylinders, in-line, with pushrod-operated overhead-valve cylinder head. Bore, stroke and capacity 66×96mm, 1971cc, built by Bristol. Maximum power 125bhp (net) at 6000rpm.; maximum torque 132lb.ft. at 4500rpm. Four-speed manual gearbox with optional Laycock overdrive in unit with engine. Hypoid bevel final drive.

Chassis: Front engine, rear drive. Separate chassis frame, with tubular members. Independent front suspension by coil springs and wishbones. Rack and pinion steering. Independent rear suspension by coil springs and semi-trailing wishbones. Front wheel disc brakes, drum rears.

Bodywork: Light-alloy skin panels on light tubular frame, in two-door 2 + 2 seater, fastback coupe style. Length 14ft. 7in.; width 5ft. 5.5in.; height 4ft. 4.5in. Unladen weight 2240lb.

Performance: Maximum speed 104mph. 0-60mph 12.7sec. Standing ¼-mile 19.1 sec. Typical fuel consumption 18mpg.

Note: Alternative 2.2-litre Bristol engines were also available.

Alfa Romeo Giulia TZ

Built: Milan, Italy, 1963-1965

Arguably one of the most exciting Alfa Romeo 'road' cars ever produced has been the TZ. Known affectionately, and world wide, as the 'Tubolare', the car was intended, purely and simply, as a competition car. There were no compromises of any nature, except, perhaps in styling, which made the car less than ideal for its purpose. Historically, the TZ was Alfa's successor to the formidable little Giulietta SZ, and proved to be an even doughtier proposition.

Unlike the SZ, however, the TZ (which stood for 'Tubolare Zagato') was constructed around an entirely special chassis. As the name would imply, this chassis was a multi-tubular structure, well triangulated around the engine bay and rear suspension area, which nevertheless allowed ample space for two passengers. All round independent suspension was a feature, with not even the front suspension having much in common with the quantity-production Alfas.

Engine and transmission, however, were identical with those fitted to the 1.6-litre Sprint Speciales and the TI Super saloons – at least in 'over the counter' form. The fact was, of course, that almost every TZ sold was subjected to considerable and expensive tuning and modification, with 1.6-litre engines often producing at least 150bhp, and with a large choice of gearbox and final drive ratios.

Not only was the TZ a rugged, nimble and potentially fast little car, but it was also incredibly noisy, and had the most stark but attractive styling by Zagato. That style was clearly descended from that of the SZ, and was initially constructed of flimsy light alloy. A few cars in the original series, however, were also constructed of glass-fibre.

It is interesting to note that development of the TZ began while the Giulietta SZ was still not yet a winning machine, and if it had not been for the demands of the new Giulia models, it is likely that the TZ would have been on the scene much earlier. Work had begun in 1959, and the first prototype was built by 1961, but it was not until 1963 that the first cars were delivered for competition use, and not until later that sporting homologation was achieved.

In its class, the TZ always had intense competition – notably from Porsche – but was often a winner, particularly where long-distance endurance in rallies like the *Tour de France,* or in the Targa Florio, were features. Aerodynamically, too, the original TZ was very efficient, and its light weight was an advantage.

Porsche took the ascendant again once the 904 mid-engined car was announced, but Alfa-Romeo riposted with the TZ2, which was a lower and restyled car built on the same chassis, and this kept the clover-leaf cars at the front of their class for another year. By then, however, Alfa's works team, Autodelta, were turning to vee-8 engines and pure sports racing cars on the one hand, or to a different type of homologation special (the light-alloy GTA) on the other, and the lovable TZ was dropped.

120 of the original-shape cars (of which 10 were in glass-fibre) were built in 1963-1964, while a further 50 of the TZ2 models were built in 1965 and 1966.

Alfa Romeo Giulia TZ

Specification (TZ)

Engine and transmission: Four-cylinders, in-line, with twin-overhead-camshaft cylinder head. Bore, stroke and capacity 78 × 82mm., 1570cc. Maximum power 112bhp (DIN) at 6500rpm.; maximum torque 98lb.ft. at 4200rpm. Five-speed manual gearbox in unit with engine. Hypoid bevel final drive.

Chassis: Front engine, rear drive. Multi-tubular chassis frame, separate from bodyshell. Independent front suspension by coil springs and wishbones. Recirculating ball steering. Independent rear suspension by coil springs and wishbones. Four-wheel disc brakes.

Bodywork: Light-alloy bodywork, in two-door two-seater fastback coupe style, by Zagato. Length 12ft. 11.5in.; width 4ft. 11.4in.; height 3ft. 11.2in. Unladen weight 1435lb.

Performance (Manufacturer's claim): Maximum speed up to 152mph. Typical fuel consumption 24mpg.

Alvis TD/TE/TF series

Built: Coventry, England, 1956 to 1967

Although the smooth Park Ward bodied Alvis cars sold in the 1960s were elegant and fast, it is also a fact that the chassis and engine design was elderly by then. In fact, it would be true to say that only one new Alvis chassis design ever appeared after the second world war, and that all subsequent cars were developed from this.

The founding model was the TA21 of 1950, with a box-section chassis frame, coil spring independent front suspension, and a brand-new six-cylinder 3-litre engine design of typically classic Alvis layout. That engine, at first, produced 85bhp at 4000rpm. TA21s (and the later TC21s) had four door saloon bodies by Mulliners of Birmingham, or convertibles by Tickford.

Graber of Switzerland produced a smart modern two-door coupe style for this chassis, which eventually went into series production in Britain at Park Ward, after more than one false start. As the 1960s opened the production car was known as the TD21, and by mechanical evolution it became the TE21, and finally (in 1966 and 1967) the TF21. Alvis, however, spent the postwar years building up their aero-engine and military vehicle interests, so that private car production was only ever an interesting and prestigious sideline.

Alvis TE 21

The six-cylinder engine had conventional overhead valve gear, but in its final form was boosted to an extremely creditable 150bhp (net) at 4750rpm, which was enough to boost the TF21 to a 120mph maximum speed. By this time, automatic transmission was an option, ordered by many Alvis customers, and there were four-wheel disc brakes to keep the performance in check. Not only that, but Alvis's own four-speed manual gearbox could be displaced by the immensely strong 5-speed ZF gearbox to special order. The whole car was massively built, and heavy (nearly 3500lb.) and 'thoroughbred' in the best 1930s manner.

That, in a way, was at once the main attraction and the main drawback to the Alvis layout, for it had been designed to standards and customs of the 1930s, for customers of the 1950s and 1960s. To drive one was to enjoy (or suffer – in terms of heavy steering and ponderous behaviour) motoring of a bygone era, in comfort and good taste of a modern British coachbuilt body. This, while enjoyable, seemed to appeal to less and less people, and well before production came to an end in 1967 Alvis were looking desperately for ways to sell the last sanction of cars.

They had looked at an entirely new design in the 1950s (and had hired Alec Issigonis to lay out the new car) but shied away from the heavy tooling costs forecast, and by the 1960s never looked like producing a new model. The fact that Rover took them over in 1965, and had more viable industrial plans in mind for the Coventry factory, merely confirmed their resolve, and the TF21 was the last Alvis private car ever made.

Specification (TD21 of 1961)

Engine and transmission: Six-cylinders, in-line, with pushrod-operated overhead-valves. Bore, stroke and capacity 84 × 90mm., 2993cc. Maximum power 115bhp (net) at 4000rpm.; maximum torque 152lb.ft. at 2500rpm. Four-speed gearbox in unit with engine. Hypoid bevel final drive. Optional Borg Warner automatic transmission.
Chassis: Front engine, rear drive. Separate chassis frame with box-section members. Independent front suspension by coil springs and wishbones. Recirculating ball steering. Rear suspension of live axle by half-elliptic leaf springs. Front wheel disc brakes, rear drums.
Bodywork: Light-alloy skinned coachbuilt shell by Park Ward, close-coupled four-seater, available as coupe or convertible. Length 15ft. 9in.; width 5ft. 6in.; height 4ft. 9.5in. Unladen weight 3425lb.
Performance: Maximum speed 104mph. 0-60mph 13.9sec. Standing ¼-mile 19.6sec. Typical fuel consumption 19mpg.

Note: The final version, the TF21, built in 1966 and 1967, had the following major differences: Maximum power 150bhp (net) at 4750rpm; maximum torque 185lb.ft. at 3750rpm. Five-speed ZF gearbox, or optional Borg Warner automatic transmission. Four-wheel disc brakes. Unladen weight 3485lb.
Performance: Maximum speed 120mph.

Aston Martin DB4GT Zagato

Built: Newport Pagnell, England, 1960-1962

Built in tiny quantities, and put on sale at an enormously high price, only so that it could be used in International sports car racing, the Zagato-bodied Aston Martin DB4GT is a perfect example of the way determined car makers get round the rules of competition. Only 25 of these sensational cars were built, and though a few of them were used on the open road, they were mainly purchased with track racing in mind.

The DB4/DB4GT series is covered in the Supercars series – for such they undoubtedly were – the Zagato derivative is of interest here only for its body, and for its extra-high engine tuning. The 3.7-litre engine, which could eventually be enlarged to 4-litres if owners used later DB5 cylinder blocks and components; produced a massive 314bhp, helped by three twin-choke Weber carburettors and a twin spark plug cylinder head layout.

Central to the design was the elegant and lightweight Zagato bodyshell, which saved well over 300lb. compared with the standard body, and was also rather more 'slippery' at high speeds. For these cars chassis were sent to Italy, where Zagato mounted their tubular-framed bodyshells, after which they were returned to Newport Pagnell for painting, trimming, and completion. Not unnaturally, the price was considerably higher than that of the DB4GT – in 1962, for instance, when road-test cars achieved more than 150mph maximum speed on 'road' gearing, a Zagato cost £3750 basic price, compared with £3200 for the standard-bodied GT.

Aston Martin DB4 GT Zagato, 1962

For road use, the flimsy light-alloy bodywork was not practical without bumpers, which were not normally supplied. Aston Martin eventually made the gesture of making bumpers available, but it is doubtful if more than one or two sets were ever fitted.

In competitions, by the way, the car was only a partial success, for it had to face the phenomenal performance of the 3-litre GTO Ferraris.

Specification

Engine and transmission: Six-cylinders, in-line, with twin-camshaft cylinder head. Bore, stroke and capacity 92×92mm, 3670cc. Maximum power 314bhp (net) at 6000rpm.; maximum torque 278lb.ft. at 5400rpm. Four-speed gearbox in unit with engine. Hypoid bevel rear axle.

Chassis: Front engine, rear drive. Fabricated steel platform chassis. Independent front suspension by coil springs and wishbones. Rack and pinion steering. Rear suspension of live axle by coil springs, radius arms, and Watts linkage. Four-wheel disc brakes.

Bodywork: Light-alloy Zagato bodyshell on DB4GT chassis, two-seater coupe. Length 14ft. 0in.; width 5ft. 5.25in.; height 4ft. 2in. Unladen weight 2765lb.

Performance: Maximum speed 153mph. 0-60mph 6.1sec. Standing ¼-mile 14.5sec. Typical fuel consumption 14mpg.

Aston Martin Lagonda (DB V8 type), 1975

Aston Martin Lagonda (DB V8 type)

Built: Newport Pagnell, England, 1974-1975

As far back as 1967, when the first Aston Martin DBS coupe was completed, its designer Bill Towns had thought that a four-door Grand Touring car could evolve from it. Aston's financial condition was such, however, that this extension of the basic style did not appear until 1974. Even then, it was almost killed off by the closure (temporary, thank goodness) of 1974/1975, and a mere handful were completed before and after this prolonged stoppage.

The 'Lagonda' (it was a model name, not a marque title, by the way,) was therefore little more than a long-wheelbase Aston Martin V8, with a near-identical front end and panelling, but with a four-door style. Mechanically, it was identical with the V8 Coupe, down to the option of manual or automatic transmission, and it kept the same coil spring front suspension and de Dion rear layout.

This particular 'Lagonda' is not significant in itself, but was important for the later, much more futuristic, Lagonda which was to folow in 1976.

Specification

Engine and transmission: Eight-cylinders in 90-degree vee-formation, with twin-camshaft cylinder heads. Bore, stroke and capacity, 100×85mm, 5340cc. Maximum power and torque figures not quoted. Five-speed ZF gearbox or Chrysler automatic transmission. Hypoid bevel rear axle.

Chassis: Front engine, rear drive. Fabricated steel platform chassis. Independent front suspension by coil springs and wishbones. Power-assisted rack and pinion steering. Rear suspension, de Dion, coil springs, radius arms, Watts linkage. Four-wheel disc brakes.

Bodywork: Shell built from light-alloy skin panels and inner steel panels, welded to platform chassis; four-door saloon. Length 16ft. 2in.; width 6ft. 0in.; height 4ft. 5.25in. Unladen weight 4400lb.

Aston Martin Lagonda

Built: Newport Pagnell, England, 1976 to date

After the revival of Aston Martin by a quartet of wealthy Aston Martin enthusiasts in 1975, their first priority was to restore the concern to health, and build existing models. Not much more than a year later, in 1976, they decided that a new model was needed, and commissioned stylist Bill Towns to design an entirely new four-door Grand Touring shape. This, christened the 'Lagonda', like the less startling four-door car built by the previous regime, made its debut at the 1976 British motor show, and went haltingly into production during 1978.

The Lagonda's chassis engineering is all based on that of the existing, and long-running Aston Martin V8, which is to say that the 5.3-litre vee-8 engine is very powerful but never has power or torque figures publicly quoted, that there is de Dion rear suspension, and that the main chassis is built up as a pressed-steel platform, on to which the steel and light-alloy bodyshell superstructure is added. The vast majority of all this work takes place in the historic Newport Pagnell factory – engine assembly and test, chassis build, body production and final completion. Production is very limited, but the price is enormously high.

The latest Lagonda has simply sensational sharp-edge styling, and manages to combine great bulk with a delicacy of touch, and a weight kept down to a very reasonable 4400lb., when the size and performance potential is considered. Although the shape itself is startling enough, the doors are large, and there is really adequate accommodation for four passengers.

On announcement, much was made of the instrumentation, the display of information, and the electronic equipment which was to be fitted to the car. The panel would be entirely black when the car was at rest, but once switched on all manner of digital displays would spring to life, including a read out of speed, fuel contents and many other functions.

Although Aston Martin engineers led by Mike Loasby, their Technical Director, strove to make these functions reliable, it was their very advanced nature which led to the car's first deliveries being long delayed. The first car was delivered in April 1978, and production has slowly been building up ever since. Already cases have been reported of cars being delivered, then immediately resold by their first owners at a considerable profit.

No authoritative road-tests have been carried out at the time of writing, but the new car is confidently expected to be capable of more than 150mph. Fuel consumption, of course, will inevitably be high, but the sort of person (or company) which buys a car like this will hardly notice such a minor detail.

Unhappily for the image of the space-age Lagonda, many of the original electronic features had to be abandoned to get the car into production, though it is expected that some will be reinstated in due course.

Specification

Engine and transmission: Eight-cylinders in 90-degree vee-formation, with twin-camshaft cylinder heads. Bore, stroke and capacity, 100×85mm, 5340cc. Maximum power and torque figures not quoted. Chrysler automatic transmission in unit with engine. Hypoid bevel rear axle.

Chassis: Front engine, rear drive. Fabricated steel platform chassis. Independent front suspension by coil springs and wishbones. Power-assisted rack and pinion steering. Rear suspension, de Dion, coil springs, radius arms, Watts linkage. Four-wheel disc brakes.

Bodywork: Composite light-alloy and steel body welded to platform chassis; four-door saloon. Length 17ft. 4in.; width 5ft. 11.5in.; height 4ft. 3.3in. Unladen weight 4400lb.

Aston Martin Lagonda, 1979

Bizzarrini GT Strada 5300

Built: Livorno, Italy, 1965-1967

At the beginning of the 1960s, Ing. Giotti Bizzarrini was a prolific engineer, and always concentrated on the super-sporting type of car. At one and the same time, he was working on the first Lamborghini model, on the Iso Grifo and Rivolta project, and on his own sports racing project! It is no surprise, therefore, to see that the GT Strada is suspiciously similar in many ways to the Iso Grifo, with which it was almost concurrent.

Announced in 1965, the GT Strada was based on a fabricated steel platform chassis frame, with coil spring independent front suspension and de Dion rear suspension, also by coil springs, and it goes without saying that this was very similar to the components used in the Iso Grifo.

The body style, by Bertone, was also very similar to that of the A3L Grifo, and might at one time have been adopted by Iso. For Bizzarrini, however, it was in light-alloy, with the very minimum of trim and furnishings, and was intended for competition use. Very few, however, were sold, as customers for that sort of car preferred to go racing behind (or preferably, ahead of) a Ferrari vee-12 rather than a much-modified North American vee-8.

Specification

Engine and transmission: Eight-cylinders, in 90-degree vee-formation, with pushrod operated overhead valve cylinder heads, manufactured by General Motors. Bore, stroke and capacity 101.6×82.55mm., 5354cc. Maximum power 365bhp (gross) at 6000rpm.; maximum torque 376lb.ft. at 3500rpm. Four speed manual gearbox in unit with engine. Hypoid bevel final drive.

Chassis: Front engine, rear drive. Separate fabricated steel platform chassis, with coachwork attached on assembly. Independent front suspension by coil springs and wishbones. Recirculating ball steering. De Dion rear suspension by coil springs, radius arms and Watts linkage. Four wheel disc brakes.

Bodywork: Light-alloy coachbuilt two-door two-seater fastback coupe body style by Bertone (built by BBM of Modena). Length 14ft. 4in.; width 5ft. 9.3in.; height 3ft. 7.7in. Unladen weight 2760lb.

Performance: Maximum speed 145mph. 0-60mph 6.4sec. Standing ¼-mile 14.6sec. Typical fuel consumption 15mpg.

Bitter CD

Built: Stuttgart, Germany, 1973 to 1979

It was once said that General Motors' top management in Detroit would undoubtedly cancel the Bitter if ever they found out how closely Opel were involved, but the truth is probably that they knew all along, and that secretly they approved of the whole idea. The Bitter, certainly, is as close to being an Opel Supercar as we are ever likely to see, and has many potential advantages over the Italian models which it so closely resembles in some ways.

The CD's conception dates from 1969, when Opel Styling, then headed by Chuck Jordan, produced their dream car for use at motor shows all round the world. This car, based on the use of Opel Diplomat running gear, had startling but quite impractical-to-produce looks. It was not until a couple of years later that Opel, aided in initial construction by Frua (which let them call the car the Opel Frua for a time), produced a much more practial prototype, with conventional screen pillars, and breathtakingly attractive styling. In many ways the general layout and style was similar to that of the Maserati Khamsin, but that car was by Bertone, and did not appear until the end of 1972; great minds, it seems, often think alike.

In 1973, however, Opel were ready for their 'dream car' to be put into limited production. It retained the underframe, suspensions, engine and transmission of the Opel Diplomat, which was a fine but not very successful 'flagship', which used mainly Chevrolet engine engineering, and always fought a losing battle against similar opposition from Mercedes-Benz. The pressed-steel bodyshell was now to be built by Baur of Stuttgart (who now build the M1 mid-engined BMW Supercars), and was to be marketed and supported by Erich Bitter, who had nagged Opel into letting this remarkably sleek car be put into production.

No more than a dozen cars a month could be built (Baur were not in the quantity-production business in the same way as Bertone or Pininfarina), but this is not the only way in which a Bitter CD differs from the products of these concerns; it is also built to the highest standards of refinement and quality, with really efficient sound insulation. It is a car which, no doubt, Opel wish they could have marketed themselves, at a more reasonable price and in larger numbers. It is also something of a relief to BMW and Mercedes-Benz that they have not done this, as it is certainly more visually attractive than anything made by these concerns.

Specification

Engine and transmission: Eight-cylinders, in 90-degree vee-formation, with pushrod-operated overhead-valve cylinder heads, manufactured by General Motors. Bore, stroke and capacity 101.6 × 82.55mm., 5354cc. Maximum power 230bhp (gross) at 4700rpm.; maximum torque 315lb.ft. at 3000rpm. Three-speed GM Turbo-Hydramatic automatic gearbox in unit with engine. Hypoid bevel final drive.

Chassis: Front engine, rear drive. Unit construction pressed-steel bodyshell, based on Opel manufactured floorpan and suspensions. Independent front suspension by coil springs and wishbones. Power-assisted recirculating ball steering. De Dion rear suspension by coil springs, radius arms and A-bracket. Four-wheel disc brakes.

Bodywork: Pressed-steel two-door 2 + 2 fastback coupe style by Baur. Length 15ft. 11.1in.; width 6ft. 0.6in.; height 4ft. 2.6in. Unladen weight 3800lb.

Performance: Maximum speed 130mph. 0-60mph 9.6sec. Typical fuel consumption 18mpg.

BMC Mini-Cooper S

Built: Longbridge, England, 1963 to 1971

The Mini-Cooper S was a direct and logical development of the basic Mini theme, but was intended to provide a very suitable base for the preparation of competition cars in both racing and rallying. Made in true quantity production (in spite of what rival firms might have thought), the basic car was civilised enough and quiet enough to provide really exciting and interesting motoring on the public road, it was sold at a very reasonable price, and it was easily serviced and maintained by run-of-the-mill garages.

Not only that, but in works-modified form, it was a remarkable little competition car. Between 1964 and 1968, for sure, when the BMC factory was actively campaigning the 1275cc engined version, it was not only a potential class winner, but a potential outright winner in rallies, and in races it could always be relied upon to embarrass the performance of far larger and more specialised cars.

The original Issigonis-designed Mini, with its transversely-mounted 848cc engine, had appeared in 1959, and the Mini-Cooper, with modifications inspired by John Cooper (of Grand Prix racing fame) followed in 1961. But this little car, in spite of a 997cc engine and tiny front wheel disc brakes, was still not a 'winner'. It was not until the lessons of Formula Junior racing were applied to the versatile engine that a truly remarkable power plant evolved.

By enterprising (and, in motor sporting terms, by 'illegal') methods, the basic cylinder block was completely redesigned, with repositioned cylinder centres, and with more strength. Formula Junior racing demanded the use of unmodified quantity-production blocks! This allowed the cylinder bore to be increased, the cylinder head breathing to be improved, and the potential to be markedly stretched.

In 1963, using the Formula Junior block and cylinder bore, but with a 'standard' stroke, the first interim Cooper S, with a 1071cc engine, was put on sale, and only a year later this car was joined by the two definitive models – the short-stroke 970cc car, and the longer-stroke 1275cc car. This last engine, incidentally, was entirely special to the Mini-Cooper S until the end of 1966, when a productionised version was fitted to Sprites and Midgets, after which it began to be specified, in detuned form, in many other BMC touring cars.

The rest of the car was essentially that of the mass-production Mini. There was a steel two-door bodyshell, no more than ten-feet long, all-independent suspension by rubber in compression, and – for the Cooper S only – front wheel disc brakes of a more reasonable size than those offered on the less-fast Mini-Cooper. For a five-year period (1964 to 1969) the new-fangled Hydrolastic suspension was standardised on all Minis, but this was never satisfactory on competition cars, which were usually built to the 'obsolete' specification of 1963 and 1964. In any case, Hydrolastic was withdrawn from Minis in 1969, as a cost saving and simplification move.

Both the 970cc and 1071cc cars were short-lived, and from the beginning of 1965 the 1275S (as it was always known) reigned alone.

In standard form, the engine was incredibly flexible and potentially economical, and the Cooper S must go down in history as one of the best-ever town cars. In fully-tuned form the engine's standard 76bhp could be boosted to well over 110bhp, which often led to overheating, and made grievous demands on the transmission. To counter this, serious competition cars used alternative straight-cut gears, which were so noisy as to preclude all normal conversation between driver and co-driver.

Without a change in corporate management (the British Leyland merger occurred at the beginning of 1968) 'works' cars might have been used for longer, but it is a fact that by 1968 they were losing their competitive edge. In the constant search for improved performance, the Cooper S came up against the power/steering/traction/-handling conundrum which afflicts all such front-wheel-drive cars. Once its nimble handling and small size was no longer enough, its potential fell away, and by the end of the 1960s it had been eclipsed. The last, rather emasculated, production Cooper S, was built in 1971.

Austin Mini-Cooper S MkII 1275cc

Specification (1275S)

Engine and transmission: Four-cylinders, in-line, with pushrod-operated overhead-valve cylinder head. Engine mounted transversely in body/chassis unit. Bore, stroke and capacity 70.6 × 81.3mm., 1275cc. Maximum power 76bhp (net) at 6000rpm.; maximum torque 79lb.ft. at 3000rpm. Four-speed manual gearbox in unit with engine and transaxle. Spur gear final drive.

Chassis: Front engine, front drive. Unit construction pressed-steel body/chassis unit. Independent front suspension by rubber in compression, and wishbones. Rack and pinion steering. Independent rear suspension by rubber in compression and trailing arms. From autumn 1964 to autumn 1969, rubber suspension was replaced by interconnected Hydrolastic suspension units. Front wheel disc brakes, rear drums.

Bodywork: Pressed-steel two-door four-seat saloon car bodywork, in unit with structure. Length 10ft. 0.25in.; width 4ft. 7.5in.; height 4ft. 5in. Unladen weight 1440lb.

Performance: Maximum speed 96mph. 0-60mph 11.2sec. Standing ¼-mile 18.4sec. Typical fuel consumption 30mpg.

Note: Also available were 970cc engines (70.6 × 61.9mm), and 1071cc engines (70.6 × 68.26mm), which were in production for one year in each case.

Bristol 406

Built: Bristol, England, 1958-1961

It may be a trifle unkind, but none the less true, to point out that Bristol is still a 'one chassis' concern. The mechanical layout chosen immediately after the second world war, which was a thoroughly updated copy of late-1930s BMW engineering, has persisted ever since. There have been many improvements, but the Bristol of the late 1970s is still recognisably derived from that of the 1940s.

The 406 model, built for three years (1958 to 1961), represents something of a watershed in the affairs of the tiny Bristol concern. It was really the last of the Grand Touring cars — all the rest have effectively been Supercars — and it was also the last Bristol to use its own six-cylinder engine.

In terms of body styling, the 406 was really the beginning of the fourth generation, and all Bristols up to the 411 were to be based on its style. Paradoxically enough, it was as a big two-door GT car that the 406 replaced the *four*-door 405, with more modern styling and altogether crisper lines.

The car's engineering, and the reason for its fine roadholding and obvious rigidity, was based on a strong steel box-section chassis. Although a live rear axle was specified, it was properly located by torsion bars, a Watts linkage and a torque arm. Four wheel disc brakes (by Dunlop) were standardised, and the well-known cross-pushrod Bristol engine (copied very closely from that of the BMW 328 layout) was enlarged to 2216cc, and gave 105bhp at 4700rpm. There was adequate four-seater accommodation, and the all-steel coachbuilt bodyshell had light-alloy skin panels. As on the 405, the 406 had its spare wheel mounted inside the front wing panel, behind the line of a front wheel.

The Bristol's appeal was that it was essentially hand-built in the best possible manner, still had its own engine and transmission, but did not hesitate to call on supreme specialist items like the Dunlop disc brakes to complete a fine specification. Production was always kept very low — anything over four cars built per week was considered unsuitably hasty by the Bristol management — and every car was therefore built to order and tailor-made for its customer.

The only major problem, in a rapidly developing market, was that the power output of 105bhp did not really match the car's 3000lb. weight, and its performance was not evidently considered to be enough by potential buyers. It was with this in mind that Bristol went shopping for vastly more power to Chrysler in Detroit, and the identically styled 407 was the result.

Specification

Engine and transmission: Six-cylinders, in-line, with pushrod-operated overhead-valve cylinder head. Bore, stroke and capacity 68.7 × 99.6mm., 2216cc. Maximum power 105bhp (net) at 4700rpm.; maximum torque 129lb.ft. at 3000rpm. Four-speed manual gearbox and overdrive in unit with the engine. Hypoid bevel final drive.

Chassis: Front engine, rear drive. Fabricated box-section steel chassis frame. Independent front suspension by transverse leaf spring and wishbones. Rack and pinion steering. Suspension of rear live axle by torsion bars, radius arm and Watts linkage. Four-wheel disc brakes.

Bodywork: Fabricated, coachbuilt, steel bodyshell, with light-alloy skin panels, in two-door four-seater GT saloon style, built by Jones Brothers of Willesden. Length 16ft. 4in.; width 5ft. 8in.; height 5ft. 0in. Unladen weight 3010lb.

Note: A few examples of the 406 were bodied by Zagato, with 130bhp (net) at 5750rpm engines. Length 15ft. 5in.; height 4ft. 7in.; width 5ft. 3in. Unladen weight 2470lb.

Bristol 406

Citroen SM

Built: Paris, and Vichy, France, 1970-1975

Although Citroen had already started thinking about a car along the lines of the SM Coupe by the mid-1960s, it was not until they took over Maserati in 1968 that they really became serious. It was not until Maserati came into their orbit, after all, that they could lay hands on a suitable engine for the project. From the day they challenged Maserati to produce a suitable engine unit, their new car became 'SM', where 'M' stood for Maserati, and technically it was a fascinating mixture.

In general layout, a Citroen SM was similar to that of the long-established DS saloons — which is to say that a conventional pressed-steel body/chassis unit housed a front-wheel-drive engine and transaxle, and that self-levelling Hydropneumatic all-independent suspension was specified. It was the engine which was so remarkable.

Citroen apparently asked Maserati if a suitable engine for their proposed high-performance coupe could be produced inside six-months. Ing. Alfieri then astounded them by quite literally producing a prototype unit in three weeks! But, in many ways, Alfieri was cheating. He produced a vee-6, at least in strictly prototype form, by cutting one pair of cylinders off the back of a Maserati vee-8, worked out a reduced crankshaft throw to reduce the capacity from 3.1-litres to 2.7-litres (for French fiscal horsepower reasons), had a new crankshaft produced from a solid billet, and — *voila* — had a 90 degree twin-camshaft vee-6 running on the test beds at Modena!

The production unit was much more refined in its construction and development than this, but it is a fact that it was produced on the rudimentary tooling already in existence for the vee-8 Maserati (which explains the strange and theoretically undesirable angle between cylinder banks — 60-degrees, or 120-degrees, would have been ideal for balancing purposes) and had the same basic breathing arrangements, combustion chambers, valve gear and other moving parts. One very unusual feature of

Citroen SM

this engine was that the drive to the camshafts was in two sections. Primary chain drive was from the crank nose to a jackshaft running the length of the engine vee, while the secondary drive was taken up, not to the end of the camshafts, but to sprockets part way along their length, effectively in the centre of the engine.

This splendid, and reputedly very reliable, 2.7-litre engine produced 170bhp in carburettor form, or – later – 180bhp in 3-litre guise with an enlarged cylinder bore; this 3-litre unit was also developed for use in the Maserati Merak mid-engined car, and was also used in the Ligier JS2 model.

Bolted to the engine, which in true big-Citroen style was behind the line of the front-wheels, just in front of the passenger toe board, was Citroen's beefy five-speed all-synchromesh gearbox, which was also to be used, incidentally, in the Maserati and Ligier models, and in the Lotus Esprit.

The steering was power-assisted, but even more complex and sophisticated than that of the DS saloons, while no fewer than six headlamps, four of which were linked to the steering linkage (so that they could pivot with the front wheels on lock), were fitted behind a curved glass cover.

For all this, and in spite of its great (16ft. 0.6in.) length, the SM was barely more than a generous 2 + 2 machine, and was, in every way, a rich man's toy or indulgence.

Like other big Citroens, it was a lot stronger and more rugged than it looked, and if well-maintained the complex hydraulics which governed everything from the suspension to the gearchange, the brakes to the self-levelling, were surprisingly reliable. It also had the incredibly satisfying combination of high performance, great refinement, and a real 'magic carpet' ride on almost every type of surface.

Although nearly 12 000 were built between 1970 and 1973, the energy crisis did the car a great deal of harm, and production of the last Ligier-produced examples tailed off badly. Only 294 were built in 1974, and 119 in 1975, after which the car was dropped; at almost the same time Citroen abandoned its links with Maserati, and sold out to de Tomaso.

Specification

Engine and transmission: (Manual gearbox version) Six-cylinders, Maserati-manufactured, in 90-degree vee-formation, with twin-camshaft cylinder heads. Bore, stroke and capacity 87 × 65mm, 2670cc. Maximum power (carburettor version) 170bhp (DIN) at 5500rpm; maximum torque 172lb.ft. at 4000rpm. Maximum torque (injection version) 178bhp (DIN) at 5500rpm.; maximum torque 164lb.ft. at 4000rpm. Five-speed gearbox, in unit with engine and final drive. Spiral-bevel final drive. **(Automatic transmission version)** Bore, stroke and capacity 91.6 × 75mm, 2965cc. Maximum power 180bhp (DIN) at 5750rpm.; maximum torque 181lb.ft. at 4000rpm. Borg Warner automatic transmission.

Chassis: Front engine, front drive. Independent front suspension by Hydropneumatic struts and wishbones. Independent rear suspension by Hydropneumatic struts and trailing arms. Self-levelling and ride height control. Power-assisted rack and pinion steering. Four-wheel disc brakes.

Bodywork: Pressed-steel, unit-construction, body chassis unit. Two-door four-seater coupe. Length 16ft. 0.6in.; width 6ft. 0.3in.; height 4ft. 4in. Unladen weight 3200lb.

Performance: (Fuel-injection version) Maximum speed 139mph. 0-60mph 9.3sec. Standing ¼-mile 17.1sec. Typical fuel consumption 20mpg.

Ferrari 275LM

Built: Maranello, Italy, 1963-1965

Ferrari's efforts to produce a limited number of sports racing cars which might just be usable on the roads were often frustrated by the bureaucrats. Nowhere was this more obvious than in the case of the 275LM. Introduced in the autumn of 1963, with the specific intention of being used in GT racing in 1964, it did not actually achieve this status until 1966, by which time it was obsolete!

First, I must justify my use of the 275LM nomenclature. When announced at the Paris Show in 1963, a 2953cc engine was fitted, and logically enough, (in view of his numbering methods, which considered the size of one cylinder in cubic centimetres) Ferrari called it a 250LM. This was the title under which homologation was requested, which was very strange as every car after the first one had a 3286cc engine, and logically should have been a 275LM. Like many writers, therefore, I choose to call the car a 275LM, and let the purists battle away over the rightness of this after I have completed the description.

250LM meant 250 Le Mans, and the new car was really nothing more than a slightly-civilised version of the 250P sports racing car which had notched up a runaway victory at Le Mans in June 1963. It had a single-overhead-camshaft 'Colombo' engine, almost the same as that used in the front-engined Testa Rossas and GTOs which raced for Ferrari with such success, mounted ahead of the line of the rear wheels, with a five-speed unsynchronised gearbox mounted behind the final drive assembly.

Such a car was shaped with an eye to function, lightweight and smooth aerodynamics; nevertheless, Pininfarina was consulted about the transition from 250P racing car to 250LM/275LM 'road car', and the cars built for sale to customers had bodies built by Scaglietti in Modena. The chassis frame, multi-tubular and complex, made no concessions to practicality or to ease of manufacture, and the all-round coil spring independent suspension, disc brakes, lack of sound-deadening, and sparse equipment all bore witness to its racing function and intent.

After the 250LM prototype had been blooded in racing conditions in North America, where it had a quite undistinguished career, the next 250LM appeared at Le Mans complete with 3.3-litre engine, and all subsequent cars were built with this increased-capacity unit. In the meantime, Ferrari had tried to get the car homologated, but failed when the governing body of motor sport (the FIA) discovered that only a

Ferrari '275LM' (250 LM)

handful of cars had been built. Ferrari's case was not helped when he complained that the 250GTO had been approved when rather less than the specified 100 had been built, for this seemed to make the authorities even more determined to deny him a shortcut to approval. His second attempt was also turned down, and in the event the car was not homologated until 1966.

The first noteworthy victory was in the Rheims 12-Hour race in July 1964, when Graham Hill and Jo Bonnier drove an example to win at 126mph, while John Surtees/Lorenzo Bandini were second in a similar car. The car was also successful in 1965, its greatest achievement being to win at Le Mans (for Jochen Rindt and Masten Gregory in a NART-entered car). By 1966, however, Ferrari was more interested in campaigning his P2s or P3s, while the massive and brutishly-powerful Ford GT40s had the legs of the 275LM in Grand Touring races.

Thus, the car never really achieved what Ferrari intended for it, and considerably fewer examples – less than 40, apparently – were sold than had been intended.

Specification

Engine and transmission: Twelve-cylinders, in 60-degree vee-formation, with single-overhead-camshaft cylinder heads. Bore, stroke and capacity 77×58.8mm., 3286cc. Maximum power 320bhp (DIN) at 7500rpm.; maximum torque 231lb.ft. at 5500rpm. Five-speed manual gearbox in unit with engine and transaxle.
Chassis: Mid-engine, rear drive. Separate tubular chassis frame. Independent front suspension by coil springs and wishbones. Worm and sector steering. Independent rear suspension by coil springs and wishbones. Four wheel disc brakes.
Bodywork: Light-alloy coachbuilt two-door two-seater closed coupe fastback style by Pininfarina/Scaglietta. Length 13ft. 5in.; width 5ft. 6.9in.; height 3ft. 7.9in. Unladen weight 1875lb.

Fiat 2300/2300S Coupe

Built: Turin, Italy, 1961-1968

As with the Healey 100, which was speedily adopted for quantity production by Austin, so with the Ghia-styled Fiat coupe, which was shown at the 1960 Turin Show as a private venture, liked by Fiat, and was taken up by the Italian giant to be marketed as an official Fiat model. In the meantime, the larger version of the Fiat six-cylinder engine was to be enlarged from 2.1-litres to 2.3-litres, so the Fiat 2100 Coupe shown by Ghia actually went into production as a 2300.

The mechanical basis of this smart Ghia creation was the underpan, suspensions, and all the running gear, of the six-cylinder Fiat saloon which had made its bow in 1959. It was the first time for some years that there had been a six-cylinder Fiat engine in production, and this one was part of a planned family of units whose smallest derivative was the 1.3-litre 'four' used in the Fiat 1300. Although the original 1800/2100 models used drum brakes, a major innovation for the 1800/2300 models which replaced them in June 1961 was that four-wheel disc brakes were specified.

The structural base of the new car was the standard steel floorpan, on to which Ghia welded a stylish steel two-door four-seater fastback coupe body. So smart was the resulting combination that the 2300S was often dubbed 'the poor man's Ferrari', and with the more powerful derivative of the engine used that was no great exaggeration.

Perhaps it is as well that no cars were sold on the original 2100 base, for that car was no great shakes in the roadholding department. The problem was that although the front end (by wishbones and longitudinal torsion bars) was fine, the rear axle was located by a rather vague combination of trailing quarter-elliptic leaf springs, coil springs over the axle, and a short Panhard rod across the axis of the car. For the 2300 of 1961 (which must mean that the decision to make the change took place soon after the 2100 had been announced!) this complex system was discarded in favour of a perfectly adequate and conventional rear suspension by half-elliptic leaf springs.

There were two versions of the car right from the start, which could not be distinguished externally by badging or style differences. The 'standard' 2300 used the unmodified Fiat 2300 engine, while the 2300S model used a much more powerful version of the same engine, which boasted no less than 150bhp (gross), and was linked to higher gearing. As the engine range had been developed under the direction of Aurelio Lampredi, that distinguished designer of Ferrari vee-12s in the 1950s, as soon as he had joined Fiat, no one doubted that it could do the job, and give long life. Even though it had a single side-mounted camshaft and pushrod-operated valves, those valves were opposed to each other in part-spherical combustion chambers, which ensured deep and efficient breathing.

Some thousands of these smart and practical coupes were built between 1961 and 1968, but their place as Fiat 'flagships' was taken over by the Ferrari-engined Dinos in 1967, and production ran out shortly afterwards when the saloon range on which they were based was discontinued.

Specification

Engine and transmission: Six-cylinders, in-line, with pushrod-operated overhead-valve cylinder head. Bore, stroke and capacity 78 × 79.5mm., 2279cc. Maximum power 150bhp (gross) at 5600rpm.; maximum torque 145lb.ft. at 4000rpm. Four-speed manual gearbox in unit with engine. Hypoid bevel final drive.

Chassis: Front engine, final drive. Unit-construction pressed-steel body/chassis unit. Independent front suspension by torsion bars and wishbones. Worm and sector steering. Rear suspension of live axle by half-elliptic leaf springs. Four wheel disc brakes.

Bodywork: Pressed-steel monocoque two-door four-seater fastback coupe style by Ghia. Length 15ft. 1.9in.; width 5ft. 4.2in.; height 4ft. 5.7in. Unladen weight 2790lb.

Performance: Maximum speed 121mph. 0-60mph 11.6sec. Standing ¼-mile 18.8sec.

Note: The 2300 coupe, a lower-powered version, had 117bhp (gross) at 5300rpm.; maximum torque of 136lb.ft. at 3000rpm.

Fiat 2300S Coupe

Fiat 124 Abarth Rally, Montecarlo 1975

Fiat 124 Abarth Rally

Built: Turin, Italy, 1973-1975

Although Fiat had not actively been involved in motor sport for many years, their announcement that they were to set up a factory team for world-championship rallying in 1971 was taken with great seriousness. There was only one minor disappointment — that they were not proposing to use the Ferrari-engined Fiat Dinos. Instead, their effort was concentrated on the evolution and development of the Fiat 124 Sport Spider model. This, though relatively heavy, had the twin-overhead-camshaft engine which had been newly-announced in 1966.

Even though they notched up successes at once, and had their first outright win with the car in 1972, it was clear that a more specialised machine would soon be needed. To make the Spiders fully competitive, Fiat asked their Abarth subsidiary (they had taken over the famous tuning concern in 1971) to develop it further, on the basis that such a specialised car would have to be sold in some numbers to ensure its homologation.

The result of this contract, first seen in 1973, was the 124 Abarth Rally, which though visually little changed was rather different under the skin. To the standard steel monocoque, Abarth had grafted an independent rear suspension layout, standardised on the five-speed gearbox, and matched this to the 1756cc engine currently fitted to the 132s and the latest 124 Coupes. The whole car was lighter than before (all sound deadening and other 'comfort' items were ruthlessly discarded), there were no bumpers, and the car was built with a glass-fibre hardtop but without provision for a hood.

Because Fiat only intended to built the minimum quantity required to achieve homologation – 500 in this case, for Group 4 classification – they arranged for Abarth to built the special mechanical parts, for Pininfarina (who built the quantity-production 124 Sport Spiders on which this body was based) to built the special bodies, and for the cars to be assembled on a special assembly line at the Fiat Lingotto plant near Turin.

The prototype car was seen in the autumn of 1972, but production and deliveries did not begin until the beginning of 1973 – by which time, incidentally, homologation had already been achieved. Although a very practical and purposeful rally car, it was clear that in heavy traffic it could be a liability, as the skin panels were largely light alloy and flimsy glass-fibre. The 'production' car had a 128bhp (DIN) engine, though most cars were instantly modified to the 170/180bhp tune used by the works, and sold (for a great deal of money) by Abarth.

It was enough for Fiat to win the Portuguese TAP Rally outright in 1974, but this win had taken time as two second places were the best which could be achieved in 1973. For 1975 the works cars were even more powerful than before (with between 180 and 200bhp being claimed, depending on how boastful the spokesman was feeling that day!), for they were being fitted with the optional 16-valve cylinder head which was also to be found on the Lancia Beta Coupes used briefly by the Lancia works team, and which would be such an important item in the specification of the next new Fiat rally car.

In 1975, however, in spite of some very determined driving, and many successes, it was clear that the 124 Abarth Rally was being outpaced. After dallying with the idea of a much-modified mid-engined X1/9, Fiat decided to go for an 'Abarth solution' to their 131 saloon, and to make ready for this production of the two-seater was run down in 1975.

Specification

Engine and transmission: Four-cylinders, in-line, with twin-overhead-camshaft cylinder head. Bore, stroke and capacity 84×79.2mm., 1756cc. Maximum power 128bhp (DIN) at 6200rpm.; maximum torque 117lb.ft. at 5200rpm. Five-speed manual gearbox in unit with engine. Hypoid bevel final drive.

Chassis: Front engine, rear drive. Unit-construction pressed-steel body/chassis unit. Independent front suspension by coil springs and wishbones. Worm and sector steering. Independent rear suspension by coil springs, wishbones and radius arms. Four-wheel disc brakes.

Bodywork: Pressed-steel two-door two-seater open sports body style by Pininfarina. Length 12ft. 10in.; width 5ft. 4.2in.; height 4ft. 0.8in. Unladen weight 2070lb.

Performance (Manufacturer's claim): Maximum speed 118mph. 0-60mph 7.5sec. Standing ¼-mile 15.9sec. Typical fuel consumption 25mpg.

Fiat 131 Abarth

Built: Turin, Italy, 1976 to 1979

Although Fiat have only been actively involved in 'works' competition since the beginning of the 1970s, they have acquired a fearsomely impressive amount of expertise in a very short time. However, they did not attempt to produce a true saloon car 'homologation special' until 1976, when the Fiat 131 Abarth was announced.

Up to that time, 'works' Fiats had been based on the 124 Sport Spider, and it was only after a much-modified X1/9 project was dropped in 1975 that it was decided to produce a very special saloon car. Abarth, who had been building the special all-independent Abarth Sport Spiders for a couple of years, were commissioned to turn the humdrum 131 saloon into a winner.

As produced in huge quantities at the Mirafiori factory, the 131 was no more and no less than a multi-model small/medium saloon car, with a choice of 1300 or 1600

Fiat 131 Abarth Rally, Canada 1977

pushrod engines, an all-steel bodyshell, and a live rear axle. Abarth, working very fast, produced the 131 Abarth, which in every way except its basic bodyshell was completely different.The first prototype was ready in the autumn of 1975, the first rally win followed within weeks, and the 'production' car was homologated in spring 1976. Since then it has been stronger, faster, and more reliable, and has helped Fiat to win two successive rallying world championships — in 1977 and 1978.

Starting from the basic two-door bodyshell, Abarth threw away all the skin panels and the entire power train. In their place, they inserted the full 2-litre, twin-overhead-cam, 16-valve version of the Fiat engine, matched it to a Colotti five-speed gearbox, and inserted the independent rear suspension system already well-proven on the two-seater 124 Spiders. All body skin panels were of glass-fibre, with slots and louvres which could be blanked off or made functional, depending on the purpose for which the car was intended. To gain Group 4 homologation, 400 examples had to be built quickly, and this was therefore done. The factory competitions department took delivery of a large number — rumoured to be no less than 50; — and set about turning the car into a winner.

As so much was already known about the engine and transmission, this took very little time, and — helped by a dedicated and very large development staff — the department were soon able to fine-tune the basic car to most events. Compared with other marques (Ford, for example), the engine would neither rev as well, nor produce as much peak power, but it was still competitive, and since the chassis was endowed with such good roadholding this made up for a lot.

Not too many cars are sold purely for road use, but in that trim the engine produces a mere 140bhp and uses only one twin-choke Weber carburettor. Fuel-injected and race-tuned works engines dispose of about 230bhp, and can be almost shatteringly noisy.

On events where practice is possible in advance (which represents most of the world's top rallies these days) the Fiat is always a potential winner, especially when its superstar drivers like Markku Alen and Walter Rohrl are in the team cars. For the last few years their running battle with the factory Fords has made rallying incredibly exciting. The marketing benefits of successful competition are there for all to see.

Specification

Engine and transmission: Four-cylinders, in-line, with twin-overhead-camshaft cylinder head. Bore, stroke and capacity 84×90mm., 1995cc. Maximum power 140bhp (DIN) at 6400rpm.; maximum torque 130lb.ft. at 3800rpm. Five-speed manual Colotti gearbox in unit with engine. Hypoid bevel final drive.

Chassis: Front engine, rear drive. Pressed-steel unit-construction body-chassis unit. Independent front suspension by coil springs and MacPherson struts. Rack and pinion steering. Independent rear suspension by coil springs, wishbones and radius arms. Four-wheel disc brakes.

Bodywork: Pressed-steel two-door four-seater GT saloon body style with glass-fibre skin panels. Length 13ft. 7.8in.; width 5ft. 11.6in.; height 4ft. 6.3in. Unladen weight 2160lb.

Performance: (Road car) Maximum speed 112mph. 0-60mph 7.2sec. Standing ¼-mile 16.5sec. Typical fuel consumption 26mpg.

Ford Lotus-Cortina

Built: Cheshunt, England, 1963 to 1966 & Dagenham, England, 1967 to 1970

My immediate problem is to define the manufacturer of these intriguing cars. The 1963-1966 model, always affectionately known as 'the Lotus-Cortina, was actually assembled by Lotus though sold by Ford dealers, while the restyled example of 1967-1970 was always assembled by Ford, and for the latter part of its life was known as a 'Cortina Twin-Cam.'

The original car was designed as part of a deal between Ford and Lotus, to provide a potential race and rally winner for both companies. Ford had just embarked on their new 'Total Performance' marketing programme. They were to supply the basic two-door bodyshells and front suspensions to Lotus, who would install their own Lotus-modified Ford engine, close-ratio gearbox, and special rear suspension, along with different fascia styling and other details.

The car was announced at the beginning of 1963, was in halting production by the summer, and was a race winner almost at once. Rally successes took time to mature, mainly because the car proved to have very fragile rear suspension, and doubtful reliability. It was only after the car was re-engineered (really reverting to standard) with leaf spring instead of coil spring rear suspension that it could begin to win rough road events as well.

When the Cortina was restyled, the original Lotus-Cortina was withdrawn from production, and when the Mark II car was revealed it was seen to be rather more of a Ford, and it was always assembled among more humdrum Cortinas at Dagenham. Although it still used the twin-cam eight-valve Lotus engine of 1558cc, the light-alloy body skin panels had gone, and items like the special gearbox and axle ratios were now only expensive options. The main reason for its existence (as a potential competition winner) disappeared in 1968, when the Escort Twin-Cam was announced, and it was only used in 'works' guise in 1967.

However, the Mark II car, which had been thoroughly redeveloped by Ford when it had been decided to make it at Dagenham, was also a fine and exhilirating road car to drive. The same could rarely be said of Mark I cars, which often suffered from leaky back axles, unreliable engines, and noisy bodies.

Both cars were offered as standard with engines of between 105 and 110bhp. In racing use, however, where fuel-injection could be used, and where there were no limits on special fittings, anything up to 180bhp was seen. Because of the nature of the suspension geometry, incidentally, it was quite usual to see Lotus-Cortinas 'three-wheeling' round tight corners, with their inside front wheels several inches off the ground.

All Mark I cars were sold in white with Lotus-green flashes, as were some of the Mark IIs, but a complete colour range became available for the later cars. The Mark IIs, too, acted as midwives for the Escort Twin-Cams, which used most of their power train components without modification. The Mark II remained on the market until 1970, but when the Cortina was once again restyled it was withdrawn completely.

Ford Lotus-Cortina MkI, 1965

Specification (Mk I model)

Engine and transmission: Four-cylinders in-line, with twin-overhead-camshaft cylinder head, Lotus-modified on Ford base. Bore, stroke and capacity 82.55×72.7mm., 1558cc. Maximum power 105bhp (net) at 5500rpm.; maximum torque 108lb.ft. at 4000rpm. Four-speed manual gearbox in unit with engine. Hypoid bevel final drive.
Chassis: Front engine, rear drive. Unit-construction pressed-steel body/chassis unit. Independent front suspension by coil springs and MacPherson struts. Rack and pinion steering. Suspension of rear live axle by coil springs, radius arms and A-bracket, or (later cars, 1965 and 1966) by half-elliptic leaf springs and radius arms. Front wheel disc brakes, rear drums.

Bodywork: Pressed-steel, two-door four-seater GT saloon style. Length 13ft. 10in.; width 5ft. 2.5in.; height 4ft. 7in. Unladen weight 1820lb.

Performance: Maximum speed 106mph. 0-60mph 9.9sec. Standing ¼-mile 17.4sec. Typical fuel consumption 22mpg.

Note: Mark II Lotus Cortina of 1967-1970 had following differences: 110bhp (net) at 6000rpm.; maximum torque 107lb.ft. at 4500rpm. Length 14ft. 0in.; width 5ft. 5in.; height 4ft. 6in. Unladen weight 2010lb.

Performance: Maximum speed 104mph. 0-60mph 11.0sec. Standing ¼-mile 18.2sec. Typical fuel consumption 24mpg.

Ford Lotus-Cortina MkII, 1967

Ford Escort Twin-Cam and RS1600

Built: Liverpool, England, 1968-1970 & South Ockendon, England, 1970-1974

To replace, and improve upon, the Lotus-Cortina as an 'homologation special' for competition, Ford decided to transform the new Ford Escort in exactly the same way. It is simpler to describe what was done than it undoubtedly was to carry out the project, but the entire power train from the Lotus-Cortina was fitted into a standard steel two-door Ford Escort bodyshell. With suitably strengthened and stiffened suspension, therefore, the new Escort Twin-Cam was born.

To get production under way as quickly as possible, the first 25 cars were actually assembled at the Ford competition department at Boreham Airfield, but thereafter the Twin-Cams were assembled in relatively small numbers among more mundane Escorts at the Halewood factory, near Liverpool.

The Twin-Cam immediately proved to be competitive in forestry-type events, but it was soon apparent that it was not a winner on tarmac events, so for 1970 it was given an entirely different engine – this time designed by Cosworth. The original Twin-Cam had used the eight-valve Lotus modified engine, but the BDA engine, by Cosworth, was based on the latest 1600cc cylinder block, and had four-valves per cylinder in best Grand Prix engine style, driven by a toothed rubber belt; this derivative was named the RS1600.

Even so, it was still only capable of being enlarged safely and predictably to about 1800cc (this enlargement was allowable under most sets of regulations), and it was not until the end of 1962, when a new light-alloy cylinder block was standardised, that it became possible for the 1601cc unit to be enlarged to the full two-litre capacity limit of its class.

The power of each production engine was limited to no more than 106bhp and 120bhp (Twin-Cam and RS1600 respectively), but for full-blooded competition these figures could be raised dramatically. Most powerful of all were the race-tuned BDAs, which could give up to 260bhp (and later units – see the RS1800 section – gave even more) and could rev to beyond 9000rpm.

Demand for the Escort performance models was healthy, and increased sharply when the Mexico (a downmarket version of the RS1600 with an ordinary pushrod ohv engine) came on to the market. To make this car, and to take over RS1600 assembly from Halewood, a special production line was installed at the small Ford South Ockendon factory, becoming the Advanced Vehicle Operation, and it was here that special Escorts were turned out until the end of 1974, when Mark I Escort production also ceased.

The Twin-Cam and RS1600 road cars used suspension which, though beefier, bore a definite close resemblance to those of the cheap little family-car Escorts. In full-house competition form, however, four wheel disc brakes were fitted, special linkages were developed for back axles, and these were matched with the fitment of 5-speed ZF gearboxes, heavy-duty axles, and extensively modified bodies.

The RS1600s, indeed, were almost infinitely variable to a customer's use, which made them ideal for many branches of the sport. Not only that, but they were essentially simple cars, which could be fettled and repaired very quickly. They did not fade from popularity, but were replaced by the rebodied RS1800 in 1975.

Ford Escort RS1600

Specification (Twin Cam)

Engine and transmission: Four-cylinders, in-line, with twin-overhead-camshaft cylinder head, Lotus-modified from Ford design. Bore, stroke and capacity 82.55×72.8mm., 1558cc. Maximum power 106bhp (net) at 6000rpm.; maximum torque 107lb.ft. at 4500rpm. Four-speed manual gearbox in unit with engine. Hypoid bevel final drive.

Chassis: Front engine, rear drive. Unit-construction pressed steel body shell. Independent front suspension by coil springs and MacPherson struts. Rack and pinion steering. Rear suspension of live axle by half-elliptic leaf springs and radius arms. Front wheel disc brakes, rear drums.

Bodywork: Pressed-steel, two-door four-seater GT saloon style. Length 13ft. 0.6in.; width 5ft. 1.8in.; height 4ft. 5in. Unladen weight 1920lb.

Performance: Maximum speed 113mph. 0-60mph 9.9sec. Standing ¼-mile 17.2sec. Typical fuel consumption 24mpg.

Note: RS1600 was same car, with different twin-overhead camshaft engine. Bore, stroke and capacity 80.97×77.6mm., 1601cc. Maximum power 120bhp (DIN) 6500rpm.; maximum torque 112lb.ft. at 4000rpm.

Performance: Maximum speed 113mph. 0-60mph 8.9sec. Standing ¼-mile 16.7sec. Typical fuel consumption 22mpg.

294

Ford Escort RS1800

Built: Saarlouis, Germany, & South Ockendon, England, 1975-1977

In essence, the Escort RS1800 was no more than a rebodied successor to the Escort RS1600, but in fact there was more to it than this. Much less emphasis was always laid on the RS1800 in marketing terms than had ever been put on the RS1600. The later models, it seems, were really only built under sufferance, because a certain minimum quantity were required for the car to re-qualify for competitions eligibility. Before the exigencies of EEC Type Approval bore on it the RS1800 was officially withdrawn from production, but for months before that only a trickle had been delivered.

Compared with the RS1600, the RS1800 had the completely revised two-door Escort II body style (including a distinctive flexible rubberised rear spoiler), and the light-alloy engine had been enlarged to 1845cc, and had only a single downdraught twin-choke Weber carburettor fitted. For competition use, however, the car could be brought up to the full specification already familiar on RS1600s, and there has been continuous development in recent years to make the car even faster, stronger, and more versatile.

Ford Escort RS1800

Although a very few of the cars were assembled in Britain (at Halewood, the South Ockendon plant having closed at the end of 1974), proper RS1800 production took place in West Germany, and the engines were finally fitted in a small workshop in Britain before being delivered to the dealers.

With its new enlarged engine, and with more docile tuning, the RS1800 road car, if kept reliable and in good shape, was a most pleasant road car. The engine was very free-revving, the handling was predictable and sporting, yet the ensemble was flexible enough to be used in heavy traffic or on motorways.

Unlike the RS1600, too, the RS1800 had more distinctive badging and decoration, and could be ordered in one of two standards of trim and furnishing. Nevertheless, it was as a competition car that it had most appeal, and it is true that many RS1800s were painstakingly built up from bare bodyshells in workshops, often as effective rebuilds as old and tired RS1600s. Almost all the factory competition cars took shape in this manner, and since 1975 they have become more and yet more effective rally winners. In 1979, without mounting an all-out effort, the marque won the World Rally Championship; it looks as if the car could go on being a winner for years to come.

It is remarkable, looking back, to think that the first Escort won its first event in 1968, and that 12 years later it has the pace and versatility to be a world champion. The 155bhp of the 1968 Twin-Cam, however, does not compare with the fuel-injected 270bhp of the latest RS1800s!

Specification

Engine and transmission: Four-cylinders, in-line, with twin-overhead-camshaft cylinder head. Bore, stroke and capacity 86.75 × 77.62mm., 1845cc. Maximum power 115bhp (DIN) at 6000rpm.; maximum torque 120lb.ft. at 4000rpm. Four-speed manual gearbox in unit with engine. Hypoid bevel final drive.

Chassis: Front engine, rear drive. Unit-construction pressed-steel body/chassis unit. Independent front suspension by coil springs and MacPherson struts. Rack and pinion steering. Suspension of rear live axle by half-elliptic leaf springs and radius arms. Front wheel disc brakes, rear drums.

Bodywork: Pressed-steel, two-door four-seater GT saloon style. Length 13ft. 0.5in.; width 5ft. 2.8in.; height 4ft. 7.5in. Unladen weight 2015lb.

Performance: Maximum speed 111mph. 0-60mph 9.0sec. Standing ¼-mile 16.9sec. Typical fuel consumption 28mpg.

Lagonda Rapide

Built: Newport Pagnell, England, 1961-1964

In 1947, industrialist David Brown took control of two ailing car manufacturers – Lagonda and Aston Martin. As part of their assets he inherited a fine chassis (Aston Martin) and a fine engine and GT car (Lagonda). The Lagonda was put into production virtually unchanged, and the first of the DB2s (which also used that engine) followed in 1950. Production of the Lagonda, in spite of a smart restyle, ran out in 1958, after which the very name disappeared from the scene for three-years.

David Brown always let it be known that he wanted to see a Lagonda saloon car back on offer, and he fulfilled this wish in 1961 when the Rapide GT saloon was introduced. As one might expect, it was broadly based on DB4 design principles and components, but was rather different in many detail respects. The platform chassis and front suspension was retained, though lengthened by 16-inches, and the Rapide's rear suspension was de Dion, by transverse torsion bars.

The engine was an enlarged version of that already fitted to the DB4 (3995 instead of 3670cc) – a size which would be standardised on the DB5 in two years time – but for a six-cylinder unit was very strangely equipped with two twin-choke Solex carburettors. Automatic transmission was standard, though manual transmission was optional.

Lagonda Rapide

In many ways, the Rapide should have been a big version of the Aston, but (and I do not say this lightly) its controversial looks were likened to those of Ford's unhappy Edsel, which somehow tainted its potential. It is also a sad historical fact that four-door cars produced by or for Aston Martin have not so far achieved success, and the Rapide did not break this trend. Only 55 cars were sold in three years, some were unreliable, and with the continuing expansion in DB5 sales at the time the company were happy, if not relieved, to drop the Rapide. There would be no further 'Lagonda' for another ten years.

Specification

Engine and transmission: Six-cylinders, in-line, with twin-camshaft cylinder head. Bore, stroke and capacity 96×92mm, 3995cc. Maximum power 236bhp (net) at 5000rpm.; maximum torque 265lb.ft. at 4000rpm. Four-speed gearbox or optional Borg Warner automatic transmission, in unit with engine. Hypoid bevel rear axle.
Chassis: Front engine, rear drive. Fabricated steel platform chassis. Independent front suspension by coil springs and wishbones. Rack and pinion steering. Rear suspension, de Dion, transverse torsion bars, radius arms, Watts linkage. Four-wheel disc brakes.
Bodywork: Shell built on Superleggera principles, with steel inner panels, tubular superstructure, and light alloy skin; four-seater, four-door saloon. Length 16ft. 3.5in.; width 5ft. 9.5in.; height 4ft. 8in. Unladen weight 3780lb.

Lancia Stratos

Lancia Stratos

Built: Turin, Italy, 1974-1975

Perhaps the only example, so far, of a purpose-built, limited-production rally car, Lancia's Stratos had a short and incredibly successful career. Its first event of all was in the 1972 *Tour de Corse*, and its last 'works' entry was in the 1978 RAC Rally. In both events it retired, which gives a completely unreliable guide to its effectiveness; it was enough to give the rallying World Championship to Lancia in 1975 and 1976, and a Stratos was *always* a likely winner, whatever the event in which a 'works' car was entered.

The story starts with a Bertone design exercise shown at the 1970 Turin Motor Show, in which a wedge-shaped dream car had a mid-mounted Lancia Fulvia 1600 engine, and a rear-hinged top opening door/passenger compartment lid. Cesare Fiorio, Lancia's competitions chief, noticed the car, saw its potential as a competition car, and persuaded his company to adopt it as a serious project. The first car to run was a Lancia-engined prototype in 1971 (the Turin Show car was only a mock-up) but before any serious development was carried out it was decided to use the Ferrari Dino 246's 2.4-litre vee-6 engine and transmission in place of the Lancia unit. As both Lancia and Ferrari were − by then − controlled by Fiat, the engine could be considered as 'in the family', and there were no commercial difficulties in making this swap.

Development continued in 1972 and 1973, with a car winning the *Tour de France* in 1973, driven by Sandro Munari and Mario Mannucci. Production, at a very limited rate, started at the Bertone body building factory in Turin early in 1973, and 'homologation' for competition use was achieved in the autumn of 1974. Thereafter,

the Stratos was *the* car to beat in international rallying; and it was very rarely beaten!

The structure, thoroughly redesigned and made more rugged once Lancia took an interest, was a simple but technically efficient steel monocoque, with all-independent suspension, topped by a stubby but entirely functional wedge-shaped glass-fibre two-seater coupe bodyshell.

Even though it was supreme on tarmac rallies, Mike Parkes, in charge of technical development until he was killed in a car crash, also developed it into a really formidable rough road car. It could so easily have won the world's two most important rough-road events – the RAC Rally and the East African Safari – but on several occasions was side-lined by misfortune or by trivial failures.

Few more than 400 production cars were built (this was the minimum number required to achieve homologation), and even Lancia admitted that a good deal of this number sat around, unsold, in Lancia factories for a long time. The Stratos, it must be admitted, was a 'nervous', cramped, and uncivilised machine for purely road use, and though some cars have been seen in use for this purpose, the vast majority have been purpose-modified competition cars.

Known affectionately as the 'plastic pig' by friend and rival alike, the Stratos became extraordinarily versatile. It could be seen with short-travel or long-travel suspension, normal or turbocharged engines, two-valve or four-valve cylinder heads, with and without aerodynamic spoilers, and – naturally – in a whole range of sponsors' colour schemes. In factory use, many Stratos entries were in Marlboro, Alitalia, or Pirelli livery, and it is in this form which many of us will always remember them. We will also recall that sensational noise, that warbling exhaust accompanied by frequent gearchanges which always seemed certain to be too noisy to get through the compulsory noise tests. But we need not have worried; they always passed – perhaps even the event organisers were reluctant to pass up an opportunity of having the Stratos grace their events.

Although it was officially 'retired' by the Fiat-Lancia team at the end of 1978, for policy reasons and in favour of the Fiat 131 Abarth, the Stratos is still good enough to win in well-sponsored but private hands, as Bernard Darniche proved by immediately winning the 1979 Monte Carlo against the might of the factory Ford Escorts. This is not surprising, as the four-valve engines could produce up to 285bhp, and the later two-valve units 270bhp, with impressive flexibility and great reliability.

Specification

Engine and transmission: Six-cylinders, in 65-degree vee-formation, transversely mounted, with twin-overhead-camshaft cylinder heads, built by Ferrari. Bore, stroke and capacity 92.5×60mm., 2418cc. Maximum power 190bhp (DIN) at 7000rpm.; maximum torque 166lb.ft. at 4000rpm. Five-speed manual gearbox in unit with engine and transaxle. Hypoid bevel final drive.

Chassis: Mid-engine, rear drive. Pressed and fabricated steel unit-construction body-chassis unit. Independent front suspension by coil springs and wishbones. Rack and pinion steering. Independent rear suspension by coil springs and wishbones Four-wheel disc brakes.

Bodywork: Glass-fibre, two-door two-seater mid-engined coupe body style by Bertone. Length 12ft. 2in.; width 5ft. 8.9in.; height 3ft. 7.7in. Unladen weight 2160lb.

Performance: Maximum speed 143mph. 0-60mph 6.0sec. Standing ¼-mile 13.5sec. Typical fuel consumption 18mpg.

NSU Prinz 1000TTS

NSU Prinz 1000 TTS

Built: Neckarsulm, Germany, 1967-1971

By the mid-1960s, almost every manufacturer with any ambitions to sporting success had produced an 'homologation special' of one sort or another. NSU, with their Prinz 1000TTS, were no exception. This rather unattractive looking little projectile, which even in standard form offered 70bhp (DIN) from a 996cc engine, was always a potential class winner, in racing and rallying, but was forced out of production in 1971 as VW (who had taken over a financially-troubled NSU in 1969) began to carry out rationalisation and economies.

As with other such homologation specials, the TTS was a case of squeezing more power into less space. The ancestor of the whole of this NSU range was the stubby little Prinz 4 of 1961, which among other things also gave birth to the Bertone-bodied Sport Prinz coupe, and to the technically-significant Wankel Spider. The Prinz 4 had a rear-mounted two-cylinder 598cc engine, but the Prinz 1000 which followed in 1963 had a closely-related four-cylinder unit of 996cc, also mounted transversely behind the line of the rear wheels. The Type 110 and the 1200 followed (the latter with an engine enlarged to 1177cc), as did the 1000TT, which was roughly equivalent to the Mini-Cooper, but it was the TTS which provided most excitement.

There were three body lengths in this series — the Prinz 4 being shortest, the 1000 lengthened, and the Type 110 and 1200s being even longer. The TTS used the middle-sized body with the four-cylinder engine designed to match it in the first place, but with the highest specific output of all the engines used in this long-running and successful series.

The TTS's biggest drawback (apart from its styling, which could best be described as USA-influenced, and rather flashy) was that its rear engine, even though constructed mainly of light-alloys, affected the handling and stability due to its position in the tail of the car. For that reason the TTS, even though powerful (and potentially very powerful after receiving the attention of West German tuners) could not match the Cooper S, even in its hard-to-buy 1-litre form, which had quite impeccable road manners.

A characteristic of these noisy but effective little cars was that their highly-tuned engines tended to overheat (the water radiators were not really adequate for the job, as they were placed in the engine bay at the rear), so to alleviate this successfully, the car was homologated complete with wedges to prop open the engine lid to allow more air to circulate. A look into the engine compartment revealed an engine dominated by two huge twin-choke Solex carburettors, and convoluted exhaust manifolding.

Specification

Engine and transmission: Four-cylinders, in-line, transversely mounted, with single-overhead-camshaft cylinder head. Bore, stroke and capacity 69 × 66.6mm., 996cc. Maximum power 70bhp (DIN) at 6150rpm.; maximum torque 61lb.ft. at 5500rpm. Four-speed gearbox in unit with engine and transaxle. Spiral bevel final drive.
Chassis: Rear engine, rear drive. Unit-construction bodyshell, in two-door four-seater saloon car style. Independent front suspension by coil springs and wishbones. Rack and pinion steering. Independent rear suspension by coil springs and semi-trailing arms. Front wheel disc brakes, rear drums.
Bodywork: Pressed-steel unit-construction shell, made by NSU. Length 12ft. 5.2in.; width 4ft. 10.7in.; height 4ft. 5.5in. Unladen weight 1545lb.
Performance: Maximum speed 97mph. 0-60mph 14.7sec. Standing ¼-mile 19.3sec. Typical fuel consumption 27mpg.

Opel Ascona 400

Built: Antwerp, Belgium, 1979 to date

Although Opel, through their dealer-financed Eurohandler Team, began a serious competitions programme in the early 1970s, they never troubled to develop a true 'homologation special' until the end of the decade. For years they concentrated on the use of Kadett GT/Es, with a variety of 1.9 and 2.0-litre engines, one version of which had the option of a twin-overhead-camshaft 16-valve cylinder head.

The team suffered mixed fortunes, and under their new manager – Englishman Tony Fall – a new car began to evolve in 1977, and was announced in the spring of 1979. Its base was the perfectly normal two-door Ascona saloon, but there were important differences for the new derivative. As a minimum of 400 cars had to be built to achieve homologation, it was decided to call the new car, appropriately enough, the Ascona 400, and more than this minimum quantity was built at Opel's Belgian assembly plant during 1979.

The 'chassis' was virtually the same as that of the normal Ascona, except that the torque tube axle location was discarded in favour of a radius arm and Panhard rod location for the coil sprung back axle; this, in fact, was a layout already in use by GM

Opel Ascona 400

South Africa. Disc brakes were fitted to the rear axle, which was a modified Commodore unit.

The heart of the car was its engine, based on the very strong Ascona *diesel* cylinder block, and having a displacement of 2.4-litres. This was topped by a developed version of the existing Opel sixteen-valve cylinder head. Road cars use Bosch fuel-injection (with inlet manifold pipes cast in to the engines top camshaft cover), though competition engines use Weber carburettors, and are prepared by Cosworth. To deal with all this power the gearbox is a robust five-speed Getrag unit as used on larger and more luxurious Opels.

Like all good 'homologation specials' the Ascona 400 is distinguished by a special colour scheme, and has plastics panels, including a big under-bumper spoiler and embryo 'running boards' along the sides. An interesting touch is the air outlet in the bonnet panel, immediately above the radiator shell, and styled into the overall decor.

Even the road car has exhilirating performance, and excellent roadholding due to the fat low-profile tyres. The Group 4 rally car proved itself on only its second event with an outright win on the 1980 Swedish rally; even on its debut, in the Monte Carlo Rally, an Ascona 400 was fourth overall.

As first seen in 1979, the Ascona 400 was only at the start of an ambitious development programme. Rally engines produce 240bhp, but may be expected to become more powerful in the next couple of years, and it is known that more effective (and more noticeable) aerodynamic spoilers and aids will be fitted in the future. The car is a little heavy and will be progressively lightened.

Specification

Engine and transmission: Four-cylinders, in-line, with twin-overhead-camshaft cylinder head. Bore, stroke and capacity 95 × 85mm., 2410cc. Maximum power 140bhp (DIN) at 5000rpm.; maximum torque 147lb.ft. at 3500rpm. Five-speed manual gearbox in unit with engine. Hypoid bevel final drive.

Chassis: Front engine, rear drive. Unit-construction pressed steel body/chassis structure. Independent front suspension by coil springs, wishbones and anti-roll bar. Rack and pinion steering. Suspension of rear live axle by coil springs, radius arms and Panhard rod. Four wheel disc brakes.

Bodywork: Pressed steel bodyshell, with plastics panels and aerodynamic aids. Two-door four-seater GT saloon style by Opel. Length 14ft. 2.1in.; width 5ft. 5in.; height 4ft. 5in. Unladen weight (approx) 2200lb.

Performance (Manufacturer's claims): Maximum speed 124mph. 0-60mph 8.0sec.

Panther de Ville

Built: Byfleet, England, 1974 to date

After Robert Jankel's Panther J72 (described elsewhere) had been in production for two-years, he decided to expand his Panther range with something entirely different. The result was the enormous and exclusive de Ville, which may or may not (depending on whom you talk to) have a resemblance to the legendary Bugatti Royale. It is made as a four-door coupe or as a two-door convertible, in tiny numbers and at a very high price, but finds ready sales in overseas markets. The bluff styling and ponderous construction ensures that it does not qualify as a Supercar, as the performance is not as outstanding as the use of a Jaguar vee-12 engine might suggest.

Mechanically and structurally, the Panther is a strange mixture of modern and obsolete construction. The engine, transmission and suspensions are all pure modern Jaguar, which ensures that the de Ville has an acceptable ride, respectable handling, great refinement and good performance. On the other hand, the tubular chassis is as simple and uncomplicated as Panther can make it, commensurate with stiffness and rigidity. The imposing bodyshell, for all that it is remarkably carefully and artistically assembled, uses age-old methods of assembly – with steel and light-alloy panelling on the basis of a hardwood bodyframe. Craftsmen, indeed, from old-established coachbuilding businesses, have been attracted to Byfleet to carry on with their skills.

The de Ville, like other Panthers, is deliberately styled in the 'manner' of the 1920s and 1930s, and this has been done because Jankel is of the opinion that cars of those actual periods are now very rare and there is a good demand for replicas of the type.

Panther De Ville

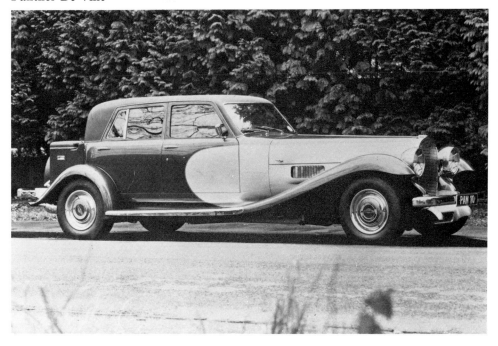

Specification

Engine and transmission: Twelve cylinders, in 60-degree vee-formation, with single-overhead-camshaft cylinder heads, Jaguar built. Bore, stroke and capacity 90 × 70mm., 5343cc. Maximum power 285bhp (DIN) at 5750rpm.; maximum torque 294lb.ft. at 3500rpm. Borg-Warner automatic transmission; manual transmission not available. Hypoid bevel final drive.

Chassis: Front engine, rear drive. Separate chassis frame with tubular members. Independent front suspension by coil springs and wishbones. Power-assisted rack and pinion steering. Independent rear suspension by coil springs, transverse wishbones, and radius arms. Four-wheel disc brakes.

Bodywork: Coachbuilt bodyshell of light-alloy panelling on wooden frame, by Panther, available as two-door GT saloon or convertible. Length 17ft. 0in.; width 5ft. 11in.; height 5ft. 1in. Unladen weight 4370lb.

Note: Optional 6-cylinder version has following differences: Six-cylinders, in-line, with twin-overhead-camshaft cylinder head, Jaguar built. Bore, stroke and capacity 92.05 × 106mm., 4235cc. Maximum power 190bhp (DIN) at 5000rpm.; maximum torque 200lb.ft. at 2000rpm. Four-speed gearbox with overdrive optional. Unladen weight 4365lb.

Panther De Ville Convertible

Renault 5 Gordini

Renault 5 Alpine or Gordini

Built: Paris, France, 1976 to date

Ever since Amadee Gordini joined forces with Renault, there has always been one sporting car in the Renault range bearing his illustrious name. The most recent of these only carries the Gordini name in some markets, and the Alpine in others. In Britain, for instance, use of the model name of Alpine would not have been allowed because of a clash with the Chrysler/Talbot Alpine.

The Renault 5 range began with a very practical series of workaday hatchbacks launched in 1972, but the Alpine derivative was delayed until March 1976, when it came in as an effective replacement for the 12 Gordini. Described at the time as the 'Renault Mini-Cooper', the similarities were obvious, for under a nominally mundane exterior was hidden a really sporting mechanical package.

The bodyshell was merely that of the Renault 5, with a practical but typically French three-door hatchback shape of no particular grace, and the all-independent torsion bar suspensions (transverse at the rear, longitudinal at the front) was different only in relation to the rates and stiffnesses. The engine, as in other Renault 5s, was placed fore-and-aft, and was behind the line of the front wheels, with a gearbox ahead of it.

307

The engine itself was the final stretch of the long-running R5/R8/R12/R15 units which had started life at 956cc. For the R5 Alpine/Gordini, the capacity had been increased to 1397cc (the bore and stroke of 76 × 77mm comparing with 65 × 72mm for the original 956cc engine), but this is also linked with the familiar but very efficient Gordini cylinder head, including inclined valves opposed to each other at 45-degrees, in a part-spherical combustion chamber, which had been used since 1964. With a power output of no less than 93bhp (DIN) in 'over-the-counter' form, and with perhaps 130/140bhp available when razor-edge tuned, it was obvious that this was a car with a competition future.

To match it, there was a five-speed manual gearbox, ahead of the final drive, which is also that used in Renault 16TX and in Renault 17TS models − and was also used in the Renault 17 Gordini of the early and mid-1970s. It is in this way that Renault can afford to produce a successful series of 'homologation specials'.

Outwardly, only special paintwork, cast alloy wheels, and a 'snow-plough' spoiler under the nose give the game away, but once on the move there can be no mistaking a 5 Gordini from its stable mates. It has stiffer suspension than the others, so rolls less, but in Renault terms this still does not make it a firm little car. Because it has front-wheel-drive, however, a 5 Gordini is undoubtedly a stable good-handling little car.

In sporting terms, its moment of glory came in 1978 when, in appallingly slippery conditions, works-sponsored cars came second and third overall in the Monte Carlo rally.

Specification

Engine and transmission: Four-cylinders, in-line, with pushrod-operated overhead-valve cylinder head. Bore, stroke and capacity 76 × 77mm., 1397cc. Maximum power 93bhp (DIN) at 6400rpm.; maximum torque 85lb.ft. at 4000rpm. Five-speed manual gearbox in unit with engine and transaxle. Hypoid bevel final drive.
Chassis: Front engine, front drive. Unit-construction pressed-steel body-chassis unit. Independent front suspension by torsion bars and wishbones. Rack and pinion steering. Independent rear suspension by transverse torsion bars and radius arms. Front wheel disc brakes, rear drums.
Bodywork: Pressed-steel two-door four-seater GT saloon style. Length 11ft. 8in.; width 5ft. 0in.; height 4ft. 6.9in. Unladen weight 1875lb.
Performance: Maximum speed 107mph. 0-60mph 10.7sec. Standing ¼-mile 17.8sec. Typical fuel consumption 33mpg.

Renault 8 Gordini

Built: Paris, France, 1964-1969

Although Renault were always interested in, and sympathetic to, competitions, at the beginning of the 1960s their Dauphine Gordinis had faded away, and the Renault image was being upheld by the rear-engined Alpine-Renaults. It was only the great surge of BMC, with their Mini-Cooper 'homologation specials', which persuaded Renault that they should carry out a similar programme of their own. They therefore paid Amadee Gordini to develop a new engine tune for their Renault 8 model, and the R8 Gordini of 1964 was the result.

As with the Mini-Cooper S, the 'chassis', coachwork and general running gear of the car were almost standard — apart from the use of French racing blue paintwork and twin 'go faster' stripes which were supplied as rolls of tape, for the customer only to apply if he felt like advertising his new toy.

The engine of the R8, of course, was a perfectly conventional wet-liner four-cylinder unit, which had first appeared as a 956cc unit in 1962. It had already been enlarged to 1108cc for the Caravelle coupe, which was one of the worst forms of 'boulevard poseur' machines known to man. For the new car, Gordini therefore chose the 1108cc engine, which fitted the existing bodyshell, and matched up perfectly to the existing transmission.

It was the cylinder head which was so remarkable, and which deserves so much attention. The bread-and-butter car had a cylinder head with in line valves and bathtub type combustion chambers. To replace it, Gordini developed an entirely new light-alloy casting, in which he found it possible to combine the existing side-mounted camshaft with pushrod-operation of the valves, but had these opposed to each other in part-spherical combustion chambers. This was achieved by clever angling of pushrods, and detailed allocation of space, so that the use of twin rocker shafts almost gave the equivalent of a twin-overhead-camshaft valve gear layout. Not only this, but large valves were used — so large that the sparking plug had to be positioned slightly remote from the main combustion chamber, with mixture impinging by way of two tiny passages from the main combustion chamber; it sounded bizarre, but it worked!

Even in 1108cc form, the engine produced a rousing 95bhp (gross) at no less than 6500rpm., and when fully race-tuned it could be urged up to something nearer 105/110bhp.

Although the R8 Gordini immediately became every amateur French driver's dream car, and soon made its name, it was clear that even more power would be needed to match the 1.3-litre engined Mini-Cooper S cars. From the middle of 1966, therefore, the standard production car was replaced by one having an enlarged engine and a five-speed all-synchromesh gearbox. The capacity increase was gained by fitting new wet liners with a cylinder bore of 74.5mm in place of the 70mm liners of the standard car, and the resulting capacity was 1255cc, close to the 1.3-litre class limit.

The R8 Gordini 1300, to give it its full title, was also recognisable by having four forward-facing driving lights, and it also had an extra auxiliary fuel tank in the front luggage compartment. As the normal R8, and the earlier Gordinis, had had a fuel tank in the rear (between the engine and the rear seats) this made the Gordini 1300 one of the few in the world ever to have fuel tanks at each end of the car.

Engine power was up to 103bhp (gross) in over-the-counter form, and it was perhaps possible for factory-tuned examples to produce between 120 and 130bhp, so it was no surprise to see these cars now being definite contenders for victory in Europe, particularly where traction (as on ice, or in loose going) was at a premium. By the end of the 1960s, however, the new generation of mid- and rear-engined sports cars (ironically enough led by the rear-engined Alpine-Renaults) were proving to be faster than the more conventional saloons, and when the mass-production R8 range was replaced by the Renault 12s in 1969 the R8 Gordini cars were dropped.

Renault 8 Gordini, 1965

Specification

Engine and transmission: Four-cylinders, in-line, with pushrod-operated overhead-valve cylinder head. Bore, stroke and capacity 70×72mm., 1108cc. Maximum power 95bhp (gross) at 6500rpm.; maximum torque 72lb.ft. at 5000rpm. Four-speed manual gearbox in unit with engine and transaxle. Hypoid bevel final drive.
Chassis: Rear engine, rear drive. Unit-construction pressed-steel body-chassis unit. Independent front suspension by coil springs and wishbones. Rack and pinion steering. Independent rear suspension by coil springs, swing axles and radius arms. Four wheel disc brakes.
Bodywork: Pressed-steel four-door four-seater GT saloon style. Length 13ft. 1in.; width 4ft. 10.5in.; height 4ft. 3.5in. Unladen weight 1755lb.
Performance: Maximum speed 106mph. 0-60mph 12.3sec. Standing ¼-mile 18.8sec. Typical fuel consumption 27mpg.

Note: Gordini 1300 replaced the original car in summer 1966. Important differences were: Bore, stroke and capacity 74.5×72mm., 1255cc. Maximum power 103bhp (gross) at 6750rpm.; maximum torque 86lb.ft. at 5000rpm. Five-speed manual gearbox. Unladen weight 1875lb.
Performance: Maximum speed 108mph. 0-60mph 10.9sec. Standing ¼-mile 17.7sec. Typical fuel consumption 25mpg.

Renault 12 Gordini

Built: Paris, France, 1970-1974

By the middle of the 1960s, Renault had gradually but persistently begun to abandon their previous faith in the rear-engined philosophy. The R8 models of 1962 were the last new range to have rear engines and rear drive, while the R4 of 1961 had been the first with front engines and front drive. The front-wheel-drive theme was carried on with the 1.5-litre Renault 16 of 1965, but it was not until the rear-engined R8 was replaced by the front-engined Renault 12, in the autumn of 1969, that the revolution was really complete. This also displaced the very effective little R8 Gordini cars, so it was no surprise when a successor, in the form of the front-wheel drive 12 Gordini, came on the scene in the summer of 1970.

The 12's layout was new, to Renault, in several ways, for the engine was ahead of the final drive unit, with the gearbox behind it — whereas both the existing Renault 4 and Renault 16 models had engines behind the final drive and transmissions ahead. Even today, however, at the end of the 1970s, Renault have not achieved uniformity in layout, and some of their engines find different positions in space, depending on the model range in which they are used.

The Renault 12 Gordini, however, which was otherwise fairly closely based on the Renault 12, had its 1565cc engine in the nose, and even this needs explanation, for the mass-production 12 had a 1289cc engine developed from the basic R8 unit, while *this* Gordini version was developed from the larger and completely different Renault 16 unit. Purely for comparison purposes, it is enough to say that the R8 Gordini 1300 unit was of 1255cc, with bore and stroke of 74.5 × 72mm, while the 12 Gordini's entirely different unit was of 1565cc, with bore and stroke of 77 × 84mm.

What was so different, however, was the effectiveness of Gordini's attention to the engine. Although the cylinder head casting had to be new, due to the 1565cc engine being of entirely different dimensions from the 1255cc unit, the design principles remained the same, the breathing was equally deep and efficient, and the result was

Renault 12 Gordini, 1971

that the 1.56-litre engine produced a very unfussed 113bhp (DIN) at 6250rpm. As with the R8 Gordini 1300, it was linked to a five-speed gearbox, but this again was of a different design, and was eventually to find a home in cars as diverse as the R17, the Renault 16TX, and the rear-engined Alpine-Renaults.

If Renault had hoped to produce another winner in the 12 Gordini, however, they were to be disappointed. The new car was considerably heavier, less nimble, and not at all as competitive in the 1970s as the old car had been in the 1960s. Renault, like other manufacturers before and since, were to discover that there was a practical limit to the performance of a front-wheel-drive competition car. Therefore, in spite of strenuous efforts to prove the car's worth on the slippery-surface events where it might shine, the works competition team eventually discarded it in favour of the last of the Alpine-Renaults.

With no viable competition programme to support, and with the private owners also finding out that these new cars were not as good as necessary, sales fell away, and the last 12 Gordini of all was built in 1974.

Specification

Engine and transmission: Four-cylinders, in-line, with pushrod-operated overhead-valve cylinder head. Bore, stroke and capacity 77 × 84mm., 1565cc. Maximum power 113bhp (DIN) at 6250rpm.; maximum torque 103lb.ft. at 4500rpm. Five-speed manual gearbox, in unit with engine and transaxle. Hypoid bevel final drive.
Chassis: Front engine, front drive. Unit-construction pressed-steel body-chassis unit. Independent front suspension by coil springs and wishbones. Rack and pinion steering. Rear suspension of axle beam by coil springs and radius arms. Four-wheel disc brakes.
Bodywork: Pressed-steel four-door four-seater GT saloon style. Length 14ft. 1.3in.; width 5ft. 3.5in.; height 4ft. 7in. Unladen weight 2160lb.
Performance (Manufacturer's claim): Maximum speed 115mph. Typical fuel consumption 28mpg.

Talbot Sunbeam-Lotus

Built: Linwood, Scotland and Hethel, England, 1979 to date

Compared with the truly committed British factories, Rootes (later Chrysler UK) were always at something of a disadvantage with their competition programme. Apart from the production of rather limited-performance Imp and Avenger 'specials', they did not produce for sale a really competitive car until 1979. That car, announced in the spring as a Chrysler, actually went into production during the summer and was eventually put on the market as a Talbot; Peugeot, having taken over the concern in 1978, were changing all the ex-Chrysler marque names to Talbot, so the Sunbeam-Lotus gets the accolade as the first 'new' Talbot model to go on the market.

Like other homologation specials put on the market in recent years, this new model uses the basic shell of a mass-production saloon car (or, more correctly, a hatchback), some of its suspension elements, and specifies a much more specialised running gear. To make the new car as potentially competitive as possible, Chrysler UK (who did the original deal and much of the development) chose to use a modified version of the wellknown 16-valve light-alloy Lotus engine; logically, therefore, as the bodyshell was Chrysler Sunbeam, it was clear that the new car should be a Sunbeam-

Talbot Sunbeam-Lotus, 1979 313

Lotus. Now that the marque name has changed, this gives the car something of a unique title – Talbot Sunbeam-Lotus – where each of the components is (or was, once) a marque on its own.

The basis of the car, therefore, is the bodyshell of the Talbot/Chrysler Sunbeam, which is a neat and rather angular hatchback, based on the shortened floorpan of a Chrysler/Talbot Avenger. That car's basic suspension – MacPherson front suspension and four-link location of a live axle at the rear – is retained, but the rest of the running gear is quite special to this car.

In the Lotus range (and, when in production, in the Jensen-Healey) the 16-valve engine has a capacity of 1971cc. In this car, however, to improve the low-speed and mid-range torque *and* to allow the car's engine to qualify for the over 2-litre class, the stroke is slightly lengthened (from 69.2mm to 76.2mm), and the resulting capacity is 2172cc. In fact, 'works' competition cars can be enlarged a little more, and in the next few years undoubtedly will be stretched even further. In production form the engine is relatively mildly tuned, producing 150bhp (DIN), but in full-blooded competition guise more than 240bhp is available.

The gearbox is the ubiquitous five-speed all-synchromesh ZF unit – the same basic unit used currently in competition versions of the Escort RS1800 and the Chevette 2300HS, and previously used in road cars as diverse as the Vauxhall Firenza and some BMWs; a much stronger rear axle than standard is also specified.

In addition to this, there are special cast-alloy roadwheels, suspension setting changes, and many other detail changes intended to make this a true basic competition car which can also be used on the road.

Talbot say they are going to produce more than 4500 of these little bombs before 1981, and are going about it in rather a complex manner. First of all the modified bodyshells are made at Linwood, in Scotland, where the normal Talbot Sunbeam is manufactured, after which they are transported to the Lotus factory at Hethel in Norfolk for engine and transmission to be fitted. Finally they return to one of the group's Coventry factories for final checking and pre-delivery road-tests.

Even in the few months following the car's launch, impressive rallying results have been obtained, and there seems to be no doubt that, given the will and the dedication from the factory competition department, the car can be a winner.

Specification

Engine and transmission: Four-cylinders, in-line, installed at 45-degrees to vertical, with twin-overhead-camshaft cylinder head, built by Lotus. Bore, stroke and capacity 95.2 × 76.2mm., 2172cc. Maximum power 150bhp (DIN) at 5750rpm.; maximum torque 150lb.ft. at 4500rpm. Five-speed manual ZF gearbox in unit with engine. Hypoid bevel final drive.

Chassis: Front engine, rear drive. Pressed-steel unit-construction body-chassis unit. Independent front suspension by coil springs and MacPherson struts. Rack and pinion steering. Suspension of live rear axle by coil springs, and radius arms. Front wheel disc brakes, rear drums.

Bodywork: Pressed-steel two-door four-seater saloon car body with hatchback. Length 12ft. 7.2in.; width 5ft. 3.1in.; height 4ft. 7.3in. Unladen weight 2115lb.

Performance: Maximum speed 121mph. 0-60mph 7.4sec. Standing ¼-mile 15.6sec. Typical fuel consumption 18mpg.

Triumph Stag

Built: Coventry, England, 1970 to 1977

The origins of the Stag are in a motor show 'dream car' which the Italian stylist, Giovanni Michelotti, built for himself in the mid-1960s. He was under contract to Triumph, who provided a Triumph 2000 to be rebuilt for this purpose; then, having seen the result, they commandeered it for their own use!

Originally the Stag used a shortened Triumph 2000 underpan, but by the time production began in the summer of 1970 its bodyshell (built in Liverpool) had become entirely special. Similarly, though the first prototypes used Triumph 2000/2.5PI engines, transmissions and suspensions, the production cars were much more specialised. As sold in large numbers, therefore, the Stag was much more of a 'bespoke' GT than it might originally have been.

The Stag's structure was a conventional pressed-steel monocoque, and in basic form it was a close-coupled four-seater convertible, distinguished by the presence of a large T-shaped roll bar. It was also sold with a heavy but stylish hardtop, which in conjunction with the big windscreen and wind-up door glasses made it into a stylish Grand Touring car. Its all-independent suspension was by coil springs, Triumph 2000 type, and the rack and pinion steering was power assisted.

The heart of the design, however, was the 2998cc vee-8 engine, which had single-overhead-camshaft cylinder heads, produced 145bhp, and was very closely related in design and machining terms to the Triumph Dolomite four-cylinder unit. It follows that it would have been possible for 16-valve cylinder heads to have been applied to this unit, with awesome potential, but it never seems to have been done.

In marketing terms the Stag was aimed at the Mercedes-Benz, Alfa-Romeo and Lancia market, and was specifically expected to appeal to the North American market. Unfortunately for Triumph, however, Stags had a great deal of reliability trouble, particularly with the vee-8 engine, and it was that reputation which, combined with the expense of meeting new legislation, caused it to be withdrawn prematurely from the United States.

Triumph Stag, 1970

The Stag's styling, too, seemed to 'date' rather quickly, which is probably because it was shaped at least five-years before it made its public debut, and because no significant changes were made to it in a seven-year life.

For all that, its engine was flexible and powerful when running properly, but expensive to repair when it gave trouble, as it often seemed to do. Warped cylinder heads, and bearing trouble, was regularly reported, and it is a fact that many surviving Stags have been given Ford vee-6 or Rover vee-8 engine transplants.

Prior to the closure of Triumph's Liverpool factory, where Stag bodies were made and trimmed, the Stag was withdrawn from production, and a long wheelbase TR7 coupe successor was cancelled.

Specification

Engine and transmission: Eight-cylinders, in 90-degree vee-formation, with single-overhead-camshaft cylinder heads. Bore, stroke and capacity, 86×64.5mm., 2998cc. Maximum power 145bhp (DIN) at 5500rpm.; maximum torque 170lb.ft. at 3500rpm. Four-speed manual gearbox and optional overdrive (standard from autumn 1972), or optional three-speed Borg Warner automatic transmission, in unit with engine. Hypoid bevel final drive.

Chassis: Front engine, rear drive. Pressed-steel, unit-construction, body/chassis unit. Independent front suspension by coil springs, MacPherson struts and wishbones. Power-assisted rack and pinion steering. Independent rear suspension by coil springs and semi-trailing wishbones. Front wheel disc brakes, rear drums.

Bodywork: Pressed-steel bodyshell, in two-door close-coupled four-seater style, as convertible, or with optional hardtop. Length 14ft. 5.8in.; width 5ft. 3.5in.; height 4ft. 1.5in. Unladen weight 2810lb.

Performance: Maximum speed 116mph. 0-60mph 9.3sec. Standing ¼-mile 17.1sec. Typical fuel consumption 22mpg.

Vauxhall Firenza 'Droopsnoot', 1975

Vauxhall Firenza 'Droopsnoot'

Built: Ellesmere Port, England, 1973 to 1975

Even though General Motors were not officially interested in motor sport, both their European subsidiaries, Opel and Vauxhall, produced cars in the 1970s which were specifically aimed at a rallying programme. Opel's car was the 1.9-litre Kadett GT/E, while Vauxhall's was the Firenza 'Droopsnoot'. Although big-engined Firenzas had been in production between 1971 and 1973 they were neither as visually distinctive nor as mechanically specialised as the later car.

The Firenzas were coupe derivatives of the Viva saloons in origin, and the 1971 to 1973 models were sold with a variety of engines and specifications; after 1973 they carried on for a time as Magnums. From the autumn of 1973, however, a new Firenza was put on the market, and apart from its basic structure and suspensions was a much more advanced car. Most obvious, of course, was the new nose styling, where a plastic nose-cone, in a wedge style and with faired-in headlamps was a feature, and the special wheels and other decorative details.

Mechanically, a tuned version of the single-cam 2.3-litre Vauxhall engine was fitted, with a very creditable 131bhp power output, and it was matched to the ubiquitous five-speed ZF gearbox. This gave the car a 114mph top speed, and acceleration to match. As with other 'homologation specials', however, the base car was only a start. For competition use, it was intended to use a twin-cam conversion of the engine, relying on the fact that the Lotus 16-valve cylinder head fitted very easily to the Vauxhall engine and that this could be prepared to give at least 240bhp.

Although announced in 1973, Vauxhall took ages to get the car into production, and it was not until mid 1974 that any production cars were delivered. Even then, only a very low rate of production was achieved — a problem compounded by tardy

delivery of nose cones, of suitable gearboxes, and of modified engines. In the meantime, it rapidly became clear that the car was both too heavy and too ponderous to be an Escort beater, and thoughts turned to a similarly-modified Chevette. The last of the droopsnoot Firenzas was built in mid 1975, making a total of only 204 in this very troubled programme. The distinctive frontal body style, incidentally, was also seen on about 200 Magnum 'Sports Hatch' estate cars built in 1975.

Specification

Engine and transmission: Four-cylinders, in-line, with single-overhead-camshaft cylinder head, mounted in bodyshell 45-degrees from vertical. Bore, stroke and capacity 97.5×76.2mm, 2279cc. Maximum power 131bhp (DIN) at 5500rpm.; maximum torque 144lb.ft. at 3500rpm. Five-speed ZF gearbox in unit with engine. Hypoid bevel final drive.

Chassis: Front engine, rear drive. Unit construction pressed-steel bodyshell, made by Vauxhall. Independent front suspension by coil springs and wishbones. Rack and pinion steering. Rear suspension of live axle by coil springs and radius arms. Front wheel disc brakes, rear drums.

Bodywork: Pressed-steel unit-construction shell, in two-door coupe style, with close coupled four-seat arrangement. Length 14ft. 1.4in.; width 5ft. 4.7in.; height 4ft. 3.3in. Unladen weight 2295lb.

Performance: Maximum speed 114mph. 0-60mph 9.4sec. Standing ¼-mile 16.9sec. Typical fuel consumption 22mpg.

318   **Vauxhall Chevette 2300HS, 1978**

Vauxhall Chevette 2300HS

Built: Luton, England, 1978 to date

To succeed their unsuccessful Firenza Droopsnoot, Vauxhall carried out a similar 'transplant' operation on their Chevette hatchback, to make an 'homologation special', and incidentally to provide a very fast and interesting road car for those who did not want to commit their cars to competition. The Chevette 2300HS (HS perhaps means High Speed) has been more successful on all counts, and has provided Vauxhall with a rallying 'winner' for the first time.

The car is based on the three-door hatchback Chevette, which is normally only made as 1256cc engined car with its own transmission assemblies, none of which is at all suitable for competition. Since the engine bay is quite roomy (it was, indeed, designed to accept several different power units for world-wide production) it was possible to fit another derivative of the 2.3-litre Vauxhall four-cylinder engine, and in this car it is matched to a five-speed Getrag gearbox (as used on other Vauxhall/Bedford models), and a heavy duty Opel Kadett GT/E axle. The whole is marketed in a single silver colour with distinctive badging and colour striping, and

special wheels, tyres and rear body spoiler.

The engine, in production form, is entirely special, because it has a twin-cam 16-valve cylinder head designed, developed and produced by Vauxhall themselves. This produces, in production form, no less than 135bhp at 5500rpm., and endows the 2300HS with a top speed of 115mph. It was the engine which provided so much controversy even before the car was properly in production.

The original car was built by Dealer Team Vauxhall for use in the 1976 RAC Rally, when it was fitted with the Lotus cylinder head, and with a ZF gearbox. Although Vauxhall had plans to introduce their production car in 1977 the competition programme went ahead in 1977 without production cars being available, rally cars started winning, and it became clear that the Lotus head and ZF box were part of the specification. Pre-production cars were seen, however, with their own cylinder head, and were not put on sale until the spring of 1978.

At this point the motor sporting authorities stepped in, and demanded that the car should only use 'production' components. This caused something of a hiatus in competition progress, though the production car sold relatively well and has now established its own market. Hard development work, however, made the Vauxhall-engined car capable of more than 240bhp in due course, and it continues in this form.

Specification

Engine and transmission: Four-cylinders, in-line, with twin-overhead-camshaft cylinder head, mounted in bodyshell at 45-degrees from vertical. Bore, stroke and capacity 97.5 × 76.2mm., 2279cc. Maximum power 135bhp (DIN) at 5500rpm.; maximum torque 134lb.ft. at 4500rpm. Five-speed Getrag gearbox in unit with engine. Hypoid bevel final drive.

Chassis: Front engine, rear drive. Unit-construction pressed-steel structure, made by Vauxhall. Independent front suspension by coil springs and wishbones. Rack and pinion steering. Rear suspension of live axle by coil springs, radius arms, Panhard rod and torque tube. Front wheel disc brakes, rear drums.

Bodywork: Pressed-steel unit-construction shell, in three-door hatchback style, with four-seat arrangement. Length 13ft. 1.2in.; width 5ft. 2.2in.; height 4ft. 6in. Unladen weight 2235lb.

Performance: Maximum speed 115mph. 0-60mph 8.5sec. Standing ¼-mile 16.5sec. Typical fuel consumption 24mpg.

Ferrari Dino 246GTS (Page 369)

Morgan Plus 8 (Page 98)

Ferrari 250GT Lusso (Page 359)

Triumph GT6 (Page 246)

Daimler SP250 (Page 162)

Aston Martin DB5 (Page 333)

BMW 3.0CSL Coupe (Page 155)

Bitter CD (Page 274)

AC Cobra 289 (Page 33)

Gordon-Keeble GK1 (Page 385)

Triumph TR4A (Page 250)

Sunbeam Tiger 4.7 (Page 241)

TVR Turbo (Page 127)

Ferrari 365 GTC/4 (Page 374)

Alvis TD21 Convertible (Page 265)

De Tomaso Pantera GTS (Page 458)

Chapter Six

The Supercars

Although this is a category which defies exact description, there is rarely much doubt about the cars which qualify. After making due allowance for the period in which they were built, and the markets for which they were developed, I think almost everyone would agree that a Supercar must have tremendous performance, great elegance, considerable exclusivity or status, and a generous dash of that elusive flavouring called style.

According to this, therefore, every Ferrari, even the 2-litre Dino, is a Supercar, and so is every Maserati, Lamborghini or de Tomaso. Although I would probably not include the earlier postwar Aston Martins on performance grounds, I have no hesitation at all over any Aston built since 1960. But the question of 'style' is critically important. There is no way that I would want to include an AC Cobra (even one with the enormously powerful 7-litre Ford engine), though I do include the AC428 — any collector of beautiful and elegant things would understand, I'm sure. For similar reasons I shun the Panther de Ville, and just because they aren't special *enough* I have not included the Ferrari-engined Fiats.

On the other hand, I most certainly want to list all the Jaguar E-Types (and, of course, the XJ-S), even though there are so many of them. These cars, like Porsche's 911 family and the Alfa Romeo Montreal, prove that a car doesn't necessarily have to come from a tiny concern to be a Supercar; in the 1950s and the early 1960s, in any case, Mercedes-Benz had already proved that.

Even so, my Supercar collection is still rather exclusive. Only eighteen European marques qualify, and I think it extremely significant that no fewer than twelve of these have used body styles conceived in Italy; six of them, indeed, are also based in Italy too. It is also heartening to know that, in spite of the supposedly fickle nature of rich buyers, twelve of these marques were already trading at the start of the 1960s, and that none of them have since disappeared. On the other hand, it is sad to note that it is not easy to break into this exclusive circle. Five concerns were founded in the 1960s, two (Gordon-Keeble and Iso) have already foundered, and one (Lamborghini) has been staggering from crisis to crisis for some time.

European Sports & GT Cars

At the beginning of the 1960s, there were really seven Supercar manufacturers – Aston Martin, Bristol, Ferrari, Jaguar, Jensen, Maserati and Mercedes – of which Bristol and Jensen owed their standing to the use of big, simple, but massively powerful North American power units. Gordon-Keeble, Lamborghini and Porsche were also thinking about ways of getting on the same level. Although the cars were being built in three countries, and all used the front engine/rear drive configuration, their layout was by no means stereotyped. Mercedes-Benz used a true spaceframe, Jaguar a combined multi-tubular frame and monocoque, Ferrari, Jensen and Maserati variations on a theme of large-tubed frames, with Aston Martin and Bristol using platforms.

There was also plenty of variety in engine layouts, with straight-sixes, vee-8s and vee-12s, pushrod overhead valves, single overhead camshaft layouts, and classic twin-cam installations. Most offered convertible bodies, and most had a choice of two-seater or four-seater layouts. Independent front suspension, of course, was universal, but independent rear suspension was not. Only Jaguar and Mercedes-Benz thought their Supercars needed that sort of thing, and Jaguar's was much the most satisfactory layout.

Since then, eleven other Supercar marques have evolved and (in some cases) faded away. AC, Alfa Romeo, BMW and Porsche were all long-established concerns, of which AC and Alfa Romeo (AC428 and Montreal, respectively) only dabbled in the Supercar business. Some of the others – Gordon-Keeble, Iso, Lamborghini, Monteverdi and de Tomaso – relied heavily on importing major components; only Lamborghini, financed by a wealthy industrialist instead of a hopeful entrepreneur, were able to design and built their own engines, while all the others relied on North American horsepower.

In view of the rapid spread of mid-engines in motor racing, it was inevitable that Supercars should be developed in the same configuration. At the time of writing, and if you include Porsche in this category, eight marques have offered mid-engined cars, while three others (AC, Jaguar and Mercedes-Benz) either sell a non-Supercar with a mid-engine, or have publicised testbed machines built to that configuration. The most exciting of them all – Ferrari's Boxers and Lamborghini's Countachs – are nothing if not cramped and impractical, but to a Supercar customer this is not thought to be important. That Porsche's Turbo is probably a better car than either of them, as an engineering and practical concept, is not enough.

Perhaps it is significant that the three manufacturers who stopped trading in the 1960s and 1970s all fell into that unkindly-named, but accurately-conceived category of 'Euro-American sports mongrels'. Gordon-Keeble, Iso and Jensen all lacked the exclusivity, the special engineering, and the style, to survive in such a restricted market, and without timely help from Ford of Detroit, de Tomaso might have gone the same way.

Technically, since 1960 there has been steady rather than shattering advance. Apart from the Countach and Boxer models, mid-engined cars from Lamborghini, Maserati and de Tomaso have sold in fair quantity (considering the size of the market), though only Porsche, with their vastly popular and continuously-developing 911 family, have really sold large numbers of cars where the engine is behind the driver. Even Porsche, for the 1980s, will be relying on the 'conventional' layout of the 928 family to enhance its high reputation.

Chassis have tended to become monocoque where the sales potential justifies it.

Porsche of course, Jaguar, some Maserati and some de Tomaso models have all adopted this, but if sales are clearly going to be limited then the halfway-house method espoused by the Italian manufacturers (where a fabricated, pressed and tubular floorpan forms the structural base, and where the coachbuilt body is added afterwards) is popular. For years, of course, firms like Ferrari and Maserati relied on very strong, but very simple, multi-tubular (large-section) chassis frames. Monteverdi copied them, as did AC with the 428 and BMW with the M1. The true spaceframe used by Mercedes-Benz proved to be quite uneconomic (and unnecessary) and was never used by any other Supercar manufacturer. Even Jaguar's D-Type-derived frame in the E-Type was dropped in favour of unit-construction when the XJ-S was being developed.

Apart from those companies who could not afford to tool up for (or even design) their own engines, it seems that twin-overhead-camshaft cylinder heads are most desirable, though emission restrictions of the 1970s have led to single-cam cylinder heads with 'clean breathing' being developed. Ferrari converted their single-cam vee-12s to twin-cams in the course of the 1960s, which caused a minor sensation, and attracted a great deal of favourable comment in the process. If a single-cam layout is powerful enough and *looks* right (as the Jaguar vee-12, Porsche 928 and 911, and the Lamborghini Urraco engines, all do) then it is perfectly acceptable; it is interesting to note that with the exception of the 911 engine, designed at the beginning of the period, all make do with in-line vertical valves and no suggestion of part-spherical combustion chambers.

Turbocharging on engines already big and powerful might be considered to be gilding a rather splendid lily, but Porsche have already done it on the 911, are supposed to be doing so to the 928, and may yet attract a rash of imitators. Who knows what BMW's motoring sporting ambitions might lead to in the case of the exciting M1 coupe?

Four-speed transmissions were normal at the beginning of the 1960s, with some models (including Aston Martin and Ferrari) offering overdrive. By the end of the 1960s, however, more and more cars had five-speed transmissions (often, in the case of the small manufacturers, from ZF in West Germany), and a majority can now be bought with automatic transmission. A feature of the Supercar scene in the late 1970s is that several models are only sold with automatic transmission, or at least with the manual transmission as a mere option. Perhaps we can come to terms with an automatic Jaguar XJ-S, but how about an automatic Ferrari?

The surprising feature on the coachwork scene is that very few Supercars have ever been sold with glass-fibre bodies. Perhaps this is a function of production output (glass-fibre makes most sense at outputs between about 1000 and 10 000 units a year – after which the space required to allow new shells to 'cure' becomes prohibitively large), and – rather undefinably – of status and a customer's expectations. Glass-fibre shells, somehow, are not quite right for this type of car. Lotus, who make all their cars this way, do not quite qualify for the Supercar category (but if their much-rumoured vee-8 engine is produced, I may have to revise my views), so the only cars which have adopted this method have been the Gordon-Keeble, the original Ferrari 308GTB (which has now reverted to a conventional method of construction), and the exciting BMW M1.

Most Supercars rely to a considerable extent on hand-building of coachwork, but really successful cars like the Porsches and Jaguars have fully-tooled pressed-steel bodies. Even in Italy, the home of high-performance coachbuilt bodies, the skills (and the patience needed to carry out the job) are on the decline, which explains Ferrari's dabble with glass-fibre, with the fact that simple press-tooling is now made for most models, and why production runs continue to lengthen.

True hand-building, however, persists at factories like those building Aston Martins, Bristols and Monteverdis. In these buildings, and at the Bertone, Scaglietti and Ghia works which had produced so many fine shapes in the last 20-years, a master jig might still be built in hardwood, and shapes might continue to be rolled on craftsmen's simple tools and machines. A surprising number of Supercars use steel panels, which are easier to work, though light-alloy still finds a home where lightness is thought to be more important than durability.

A look down the lists proves that there is no likelihood of the Supercar disappearing. The North Americans may throw exhaust emission limitations and safety regulations at the Supercar, but it refuses to be daunted. The USA, and much of the civilised world, may now be subject to stupid and restricting speed limits, but cars with maximum speeds of 160mph and 170mph continue to sell well. The fact that many only have space for two people and the proverbial toothbrush is no deterrent, neither is the terribly high price asked for all of them.

At the beginning of the 1960s I commented that there were seven active Supercar manufacturers. As the 1970s draw to a close, I am happy to report that this number has risen to eleven, and it is highly likely that more will join them in the 1980s. Mercedes-Benz, for instance, now have a really splendid light-alloy five-litre vee-8 engine which is crying out for a Supercar chassis, Lotus have always had a desire to join their Elites with the elite. There must be others....

AC 428 Fastback

AC 428

Built: Thames Ditton, England, 1966-1973

Although AC had probably never been as busy as they were in the phenomenal years when the AC Cobra was in such demand, their management always worried about the lack of a more plushy car in the range, as there had always historically been this sort of AC in their range. From the autumn of 1966, therefore, they put the AC428 on the market.

In regard to the chassis, the work involved was relatively small. The AC428, in effect, merely had the strongest derivative of the Cobra's chassis, with a wheelbase extended by six-inches, something which was easy to arrange due to the simple tubular construction of the chassis frame. When the first prototype had been shown in the autumn of 1965, there was initial confusion between the engine fitted to the 7-litre Cobra, and that to be used in this new car; initially, indeed, there was talk of this car being called AC427, which it most assuredly was not.

The difference between AC427 and AC428 is much more than a nominal one-cubic-inch of engine capacity. The Ford '427 CID' engine fitted to Cobra chassis was a highly tuned 6989cc unit with the accent on performance, while that fitted to the AC428 was a 7016cc unit built with considerably fewer 'high performance' parts, and as normally fitted to some premium-price Fords in the United States.

AC felt unable to do justice to the coachbuilding of such a car, at the price and for the market they envisaged, so for the first time in postwar years they contracted an outside coachbuilder to do the job. Frua of Turin were chosen, and their first offering

was a massive but impressive two-seater convertible. This was the type which went into strictly limited production at the end of 1966, but from the spring of 1967 it was joined by a fastback coupe which, in spite of its 14ft. 6in. length, could still only accommodate two people. Since Frua were also responsible for the Mistrale variety of Maserati, which was being built at the same time, it is not surprising to see that there was much in common (with many common components) between the two designs.

Production of AC428s was very limited, even when AC found themselves with more space after the Cobra was dropped towards the end of the 1960s, and this is not surprising as they first had to send rolling chassis to Frua for bodies to be erected, painted and trimmed, wait for the bodies to be returned to England, and complete the job at Thames Ditton. With more and more labour trouble erupting periodically in Italy, with costs rising, and with the legislation burden becoming more severe every year, AC decided to drop their big 'flagship' in favour of a new, mid-engined, sports coupe, the AC ME3000.

AC 428 Convertible

Specification

Engine and transmission: Eight-cylinders, in 90-degree vee-formation, with pushrod-operated overhead-valve cylinder heads, manufactured by Ford USA. Bore, stroke and capacity 104.9 × 101.1mm., 7016cc. Maximum power 345bhp (gross) at 4600rpm.; maximum torque 462lb.ft. at 2800rpm. Four-speed manual transmission, or optional Ford three-speed automatic transmission, in unit with engine. Hypoid bevel final drive.
Chassis: Front engine, rear drive. Independent front suspension by coil springs and wishbones. Rack and pinion steering. Independent rear suspension by coil springs and wishbones. Four-wheel disc brakes.
Bodywork: Light-alloy coachbuilt bodyshell by Frua, in two-door two-seater convertible or coupe styles. Length 14ft. 6in.; width 5ft. 7in.; height 4ft. 3in. Unladen weight 3145lb.
Performance: (Automatic transmission) Maximum speed 142mph. 0-60mph 6.2sec. Standing ¼-mile 14.2sec. Typical fuel consumption 17mpg.

Alfa Romeo Montreal, front end styling

Alfa Romeo Montreal

Built: Milan, Italy, 1971-1975

Alfa's Montreal coupe was one of those cars which grew, unstoppably, out of a 'dream car' at a show – in this case at Expo '67 in Montreal, in 1967. At the World Fair, Bertone had electrified the motoring enthusiasts by producing a very good looking coupe which many thought to be mid-engined. What they did not know, then, was that it was fitted with rather ordinary Giulia running gear.

Original plans had been to build a limited number of cars, but these were hastily revised upwards, more systematic development followed, and the production car was shown – prematurely, as it turned out – at the Geneva Motor Show of 1970. Although the Bertone shape had scarcely been changed – featuring, among other things, slatted covers over the quadruple headlamps and a hatchback giving space to a roomy loading area – there was much to be excited about under the skin.

Perhaps observers were disappointed to learn that not only was the Montreal not mid-engined, but that it was based on the quantity-production Alfa Giulia floorpan, suspensions and steering gear. The engine, however, was something else, being nothing less than a road-tuned version of the Type 33 racing vee-8 unit, with twin-overhead-camshafts, a capacity of 2.6-litres, and Spica fuel injection. It drove through a five-speed ZF gearbox, and with an output of exactly 200bhp (DIN) it was sure to put the car into the Supercar category.

As happens so often in Italy, the start of series production was delayed by strikes   327 in the Italian motor industry, but at the beginning of 1971 the floorpans were being delivered to Bertone's plant, where the distinctive bodyshell was built, painted, trimmed, and fixed to the 'chassis', before delivery to the customer. For four years it was Alfa's 'flagship' − they had not been able to sell such a large-engined car since the 2.6-litre straight-six had gone out of production a few years earlier − and as such it was not, perhaps, expected to make much money for them.

Production, however, lasted for only five years. One reason was that no right-hand drive version was produced until the summer of 1974, which precluded sales in certain important markets, including Great Britain, and another was that the vee-8 engine was never properly manufactured on serious tooling equipment. When Alfa Romeo's racing department turned to a flat-12 engine for racing, abandoning further developed versions of the vee-8 (which could be enlarged to 3-litres for this purpose), interest in the Montreal waned. Alfa, too, being state-owned, were under some pressure to cut their mounting losses as much as possible, and one victim of a rationalisation programme was the Montreal. Now, as at the end of the 1960s, Alfa make mainly four-cylinder cars again, and they have no exciting coupe to give their marque prestige.

Specification

Engine and transmission: Eight-cylinders, in 90-degree vee-formation, with twin-overhead-camshaft cylinder heads. Bore, stroke and capacity 80×64.5mm., 2593cc. Maximum power 200bhp (DIN) at 6500rpm.; maximum torque 173lb.ft. at 4750rpm. Five-speed ZF manual gearbox in unit with engine. Hypoid bevel final drive.

Chassis: Front engine, rear drive. Pressed-steel unit construction floorpan and structure. Independent front suspension by coil springs and wishbones. Recirculating ball steering. Rear suspension of live axle by coil springs, radius arms and A-bracket. Four-wheel disc brakes.

Bodywork: Coachwork in pressed-steel by Bertone, in two-door, two-seat fastback coupe style. Length 13ft. 0in.; width 5ft. 6in.; height 3ft. 11.5in. Unladen weight 2830lb.

Performance: Maximum speed 137mph. 0-60mph 7.6sec. Standing ¼-mile 15.4sec. Typical fuel consumption 17mpg.

Alfa Romeo Montreal, side view

Aston Martin DB4

Built: Newport Pagnell, England, 1958-1963

To replace the successful and long-running DB2/DB2/4 and DB Mk 3 range of cars, and to utilise their newly-purchased Newport Pagnell factory to the full, Aston Martin decided to design an entirely new car. Every important component of the DB4, as the car was to be known, was new, and the design was not to be hampered by consideration of any 'carry over' parts. Helped by a magnificent new engine, the DB4 put Aston Martin into an entirely new league of performance, and made the cars equals of Ferrari and Maserati in all ways except that of status; that would take years to build up — but has successfully been achieved.

Whereas the earlier DB-type Aston Martins had been built around a multi-tube chassis frame, the DB4's design centred around a pressed and fabricated steel platform chassis. Front and rear suspensions were, for Aston Martin, conventional — which is to say that coil spring and wishbone i.f.s. was matched to a well-located live rear axle, and there were disc brakes at all corners.

It was the engine which was the cornerstone of the design. Tadek Marek had designed a brand-new twin-overhead-camshaft unit, physically rather larger than that of the 2.6-litre or 2.9-litre engine which had its origins in a W.O. Bentley inspiration of the 1940s. The new unit was of 3670cc, though there was a little room for expansion in later models. It had already been tested successfully in the DBR2 racing sports cars, and in its initial form (producing 240bhp) it was under-stressed and obviously capable of a long life. Drive was through a massive David Brown four-speed gearbox, and overdrive became optional from 1961 onwards.

Even though Aston Martin's manufacturing process was now centred on the old Tickford body building works at Newport Pagnell, and many of that company's craftsmen remained on the payroll, the company decided to commission a new body style from overseas. It was Touring of Milan who shaped the final product, and it was this company's Superleggera type of body construction which was used. The shape, then and now quite unmistakeable, was formed on a network of lightweight steel tubes which accurately defined the profile.

Once production of the DB4 got under way at the end of 1958, Aston Martin were able to begin evolution and development of the range. Before too long they were also able to offer a convertible derivative, which had rather less back seat space, and a hardtop version of this convertible body was also made available.

Mechanically, however, there was not much that could be done to make the colossal performance even more impressive, but for the DB4 the company merely contented themselves with offering a 'Vantage' version, with 266bhp instead of 240bhp, from the start of 1962 model year production. They also confused the casual observer slightly, by later adopting the fared-in headlamp nose which had previously been limited to DB4GT cars.

Five separate series of DB4s were built up to October 1963, each having a number of improvements built in, and a total of 1119 cars were built in that time.

At Aston Martin at the time, however, rapid development was always going ahead, and even before it began to lose its popularity the DB4 was replaced by the DB5.

Aston Martin DB4, 1958

Specification

Engine and transmission: Six-cylinders, in-line, with twin-camshaft cylinder head. Bore, stroke and capacity, 92 × 92mm., 3670cc. Maximum power 240bhp (net) at 5500rpm.; maximum torque 240lb.ft. at 4250rpm. Four-speed gearbox in unit with engine. Hypoid bevel rear axle. Overdrive became available from spring 1961, and a 'Vantage' version with 266bhp at 5750rpm became available for 1962 models.

Chassis: Front engine, rear drive. Fabricated steel platform chassis. Independent front suspension by coil springs and wishbones. Rack and pinion steering. Rear suspension of live axle by coil springs, radius arms and Watts linkage. Four-wheel disc brakes.

Bodywork: Hand-built shell on Superleggera principles, with steel inner panels, tubular superstructure, and light-alloy skin, close-coupled four-seater, made as coupe, convertible, or hardtop. Length 14ft. 8.4in.; width 5ft. 6in.; height 4ft. 3.5in. Unladen weight (1958 coupe) 2885lb.

Performance: Maximum speed 141mph. 0-60mph 8.5sec. Standing ¼-mile 16.1sec. Typical fuel consumption 16mpg.

Aston Martin DB4GT

Built: Newport Pagnell, 1959-1960

In 1959 and 1960, Aston Martin built just 75 special DB4GT cars, which were derived from the DB4 production. Quite simply, these cars were intended to provide Aston Martin customers with cars suitable for use in racing events for Grand Touring cars, and so it was never expected that production would last for long, nor that a great number would be built.

The DB4GT's engineering was very closely based on that of the DB4, except that it had a five-inches shorter wheelbase to trim the weight and bulk, and to make the car that much more nimble on racing circuits. The prototype, in fact, won its maiden race at Silverstone in 1959 when driven by Stirling Moss.

To accommodate that five inches cut in length, the doors were shortened, along with the appropriate floor and roof panels, the occasional rear seats of the DB4 were discarded, and the trim and fittings made altogether more simple. To improve the aerodynamics and (quite unintended, it seems) to make the two cars instantly recognisable from each other, the DB4GT was also given headlamps fared in to the front wings behind smoothly contoured covers; this change, however, was later adopted for the standard DB4s.

Although the DB4GT achieved a limited degree of success, the Zagato version of this chassis (reviewed in the GT and Homologation Specials chapter) was even more suitable for its purpose. To make sure, incidentally, that the DB4GT was as competitive as possible, it was fitted with a 302bhp engine, which was even more powerful than that of the DB4 'Vantage' unit, and was distinguished by the use of three twin-choke Weber carburettors.

Because DB4GTs are so rare, they are now real collector's items, and are now generally considered too precious to be raced.

Specification

Engine and transmission: Six-cylinders in-line, with twin-camshaft cylinder head. Bore, stroke and capacity 92×92mm., 3670cc. Maximum power 302bhp (net) at 6000rpm.; maximum torque 270lb.ft. at 5000rpm. Four-speed gearbox in unit with engine. Hypoid bevel rear axle.
Chassis: Front engine, rear drive. Fabricated steel platform chassis. Independent front suspension by coil springs and wishbones. Rack and pinion steering. Rear suspension of live axle by coil springs, radius arms and Watts linkage. Four-wheel disc brakes.
Bodywork: Hand-built shell on Superleggera principles, with steel inner panels, tubular superstructure, and light-alloy skin, two-seater coupe. Length 14ft. 3.8in.; width 5ft. 6in.; height 4ft. 4in. Unladen weight 2705lb.
Performance: Maximum speed 152mph. 0-60mph 6.4sec. Standing ¼-mile 14.0sec. Typical fuel consumption 15mpg.

Aston Martin DB4 GT

Aston Martin DB5

Built: Newport Pagnell, England, 1963-1965

Although the DB5 was the shortest-lived of this model family – it was only in production for two years – it was also the most popular. That success was not entirely due to the enormous publicity generated by the use of an Aston Martin DB5 in the James Bond film *Goldfinger*, but due to the build up in demand as a result of the DB4's success in earlier years.

The DB5 was no more and no less than a thoroughly logical re-work of the original DB4 layout, with the accent on mechanical improvement and versatility. In particular, Aston Martin acknowledged that not only did they have wealthy customers interested in the ultimate in sporting motoring, but customers also interested in ultra-fast, ultra-exclusive relaxed motoring. This meant not only that they had to be offered even more performance than the DB4 had offered, but there should be a choice of transmission too.

To make the car more flexible than before, the big six-cylinder engine was enlarged (by a 4mm bore increase) to 3995cc – a size which was not to be altered in future years – and the power output, using what had originally been the 'Vantage' tune, went up to 282bhp (net) at 5500rpm, with a great deal of torque over a wide range of engine speeds.

This engine could be matched to no fewer than four types of transmission – the original David Brown four-speeder, the same box with overdrive fitted, a ZF five-speed gearbox, or a Borg Warner automatic transmission. The ZF gearbox, incidentally, was that developed for the Maserati 5000GT vee-8 model, and was used by several other manufacturers.

Almost as soon as the DB5 had been announced, a drophead coupe was also made available, and during 1964 a further-tuned 'Vantage' engine option – this time with no fewer than 325bhp at 5500rpm, became optional.

Like the later DB4 models, and the DB4GT, the DB5 had its headlamps hidden behind glass covers, and its basic bodywork was in fact just like that of the late-model DB4s.

In the two years that the car was in production, no fewer than 1150 of the coupes and convertibles were built, and in 1965 a further 37 of the rather different DB5-based Volante convertibles were also built. By then, however, Aston Martin had pushed on with another version of the car, and the DB6 was the result.

Specification

Engine and transmission: Six-cylinders, in-line, with twin-camshaft cylinder head. Bore, stroke and capacity, 96×92mm., 3995cc. Maximum power 282bhp (net) at 5500rpm.; maximum torque 288lb.ft. at 3850rpm. A 'Vantage' engine became available in 1964: Maximum power 325bhp (net) at 5500rpm.; maximum torque 290lb.ft. at 4500rpm. Five-speed ZF gearbox, 4-speed gearbox, or 4-speed gearbox with overdrive, or automatic transmission alternatives, all in unit with engine. Hypoid bevel rear axle.

European Sports & GT Cars

Chassis: Front engine, rear drive. Fabricated steel platform chassis. Independent front suspension by coil springs and wishbones. Rack and pinion steering. Rear suspension of live axle by coil springs, radius arms and Watts linkage. Four-wheel disc brakes.

Bodywork: Hand-built shell on Superleggera principles, with steel inner panels, tubular superstructure, and light-alloy skin, close-coupled four-seater, made as coupe or convertible. Length 15ft. 0in.; width 5ft. 6in.; height 4ft. 5in. Unladen weight 3235lb.

Performance: Maximum speed 141mph. 0-60mph 8.1sec. Standing ¼-mile 16.0sec. Typical fuel consumption 15mpg.

Aston Martin DB5

Aston Martin DB6 MkII, 1970

Aston Martin DB6 series

Built: Newport Pagnell, England, 1965-1971

Because it remained in production for more than five years, the DB6 might be considered as the definitive version of this Aston Martin family, which began with the DB4 of 1958. In many ways, too, it was a rather different car from the original DB4, which proved just how much the market for Aston Martins changed during the time that these six-cylinder cars remained in production.

Although based on the same chassis layout, and although looking superficially the same as earlier models, the DB6 bodyshell was almost entirely different from that of the DB5. Aston Martin decided that their new model needed rather more space than the DB5 which it was to replace, so the first thing was to stretch the well-proven wheelbase by 3.75in., the extra length being allocated to the rear seat area. This required little change to the chassis engineering, except for modifications to rear suspension geometry.

With more rear seat space, and with more headroom required, the body profiles were extensively, but subtly, changed. The screen was deeper, the passenger compartment longer (you recognise the DB6 in side view by its squared-off rear quarter

335

windows — those of the DB5 swoop gracefully to a sharp apex at the rear), and the roof altogether squarer in side view. The dip to the tail was less pronounced, and terminated in a swept-up spoiler neatly shaped into a squared-off boot lid.

There were absolutely no mechanical changes to engine and transmission, except that the old David Brown four-speed gearbox was no longer offered. Many cars, indeed, were built with the optional automatic transmission, which was not an 'extra' in terms of pricing. In the same way, the normal or 'Vantage' engines could also be ordered without any price changes.

Under the skin, incidentally, Superleggera body construction principles were abandoned, though square-section tubing was still used to build up the framework around which the light-alloy body was erected. Although there was a short-lived overlap in models, where the convertible car in the range, the Volante, was based on the DB5 chassis, a DB6-based Volante followed in autumn 1966.

From the autumn of 1969, almost coincidental with the launch of the much more expensive DBS V8, the DB6 was uprated to become the DB6 Mk II. This involved little more than the use of DBS wheels and tyres, flared wheel arches to make sure that the wider footwear did not foul the bodywork, and other touches.

At the same time, the Associated Engineering fuel-injection installation (which was never taken up by any other customer) was offered as an optional extra on DB6 Mk II models. By this time, however, Aston Martin had ceased quoting power outputs for their engines, and the extra benefit of fuel-injection was never quantified. In fact the injection installations often gave trouble, and the experiment was not continued with great resolve. Many surviving DB6 Mk II models have been re-converted to one or other of the carburettor installations.

1330 of the DB6 (Mark I, as it was retrospectively known) were built between 1965 and 1969, while 423 of the Mk II models were built before the car was withdrawn in February 1971. By then, the DBS model was dominating the scene at Newport Pagnell, and was taking the lion's share of sales, as a comparison between Mk I and Mk II deliveries proves. With the withdrawal of the DB6 models, the six-cylinder engine was found only in the DBS car, and even this model only lasted until 1973.

Specification

Engine and transmission: Six-cylinders, in-line, with twin-overhead-camshaft cylinder head. Bore, stroke and capacity, 96 × 92mm., 3995cc. Maximum power 282bhp (net) at 5500rpm.; maximum torque 288lb.ft. at 3850rpm. Optional 'Vantage' tune, 325bhp (net) at 5500rpm.; maximum torque 290lb.ft. at 4500rpm. Five-speed ZF manual gearbox, or optional three-speed Borg Warner automatic transmission, in unit with engine. Hypoid bevel rear axle.

Chassis: Front engine, rear drive. Fabricated steel platform chassis frame. Independent front suspension by coil springs and wishbones. Rack and pinion steering (later optionally power-assisted). Rear suspension of live-axle by coil springs, radius arms and Watts linkage. Four-wheel disc brakes.

Bodywork: Two-door, close-coupled four-seater body style by Aston Martin, available as fastback coupe, or convertible, of steel and light-alloy, with square-section tube frame work of shell. Length 15ft. 2in.; width 5ft. 6in.; height 4ft. 5.5in. Unladen weight 3250lb.

Performance: (Vantage version) Maximum speed 148mph. 0-60mph 6.5sec. Standing ¼-mile 14.5sec. Typical fuel consumption 15mpg.

Aston Martin DBS and Vantage

Built: Newport Pagnell, England, 1967-1972

The new model announced by Aston Martin in 1967 was effectively only the third new concept from the David Brown-owned concern since the end of the 1940s – the DB2 of 1950 and the DB4 of 1958 being the other two – and set the standard and style for Aston Martins still being built as the firm looks into the 1980s. Even so, much of the chassis engineering looked back to the DB4 series.

The DBS of 1967 was not at all the DBS which Aston Martin had wanted to introduce, but economic problems in the previous year made them change their course. The DBS production car, which was always laid out with a new vee-8 engine in mind, was much wider than the DB6 which it joined in production, so although the same basic steel platform chassis frame was used it was effectively new, as wheel tracks were increased along with body width, and there was a further one-inch increase in the wheelbase. Front suspension and optionally power-assisted rack and pinion steering were much as before, but at the rear there was a newly-developed de Dion suspension layout, better and altogether more refined than that recently seen on the short-lived and none-too-popular Lagonda Rapide car.

Because the engine bay was laid out with a much wider engine in mind, there was a great deal of space for the unchanged six-cylinder 3995cc engine to be installed, and this was available in either of the engine tunes already offered in the DB6; the fuel-

Aston Martin DBS

injection option later applied to the DB6, however, would never be available on the DBS. Although the ubiquitous ZF five-speed gearbox remained for customers insisting on manual transmission (a diminishing band), new automatic transmission option was much more popular than before.

Mechanically the DBS was more or less 'as expected', but the body style was outstanding and completely new. Gone were the last traces of a Touring style, and in came a smart and entirely special two-door four-seater style by Aston Martin themselves, in fact by their employee William Towns, who later went on to become a distinguished freelance industrial designer. At the time it featured a tiny air intake in the bonnet, and a four-headlamp nose. No spoilers were thought necessary, in spite of the fact that speeds of up to 150mph were envisaged even with this six-cylinder engine, and the whole design was as smart and integrated as anything which might have been bought at great expense from one or other of the Italian styling houses.

This basic body has persisted in production at Newport Pagnell to this day, but it was not until 1978 that a convertible version was ever developed, and no such body was ever offered on the six-cylinder chassis.

DBS cars were put on sale immediately after the 1967 motor show at Earls Court, and because they were considerably more costly than the DB6 cars they did not sell in such large quantities. Once the V8-engined car arrived, too, they became less fasionable, and demand dropped a little further.

In 1972 there came a big change in company structure. Financial considerations (Aston Martin had never made a true profit) meant that the David Brown Group were forced to sell out to a property company, Company Developments Ltd., and one immediate result was that the 'DB' part of the model titles was dropped. At the same time the cars were given a rather simpler nose, with single seven-inch headlamps instead of the pair five-inch lamps of the original style, and it was in this guise, known as the Aston Martin Vantage, that production ran on to 1973. A total of 787 DBS six-cylinder cars, and 70 Aston Martin Vantage models were built.

Specification

Engine and transmission: Six-cylinders, in-line, with twin-overhead-camshaft cylinder head. Bore, stroke and capacity 96 × 92mm., 3995cc. Maximum power 282bhp (net) at 5500rpm.; maximum torque 288lb.ft. at 3850rpm. Optional 'Vantage' engine: 325bhp (net) at 5500rpm.; maximum torque 290lb.ft. at 4500rpm. Five-speed ZF gearbox or Borg Warner three-speed automatic transmission, in unit with engine. Hypoid bevel final drive.

Chassis: Front engine, rear drive. Fabricated steel platform chassis frame. Independent front suspension by coil springs and wishbones. Optional power-assisted rack and pinion steering. Rear suspension, de Dion, coil springs, radius arms and Watts linkage. Four-wheel disc brakes.

Bodywork: Two-door, four-seater fastback coupe body style by Aston Martin, of steel and light-alloy panels. Length 15ft. 0.5in.; width 6ft. 0in.; height 4ft. 5in. Unladen weight 3760lb.

Performance: (Vantage version): Maximum speed 148mph. 0-60mph 8.6sec. Standing ¼-mile 16.3sec. Typical fuel consumption 13mpg.

Aston Martin DBS V8 family

Built: Newport Pagnell, England, 1969 to date

When Aston Martin conceived the new chassis and bodyshell first seen in 1967 as the DBS, they designed it around a brand new vee-8 engine. As it happened, the vee-8 engine was not ready for production along with the rest of the car, so the six-cylinder DBS was built for two-years before it was joined by the definitive DBS V8 in the autumn of 1969.

Structurally and visually, the DBS V8 was almost exactly the same as the DBS-6, as the original car came to be known. Recognition points were the cast-alloy wheels, and the badging.

Mechanically, only the engine and the optional automatic transmission were new – the manual transmission continuing to be the ZF five-speed unit. The engine was a massive vee-8 with light-alloy cylinder block and heads, and had twin-overhead-camshaft cylinders and chain driven cams in the traditional Aston Martin manner. Though philosophically related to the 'six', there were no common parts, and as Aston Martin had, by now, decided that there was no point in claiming accurate power outputs when their competitors were claiming higher and quite erroneous ones, it was decided that they would never reveal the true output of this vee-8. A recently published book by a director of the company, however, suggests that an average power output of 345bhp was achieved, with great flexibility and a good spread of torque.

Most cars were built with automatic transmission, which tells us a lot about the type of clientele which Aston Martin were attracting by the end of the 1960s, and for this engine, the sophisticated Chrysler Torqueflite transmission was offered in favour of the Borg Warner unit matched to the six-cylinder engine.

The engine had first been seen in racing Lola sports-racing cars owned by John Surtees, though that project had been unsuccessful. In that form the engine was equipped with Weber carburettors, but in its initial production form Bosch fuel-injection was fitted.

Following the company takeover of 1972, when the David Brown influence disappeared, the name of the car was changed to Aston Martin V8, and at the same time the simplified two-headlamp nose was adopted. Not much more than a year later – in the summer of 1973 – and with sales to North America in mind, the finicky Bosch injection installation was abandoned, and a quartet of downdraught twin-choke Weber carburettors took its place. This slightly reduced the maximum power output, but improved the exhaust emission performance.

At the end of 1974, of course, the company went into financial liquidation, and production of V8s ceased for several months. From mid-1975, however, a rejuvenated concern began to build cars again, at a rate of approximately six units a week. Changes in engine specification resulted in a more powerful engine from mid-1977, and it is in this form that Aston Martin V8s continue to be built at the beginning of the 1980s.

Aston Martin V8

Specification

Engine and transmission: Eight-cylinders in 90-degree vee-formation, with twin-camshaft cylinder heads. Bore, stroke and capacity 100×85mm. 5340cc. Maximum power and torque figures not quoted. Five-speed ZF gearbox or Chrysler automatic transmission, in unit with engine. Hypoid bevel rear axle.

Chassis: Front engine, rear drive. Fabricated steel platform chassis. Independent front suspension by coil springs and wishbones. Power-assisted rack and pinion steering. Rear suspension, de Dion, coil springs, radius arms and Watts linkage. Four-wheel disc brakes.

Bodywork: Shell built from light-alloy skin panels and inner steel panels, welded to platform chassis; four-seater coupe. Length 15ft. 0.5in.; width 6ft. 0in.; height 4ft. 5in. Unladen weight 3800lb.

Performance: (Injection version) Maximum speed 161mph. 0-60mph 6.0sec. Standing ¼-mile 14.1sec. Typical fuel consumption 13mpg.

Note: From 1972 the model was renamed 'Aston Martin V8', and from mid-1973 engines with Weber carburettors replaced those with fuel-injection. Convertible also available.

Performance: (Carburettor version) Maximum speed 145mph. 0-60mph 6.2sec. Standing ¼-mile 14.7sec. Typical fuel consumption 13mpg.

Aston Martin Vantage (V8 type)

Built: Newport Pagnell, England, 1977 to date

Following the re-birth of the Aston Martin concern in 1975, engineering development work got under way again, and at the beginning of 1977 the company produced one of the most astonishingly-fast versions of a road car that anyone could imagine. Without doing more than make minor changes to the long-established coupe shape, and by strictly conventional tuning methods, the engineers squeezed a claimed 40 percent more power out of the 5.3-litre engine (no figures were ever released), and ensured that a maximum speed of more than 170mph was assured. Although this was only 10mph more than the original DBS V8, it was at least 20 to 25mph more than that of the Aston Martin V8 when equipped with carburettors (which were retained on the Vantage), and had the most remarkable accelerative powers. There are grounds for thinking that this car must vie with Ferrari's Daytona as the fastest road car ever sold to the public.

   Visually the changes were concentrated on the nose, where there was a large but effective air dam under the front bumper, and where the grille and air intake on the

Aston Martin Vantage (V8)

bonnet had been blanked off. Journalists who expressed surprise at this move were told that there was ample air circulating in the engine bay at the speeds of which the Vantage was capable; the truth was, it seems, that at high speeds the aerodynamics of the body were such that very little air actually penetrated the grille in any case!

Production of Vantage models, only sold as closed coupes, is strictly by special order, and never more than one every week is manufactured at Newport Pagnell. It was on the basis of the Vantage that Robin Hamilton's Le Mans Aston Martins have been prepared.

Specification

Engine and transmission: Eight-cylinders in 90-degree vee-formation, with twin-camshaft cylinder heads. Bore, stroke and capacity 100 × 85mm, 5340cc. Maximum power and torque figures not quoted. Five-speed ZF gearbox or Chrysler automatic transmission, in unit with engine. Hypoid bevel rear axle.

Chassis: Front engine, rear drive. Fabricated steel platform chassis. Independent front suspension by coil springs and wishbones. Power-assisted rack and pinion steering. Rear suspension, de Dion, coil springs, radius arms and Watts linkage. Four-wheel disc brakes.

Bodywork: Shell built from light-alloy skin panels and inner steel panels, welded to platform chassis; four-seater coupe. Length 15ft. 3in.; width 6ft. 0in.; height 4ft. 5in. Unladen weight 4000lb.

Performance: Maximum speed 170mph. 0-60mph 5.4sec. Standing ¼-mile 13.7sec. Typical fuel consumption 14mpg.

BMW M1

Built: Stuttgart, W. Germany, 1978 to date

Although it was a great temptation to classify the very first mid-engined BMW coupe as an 'homologation special', it must also be looked on as a Supercar in every way. Considering that it has been sponsored, if not entirely designed and produced, by a company which makes more than 200 000 cars a year, its very existence is remarkable.

The origins of the M1 ('M' stands for mid-engined, '1' presumably for the fact that it is BMW's first such car) date back to 1975. By then the battle between Ford and BMW for the European Touring Car championship had evaporated, and BMW turned their attention to the more rarified but very prestigious sports-racing category, where cars like the 934/935 range of Porsches ruled the roost. Apart from having a very suitable engine, as proved in the much-modified 3.0CSL models, they had to start from scratch. They would produce a Group 4 car first, then detune it and make it suitable for road use because they had to sell a certain minimum number. The M1 was the result.

Initially, BMW entrusted the design to Lamborghini, on the basis that the S'Agata firm would also build the production cars alongside its own models in Italy. That arrangement fell through when Lamborghini fell into financial problems, but their design (and their sourcing of major sections of the car) have persisted. The multi-tube chassis frame, owing much in its layout to Ferrari, Maserati and Lamborghini models of the 1970s, is built by Marchesi of Modena, and the glass-fibre bodyshell, styled by Ital Design on BMW's behalf, is manufactured by Transformazione Italiana Resina of Reggio Emilia, also in Italy. The two major components are mated at Ital Design's premises, after which they are transported to the German body makers, Baur of Stuttgart, for final assembly and testing. Thus, apart from their sponsorship and the use of their engine, BMW are not really involved until the marketing takes place.

The engine, a 3453cc unit, is a direct descendant of those developed during BMW's active racing programme with the 3.0CSL coupes. Its roots are in the six-cylinder engine first seen in BMW cars in 1968, but it is installed in a vertical position in the M1, rather than canted over as in every one of the six-cylinder quantity-production cars. A twin-overhead-camshaft, 24-valve cylinder head is used, with 38-degrees between lines of valves, and the combustion chamber and valve gear layout is obviously based on Ford's successful BDA/DFV assembly. Fuel metering is by a Bosch fuel-injection system, and in road form the power output is a mere 277bhp; the word 'mere' is used, because in racing form the same basic engine, using the same cylinder block and head castings, can be persuaded to develop up to 500bhp, which is an astonishing 143bhp/litre and worthy of note by out-and-out racing car engine designers.

This power output is harnessed by a large ZF five-speed transaxle, which also has to cope with the turbocharged derivative of the engine (when up to 850bhp may be – literally – 'on tap'), and roadholding is helped by four-wheel coil spring and wishbone independent suspension. Even in untuned form, a maximum speed of more than 160mph is claimed (along with 130mph in fourth gear!) and in racing form it is certain that well over 200mph is possible with appropriate gearing.

Clearly the M1, whose first full season was 1979, when it starred in the Procar circus before every Grand Prix in the European events of that series, is only at the beginning of its development, and it could be that other large firms like Ford might be encouraged to undertake similar enterprises.

BMW M1

Specification

Engine and transmission: Six-cylinders, in-line, with twin-overhead camshaft cylinder head. Bore, stroke and capacity 93.4 × 84mm., 3453cc. Maximum power 277bhp (DIN) at 6500rpm.; maximum torque 243lb.ft. at 5000rpm. Five-speed manual gearbox in unit with engine and transaxle. Hypoid bevel final drive.

Chassis: Mid-engine, rear drive. Separate box section and tubular chassis frame. Independent front suspension by coil springs and wishbones. Rack and pinion steering. Independent rear suspension by coil springs and wishbones. Four-wheel disc brakes.

Bodywork: Glass-fibre bodyshell, in two-door, two-seater fastback coupe style, styled by Giugiario, built by Baur. Length 14ft. 3.7in.; width 5ft. 11.8in.; height 3ft. 8.9in. Unladen weight 2870lb.

Performance: Maximum speed 161mph. 0-60mph 5.6sec. Standing ¼-mile 13.8sec. Typical fuel consumption 17mpg.

Bristol 407 to 411 family

Built: Bristol, England, 1961-1976

By the beginning of the 1960s, the original Bristol six-cylinder engine (whose design they had 'liberated' from BMW at the close of the second world war) was beginning to look rather outdated and long-in-the-tooth. It could not be stretched any further, nor made any more powerful without a loss of flexibility. For their next new model, therefore, Bristol decided to buy engines and transmissions from Chrysler in North America.

In one move, therefore, Bristol converted their product from a 406 which qualifies as a Grand Touring car, to the 407, which was quite definitely a Supercar. The new car was capable of 122mph in its original form, and in the next few years steady increases in power pushed this up to around 135/140mph.

In fairness to Bristol, one must point out that they had more ambitious ideas than merely to buy their power from the United States, which included designing a new chassis (the Type 220), a new six-cylinder engine, and new transmissions to match. It was only a change in corporate policy (for Bristol Cars were still, then, a subsidiary of the Bristol Aircraft company) which caused serious cutbacks in investment, and made

Bristol 410

Bristol 411, London Motor Show 1971

abandonment of these exciting programmes inevitable.

The engine chosen by Bristol, after a great deal of study, was actually a Canadian-built unit (there were good 'Imperial preference' tax reasons for this) of the Chrysler Detroit Hemi-engine, and in its 5.1-litre guise it developed 250bhp (gross), which was probably more like 180bhp (net) due to the way all North American concerns tended to exaggerate their power outputs in the early 1960s. It was matched very successfully to Chrysler's own Torqueflite automatic transmission, and for the first time on a Bristol there was no manual gearbox available at all.

The chassis and suspensions of the 407 were effectively those of the 406, and the two-door saloon bodyshell was only a lightly-modified derivative of that originally designed for the 406 – made in London and transported to Bristol for final assembly. Even so, the massively powerful new engine meant that the 407 felt like a completely new model, so it was appropriate that at about this time the company was hived off by the aircraft company, and purchased by Sir George White and Anthony Crook, who had been Directors of the concern for some years.

Until the arrival of not one, but two new shapes, in the mid-1970s, this basic structure – platform-type chassis, coachbuilt two-door bodyshell, and Chrysler vee-8 engine – dominated the scene at Bristols. Significant changes were made to the specification from time to time, which usually meant that the model name was changed at the same time.

The 408 of 1963, for instance, which replaced the 407, had only minor mechanical and style changes, but the 409 of 1965 had a slightly enlarged (5211cc) Chrysler engine, Girling instead of Dunlop disc brakes, many other minor changes, and a claimed maximum speed which had risen to 132mph. The 410 of 1967 was much like the 409, except that power-assisted steering (introduced late in the run of the 409) was standardised, and other minor styling and mechanical changes were phased in.

European Sports & GT Cars

The 411 of 1969, which replaced the previous model, still kept to the well-established formula, but used a completely different, and much larger (6277cc) Chrysler engine. This was not the final derivative of the famous 'Hemi' design, but was one of the more modern but much less sophisticated units from Chrysler. Not only this, but radial-ply tyres were fitted for the first time.

411s then continued to be developed in the 1970s, such that the final Mk V 411 model had a 6556cc engine producing 264bhp (DIN) − a much more impressive and believable figure than the 250bhp (gross) of the first 407. Even by patrician Bristol standards, however, the 411 was now outdated, and by 1976 it had been replaced by two different designs − the 412 and the rather different 603.

Specification (407)

Engine and transmission: Eight-cylinders, in 90-degree vee-formation, with pushrod-operated overhead-valve cylinder heads, manufactured by Chrysler. Bore, stroke and capacity 98 × 84.1mm., 5130cc. Maximum power 250bhp (gross) at 4400rpm.; maximum torque 340lb.ft. at 2800rpm. Three-speed automatic (Chrysler) transmission in unit with the engine. Hypoid bevel final drive.

Chassis: Front engine, rear drive. Fabricated steel chassis frame, with box-section members. Independent front suspension by coil springs and wishbones. Cam and roller steering. Suspension of rear live axle by torsion bars, radius arms and Watts linkage. Four-wheel disc brakes.

Bodywork: Light-alloy coachbuilt bodyshell on steel framing, in two-door four-seater GT saloon style. Length 17ft. 7in.; width 5ft. 8in.; height 5ft. 0in. Unladen weight 3585lb.

Performance: Maximum speed 122mph. 0-60mph 9.9sec. Standing ⅛-mile 17.4sec. Typical fuel consumption 16mpg.

Note: The 408 of 1963 had minor changes. The 409 of 1965 had a slightly enlarged (5211cc) Chrysler engine, and power-assisted worm-and-roller steering. The 410 of 1967 had further minor changes. The 411 of 1969 had a further enlarged (6277cc) engine, with 335bhp (gross) at 5200rpm.; maximum torque 425lb.ft. at 3400rpm. The Mk IV 411 had 6556cc (110.3 × 85.7mm).; maximum power 264bhp (DIN) at 4800rpm.; maximum torque 335lb.ft. at 3600rpm. Unladen weight 3775lb.

Performance (410): Maximum speed 130mph. 0-60mph 8.8sec. Standing ¼-mile 16.2sec. Typical fuel consumption 14mpg. **(411, 6277cc):** Maximum speed 138mph. 0-60mph 7.0sec. Standing ¼-mile 15.0sec. Typical fuel consumption 15mpg.

Bristol 411 MkV

Bristol 412

Built: Bristol, England, 1975 to date

To bring a new and modern image to their range of cars, Bristol commissioned Zagato (who had styled some startling Bristols in the 1950s and 1960s) to produce a new body style on their existing chassis. The result was called the 412, and was first revealed in May 1975, when it was shown only as a convertible.

Perhaps a decision to make a convertible was only the first of a series of moves, for a 'Convertible-saloon' version of the car, in which the permanent roll-over 'Targa' bar was incorporated into a coupe/hardtop style, followed less than a year later.

In each case, the 412 was little more than a new body style on an existing chassis, and it is worth pointing out at this stage that that chassis had originated for the Bristol 400 of the 1940s, and had roots in a BMW 326 layout of the late 1930s. It is a tribute to the painstaking way that Bristol continued to develop their products that its road manners with much more power, and when carrying a lot more weight, were still completely acceptable in the 1970s.

Anthony Crook, by then the sole owner of Bristol, hoped that 411s and 412s would sell alongside each other for some time to come – and said at the time that he was only interested in Bristol making about three cars every week. Since the announcement of the 400, he said, about 6000 cars had been delivered before the 412 was revealed. However, the styling of the 412 was so much in advance of that of the 411 that the balance of sales soon shifted away from the old design, and the 603 had to be brought along to restore equilibrium.

Although the rolling chassis has not been changed since announcement, the engine specification has been affected by the necessity of 'down-sizing' for Chrysler in North America; although the first 412s had 6556cc engines (with power and torque not quoted – Bristol had followed Aston Martin in maintaining discreet silence over these matters), cars built from autumn 1977 have 5898cc engines. Performance, inevitably, has suffered somewhat, but a measure of the Zagato style's efficiency is that the 6.6-litre car was capable of 140mph, and used petrol at the rate of about 14mpg.

Specification

Engine and transmission: Eight-cylinders, in 90-degree vee-formation, with pushrod-operated overhead-valve cylinder heads, built by Chrysler. Bore, stroke and capacity 110.3 × 85.7mm., 6556cc. Maximum power and torque not revealed. Three-speed Chrysler automatic transmission in unit with the engine. Hypoid bevel final drive. From autumn 1977 engine changed to 101.6 × 90.9mm., 5898cc. Maximum power 172bhp (DIN) at 4000rpm.; maximum torque 270lb.ft. at 2000rpm.
Chassis: Front engine, rear drive. Fabricated steel chassis frame, with box section members. Independent front suspension by coil springs and wishbones. Power-assisted recirculating ball steering. Rear suspension of live axle by torsion bars, radius arms and Watts linkage. Four-wheel disc brakes.

Bristol 412, 1976

Bodywork: Light-alloy coachbuilt shell on steel framing, in two-door four-seater convertible (1975-1976) and 'Convertible saloon' (1976 onwards) styles. Length 16ft. 2.5in.; width 5ft. 9.5in.; height 4ft. 8.5in. Unladen weight 3780lb.
Performance: (6.5-litre engine) Maximum speed 140mph. 0-60mph 7.4sec. Standing ¼-mile 15.9sec. Typical fuel consumption 14mpg.

351

Bristol 603

Built: Bristol, England, 1976 to date

For Bristol Cars to announce a new model with radically different styling from the last is something of an event. For them to do this twice in less than two-years is quite earth-shattering! Having greeted the 412 'Convertible-Saloon' in 1975, the Bristol enthusiasts were quite bowled over to see that another new car — the 603 — followed it in 1976.

It was something of a celebration for Bristol, for the 603 came along just 30 years after their first-ever model, the 400, had been put on the market. However, whereas the 412, which had preceded it by more than a year, was establishing its own particular market, the 603 was specifically designed to replace the last of the 411s, the Mk V version. As with the Zagato-bodied 412, the Bristol-styled 603 was quite unlike any previous Bristol, except that it had a two-door four-seater bodyshell. It had a full-width grille style with four headlamps, but a sweeping tail which contrasted sharply with the notchback arrangement of the 407 to 411 series.

However, it was based on the faithful and long-running Bristol chassis frame, with its 9ft. 6in. wheelbase, and it used a choice of Chrysler vee-8 engines. Originally there were two versions — the 603-S, which had a 5898cc engine like the latest 412 model, and the 603-E ('E' for Economy?) which had a 5211cc engine, of the size last seen in the 409 of 1965-1967 — but after a short period the 5.2-litre engine was withdrawn, and both current Bristols are built with the same 5.9-litre engine.

As almost all traditional Bristol features remain — spare wheel mounted in the left front wing, with battery, brake servo and other details in the right wing to match — the 603 can be considered, simply, as a rebodied 411.

Specification

Engine and transmission: Eight-cylinders, in 90-degree vee-formation, with pushrod-operated overhead-valve cylinder heads, manufactured by Chrysler. Alternative engines: Bore, stroke and capacity 99.3 × 84.1mm., 5211cc. Maximum power 147bhp (DIN) at 4000rpm.; maximum torque 245lb.ft. at 1600rpm (1976 and 1977 only). Or Bore, stroke and capacity 101.6 × 90.9mm, 5898cc. Maximum power 172bhp (DIN) at 4000rpm.; maximum torque 270lb.ft. at 2000rpm. Three-speed Chrysler automatic transmission in unit with engine. Hypoid bevel final drive.
Chassis: Front engine, rear drive. Fabricated steel chassis frame, with box-section members. Independent front suspension by coil springs and wishbones. Power-assisted recirculating ball steering. Rear suspension of live axle by torsion bars, radius arms and Watts linkage. Four-wheel disc brakes.
Bodywork: Light-alloy coachbuilt shell on steel framing, in two-door four-seater fastback coupe style. Length 16ft. 1.3in.; width 5ft. 9.7in.; height 4ft. 8.7in. Unladen weight 3935lb.
Performance: Maximum speed 140mph. 0-60mph 8.6sec. Standing ¼-mile 16.5sec. Typical fuel consumption 13mpg.

Bristol 603

Facel Vega, HK500 and Facel II

Built: Colombes, France, 1954-1964

Although the Chrysler-engined Facel Vega of 1954 was a new marque name, there was nothing new about the concern who would be building it. Jean Daninos had founded *Forges et Ateliers de Construction d'Eure et de Loire* (whose initials form the name of Facel), before the second world war. At first they produced tools and dies for the aircraft industry, later moving into almost anything which could be made from pressed-metal, and by the early 1950s were supplying complete bodies to customers like Panhard, Simca, Ford-France and Delahaye. The Facel Vega car was born because the abandonment of the original ugly Dyna-Panhard for a new Panhard-produced car left lots of spare capacity, which Daninos wanted to fill.

The basis of all Facel Vegas of the Supercar type were a simple tubular chassis frame, with coil spring independent front suspension, to which a stylish (self-styled by Daninos's team, incidentally) pressed-steel bodyshell was welded on assembly at the Colombes factory, near Paris. Although a few cars had four-door bodies, the vast majority had two-door styles, usually closed coupes, but sometimes convertibles. Power was by Chrysler (at first using the 4.5-litre Dodge 'hemi' unit), matched to a massive Pont-a-Mousson gearbox or to Chrysler three-speed automatic transmission, while the back axle was by courtesy of Salisbury in Great Britain.

In the first few years, engines grew progressively bigger, and the handling, reliability, and general reputation all improved. The 'Excellence' was the only four-door model, but this was sold in a pillarless style where the bodyshell was none-too-rigid. The word got round, and though the model was listed to the very end, in 1964, only 230 examples were sold.

Facel Vega HK500, 1961

Original cars were quite simply called Facel Vegas, but the revised model of 1959 saw significant mechanical and style changes, to a model which was dubbed the HK500. This was the Facel Supercar which greeted the 1960s, and was the single most important model in this series. The Chrysler vee-8 engine grew to 6276cc − a size familiar to Jensen CV8 owners, for instance − and before long the rather poor drum brakes were dropped in favour of four-wheel Dunlop discs. For a time, however, the HK500 was unique in European terms, as no British firm would adopt Chrysler power until 1961, and that Gordon GT prototype did not mature as a production Gordon-Keeble until 1964.

The Facel Vegas were massive and impressive cars which looked as impressive as their performance. They were heavy and ponderous, but their straight-line, or 'motorway' performance was quite outstanding, and they appealed to a limited number of wealthy men who did not want the aggravation of a Ferrari or Maserati road car.

HK500 became Facel II in 1962, retaining the same chassis, and most of the power train, though the engine was potentially even more powerful than before, and maximum speed could be as high as 150mph on a suitable wide-open road. The body style had been completely revised, was more rakish, and had much in common (artistically, if not in terms of panels) with the Facellia coupe.

Facel II, like the earlier cars, was so big, fast and expensive, that it could not be expected to sell very fast. However, it was the debacle of the small-engined Facel Vegas which caused the company to go into liquidation in 1964. No more than 750 of these big cars were ever made in a full year, and the usual rate was less than a half of this. Some sources suggest that less than 500 HK500s were built, along with about 400 of the original cars, and rather less Facel IIs.

Specification (HK500)

Engine and transmission: Eight-cylinders, in 90-degree vee-formation, with pushrod-operated overhead-valve cylinder heads, manufactured by Chrysler. Bore, stroke and capacity 107.95×85.85mm., 6286cc. Maximum power 360bhp (gross) at 5200rpm.; maximum torque not quoted. Four-speed manual transmission or three-speed Chrysler automatic transmission in unit with the engine. Hypoid bevel final drive.

Chassis: Front engine, rear drive. Separate design steel chassis frame, with tubular and channel section members, welded to body on assembly. Independent front suspension by coil springs and wishbones. Cam and roller (power assisted with automatic transmission) steering. Rear suspension of live axle by half-elliptic leaf springs. Four-wheel disc brakes.

Bodywork: Coachbuilt steel and light-alloy bodyshell, welded to chassis on assembly, in two-door close-coupled four-seater coupe or convertible. Length 15ft. 1in.; width 5ft. 11in.; height 4ft. 5.5in. Unladen weight 4035lb.

Performance: Maximum speed 140mph. 0-60mph 8.4sec. Standing ¼-mile 16.3sec. Typical fuel consumption 15mpg.

355

Facel Vega Facel II, 1965

Note: Facel II model of 1962 had similar basic engineering, but 390bhp (gross) at 5400rpm (for manual transmission) or 355bhp (gross) at 4800rpm (automatic transmission). Length 15ft. 5.5in.; width 5ft. 8.7in.; height 4ft. 3in.
Performance: (Manual) Maximum speed 149mph. 0-60mph 8.3sec. Standing ¼-mile 16.5sec. Typical fuel consumption 15mpg.

Ferrari 400 Superamerica Coupe by Pininfarina

Ferrari 400 Superamerica and Superfast

Built: Maranello, Italy, 1955-1966

The Super America and Superfast series of Ferraris were at one and the same time the most expensive, the most powerful, and the most exclusive of the Maranello company's road cars. The Super America, known at first as the Type 410 model, was first revealed towards the end of 1955, when it was seen to have a road version of that incredible 4.9-litre Le Mans-winning vee-12 engine (the largest of all the Lampredi-designed vee-12 engines), linked to a four-speed gearbox, and with the usual (for Ferrari) tubular chassis, rudimentary rear suspension, and Pininfarina body style. This car, in itself, was a descendant of the Type 342 and Type 375 America models, all being made in very limited numbers.

By the beginning of the 1960s, however, the standard 'America' model was the Type 400 Superamerica, which revolved around the 3968cc vee-12 engine which would later be found in the '330' models of the mid-1960s (and which were made in considerably larger quantities). In fairness, and without being cynical, most of the interest of new road-going Ferraris was in the choice of engine (Maranello seemed to have an inexhaustible supply of new versions for any particular need!) and in the latest Pininfarina body style. The chassis of all road going Ferraris made up to 1964, and the arrival of the all-independent 275GTB, were based on a simple tubular 'ladder frame' layout, with big diameter tubes and a certain blacksmith cunning to provide stiffness

and some torsional rigidity. All, including the successful Berlinettas, seemed to have live rear axles located by nothing more enterprising than half-elliptic leaf springs and radius arms to discourage wind-up.

The Superamericas bodied by Pininfarina were very self-indulgent machines, as they were physically large, with enormously powerful engines, but provided only two seats and a minimum of luggage accommodation. Eventually, in 1964, they were replaced by the 500 Superfast model, which reverted to the use of the 4.9-litre engine, this time with a power output of no less than a claimed 400bhp (DIN) at 6500rpm, and torque of no less than 350lb.ft. at 4750rpm. This made it *the* most powerful 'production' car in the world, and it almost certainly made it the fastest car too. The car's coupe styling was derived from that of the Superamerica, and was not altered before it was finally withdrawn in 1966.

Even though it had such massive performance, the car was never seriously marketed outside North America, for whose wealthy citizens it was really intended, and it was only delivered in tiny quantities as the body and some of the chassis was not completely tooled for being produced any faster.

It was really the last of the lumberingly big and heavy Ferrari road cars with that obsolete chassis layout, as the image of the very largest Ferraris was completely changed by the 365GT 2+2 of 1967.

Specification (Type 400)

Engine and transmission: Twelve-cylinders, in 60-degree vee-formation, with single-overhead-camshaft cylinder heads. Bore, stroke and capacity 77×71mm., 3968cc. Maximum power 360bhp (gross) at 7000rpm.; maximum torque 260lb.ft. at 5500rpm. Four-speed manual gearbox and overdrive in unit with engine. Spiral bevel final drive.
Chassis: Front engine, rear drive. Separate tubular section chassis frame. Independent front suspension by coil springs and wishbones. Suspension of rear live axle by half-elliptic leaf springs and radius arms. Four-wheel disc brakes.
Bodywork: Light-alloy coachbuilt two-door two-seater fastback coupe style, or cabriolet, by Pininfarina. Length 14ft. 3.75in.; width 5ft. 7in.; height 4ft. 3.5in. Unladen weight (approx) 2860lb.
Performance: Maximum speed (approx) 150mph. 0-60mph 9.2sec. Standing ¼-mile 17.0sec. Typical fuel consumption 15mpg.

Note: The 500 Superfast model of 1964-1966 was mechanically similar to the Superamerica, with the following important differences: **Engine:** 88×68mm., 4963cc. Maximum power 400bhp (DIN) at 6500rpm.; maximum torque 350lb.ft. at 4750rpm. Length 15ft. 9.8in.; width 5ft. 10in.; height 4ft. 2.4in. Unladen weight (approx) 3100lb.
Performance: Up to 180mph maximum speed. 0-60mph 7.8sec. Standing ¼-mile 15.8sec. Typical fuel consumption 13mpg.

Ferrari 250GT

Built: Maranello, Italy, 1959-1964

Until the mid-1950s, Ferrari was not really very interested in producing proper production cars for road use — not, at least, cars which all had the same standard mechanical specification, and shared the same body style. It was the 250GT series, which really evolved from the 250 Europas and Berlinettes towards the end of the 1950s, which changed his mind.

By 1959 a new Ferrari chassis had been developed — a multi-tubular affair as usual, with independent front suspension, but with a live rear axle sprung on half-elliptic leaf springs and located by nothing more ambitious than radius arms. This had a 7ft. 10.5in. wheelbase — considerably shorter than previous 250GT types had used — and it was powered by the classic single-overhead-camshaft 'Colombo' 2953cc engine. This was backed by a solid four-speed manual gearbox, which in later years was backed by an overdrive on road cars or was supplanted by a five-speed manual gearbox on racing derivatives like the 250GTO, which were the final flowering of this great design.

Between 1959 and 1962, probably about 250 of the short wheelbase Berlinettas were built, with probably less than a quarter of these having lightweight competition bodywork. From then on, however, various other coachbuilders supplied coupe and convertible bodies, all of which at least shared the same rugged and simple chassis.

With the more spacious 250GT 2 + 2 also appearing on the same chassis in 1961, Ferrari were able to consider further and more specialised derivatives of the production two-seater cars. On the purely touring car front (if any Ferrari could be considered as a pure tourer in those days) this led to the 250GT Lusso, and for competition to the 250GTO. Both were absolute classics of their type.

The Lusso was magnificently and delicately shaped by Pininfarina for Scaglietti to build, with astonishingly sleek lines. At one and the same time it was more beautiful, more practical, and more of a road car than the original 250GT Berlinettas had ever been. It made many friends for Ferrari, from wealthy customers who had previously shied away from something they thought to be a detuned racing coupe.

The most remarkable 250GT of all, of course, was the fabulous and now priceless GTO. The only difference in model naming, of course, was the 'O', which in Italian stands for Omologato — denoting that this particular version of the car was specially built and homologated for GT racing. The basic chassis and suspensions were those of the 250GT production car, except that the engine's power output was boosted to 300bhp at 7500rpm, and that a truck-like but reputedly very strong five-speed gearbox was fitted.

It was the GTO's bodywork, however, which was so striking. Revealed at the beginning of 1962 at Ferrari's press conference, though already seen because of 'sneak' pictures which seemed to suggest a mid-engined layout, the GTO was bodied by Scaglietti to Ferrari's own design. From its low 'anteater' nose, with removable nostril panels to provide more air to the radiator and engine bay if required, to its upswept tail, with a spoiler, it was rakish, efficient and quite unmistakeable. It was also very light in weight, and as a result the GTO was always a potential winner in the GT category of any race, or road event.

It was never necessary for 100 GTOs to be built, as approval was gained on the grounds of the car being an evolution of the short-wheelbase 250GT Berlinetta. Between 1962 and 1964, in fact, when production ceased as the 250GT chassis faded away, 42 true GTOs were built, along with three similar cars with 4-litre engines.

Specification (250GT)

Engine and transmission: Twelve-cylinders, in 60-degree vee-formation, with single-overhead-camshaft cylinder heads. Bore, stroke and capacity 73×58.8mm., 2953cc. Maximum power 240bhp at 7000rpm.; maximum torque 181lb.ft. at 5000rpm. Four-speed manual gearbox and overdrive in unit with engine. Spiral bevel final drive.

Chassis: Front engine, rear drive. Tubular separate chassis frame. Independent front suspension by coil springs and wishbones. Worm and sector steering. Suspension of rear live axle by half-elliptic leaf springs and radius arms. Four-wheel disc brakes.

Bodywork: Light-alloy coachbuilt two-door two-seater fastback coupe or cabriolet style by Pininfarina. Length 15ft. 5in.; width 5ft. 7in.; height 4ft. 5in. Unladen weight 2815lb.

Performance: Maximum speed 150mph. 0-60mph 8.0sec. Typical fuel consumption 15mpg.

Note: 250GT Berlinetta had similar mechanical components, but 280bhp at 7000rpm.; maximum torque 192lb.ft. at 6000rpm. Overdrive not fitted. Light-alloy coachbuilt fastback coupe bodyshell by Pininfarina, usually built by Scaglietti. Length 13ft. 8in.; width 5ft. 6in.; height 4ft. 2in. Unladen weight 2110lb.

Performance: Maximum speed 145mph. 0-60mph 6.6sec. Standing ¼-mile 14.8sec. Typical fuel consumption 12mpg.

Note: 250GTO was effectively the GT Berlinetta with special light-alloy coachwork. Maximum power was 300bhp (net) at 7500rpm.; maximum torque 217lb.ft. at 5500rpm. Five-speed manual gearbox. Length 14ft. 5.2in.; width 5ft. 5.9in.; height 4ft. 1in. Unladen weight 2095lb.

Ferrari 250GT 2 + 2 & 330GT

Built: Maranello, Italy, 1961 to 1967

If for no other reason, the Ferrari 250GT 2 + 2 was important as the first car from the famous Maranello factory to offer more than two seats. Although rear-seat legroom was strictly limited, and would probably not have been comfortable for an adult faced with a long high-speed journey, it was nevertheless something of a watershed in Ferrari's affairs. Before then, the reasoning went, anyone buying a Ferrari only ever wanted his girlfriend or wife, but never his relatives or children, to travel with him.

Miraculously, this seating capacity was achieved without lengthening the well-proven wheelbase, or seriously altering the chassis layout, of the famous 250GT, on which it was based. The length of the body, however, was increased by 12 inches, the front seats were moved forward by a similar amount (which meant extensive changes to the steering gear and other driving equipment), and the fuel tank was relocated.

The engine, that famous single-cam 60-degree 2953cc vee-12, was not changed, and like the existing 250GT it produced a maximum of 240bhp at 7000rpm.

One glaring problem, not rectified by Ferrari on this model, was that a Laycock overdrive was fitted behind the four-speed gearbox, which was theoretically an excellent idea, except that the gearbox required one type of oil and the overdrive another. Inevitably, this resulted in the correct gearbox oil being chosen, and the overdrive giving trouble!

Even with the 3-litre engine fitted, the 2 + 2 car could reach about 135mph. However, later cars had the larger 3967cc 'Lampredi' engine installed, in which case they became 330GTs, and as they were equipped with a new Ferrari five-speed manual gearbox and no overdrive, they were considerably more reliable and long-lived. For some years, until replaced by the 365GT 2 + 2, this model was the largest, if not the most expensive Ferrari, and found favour particularly in North America. By 1967, however, its engineering was outdated, as it did not have independent rear suspension. The 365GT 2 + 2 would rectify this.

Specification (250GT 2 + 2)

Engine and transmission: Twelve-cylinders, in 60-degree vee-formation, with single-overhead-camshaft cylinder heads. Bore, stroke and capacity 73×58.8mm., 2953cc. Maximum power 240bhp at 7000rpm.; maximum torque 181lb.ft. at 5000rpm. Four-speed manual gearbox and overdrive in unit with engine. Spiral bevel final drive.
Chassis: Front engine, rear drive. Separate tubular chassis frame. Independent front suspension by coil springs and wishbones. Worm and sector steering. Rear suspension of live axle by half-elliptic leaf springs and radius arms. Four-wheel disc brakes.
Bodywork: Coachbuilt light-alloy two-door 2 + 2 seater fastback coupe by Pininfarina. Length 15ft. 5in.; width 5ft. 7.5in.; height 4ft. 5.5in. Unladen weight 2820lb.
Performance (250GT 2 + 2): Maximum speed 150mph. 0-60mph 8.0sec. Standing ¼-mile 16.3sec. Typical fuel consumption 19mpg.

Note: 330GT was basically the same car, with these important differences: Bore, stroke and capacity 77×71mm., 3968cc. Maximum power 300bhp (net) at 6600rpm.;

maximum torque 288lb.ft. at 5000rpm. Five-speed manual gearbox in unit with engine. Hypoid bevel final drive. Unladen weight 3040lb.

Performance: (330GT) Maximum speed 142mph. 0-60mph 7.4sec. Standing ¼-mile 15.5sec. Typical fuel consumption 15mpg.

Ferrari 330GT

Ferrari 275GTB

Built: Maranello, Italy, 1964-1968

Although the many versions of the famous 250GT model can be considered as Ferrari's first true production car, the 275GTB which arrived in 1964 was certainly the first Ferrari produced by series-production methods, with the same basic coachbuilt body-style for each example. But the 275GTB was much more than this, as it ushered in a completely new wave of Ferrari road car design thinking in chassis and transmission terms.

First, however, the model's title should be explained, as it typifies Ferrari's naming methods for some years. 275 was the individual capacity, in cubic centimetres, of one of the engine's 12-cylinders, 'GT' meant Gran Tourismo, and 'B' stood for Berlinetta, whose literal Italian translation was 'small saloon.'

Introduction of this car coincided with a big expansion at the Ferrari factory, and it could be built in considerably larger quantities than any previous Ferrari road car. The basis of the design was a multi-tube chassis frame, of the type favoured by many Italian constructors in the 1950s and 1960s, on to which one of two bodies – the 275GTB coupe shell or an open-spider 275GTS derivative were mounted. That body, incidentally, had been styled by Ferrari's most consistent consultant, Pininfarina. The production coupes were built by Scaglietti, while the spiders were built at the Pininfarina workshops. Both cars, incidentally, had only one row of seats, but whereas the closed car had two individual seats, that of the spider was arranged to give a driver's seat, and a double width passenger's bench seat, effectively turning this open machine into a three-seater.

The core of the new design, however, was its driveline and suspension layout. For the first time on a Ferrari road car, the transmission was separated from the engine. Whereas the vee-12 engine was front mounted as usual, the five-speed gearbox was ahead of, but in unit with, the chassis-mounted final drive casing. Connecting them, at first was a very slim and solid propellor shaft with a single centre steady bearing. This in fact, was not completely satisfactory, and was replaced by a fat and solid torque tube connecting the engine to the final drive, with the slim driveshaft enclosed in it. At one and the same time it cured the transmission vibrations, and imparted considerable extra stiffness to the rather shallow and flexible chassis frame.

The rear-mounted transmission meant that a live axle could not be used, so a double-wishbone form of independent rear suspension was adopted, with remarkably similar geometry to that of the front suspension.

The engine, need it be said, was a 3.3-litre version of the famous 60-degree vee-12 which Ing. Colombo had designed way back in the 1940s for fitment to the first Ferrari competition car (when it had been a 1.5-litre unit). In its original guise it had a single-overhead-camshaft per cylinder bank, and the power output was 280bhp (net) at 7500rpm.

The progress of the competitors (and the need to give the 275GTB even more race-winning potential) meant that more power was needed, so after only two years of production the 275GTB became the 275GTB4, with twin-overhead-camshaft cylinder heads. The '4' denoted the number of camshafts and the improved breathing of this engine resulted in a power output of no less than 300bhp (net) at a rousing 8000rpm.

Thus modified, this very successful Ferrari road car carried on for another two years, until it was replaced by the even more startling Daytona of 1968.   363

Specification

Engine and transmission: Twelve-cylinders, in 60-degree vee-formation, with single-overhead-camshaft cylinder heads. Bore, stroke and capacity 77 × 58.8mm., 3286cc. (275GTB) Maximum power 280bhp (net) at 7500rpm.; maximum torque 188lb.ft. at 5500rpm. Five-speed manual gearbox in unit with final drive. Hypoid bevel final drive. (275GTB4) Twin-overhead-camshaft cylinder heads. Maximum power 300bhp (net) at 8000rpm.; maximum torque 217lb.ft. at 5500rpm.

Chassis: Front engine, rear drive. Separate tubular chassis frame. Independent front suspension by coil springs and wishbones. Worm and sector steering. Independent rear suspension by coil springs and wishbones. Four-wheel disc brakes.

Bodywork: Coachbuilt light-alloy two-door two-seater coupe (Scaglietti) or GTS Cabriolet (Pininfarina). Length 14ft. 6in.; width 5ft. 7in.; height 4ft. 0.5in. Unladen weight 2490lb.

Performance (275GTB): Maximum speed 153mph. 0-60mph 6.0sec. Standing ¼-mile 14.0sec. Typical fuel consumption 18mpg. **(275GTS Spider):** Maximum speed 145mph. 0-60mph 7.2sec. Standing ¼-mile 15.7sec. Typical fuel consumption 17mpg. **(275GTB/4):** Maximum speed 155mph. 0-60mph 5.5sec. Standing ¼-mile 14.0sec. Typical fuel consumption 16mpg.

Ferrari 275GTB

Ferrari 330GTC/GTS and 365GTC/GTS

Built: Maranello, Italy, 1966-1970

In many ways the 330GTC (Coupe) and 330GTS (Spider) cars were classic examples of the way that Ferrari could 'product plan' his various mechanical components, clothe one combination in an attractive and distinctive body, and produce yet another new model. The 330GTC, for instance, was really the rolling chassis of the 275GTB, matched to the larger 'Lampredi' engine, and given a sleek two-seater coupe Pininfarina body.

The 330GTC, therefore, featured the multi-tube frame, the rear-mounted gearbox and final drive, the four-wheel independent suspension, and the fat torque tube linking the transmission direct to the engine, all as found in the 275GTB4. The engine was the 4.0-litre Lampredi-designed vee-12 unit.

The 330GTS, however, was not just a spider version of the coupe, but was actually an up-engined derivative of the 275GTS which had originally complemented the 275GTB coupe on the production line.

In an effort to keep the performance of these cars ahead of that achieved by Maserati and Lamborghini, the two great rivals, the 330GTC/GTS cars became 365s from the beginning of 1969. This was done merely by fitting the enlarged 4390cc engine in place of the 3967cc unit (both were physically the same size — the difference being in the cylinder bore). Maximum power was increased from 300bhp to 320bhp, both figures being achieved at 6600rpm. However, this was not a popular type of Ferrari, and in 1970 it was replaced by yet another new car, the 365GTC/4.

Specification

Engine and transmission: Twelve-cylinders, in 60-degree vee-formation, with single-overhead-camshaft cylinder heads. Bore, stroke and capacity 77×71mm., 3967cc. Maximum power 300bhp (net) at 6600rpm.; maximum torque 288lb.ft. at 5000rpm. From 1969 (for the 365GTC/GTS) bore, stroke and capacity of 81×71mm., 4390cc. Maximum power 320bhp (DIN) at 6600rpm.; maximum torque 268lb.ft. at 5000rpm. Five speed manual gearbox in unit with hypoid bevel final drive.

Chassis: Front engine, rear drive. Separate tubular chassis frame; engine and rear mounted transmission joined by rigid steel tube enclosing propellor shaft. Independent front suspension by coil springs and wishbones. Worm and sector steering. Independent rear suspension by coil springs and wishbones. Four wheel disc brakes.

Bodywork: Coachbuilt steel and light-alloy two-door two-seater fastback coupe body (GTC) or cabriolet (GTS) styles by Pinifarina. Length 14ft. 5.2in.; width 5ft. 6in.; height 4ft. 2.4in. Unladen weight (GTC) 2860lb., (GTS) 2650lb. (365GTC) 3195lb.

Performance (330 GTC): Maximum speed 143mph. 0-60mph 6.8sec. Standing ¼-mile 15.1sec. Typical fuel consumption 18mpg. **(365GTC):** Maximum speed 151mph. 0-60mph 6.3sec. Standing ¼-mile 14.5sec. Typical fuel consumption 12mpg.

Ferrari 330GTC, 1966

Ferrari 365GT 2 + 2

Built: Maranello, Italy, 1967-1971

Physically, at least, the 365GT 2 + 2 was the Ferrari 'with the mostest' when it was revealed at the Paris Motor Show in 1967. As the spiritual descendant of the massive Type 500 Superfast, and the actual successor to the 330GT, this new car was quite literally the biggest and the most expensive, if not the fastest, Ferrari on the market.

It was large by any standards – and the overall length of 16ft. 4in. was somewhat at odds with its rather cramped four-seater accommodation. This was mainly due to the majestic sweep of the Pininfarina styling, which included a long and graceful tail, and an impressive yet delicately detailed nose which swooped down to a relatively small oval air intake for the radiator.

It was the first of all Ferraris to offer power steering and air-conditioning, and although it was a truly large car, it was by no means the truck that ill-informed critics

(who never drove the car!) sometimes suggested. The solid and very simple (technically) chassis frame, built up of oval and circular section steel tubes, formed the usual base found in almost all Ferraris, and there was four-wheel independent suspension by coil springs and wishbones for the first time on a Ferrari of this size. The frame, however, incorporated the big 'Lampredi' 4.4-litre vee-12, a five-speed gearbox in unit with it, and the chassis-mounted differential was all on its own at the tail of the car. One must remember that the 275GTB/4, which was Ferrari's current two-seater coupe, had the gearbox in unit with the final drive.

Production of this graceful and very fast (more than 150mph was possible) four-seater Ferrari ran out in 1971, when the 365GTC/4 arrived. Sales of a full four-seater Ferrari had not been as high as hoped.

Specification

Engine and transmission: Twelve-cylinders, in 60-degree vee-formation, with single-overhead-camshaft cylinder heads. Bore, stroke and capacity 81×71mm., 4390cc. Maximum power 320bhp (net) at 6600rpm.; maximum torque 268lb.ft. at 5000rpm. Five-speed manual gearbox in unit with engine. Hypoid bevel final drive.
Chassis: Front engine, rear drive. Separate tubular chassis frame. Independent front suspension by coil springs and wishbones. Power-assisted recirculating ball steering. Independent rear suspension by double coil springs and wishbones, with self-levelling. Four-wheel disc brakes.
Bodywork: Coachbuilt steel and light-alloy two-door close-coupled four-seater fastback coupe by Pininfarina. Length 16ft. 4in.; width 5ft. 10.5in.; height 4ft. 5.5in. Unladen weight 3490lb.
Performance: Maximum speed 152mph. 0-60mph 7.1sec. Standing ¼-mile 15.2sec. Typical fuel consumption 14mpg.

Ferrari Dino 206/246 family

Built: Maranello, Italy, 1967-1973

The first mid-engined Ferraris were racing cars — Formula 2 and Grand prix single seaters — and the evolution of mid-engined sports-racing cars followed. The first of the sports-racing Dinos (the name was in memory of Enzo Ferrari's son, who died tragically when a young man, in the 1950s) appeared in the 1960s, and it was almost inevitable that road cars would follow.

Central to their design was the use of a vee-6 engine of between 1.5-litres and 2.5-litres. The original Dino vee-6 had raced in 1957, and was based on the rather odd angle of 65-degrees between cylinder banks. 60-degrees (or 120-degrees, for that matter) is ideal for dynamic balancing purposes, and Ferrari had merely changed the narrow 'ideal' angle to 65-degrees to gain more space between cylinder banks for carburettors and auxiliaries to be fitted.

However, the first prototype Ferrari Dino road car, shown at the Paris Salon in 1965, looked visually like the car that eventually went into production, but at that time had a normally-located (by mid-engined standards) engine driving to a combined gearbox and transaxle. By the time Ferrari got round to putting such a small car on the market, at the end of 1967, this layout had changed completely. Tucked away behind the seats, but hidden under the same sleek and unmistakeable exterior style, the 2-litre vee-6 engine was now set transversely across the chassis, driving through a train of gears to a five-speed gearbox and transaxle mounted immediately behind it.

That said, this new Dino was almost typical Ferrari in other details. A strong but simple multi-tubular chassis frame was the base of the structure, along with four-wheel independent rear suspension by coil springs and wishbones. Styling was by Pininfarina, who in this case also looked after construction of production shells; Scaglietti, who

Ferrari Dino 206GT, 1967

normally built Ferrari's road bodyshells, could not cope with the quantity expected (and achieved) for this model.

Production, with the original 2.0-litre engine, got under way at the end of 1967, but it was soon obvious that the Dino 206 could not cope with competition from the latest Porsche 911S cars, whose engines were more powerful already, and were rumoured for enlargement in due course. From the Geneva Motor Show of 1969, therefore, the Dino became the 246GT, complete with the 2418cc which had already become a famous engine size in the front-engined Grand Prix cars of 1958 onwards.

Because the Dino was completely out of the mainstream of normal Ferrari thinking and marketing, it was usually called a Dino rather than a Ferrari, though there is no evidence to suggest that any potential buyers were fooled or, indeed, impressed by this.

Because it could be sold at such a bargain price compared with the Daytonas and other vee-12-engined Ferraris, it sold in considerable numbers. From 1971 a Spider derivative (which effectively meant that a removable roof panel was provided in an otherwise unchanged bodyshell) became available, and the two models carried on strongly until 1973. It was at this time that a major change occurred in Ferrari's offerings, for the use of the vee-12 and vee-6 engines was cut only to one front-engined car, the flat-12 Boxer at last came into production, and a new vee-8 Dino 308 range was phased in.

The 246GTs, incidentally, are now so revered that they have become collectors' items. No other car built by Ferrari, after all, has been able to combine small size, high performance, and reasonable operating economy all in the same package, and collectors appreciate this. The Dino's place in motoring history is assured.

Specification

Engine and transmission: Six-cylinders, in 65-degree vee-formation, with twin-overhead-camshaft cylinder heads. Bore, stroke and capacity (206GT) 86×57mm., 1987cc. Maximum power 180bhp (DIN) at 8000rpm.; maximum torque 138lb.ft. at 6500rpm. (246GT) 92.5×60mm., 2418cc. Maximum power 195bhp (DIN) at 7600rpm.; maximum torque 166lb.ft. at 5500rpm. Five-speed manual gearbox in unit with engine and transaxle. Hypoid bevel final drive.
Chassis: Mid-engine, transversely-mounted, rear drive. Separate tubular chassis frame. Independent front suspension by coil springs and wishbones. Rack and pinion steering. Independent rear suspension by coil springs and wishbones. Four-wheel disc brakes.
Bodywork: Coachbuilt light-alloy two-door two-seater coupe or open top fastback style, by Pininfarina. Length 13ft. 9in.; width 5ft. 7in.; height 3ft. 8in. Unladen weight 2375lb.
Performance (206GT): Maximum speed 140mph. 0-60mph 7.5sec. Standing ¼-mile 15.5sec. Typical fuel consumption 18mpg. **(246GT):** Maximum speed 148mph. 0-60mph 7.1sec. Standing ¼-mile 15.4sec. Typical fuel consumption 23mpg.

Ferrari Dino 246GT, 1973

Ferrari 365GTB Daytona

Built: Maranello, Italy, 1968-1974

If the 275GTB4 had been received with acclaim, the 365GTB Daytona which replaced it in 1968 caused an enormous sensation. It was bigger, better, faster, nicer looking, more exclusive... it was quite simply the most remarkable Ferrari road car anyone could have wished for. What we did not know at the time was that it was also extraordinarily fast, and with a maximum speed of about 175mph it was (and is, still) probably the fastest road car in the world.

Like the car it replaced, the 365GTB4 used a multi-tube chassis frame, very closely based on that of its predecessor, which is to say that it also had a rear-mounted transmission and final drive unit, the engine joined to that transmission by a rigid torque tube, and with all-round coil spring and wishbone independent suspension. The bodystyle, of course, was completely new, but as before the style was by Pininfarina, and actual construction by Scaglietti in Modena.

Apart from the dramatically new shape, in which the four headlamps were recessed behind clear panels in the smooth but sharply-profiled nose, the big news was that a much larger engine than before was fitted. In place of the four-camshaft 3.3-litre engine of the 275GTB4, itself a formidably powerful unit, was a four-camshaft engine of no less than 4390cc, which was a further-developed version of the Lampredi engine which had begun life as a Grand Prix design in 1950. (This engine, of course, was physically much larger than the original Colombo engine). The power output was a

Ferrari 365GTB Daytona

monstrous 352bhp (net) at 7500rpm, and nobody doubted the performance claims made for the car itself.

Its name, incidentally – Daytona – was adopted as a tribute to the way Ferrari's P4s had dominated the 1967 event, a World Championship sports car qualifier, at the American circuit, and it wasn't long before the car was never called anything else. Although it was meant to be the ultimate in road cars – many looked on it as Ferrari's answer to the Lamborghini Miura – a Daytona could also be race-modified and used with distinction in International competition, as its record at Le Mans and in other endurance races show.

Unlike the 275GTB design, there was no convertible derivative of the Daytona, but this never hampered sales of this remarkable design. Not only was a Daytona endowed with colossal performance, but it was docile in heavy traffic, had a good ride, and was possessed of truly race-bred roadholding. Over and above all that was the wonderful sight, sound and torque delivery of the well-developed vee-12 engine. These qualities, and the indefinable and quite unmatchable aura of the 'Ferrari' badge, made the Daytona *the* car to own in the early 1970s.

However, because rich men's toys tend to be thrown away when they become too common and too readily available, the Daytona was bound to be discarded sooner or later. Its successor was the Berlinetta Boxer which, though delayed in passing from prototype to production, and with considerable overlap when both cars were on sale together, eventually took over in 1974.

Specification

Engine and transmission: Twelve-cylinders, in 60-degree vee-formation, with twin-overhead-camshaft cylinder heads. Bore, stroke and capacity 81×71mm., 4390cc. Maximum power 362bhp (DIN) at 7500rpm.; maximum torque 318lb.ft. at 5500rpm. Five-speed manual gearbox in unit with final drive. Hypoid bevel final drive.
Chassis: Front engine, rear drive. Separate tubular chassis frame. Independent front suspension by coil springs and wishbones. Worm and nut steering. Independent rear suspension by coil springs and wishbones. Four wheel disc brakes.
Bodywork: Coachbuilt steel and light-alloy two-door two-seater fastback coupe by Pininfarina/Scaglietti. Length 14ft. 6in.; width 5ft. 9.25in.; height 4ft. 1in. Unladen weight 3530lb.
Performance: Maximum speed 174mph. 0-60mph 5.4sec. Standing ¼-mile 13.7sec. Typical fuel consumption 14mpg.

Ferrari 365GTC/4

Built: Maranello, Italy, 1971-1973

Looked at in relation to Ferrari's model range before its arrival, and that which would soon develop, the 365GTC/4 was a short-lived and unsuccessful aberration. It arrived in the spring of 1971, as a theoretical replacement for both the 365GT 2+2 and for the 365GTC, but within two-years it had been overtaken by the 365GT4 2+2, and was quietly dropped.

Like other Ferrari touring cars of its period, it was developed around the fine tubular chassis first seen in the 275GTB, equipped with four-wheel independent suspension and all, but in this case the five-speed gearbox was in unit with the engine, although it was connected to the chassis-mounted final drive by a rigid torque tube. The engine was yet another version of the ubiquitous 4.4-litre 'Lampredi' vee-12, this time with inlet ports down the 'vee' between the camshafts, and carburettors on the outside of the engine.

Although the body style was something like that of the Daytona (it was, after all, by Pininfarina, who did almost all Ferrari's work), it was a little bit more spacious. This, and the fitment of a front-mounted gearbox allowed 2+2 seats to be added. Though this car was by no means as roomy as the 365GT 2+2, for instance, Ferrari's dealers were not at all sure that they needed a full four-seater in their range. They were wrong, as the 365GT4 2+2 was to prove, and that car followed less than two years after the GTC/4, thus sealing its fate.

Specification

Engine and transmission: Twelve-cylinders, in 60-degree vee-formation, with twin-overhead-camshaft cylinder heads. Bore, stroke and capacity 81×71mm., 4390cc. Maximum power 340bhp (DIN) at 6800rpm.; maximum torque 311lb.ft. at 4600rpm. Five-speed manual gearbox in unit with engine, and rigid torque tube to hypoid bevel final drive.

Chassis: Front engine, rear drive. Separate tubular chassis frame. Independent front suspension by coil springs and wishbones. Power-assisted worm and sector steering. Independent rear suspension by coil springs and wishbones. Four-wheel disc brakes.

Bodywork: Coachbuilt steel and light-alloy two-door 2+2-seater GT coupe by Pininfarina. Length 15ft. 0in.; width 5ft. 10in.; height 4ft. 2in. Unladen weight 3205lb.

Performance: Maximum speed 152mph. 0-60mph 7.3sec. Standing ¼-mile 15.7sec. Typical fuel consumption 16mpg.

Ferrari 365GT4 2 + 2

Ferrari 365GT4 2 + 2/400GT

Built: Maranello, Italy, 1972 to date

The Ferrari four-seater, now fitted with a 4.8-litre engine, but originally equipped with a 4.4-litre engine, is still in production as the 1980s begin, and is one of the longest-lived of all cars to be built at Maranello. It has been a surprisingly successful formula, and still looks as smart and up-to-the-minute as it did when announced in time for showing at the 1972 Paris Show.

The rather smaller, if more stylish, 365GTC/4 coupe, had only been on the market for 18 months when the new car was announced, and it is a fact that the birth of the later car affected the life of the other, which was soon terminated. Ferrari, however, had not made a monumental mistake in this, as the chassis of the later car was no more than a stretched (by 15cm, or six-inches, in the wheelbase) version of the other.

Like all Ferraris of modern times, it had a multi-tubular chassis frame and all-round coil spring and wishbone independent suspension. Like the other four-seater Ferraris of the late 1960s and early 1970s, the big 'Lampredi' vee-12 engine was up   375 front, with a five-speed gearbox mounted directly to it, and there was a solid three-inch torque tube linking the power train to the chassis-mounted final drive.

The body style, by Pininfarina, was rather more angular than that styling house had produced for Ferrari in previous years, but it conferred the twin benefits of more interior space, and larger luggage accommodation. Even though the GT4 2 + 2 had only two doors, it was still a 15ft. 9in. long car, which made it as bulky as a long-wheelbase Jaguar XJ4.2, even though its delicate lines belied this.

The styling was 'different' enough to excite much comment when it was announced in 1972, but developments made public in 1976 were even more controversial. The 4.4-litre engine, whose 81 × 71mm cylinder dimensions were so well known that many Ferrari buffs recited them in their sleep, was discarded in favour of a larger and further civilised version. This, which helped transform the car into the 400GT, had a bore and stroke of 81 × 78mm, and a capacity of 4823cc. Compared with the old engine, therefore, the stroke had been increased (actually to a dimension already seen on the Lampredi engine in previous years), and the torque curve flattened, to make it more flexible and suitable for use with – horror of horrors, to diehard

Ferrari 400 Automatic

Ferraristas — a General Motors automatic transmission.

The transmission in question is the highly-respected GM400 unit, as used in Cadillacs, and — in Britain — in the latest Rolls Royce and Jaguar models. It is interesting to note that the cylinder bore is precisely 1mm different from that of the latest Ferrari Boxer, which in 4.4-litre form had shared pistons and other moving parts with the 4.4-litre vee-12.

This quantum leap in marketing strategy (no previous Ferrari had ever been offered with automatic transmission) was made to tailor the car for the type of clientele it was now attracting. North Americans, of course, who always queued up to buy the latest in Ferraris, but also many businessmen, tycoons, and the merely wealthy in other parts of the world who could not be troubled to change their own gears. In theory the GM automatic transmission was standardised, but Ferrari let it be known, discreetly, that manual versions would continue to be supplied to special order.

It is interesting to see that although the maximum power output of the enlarged engine was no more than before, it developed an appropriate extra amount of torque, and was altogether easier and more flexible to drive. But that, in terms of Ferrari's legendary vee-12s, is merely a relative value.

Specification

Engine and transmission: Twelve-cylinders, in 60-degree vee-formation, with twin-overhead-camshaft cylinder heads. Bore, stroke and capacity 81×71mm., 4390cc. Maximum power 340bhp (DIN) at 6800rpm.; maximum torque 311lb.ft. at 4600rpm. Five-speed manual gearbox in unit with engine. Hypoid bevel final drive.

Chassis: Front engine, rear drive. Separate tubular chassis frame. Independent front suspension by coil springs and wishbones. Power-assisted recirculating ball steering. Independent rear suspension by coil springs and wishbones, with self-levelling. Four-wheel disc brakes.

Bodywork: Coachbuilt steel and light-alloy two-door 2 + 2 GT saloon by Pininfarina. Length 15ft. 9in.; width 5ft. 10.8in.; height 4ft. 3.8in. Unladen weight 3310lb.

Performance: Maximum speed 150mph. 0-60mph 7.1sec. Standing ¼-mile 15.2sec. Typical fuel consumption 12mpg.

Note: The 400GT replaced the 365GT4 from the autumn of 1976. Important differences were: Bore, stroke and capacity 81×78mm., 4823cc. Maximum power 340bhp (DIN) at 6500rpm.; maximum torque 347lb.ft. at 3600rpm. Optional GM Hydramatic automatic transmission (3-speed) in unit with engine. Unladen weight 4180lb.

Performance (400GT Automatic): Maximum speed 156mph. 0-60mph 8.0sec. Standing ¼-mile 16.0sec. Typical fuel consumption 9mpg.

Ferrari Dino 308 series

Built: Maranello, Italy, 1973 to 1980

Although the demise of the Dino 246 series was greeted with real sorrow, Ferrari were unrepentant. For one thing, they thought they had identified the need for a more spacious 'small' Ferrari, and for another they were ready to drop the vee-6 engine altogether. Although the engine would be fitted to the Lancia Stratos, it seems that the required number of units to ensure homologation of this car would be built at once, and used up as production of the Stratos, which began in 1974, proceeded.

The new Dino was really new in many ways. It had a vee-8 engine (something never before specified on a road going Ferrari, though racing cars had used such a layout in the 1960s), and – of more significance – it had a Bertone body style. Almost every road Ferrari built in any numbers up to that time had been equipped with a Pininfarina styled/Scaglietti built bodyshell.

The layout of the new Dino's engine and transmission as like that of the original car – which is to say that the engine was transversely mounted across the car, ahead of the line of the rear wheels, with the transmission and final drive tucked in behind it, and effectively under the rear bank of cylinders. The engine, however, was a new 90-degree vee-8 layout, even though it shared cylinder dimensions, piston, connecting rods, valve gear and breathing arrangements with the vee-12 Daytona engine. In general terms, the new 2926cc unit could be considered as a vee-8 version of the famous vee-12, with the cylinder banks now angled at 90-degrees, although an important difference was that the four-overhead-camshafts were driven by toothed belts (the Daytona's engine used chain drive).

The chassis, a multi-tubular affair in typical Ferrari/Latin manner, was effectively no more than a long-wheelbase version of that already well-proven on the Dino 246, and used that car's coil spring suspensions, and steering gear. It was the body of the 308GTB4, however, which caused some discussion, not only because it was by Bertone, but because it provided rather limited 2 + 2 accommodation.

The public, of course, is perverse, even at this rarified level. No sooner had the 2 + 2 car been launched, than demands flooded in for a two-seater version to be made available. For two-years, however, there was no response, until in the autumn of 1975 the Pininfarina-styled 308GTB two-seater came along. This car reverted to the old Dino 246GT's wheelbase of 92in. (no less than 8.4-inches less than the Bertone 2 + 2), and had an updated version of that much-loved car's lines. It caused something of a stir at the time by having a glass-fibre bodyshell (by Scaglietti to Pininfarina's style), so much so that by 1977, when the 308GTS, an open-topped Spider derivative, arrived the construction reverted to conventional steel and light-alloy.

The engine, in terms of power output per litre, is more efficient than the Daytona from which it was derived, so it is no surprise to know that any of the Dino 308s is capable of more than 150mph.

Ferrari Dino 308GT 2 + 2, by Bertone   379

Ferrari Dino 308GTS, 1977

Specification

Engine and transmission: Eight-cylinders, in 90-degree vee-formation, with twin-overhead-camshaft cylinder heads. Bore, stroke and capacity 81×71mm., 2926cc. Maximum power 255bhp (DIN) at 7700rpm.; maximum torque 209lb.ft. at 5000rpm. Five-speed manual gearbox in unit with engine and transaxle. Hypoid bevel final drive.
Chassis: Mid-engine, transversely mounted, rear drive. Separate tubular chassis frame. Independent front suspension by coil springs and wishbones. Rack and pinion steering. Independent rear suspension by coil springs and wishbones. Four wheel disc brakes.
Bodywork: (308GTB/GTS) Coachbuilt steel/light-alloy coachwork by Pininfarina in fastback coupe (GTB) and spider (GTS) styles. Glass-fibre on pre-1977 cars. Length 13ft. 10.5in.; width 5ft. 7.8in.; height 3ft. 8in. Unladen weight 2790lb. **(Dino 308GT4)** Coachbuilt steel/light-alloy by Scaglietti (styled by Bertone) in fastback 2+2 style. Length 14ft. 1.3in.; width 5ft. 7.3in.; height 3ft. 11.6in. Unladen weight 3010lb.
Performance: (GTB) Maximum speed 154mph. 0-60mph 6.5sec. Standing ¼-mile 14.8sec. Typical fuel consumption 21mpg. **(GT4 2+2)** Maximum speed 154mph. 0-60mph. 6.9sec. Standing ¼-mile 14.9sec. Typical fuel consumption 22mpg.

Note: Dino GT4 2+2 also sold with 2-litre engine, 66.8×71mm., 1991cc. Maximum power 170bhp (DIN) at 7000rpm.; maximum torque 137lb.ft. at 4900rpm.

Ferrari Boxer

Built: Maranello, Italy, 1973 to date

The Boxer, undoubtedly, is the most super of all Ferrari's Supercars, and is arguably the most desirable road car yet offered for sale. First seen in 1971, when the world had not been plunged into an era of fuel shortages, massive inflation, and social upheaval, the Boxer was Ferrari's idea of the ultimate expression of what a road car based on the layout of his world-beating racing sports cars should be.

Only in its engine layout was the Boxer a unique road-going Ferrari. Mid-engined cars had been produced before (the 'little' Dino Ferrari was then in relatively large-scale production), but nothing had yet been seen of the new flat-12 engine. Rated, initially, at 380bhp (DIN) and 4.4-litres, it was like no other engine previously seen from Maranello.

Two previous Ferrari flat-12s had been used in racing cars — the first being that of the 1964-1965 1.5-litre Grand Prix car, and the second that first seen in 1969 in 3-litre form, and since used in sports racing and Grand Prix cars in great profusion and with enormous success. But the Boxer's 4.4-litre engine had nothing but its basic layout in common with either of these. It had the same cylinder dimensions — 81×71mm — and the same swept volume — 4390cc — as that of the Daytona which it would eventually succeed. However, although there were some common components, this was much more than a 'flattened' version of the old 60-degree vee-12, as was proved by the fact that the four-camshafts were driven by toothed belt; pistons, connecting rods and valve gear, however, *were* interchangeable with those of the Daytona.

If the 275GTB of 1964 had been Ferrari's layout for the 1960s, that of the Boxer — or 365GT4/BB as it was fully titled — was the Maranello layout of the 1970s, and deserves more detailed description. Apart from the mechanical layout it accepts, there is nothing remarkable, in Ferrari terms, about the chassis or the bodyshell. The chassis is a multi-tubular frame, this time with square-section tubing, and sheet-metal skins welded above and below the main centre section to add stiffness, with all-independent suspension distinguished by the use of double coil spring and damper units at the tail. The two-seater bodyshell, wedge-styled, as it inevitably had to be due to the mechanical layout, and the performance required, was by Pininfarina, but constructed by Scaglietti in Modena and for the first time on a road-going Ferrari included glass-fibre sections around the lower section.

To get the weight distribution right, and to keep the intrusion of the engine into the passenger space as limited as possible, the engine and transmission unit was compact and uniquely detailed. Although the Boxer qualifies as a mid-engined car, in fact the engine is above and only partly ahead of the line of the rear wheels and final drive, with the five-speed gearbox mounted below it and ahead of that line. Drive from the thunderously powerful flat-twelve, therefore, is transferred down by a chain of gears to the level of the transmission behind the final drive, and drive from the box is then back to the final drive itself. It is a very sophisticated, expensive, but undeniably effective layout, and leaves a space behind the engine where luggage not likely to be affected by heat can be stowed. The normal, but small, luggage space, is up in the nose, where it has to jostle with an undersized 'get you home' spare wheel.

The Boxer was such a complex design that even Ferrari could not begin making production cars immediately, so after the launch at Turin in 1971 there was a delay   381

Ferrari Berlinetta Boxer, 1975   383

until mid 1973 before replicas of that remarkable prototype were delivered.

Almost immediately, there was controversy over the performance, which came nowhere near the 185 or even 200mph mentioned when the car was first seen. 4.4-litre cars could rarely be urged over 170mph, which suggested that there were either considerable transmission losses, or less efficient aerodynamics than those exhibited by the obsolescent front-engined Daytona.

When the original 365BB was replaced by the 512BB in 1976, this controversy was redoubled, for although the latest version had a larger engine, it was less powerful, if more torquey, and completely trustworthy magazine tests showed that 163/165mph was nearer the mark. It was interesting to note that although Ferrari enthusiasts were appalled by this, and accused the magazine concerned of incompetence, there was no protest from the factory or from Ferrari dealers, who knew about this already.

The 512BB's engine had a slightly larger bore, and a considerably longer stroke, which helped to make the engine less free-revving. At the same time the body was given a 'chin' spoiler under the nose, and NASA ducts ahead of the rear wheels to channel cool air to the exhaust manifolds.

Specification

Engine and transmission: Twelve-cylinders, in horizontally-opposed formation, with twin-overhead-camshaft cylinder heads. Bore, stroke and capacity (365GT4 Boxer) 81 × 71mm., 4390cc. Maximum power 380bhp (DIN) at 7200rpm.; maximum torque 318lb.ft. at 3900rpm. Five-speed manual gearbox in unit with engine and transaxle. Hypoid bevel final drive.
Chassis: Mid-engine, rear drive. Multi-tubular chassis frame, with square section tubes, separate from body. Independent front suspension by coil springs and wishbones. Rack and pinion steering. Independent rear suspension by coil springs and wishbones. Four-wheel disc brakes.
Bodywork: Light-alloy coachwork by Pininfarina/Scaglietti, in two-door, two-seater fastback coupe style. Length 14ft. 3.7in.; width 5ft. 10.9in.; height 3ft. 8.1in. Unladen weight 2470lb.
Performance: (Boxer 365GT4) Maximum speed 171mph. 0-60mph 6.5sec. Standing ¼-mile 14.0sec. Typical fuel consumption 14mpg.

Note: 512BB Boxer has the following important differences: Bore, stroke and capacity 82 × 78mm., 4942cc. Maximum power 360bhp (DIN) at 6200rpm.; maximum torque 332lb.ft. at 4600rpm. Unladen weight 3340lb.
Performance: (512BB Boxer) Maximum speed 163mph. 0-60mph 6.2sec. Standing ¼-mile 13.6sec. Typical fuel consumption 17mpg.

Gordon-Keeble GK1 and IT

Built: Eastleigh, then Southampton, England, 1964-1966

Although the Gordon-Keeble was not the first such car actually to be put on sale, it was probably the first *design* of Supercar to combine an Italian body style with a big and powerful North American vee-8 engine. For although the first production car was not ready until 1964, a prototype – then simply called the Gordon GT – had been revealed in 1960.

The germ of the idea came when an American customer asked for a Chevrolet vee-8 engine to be installed in a Peerless chassis. Although this worked well, when John Gordon and Jim Keeble (both of whom were involved in the Peerless project, which eventually became the Warwick GT, described elsewhere in this book) came to design another car, they started again from scratch.

Like the Peerless, however, the new car had a multi-tube chassis frame, not a scientifically laid-out and stressed spaceframe, but complex enough and light for the job it had to do. Front suspension was by coil spring independent layout, while the basic Peerless de Dion system was adapted to use coil springs instead of half-elliptic springs. Central to the design was a big Chevrolet vee-8 engine, and a matching gearbox.

The Gordon's style, which was bulky but still elegant, and which featured four headlamps installed at a slant, in a rather oriental style, was by Bertone of Italy. The ensemble was attractive, docile, and fast, so it was extremely puzzling that nothing more was then heard of the car until 1964. This was, in part, due to the financial problems first of Peerless and then of Warwick – in which designer Jim Keeble was interested.

In 1964, however, industrialist George Wansborough, who had once been chairman of Jowett in the 1940s and 1950s, formed a new company in 1963, specifically to make the new car, which was now renamed Gordon-Keeble after its original sponsors. However, although the little factory was supposedly equipped to make up to three cars a week, and in spite of the price being well under that of cars like the Aston Martin DB5, sales were hard to come by. Jim Keeble left the company early in 1965, and by the summer the original company was in liquidation with just 80 cars built and sold. Towards the end of 1965 Harold Smith, who had been a Gordon-Keeble agent, bought the manufacturing rights, moved to another small factory in Southampton, and started selling revived cars renamed Gordon-Keeble ITs. Even though the cost had been pushed right up – it rose from £2798 in 1964 to £3989 in the winter of 1965/1966 – these cars were still not profitable to make, and after a further nineteen examples had been made – bringing total production to ninety-nine cars in all – the company went into liquidation once again. Although yet another businessman (John de Bruyne of Newmarket) bought up the rights in 1968, nothing more was heard of this interesting project.

It is worth recalling that although the Gordon prototype was built up in steel by Bertone, production cars had glass-fibre bodies, and this may explain why they did not truly appeal to well-heeled customers. Even though the shape of the Gordon-Keeble was very attractive, the type and quality of manufacture was not of the same category, and many must have thought that even at the relatively low initial price they were not getting value for money.

Due to their rarity, and to the fact that the glass-fibre shells do not rot away, most of the cars built have survived, and they are now much sought after as cars of character.

Gordon-Keeble GK1, 1965

Specification

Engine and transmission: Eight-cylinders, in 90-degree vee-formation, with pushrod-operated overhead-valve cylinder heads, built by Chevrolet. Bore, stroke and capacity 101.6 × 82.55mm., 5355cc. Maximum power 300bhp (gross) at 5000rpm.; maximum torque 360lb.ft. at 3000rpm. Four-speed gearbox in unit with engine. Hypoid bevel final drive.

Chassis: Front engine, rear drive. Multi-tubular chassis frame. Independent front suspension by coil springs and wishbones. Worm and wheel steering. De Dion rear suspension, by coil springs, radius arms and Watts linkage. Four-wheel disc brakes.

Bodywork: Glass-fibre bodywork, in four-seater notchback GT coupe style. Length 15ft. 9.5in.; width 5ft. 8in.; height 4ft. 6in. Unladen weight 3165lb.

Performance: Maximum speed 136mph. 0-60mph 7.5sec. Standing ¼-mile 15.6sec. Typical fuel consumption 18mpg.

Iso Rivolta

Built: Milan, Italy, 1962-1970

When the Rivolta was released at the Turin Motor Show of November 1962, it could not possibly have been more of a contrast with Iso's previous efforts. Here was a fast, interestingly-styled, four-seater Supercar – which did not begin to compare with their previous product, which was the Isetta 'bubble' cars of the 1950s!

The Rivolta, which actually went into production in mid-1963, was one of the growing number of Supercars which might be described as 'mongrels' – which is to say that they combined Italian engineering and styling with Detroit horsepower. The basis of the design was a platform-type chassis, of pressed and fabricated steel sections, with coil spring independent front suspension, and de Dion rear suspension. It was certainly not strong enough to be self-supporting, and relied to a great deal on the steel bodyshell, which was styled and constructed by Bertone.

Iso chose General Motors vee-8 engines of 5.4-litres, as used in the Corvette and other less-exciting GM models, and linked this either to an appropriate General Motors automatic transmission, to a four-speed manual gearbox from the same stable, or to a five-speed manual ZF gearbox which was freely available to such customers, including clients like Maserati and Aston Martin.

Isos, due to their construction (American power, proprietary transmission, suspension, and brakes), were never as exclusive, or as desirable as the more glamorous rivals made in or near to Modena, and even though they were usually possessed of colossal performance, their image always suffered somewhat because of this. It is probably no more than a strong coincidence that the early Isos resembled the Gordon/Gordon-Keeble project so closely in everything but chassis construction (Bertone, after all, had styled both cars), but it is possible that Bertone's work on the Gordon prompted Iso to get into the same sort of market themselves.

The Iso Rivolta, however, which sold in two forms – IR300 with 300 gross horsepower and IS340 with 355-horsepower – was a much more refined product in every way, thanks to the solid worth of its chassis (designed, incidentally, by Bizzarrini before he settled down to design the first of the vee-12 Lamborghinis), and to the high quality of the Bertone bodyshells. The basic design, too, of that chassis, gave rise to other models, not least of which was the fierce Grifo coupe, and the smarter and sleeker Lele and Fidia models which followed towards the end of the 1960s. The Fidia, of 1968, incidentally, was a four-door saloon intended to replace the Rivolta, but there was a pleasing overlap, as the Rivolta was still in demand, and was price-listed until 1970.

Specification

Engine and transmission: Eight-cylinders, in 90-degree vee-formation, with pushrod-operated overhead-valve cylinder heads, built by General Motors. Bore, stroke and capacity 101.6×82.55mm., 5359cc. Maximum power **(IR 300)** 300bhp (gross) at 5000rpm.; maximum torque 360lb.ft. at 3200rpm. **(IR340)** 355bhp (gross) at 5800rpm.; maximum torque 360lb.ft. at 3600rpm. Four-speed manual, five-speed ZF manual, or GM automatic transmission, mounted in unit with engine. Hypoid bevel final drive. 387

Iso Rivolta IR340, by Bertone

Chassis: Front engine, rear drive. Separate pressed-steel platform-type chassis frame. Independent front suspension by coil springs and wishbones. Recirculating ball steering. De Dion rear suspension by coil springs, Watts linkage and radius arms. Four-wheel disc brakes.

Bodywork: Light-alloy and steel two-door close-coupled four-seater GT saloon by Bertone. Length 15ft. 8.75in.; width 5ft. 10in.; height 4ft. 6in. Unladen weight 3420lb.

Performance: (IR 340) Maximum speed 142mph. 0-60mph 8.0sec. Standing ¼-mile 15.9 sec. Typical fuel consumption 13mpg.

Iso Grifo series

Built: Milan, Italy, 1965-1974

After the relatively staid styling of the Iso Rivolta coupe, which had first been shown in 1962, the sleek and rakish lines of the Grifo A3L caused a great stir when they were first seen at the Turin Show in 1963. This, however, was something of a premature birth, as the production version did not appear until the autumn of 1965. The Grifo, however, was as attractive — and as fast — as any other Italian Supercar of the period. It is a measure of Iso's financial problems that the Grifo struggled on, virtually unmodified except in the use of other Chevrolet engines, until 1974, when the company folded.

In chassis terms, the Grifo was really a short-wheelbase derivative of the original Rivolta, for it used the same basic platform-type of chassis, the same suspensions, Chevrolet vee-8 engine, and choice of transmissions. Only the attractive two-door two-seater fastback body style by Bertone, was truly new.

Over the years, Grifos were sold with Chevrolet Corvette engines as (relatively) tame as the 300bhp (gross) 5.4-litre vee-8, which was still capable of moving the Grifo coupe at well over 140mph, more normally with the 365bhp (gross) engine, in which case maximum speed was more than 160mph, and sometimes even with 7-litre or 7.4-litre vee-8 engines, where the maximum speed was certainly over 170mph, and the

Iso Grifo 7-litre, 1968

performance was approaching that of the supreme Ferrari Daytona.

Early Grifos had a Bertone bodyshell, welded to the platform chassis to provide a stiff and torsionally rigid structure, with four headlamps and a conventional radiator grille and air inlets, but by the beginning of the 1970s, when production was well down due to Iso's concentration on their more modern styles, the nose had been sharpened up, Ferrari-style, to include flaps over the headlamps and a much more shallow and wind-cheating style.

Grifos, like the Rivoltas from which they evolved, were engineered by Ing. Bizzarrini, whose own A3C model had much in common with the layout, though intended purely for competition work.

Specification

Engine and transmission: Eight-cylinders, in 90-degree vee-formation, with pushrod-operated overhead-valves, built by General Motors. Various engines between 5.3-litres and 7-litres, all GM supplied. Typical engine (Grifo 300 model) bore, stroke and capacity 101.6 × 82.55mm., 5359cc. Maximum power 300bhp (gross) at 5000rpm.; maximum torque 360lb.ft. at 3200rpm. Four-speed manual transmission or optional GM automatic transmission, in unit with engine. Hypoid bevel final drive.

Chassis: Front engine, rear drive. Separate pressed-steel platform-type chassis frame. Independent front suspension by coil springs and wishbones. Recirculating ball steering. De Dion rear suspension by coil springs, Watts linkage and radius arms. Four-wheel disc brakes.

Bodywork: Steel two-door two-seater fastback coupe style by Bertone. Length 14ft. 6.75in.; width 5ft. 9.5in.; height 3ft. 11in. Unladen weight (depending on engine fitted) 3180lb to 3250lb.

Performance: (GL 365 with 365bhp gross) Maximum speed 161mph. 0-60mph 7.4sec. Standing ¼-mile 14.9sec. Typical fuel consumption 16mpg.

Iso Lele and Fidia series

Built: Milan, Italy, 1967-1974

By the mid-1960s, Iso were sufficiently well-established as makers of Supercars to consider expanding, or modifying their range of cars. The Rivolta (four-seater) and Grifo (two-seater) coupes both had a reputation for combining high-performance with simple engineering. Even though Iso could not consider a wholesale redesign of their cars' chassis and suspensions — which had been done for them on a contract basis by Ing. Bizzarrini — they could commission new body styles. The Fidia of 1967 and the Lele of 1969 were the results.

The Fidia came first, and broke new ground as far as Iso were concerned. Not only was the new style a four-door saloon model, but it was by Ghia; all previous bodywork for Iso had been by Bertone. Built on the same chassis (but extended wheelbase) as the Rivolta, it was a distinctive style, distinguished by the use of four rectangular headlamps, was equipped with full air-conditioning, and had a plain but well-appointed and purposeful interior.

Iso Fidia

The Lele, of spring 1969, was a two-door fastback coupe with 2 + 2 seating, which was something of a disappointment as it was also built on the Rivolta's wheelbase. Bertone was responsible for the Lele's style, and built the bodies, and there were touches reminiscent of other current Bertone-styled models.

In character, the Fidia, which was originally named the S4 (for 'four-seater', no doubt), was very much the executive saloon, the businessman's express, the prestige luxury transport. The Lele, on the other hand, which stayed faithful to the same basic mechanical layout, was much more of the ultra-fast *autostrada* cruiser, the sporting coupe, and the flashy status-machine. It was also, arguably, the most up-to-the-minute bodystyle of all four types — Rivolta, Grifo, Fidia and Lele.

By the beginning of the 1970s, however, Iso were in financial trouble, and although they struggled on for a time, the after effects of the Suez war and subsequent energy crisis of 1973/1974 put the finishing touches to their problem. The last Isos of all were built in 1974.

Specification (Lele and Fidia)

Engine and transmission: Eight-cylinders, in 90-degree vee-formation, with pushrod-operated overhead-valve cylinder heads, built by General Motors. Bore, stroke and capacity 101.6×82.55mm., 5359cc. Maximum power 300bhp (gross) at 5000rpm.; maximum torque 360lb.ft. at 3200rpm. Four-speed manual transmission in unit with engine. Hypoid bevel final drive.

Chassis: Front engine, rear drive. Separate pressed-steel platform-type chassis frame. Independent front suspension by coil springs and wishbones. Recirculating ball steering. De Dion rear suspension by coil springs, Watts linkage and radius arms. Four wheel disc brakes.

Bodywork: Steel shells welded to platform chassis on assembly (Fidia) Four-door, four-seater GT saloon style by Ghia. Length 16ft. 4in.; width 5ft. 10in.; height 4ft. 4in. Unladen weight 3580lb. (Lele) Two-door, 2+2 seater fastback coupe style by Bertone. Length 15ft. 4.6in.; width 5ft. 9.1in.; height 4ft. 5in. Unladen weight 3045lb.

Performance (Fidia): Maximum speed 133mph. 0-60mph 8.1sec. Standing ¼-mile 16.2sec. Typical fuel consumption 12mpg. **(Lele):** Maximum speed 132mph. 0-60mph 7.3sec. Standing ¼-mile 15.5sec. Typical fuel consumption 13mpg.

Jaguar E-Type FHC 'Series 1½'

Jaguar E-Type (6-cylinder)

Built: Coventry, England, 1961-1971

It is doubtful if any new car equalled the impact achieved by the brand-new E-Type, when it was revealed at the Geneva motor show in March 1961. It was the nearest thing to a racing sports car, for road use, that had ever been seen. Compared with the well-respected old XK150, which it replaced, the E-Type was a generation ahead in design thinking, in styling, and even in performance.

And yet, the marketing of the E-Type as a road car was not completely premeditated. It had been conceived in 1956/1957 as a racing successor to the famous D-Type, and the very first prototype was little more than a racing sports car hastily converted to road use. From 1958, however, with Jaguar's proposed return to racing (they retired at the end of 1956) deferred once again, the E-Type was completely productionised, and a truly remarkable road car was born.

For one thing, its shape made no concessions to fashion, or to practicality; aerodynamic efficiency, as evolved by Malcolm Sayer (Jaguar's renowned aerodynamicist) and by a great deal of wind tunnel work, was all that mattered. For another, a development of the D-Type's combined space frame and monocoque body/chassis construction was used, even though it was known to be expensive and tricky to manufacture.

Even though the famous six-cylinder XK engine was used in the same tune as that chosen for the obsolete XK150S – which is to say that a somewhat boastful 265bhp (gross) at 5500rpm was claimed – along with the slow-changing four-speed gearbox used on all Jaguars since the 1940s, it was still enough to endow the car with a top speed

of up to 150mph, and with acceleration to match. There was four-wheel independent suspension for the first time on a Jaguar, and the twin combined coil spring/damper layout at the rear, along with a massive pressed-steel subframe mounting, which was to be the first of many similar installations on future Jaguar touring cars.

The result was a sleek, startlingly-styled road car, with flashing performance, but with surprisingly cramped interior accommodation, poor ventilation, and some vulnerability in heavy traffic and close-driving conditions. Every new E-Type owner, it seems, had to learn the hard way that there was more nose ahead of him than could be seen from the driving seat!

At first there was a choice of body styles, both based on the same sleek shape — an open two-seater roadster, and a fastback two-seater coupe with a side-opening window/hatch at the rear. These two styles, supplemented by a detachable hardtop version of the tourer, which few customers actually specified, carried on throughout the life of the model. In the spring of 1966, too, they were joined by a longer wheelbase (by nine-inches) fixed-head coupe car with 2 + 2 seating accommodation. This derivative, due to its substantially retooled centre floor section, was also made available with optional Borg Warner automatic transmission, which was never offered on the two-seaters.

Major development changes occurred in 1964, when the 3.8-litre engine and the gearbox with unsynchronised bottom gear were replaced by the enlarged 4.2-litre engine, and a new all-synchromesh gearbox. Series I cars, too, evolved (unofficially) into 'SI½' models in 1968, and to official Series II E-Types from the autumn of 1968.

Slowly, and inexorably, the razor-sharp edge of performance was lost as the years passed. Most E-Types were sold in North America, and as that country applied more legislation, and clamped down hard on engine exhaust emissions, so the XK's power output had to be reduced. Late-model six-cylinder cars were capable of little more than 130mph, a drop as much due to the less-efficient aerodynamics caused by exposed headlamps, larger air intakes and bigger bumpers, as by the loss of engine power.

Nothing, however, could detract from those looks, from the docility of the engine, and from the ride which was out of all expectations for such a fast car. When the six-cylinder cars were dropped at the beginning of 1971, no fewer than 57 220 cars — 10 924 of them being 2 + 2 models — had been built.

Specification

Engine and transmission: Six-cylinders, in-line, with twin-overhead-camshaft cylinder head. Bore, stroke and capacity **(1961 to 1964)** 87 × 106mm., 3781cc. Maximum power 265bhp (gross) at 5500rpm.; maximum torque 260lb.ft. at 4000rpm. **(1964 to 1971)** 92.05 × 106mm., 4235cc. Maximum power 265bhp (gross) at 5400rpm.; maximum torque 283lb.ft. at 4000rpm. Four-speed manual gearbox in unit with engine. Hypoid bevel final drive.

Chassis: Front engine, rear drive. Multi-tubular front section, bolted to pressed-steel monocoque centre/tail section. Independent front suspension by torsion bars and wishbones. Rack and pinion steering. Independent rear suspension by double coil springs, fixed length driveshafts and lower wishbones. Four-wheel disc brakes.

Bodywork: Pressed-steel, two-door two-seater in open sports, detachable hardtop, or fastback coupe style. Length 14ft. 7.3in.; width 5ft. 5.25in.; height 4ft. 0in. Unladen weight (from) 2625lb.

Performance: (3.8-litre version) Maximum speed 153mph. 0-60mph 7.2sec. Standing ¼-mile 15.1sec. Typical fuel consumption 20mpg. **(4.2-litre version):** Maximum speed 153mph. 0-60mph 7.6sec. Standing ¼-mile 15.1sec. Typical fuel consumption 20mpg.

Note: Also available was the 2 + 2 E-Type, in 4.2-litre engined form. This had optional automatic transmission (Borg Warner), had only a closed fastback body style, was 15ft. 4.3in. long, and weight 2745lb.

Performance: (4.2-litre version) Maximum speed 139mph. 0-60mph 7.4sec. Standing ¼-mile 15.4sec. Typical fuel consumption 21mpg.

Jaguar E-Type Series III (vee-12)

Built: Coventry, England, 1971-1975

Like the original E-Type, the vee-12 E-Type came into existence in rather less of a planned manner than might be thought. When Jaguar launched the big and luxurious XJ6 saloons in the autumn of 1968, they let it be known that a brand new vee-12 engine was under preparation, and that it would be fitted to these cars 'within two-years'. In the event, the vee-12 engine took rather longer than that to prepare, and it was not offered in a Jaguar saloon until 1972. It was first revealed, however, in the much-changed Series III E-Type of 1971.

At a casual glance, the Series III model looks much like earlier E-Types, but a side-by-side comparison shows just how much basic change took place. The construction – a complex square-section tubular front 'chassis' bolted to a centre and tail section monocoque, with a choice of open or coupe body styles – was the

Jaguar E-Type Coupe & Roadster, Series III V12

same as before, but all cars were now built on the same longer wheelbase monocoque, disc wheels were standard wear (they had been optional since the end of 1968, on SII 6-cylinder cars), the air intake in the bonnet was even larger than before, the wheelarches were flared to clear the fatter tyres, and there was an impressive display of four exhaust pipes under that swept up tail.

Shoehorning the 60-degree 5.3-litre vee-12 engine into the chassis of the E-Type had been difficult, but had been accomplished, and since it was not a dramatically heavy engine the balance of the car had not been ruined. The power output – 272bhp (DIN), rather less on North American models – was substantially more than any previous six-cylinder car had been able to call up, and the flexibility of delivery was even more marked than before. Behind the engine, the choice of four-speed manual or three-speed automatics was as before, and the suspension layout was merely trimmed to take account of the XJ6-style wheels and tyres. Power-assisted rack and pinion steering was standard.

Since the open two-seater was now built on the longer-wheelbase floorpan, there was much more interior space than before, but only one type of fastback coupe – the 2 + 2 – was on offer.

At a stroke, this engine transplant restored the 140mph-plus performance, and acceleration was even more striking than before. However, although it rejuvenated the car for a while, this magnificent engine brought other shortcomings of the E-Type's layout – not least the ventilation and the lack of space – into sharp relief, and it became clear that this could not be a long-lasting model. Due to those infuriating North American regulations, the fixed-head coupe was withdrawn at the end of 1973, and the last vee-12 of all was built in the winter of 1974/1975. The XJ-S which arrived at the end of 1975 was an entirely different type of car. 7990 open vee-12 cars and 7297 coupes had been built, making a total E-Type production of 72 507 in all. No other Supercar has ever been built in such numbers....

Specification

Engine and transmission: 12-cylinders, in 60-degree vee-formation, with single-overhead-camshaft cylinder heads. Bore, stroke and capacity 90 × 70mm., 5343cc. Maximum power 272bhp (DIN) at 5750rpm.; maximum torque 304lb.ft. at 3600rpm. Four-speed manual or Borg Warner automatic transmission in unit with engine. Hypoid bevel final drive.

Chassis: Front engine, rear drive. Multi-tubular front section, bolted to pressed-steel monocoque centre/tail section. Independent front suspension by torsion bars and wishbones. Power assisted rack and pinion steering. Independent rear suspension by double coil springs, fixed length driveshafts, and lower wishbones. Four-wheel disc brakes.

Bodywork: Pressed-steel, two-door car in two-seat open sports or 2 + 2 closed fastback coupe styles. Length 15ft. 4.3in.; width 5ft. 6.1in.; height 4ft. 3.4in. Unladen weight 3230lb.

Performance: Maximum speed 142mph. 0-60mph 6.8sec. Standing ¼-mile 14.6sec. Typical fuel consumption 16mpg.

Jaguar XJ-S front end styling

Jaguar XJ-S

Built: Coventry, England, 1975 to date

After the last Jaguar E-Type was built, early in 1975, nearly a year was to elapse before a new sporting Jaguar went into production. That new car, the XJ-S, had an entirely different character and pedigree. It was certainly not a replacement for the E-Type, which even Jaguar themselves seemed to understand was irreplaceable. When the public saw the nature of the XJ-S, they instantly realised this, and the obsolete E-Type became an obvious 'classic'.

Ever since the E-Type had been given its vee-12 engine, which was so much in advance of the rest of the car, a successor had looked inevitable. However, whereas the E-Type had its own chassis, and its own layout, the new XJ-S was little more than a specially developed and rebodied version of the XJ saloon range. If the E-Type had been an excellent example of the Supersports car, the XJ-S was a GT Supercar.

The XJ-S style was an amalgam of Sir William Lyon's ideas, Malcolm Sayer's aerodynamic studies, and various retouching after Sir William had retired from his own concern. For that reason it looked, and was, a mixture of themes, and was by no means as attractive or as 'clean' as the original E-Type had been. For all that, with the single exception of the three-quarter-rear view, which was spoiled by those tail lights and vestigial roof spines, the XJ-S was an impressive car, bigger, heavier and much more completely equipped than the E-Type had ever been.

Its 'chassis' – actually the underpan of its unit-construction steel monocoque – was a short-wheelbase version of that already in use on Jaguar XJ

4.2-litre and XJ 5.3-litre saloons and coupes, with the same well-developed front and rear suspensions, power-assisted rack-and-pinion steering, and that wonderful freedom from road noise transmission. Its wheelbase, 8ft. 6in., was 6.8-inches less than that of the XJ Coupes, and 10.8-inches less than that of the longer-wheelbase four-door saloons.

The engine and transmission, too, was familiar, to E-Type and XJ saloon owners alike. The massive and incredibly silky vee-12 engine was provided, in 285bhp fuel-injected form, and – in theory at least – there was a choice between Jaguar's ageing four-speed all-synchromesh gearbox or the Borg Warner Type 12 three-speed automatic transmission. In fact, almost all XJ-S cars were initially built with automatic transmissions, and by the end of 1978 the manual gearbox option had been withdrawn completely.

Compared with the E-Type, the XJ-S was a little longer, considerably wider, much more squared-up in its styling and – this was a great surprise – even more aerodynamically smooth than that famous car. This was a great bonus which Jaguar had not initially taken for granted. The new car was also considerably more roomy inside, with a close-coupled but still practical four-seater layout, it had a much more comprehensive and logically laid-out fascia and instruments, and a ventilation system which was at last worthy of the rest of the car. Nobody seemed to mind that it was also very much more expensive than the E-Type, which had been deliberately underpriced in its final years to keep demand going.

More XJ-Ss are now sold than E-Types in a given period, which proves perhaps that the XJ-S has a more universal appeal. It may not be as 'pure' a sports car, not as 'sexy', and not as visually startling, but it is certainly a remarkably efficient and integrated design, still with that colossal surge of performance, that flexible engine, and that daunting under-bonnet complexity.

In the five years since the car was launched, Jaguar have changed the car very little. The most significant improvement was that, from the spring of 1977, the Borg Warner automatic gave way to the latest General Motors automatic transmission, which is now finding a home in some of the world's other really fine cars.

Controversy over the looks of the XJ-S will no doubt continue for years, but its remarkable value for money is never disputed. When matched against Ferrari, Maserati and other Supercars, the XJ-S is often as fast, but invariably several thousand pounds, or dollars less expensive. And that, in these inflationary days, is a great selling point.

Specification

Engine and transmission: 12-cylinders, in 60-degree vee-formation, with single-overhead-camshaft cylinder heads. Bore, stroke and capacity 90×70mm., 5343cc. Maximum power 285bhp (DIN) at 5500rpm.; maximum torque 294lb.ft. at 3500rpm. Four-speed manual or three-speed Borg Warner automatic transmission in unit with engine. Hypoid bevel final drive.

Jaguar XJ-S side view

Chassis: Front engine, rear drive. Pressed-steel unit-construction body/chassis unit. Independent front suspension by coil springs and wishbones. Power assisted rack and pinion steering. Independent rear suspension by double coil springs, fixed length driveshafts and lower wishbones. Four-wheel disc brakes.
Bodywork: Pressed-steel two-door close-coupled four-seater coupe style. Length 15ft. 1.7in.; width 5ft. 10.6in.; height 4ft. 2in. Unladen weight 3900lb.
Performance: Maximum speed 153mph 0-60mph 6.9sec. Standing ¼-mile 15.2sec. Typical fuel consumption 17mpg.

Jensen CV8 series

Built: West Bromwich, England, 1962-1966

After building cars with big and lazy Austin engines since the start of the 1950s, Jensen finally succumbed to the attractions of North American horsepower in 1962, when they launched the CV8 to replace the 541S. Although there was much of the 541S still to be found in the design, the 5.9-litre Chrysler engine propelled the new car firmly into the Supercar league, with a top speed of more than 130mph.

The tough chassis frame of the car, developed from that of the 541S, combined four-inch diameter main chassis longerons with a steel platform centre section, a very rigid steel scuttle and tail sections. One interesting feature was that the big chassis tubes were sealed to provide convenient vacuum reservoirs for the brake servo circuitry. Coil spring independent front suspension and a live rear axle sprung on half-elliptic leaf springs were 'carry-over' items from the 541S.

So, too, was the glass-fibre bodyshell, which was, however, considerably restyled around the nose and incorporated four headlamps, each individually mounted. The swivelling radiator flap of the 541 and 541R cars had long since disappeared, of course. The most exciting part of the whole design, however, was that a big Chrysler vee-8 engine of 5.9-litres, with an advertised gross output of 305bhp at 4800rpm, was chosen. By comparison with the 4-litre 'six' previously supplied by Austin, this was an enormous gain in power and torque, and performance benefitted accordingly.

Jensen, preoccupied with quantity production of bodyshells or complete cars for people like BMC (Austin-Healey 3000), Rootes (Sunbeam Tiger) or Volvo (the P1800 Coupe), were never able to make too much of their own products, and it is doubtful if CV8 production ever exceeded four or five cars a week. It was revised twice – the Mk II followed in the autumn of 1963, and that car was given the enlarged 6276cc engine at the beginning of 1974, and it was again retouched as the CV8 Mk III in 1965. Production eventually ran out at the end of 1966, in favour of the stylish and impressive Interceptor/FF cars. Like the earlier Jensens, the CV8's appeal was due to its long-legged nature, and its rather exclusive character.

Specification

Engine and transmission: Eight-cylinders, in 90-degree vee-formation, with pushrod-operated overhead-valve cylinder heads, built by Chrysler USA. **(Mk I model)** Bore, stroke and capacity 105×86mm., 5916cc. Maximum power 305bhp (gross) at 4800rpm.; maximum torque 395lb.ft. at 3000rpm. **(Mk II and Mk III models)** Bore, stroke and capacity 108×86mm., 6276cc. Maximum power 330bhp (gross) at 4600rpm.; maximum torque 425lb.ft. at 2800rpm. Four-speed manual or optional three-speed Chrysler automatic transmission in unit with engine. Hypoid bevel final drive.

Chassis: Front engine, rear drive. Separate tubular and fabricated steel platform chassis frame. Independent front suspension by coil springs and wishbones. Rack and pinion steering. Rear suspension of live axle by half-elliptic leaf springs and Panhard rod. Four wheel disc brakes.

Jensen CV8, 1965

Bodywork: Glass-fibre two-door close-coupled four-seater notchback coupe style. Length 15ft. 4.5in.; width 5ft. 7.5in.; height 4ft. 7in. Unladen weight (Mk I) 3360lb., (Mk III) 3515lb.
Performance: (Mk I, 5916cc) Maximum speed 131mph. 0-60mph 8.4sec. Standing ¼-mile 16.0sec. Typical fuel consumption 15mpg. **(Mk III 6276cc)** Maximum speed 129mph. 0-60mph 6.7sec. Standing ¼-mile 14.6sec. Typical fuel consumption 14mpg.

Jensen Interceptor and FF series

Built: West Bromwich, England, 1966-1976

It is not going too far to suggest that the dramatically-styled (by Vignale) Interceptors and FFs were responsible for Jensen becoming fully-fledged manufacturers of Supercars – and for the fact that the company was forced into liquidation during 1976. For although it was the appeal of the Interceptors which allowed so many to be built and sold, it was the fact that they were expensive-to-build, huge-engined gas-guzzlers which helped to make survival perilous after the Suez war and the energy crisis, and impossible by 1976.

With the CV8 getting very long in the tooth (the original bodystyle, now much modified, had been evolved for the 541 of the mid-1950s), a new bodystyle, using the same basic CV8 chassis, was needed. The decision to go ahead came at the end of 1965, and after it became clear that outside styling advice should be chosen, the company's staff went on a whirlwind tour of Italian designers, asking for submissions. Due to all manner of complications, Touring's style was accepted, but Vignale were contracted to produce press tools, and the whole job had to be completed by the British Earls Court motor show of October 1966! This breakneck pace was actually met by Vignale, who supplied the first panel sets themselves before delivering the tools to Jensen at West Bromwich, near Birmingham.

Although the basic chassis design of the new car was to be unchanged, to be that already well-proven on the CV8, there was one enormously significant difference.

Jensen Interceptor III

Apart from the conventional front-engine/rear-drive layout, Jensen also proposed to make a *four*-wheel-drive version. A prototype of the FF (which stood for Ferguson Formula – the system of four-wheel-drive chosen) had already been built and exhibited in 1965, under the old CV8 body. Apart from the problem of locating, driving, and controlling the four-wheel-drive, the front wheels had to be moved forward four inches relative to the engine to allow insertion of a front differential, which meant that on the new car the entire front ends – wings, bonnet, and inner panels – would have to be different between the two models.

Even so, Jensen were ready to begin production in the winter of 1966/1967, calling the conventional drive car an Interceptor (a throwback to an earlier Jensen model) and the four-wheel-drive car an FF. The striking Touring/Vignale bodystyle, in pressed and fabricated steel, was a reasonably comfortable four-seater coupe, distinguished by that huge rear window. Cogniscenti also know that two wheel drive cars had single air-outlet vents behind the front wheels, while FFs had twin vents.

From 1966 to 1976, when the company was finally forced out of business, there were no sheet metal changes to the design of the car, and only right at the end of the run – in 1974 – was a convertible version of the Interceptor made available.

The FF, although a functional success, was extremely difficult to manufacture, and each production unit needed individual setting up before it could be delivered. As there was a considerable price premium, and as there were recurring problems in service (and, also, no doubt, because some customers were frightened off by the complexity of it all), FFs always sold slowly, and the last of all was built in December 1971, after only 318 cars had been built.

The conventional car, however, sold well by the standards of the day, and in its class. Mk Is became Mk IIs in October 1969, and Mk IIIs in October 1971. At the same time as the Mk III made its appearance, the SP version was announced, which had a more powerful 7.2-litre type of Chrysler engine. Then, late in 1973, Jensen rationalised by making the 7.2-litre engine standard on all models.

Like many other modern Supercars, the Interceptor was only available with (Chrysler) automatic transmission, though a very few manual transmission cars were built at first. All FFs, as part of their four-wheel-drive package, had automatic transmission too.

When Jensen foundered, financially, work was going ahead on a reshaped successor to the Interceptor, which would surely have been even more attractive than that car. About 1500 Interceptors of all types were built.

Specification

Engine and transmission: Eight-cylinders, in 90-degree vee-formation, with pushrod-operated overhead-valve cylinder heads, built by Chrysler USA. Bore, stroke and capacity **(Mk I and Mk II models)** 108 × 86mm., 6276cc. Maximum power 325bhp (gross) at 4600rpm.; maximum torque 425lb.ft. at 2800rpm. **(Mk III and SP models)** 109.7 × 95.25mm., 7210cc. **(Mk III)** Maximum power 330bhp (gross) at 5000rpm.; maximum torque 425lb.ft. at 2800rpm. **(SP)** 385bhp (gross) at 4700rpm.; maximum torque 490lb.ft. at 3200rpm. Four-speed manual gearbox or three-speed Chrysler automatic gearbox (depending on model) in unit with engine. Hypoid bevel final drive (final drives in case of FF).

Chassis: Interceptors had front engine, rear drive. FFs had front engine, four wheel drive. Separate tubular and fabricated platform type pressed-steel chassis frame. Independent front suspension by coil springs and wishbones. Rack and pinion steering (power-assisted steering on later models). Rear suspension of live axle by half-elliptic leaf springs and Panhard rod. Four-wheel disc brakes.

Bodywork: Pressed-steel two-door close-coupled four-seater fastback GT style, with hatchback, by Superleggera Touring/Vignale; a convertible style was also available. Length (Interceptor and SP) 15ft. 6in (FF) 15ft 11in.; width 5ft. 9in.; height 4ft. 5in. Unladen weight (Interceptor, depending on engine) from 3500lb. (FF) 4030lb.

Performance: (1967 Interceptor) Maximum speed 133mph. 0-60mph 7.3sec. Standing ¼-mile 15.7sec. Typical fuel consumption 14mpg. **(1967 FF)** Maximum speed 130mph. 0-60mph 8.4sec. Standing ¼-mile 15.9sec. Typical fuel consumption 14mpg. **(SP)** Maximum speed 143mph. 0-60mph 6.9sec. Standing ¼-mile 14.8sec. Typical fuel consumption 14mpg **(Mk III Convertible)** Maximum speed 126mph. 0-60mph 7.6sec. Standing ¼-mile 15.8sec. Typical fuel consumption 14mpg.

Jensen Interceptor III Convertible, 1974

Lamborghini 350GT, 400GT and Islero

Built: S'Agata, Italy, 1964-1970

Ferruccio Lamborghini, having made his personal fortune as a manufacturer of specialised tractors, and of domestic and industrial heating appliances, turned his attention to cars at the beginning of the 1960s. Having owned various Italian Supercars in recent years, he was sure that he could encourage a team of engineers to do a better job, in terms of both engineering and reliable quality.

To design the engine he hired Giotti Bizzarrini, who already had an impressive record with Alfa-Romeo and Ferrari, and the same engineer was also responsible for the general layout of the chassis and suspensions of the new car. All this, incidentally, took place while Bizzarrini was working on the Iso Rivolta and Grifo models, and on his own sports-racing project!

The very first Lamborghini engine ran in the summer of 1963, and the prototype car was displayed (with Sargiotto bodywork and a chassis by Neri and Bonacini) at the Turin Show in November of that year. Although the looks were strange, and the car was not ready for production, the engine caused a great stir, as it was a dramatically

Lamborghini 350GT

carved 3.5-litre vee-12 unit which looked as if it could be used in racing cars − and it was undoubtedly very powerful.

Cynics who suggested that this would be no more than a 'one-off' dream car for the rich Lamborghini to use himself were proved wrong in the spring of 1964 when the first production cars began to be made at the new S'Agata factory. However, Lamborghini had heeded criticism of the original body, and gave the production car contract to Touring of Milan, who produced a similar but altogether more elegant and practical two-seater style. In the ensuing years, all but a very few would be closed coupes − the balance being essentially hand-built convertibles, which were really not very practical due to the very high performance of which this chassis was capable.

Lamborghini had to have the chassis and body assemblies built for him by specialists, at the prototype stage, but built his own chassis frames at S'Agata. Engines were machined and assembled by Lamborghini − a process he would never trust to any outside supplier.

Until 1966 the 350GT was the only production Lamborghini, and this was joined in that year by the 400GT 2 + 2, which was essentially the same except for an enlarged (4-litre) vee-12 engine, a Lamborghini gearbox in place of the original ZF, and a steel-panelled Touring shell. Touring had also managed to squeeze ' + 2' seating − two extra seats − behind the front seats of the original car, without materially altering the body style. At first only the 2 + 2 cars had the 4-litre engines, but these were later made available on the two-seater car as well. Thus, there is a 400GT and a 400GT 2 + 2, which are rather different in practical terms.

Lamborghini's new products − the Miura in particular − now began to make the original style look out of date, so it was no surprise that the original 350GT was dropped in 1967. The 400GT, too, needed attention, and for 1968 was completely restyled, equipped with a new 2 + 2 coupe shell by Marazzi of Milan. It was − by Supercar standards − a rather ordinary looking car, but still surprisingly fast (an Islero could achieve more than 140mph, after all), and sold steadily until 1970, when it was finally dropped in favour of the differently-engineered Jarama.

All in all, about 380 350/400 models with Touring bodywork were built, along with 225 Isleros.

Specification

Engine and transmission: Twelve-cylinders, in 60-degree vee-formation, with twin-overhead-camshaft cylinder heads. (350GT) bore, stroke and capacity 77×62mm., 3464cc. Maximum power 280bhp (DIN) at 6500rpm.; maximum torque 227lb.ft. at 4800rpm. (400GT) bore, stroke and capacity 82×62mm., 3929cc. Maximum power 330bhp (DIN) at 6500rpm.; maximum torque 262lb.ft. at 4700rpm. Five-speed manual gearbox in unit with engine, ZF on 350GT, Lamborghini on subsequent models. Hypoid bevel final drive.

Chassis: Front engine, rear drive. Separate tubular chassis frame, with square and round section tubes. Independent front suspension by coil springs and wishbones. Worm and sector steering. Independent rear suspension by coil springs and wishbones. Four-wheel disc brakes.

Bodywork: Light-alloy two-door two-seater or 2 + 2 seater fastback coupe by Carrozeria Touring; two-seater Touring Spider also offered. Length 15ft. 2.7in.; width 5ft. 7.9in.; height 4ft. 2.0in. Unladen weight (2-seater) 2650lb. (2 + 2 seater) 2735lb.

Performance (350GT): Maximum speed 152mph. 0-60mph 6.8sec. Standing ¼-mile 14.9sec. Typical fuel consumption 19mpg. **(400GT):** Maximum speed 156mph. 0-60mph 7.5sec. Standing ¼-mile 15.5sec. Typical fuel consumption 17mpg.

Note: Islero model was mechanically the same, with the following different dimensions: Length 14ft. 10.1in.; width 5ft. 8.1in.; height 4ft. 2in. Unladen weight 2795lb.

Lamborghini Islero

Lamborghini P400 Miura by Bertone

Lamborghini Miura

Built: S'Agata, Italy, 1966-1972

It is surely not exaggerating to suggest that the very first appearance of the Lamborghini Miura caused a sensation. When the partly-completed rolling chassis was displayed at the Turin Show in 1965, it was so excitingly engineered as to look completely impractical. Not only was it the first time a 3.5-litre vee-12 engine had ever been mounted behind the driver in the transverse position, but it was the first time such a mid-engined product had been intended for road-car use; the 'homologation special' Ferrari 275LM does not count. Ferruccio Lamborghini blandly told all enquirers that he was going to put the car into small-scale production.

And so he was, but no-one believed him until the completed prototype, with its sleek Bertone coupe bodyshell, was shown at Geneva the following spring. Incidentally, although Lamborghini thought he could sell perhaps 20 cars in all, more than this was ordered before production commenced at the end of 1966, and about 900 were built before the last Miura of all rolled out of the factory in 1972.

The mid-engined concept and engineering is credited to Gianpaulo Dallara. The 4-litre vee-12 engine was a derivative of that used on all other Lamborghini production

409

cars except the Urraco, and was mated to Lamborghini's own five-speed gearbox. The basis of the design was an extensively lightened steel punt-type platform chassis frame, built on Lamborghini's behalf by Marchesi in Modena, and of course Bertone were awarded the contract to supply all the production bodyshells.

The Miura was different from other 'rich men's toys', not only because it was mid-engined, but because it combined enormous performance with great stability, racing-car roadholding, unique styling, and Lamborghini's already notable reputation for quality and reliability. It was built so low that pop-up headlamps were necessary to ensure adequate night-time visibility and compliance with legal requirements in certain countries. For at least the first three years of its six-year existence, the Miura was *the* most desirable car in the world; now that production has ceased, the price commanded by surviving examples is enormous.

Three varieties of Miura were built, each new variant being faster and fiercer than the last. The original P400 of 1966 boasted 350bhp from its 4-litre engine, while the P400S of 1970 had 370bhp, and the final P400SV of 1971 and 1972 had no less than 385bhp, the last figure being produced at a rousing 7850rpm. As the power increased, so was the chassis improved to match, and the SVs had wide rear wheels, stronger suspension and a widened track.

All Miura production cars had a closed two-seater coupe body, though the one-off Jota had a spider derivative, but this had been made as an 'ideas' model rather than a possible production machine.

In its day the Miura was, quite literally, one of the fastest cars in the world, and a maximum speed of 180mph was possible with the P400SV version. Not many owners, however rich, were capable of handling a Miura at very high speeds, even though their handling had been developed with high-speed stability very much in mind.

Nowadays it is often said that the Miura was dropped prematurely – to make way for the Countach, which did not actually go on sale until 1974 – and there are those who suggest that it was still an altogether better car than its successor. Owners of surviving Miuras no doubt agree.

Specification

Engine and transmission: Twelve-cylinders, in 60-degree vee-formation, with twin-overhead camshaft cylinder heads, mounted transversely in chassis. Bore, stroke and capacity 82 × 62mm., 3929cc. **(P400)** Maximum power 350bhp (DIN) at 7000rpm.; maximum torque 278lb.ft. at 5000rpm. **(P400S)** Maximum power 370bhp (DIN) at 7700rpm.; maximum torque 286lb.ft. at 5500rpm. **(P400SV)** Maximum power 385bhp (DIN) at 7850rpm.; maximum torque 294lb.ft. at 5750rpm. Five-speed manual gearbox in unit with engine and transaxle. Spur gear final drive.

Chassis: Mid-engine, rear drive. Separate pressed steel punt-type platform chassis frame. Independent front suspension by coil springs and wishbones. Rack and pinion steering. Independent rear suspension by coil springs and wishbones. Four-wheel disc brakes.

Bodywork: Light-alloy and steel two-door two-seater fastback coupe body style by Bertone. Length 14ft. 3.5in.; width 5ft. 11in.; height 3ft. 6in. Unladen weight 2850lb.

Performance: (P400S) Maximum speed 172mph. 0-60mph 6.7sec. Standing ¼-mile 14.5sec. Typical fuel consumption 14mpg.

Lamborghini Espada

Built: S'Agata, Italy, 1968 to date

If the Miura was Lamborghini's mid-engined masterpiece, then the Espada was its front-engined equivalent. The chassis was exciting enough — anything which could combine a 150mph top speed with a four-seater capacity, and the incredibly sensual sight and sound of that fabulous vee-12 engine had to be — but it was combined with a splendidly individual fastback style of body by Bertone. Even at the end of the 1960s, when many Supercars looked much like each other, the Espada was unmistakeable.

In style, the body was probably influenced by the one-off Lamborghini Marzal dream car, though that car's gullwing doors were not adapted for use in the Espada. Even though the four seats could charitably be described as 'close-coupled', there was much more interior space than in any previous Lamborghini. It was the S'Agata firm's first true four-seater, and — at 15ft. 4in. long — was the largest Lamborghini so far built.

In many ways the chassis engineering was like that of the Miura, for Marchesi of Modena built a pressed and fabricated steel platform frame which was clearly much stronger and more rigid than the tubular frame of the 350GT/400GT Lamborghinis which had come before it. All-round independent suspension was a feature, and the 4-litre engine produced 325bhp in initial form (which was progressively improved to 365bhp by the mid-1970s), and drove through Lamborghini's own five-speed gearbox, which was notable for even having synchromesh on reverse gear!

Unlike other Lamborghinis, which carried the name of one or other type of fighting bulls, the Espada was a derivative of the Italian name 'spada', which means 'sword'. The styling, in spite of being by Bertone, who was then one of the masters of Italian bespoke shapes, was controversial, and it attracted widely different response. The few who thought it ugly (comments mainly being directed towards the sharply cut-off rear) were greatly outnumbered by those who thought it beautiful and distinctive, and in terms of accommodation it was clearly quite practical.

Lamborghini Espada, rear end styling

Lamborghini Espada by Bertone, 1968

Even though it was a Supercar in every respect, the Espada always suffered by comparison with its exotic stable mates — the Miura and Countach which replaced it. Even so, its engineering and chassis was good enough to be adapted for another Lamborghini model — the 2 + 2 Jarama — which arrived on the scene in 1970.

More than 1000 Espadas have been made, and although it nominally remained in production until the end of the 1970s, due to Lamborghini's much-publicised financial problems not many were built after 1975 or 1976.

Specification

Engine and transmission: Twelve-cylinders, in 60-degree vee-formation, with twin-overhead-camshaft cylinder heads. Bore, stroke and capacity 82 × 62mm., 3929cc. **(Original cars)** 325bhp (DIN) at 6500rpm.; maximum torque 276lb.ft. at 4500rpm. **(Later cars)** power progressively increased to 365bhp (DIN) at 7500rpm.; maximum torque 300lb.ft. at 5500rpm. Five-speed manual gearbox in unit with engine. From 1974, three-speed Chrysler Torqueflite automatic transmission became optional. Hypoid bevel final drive.

Chassis: Front engine, rear drive. Separate pressed-steel and fabricated platform chassis structure. Independent front suspension by coil springs and wishbones. Optionally power-assisted worm and roller steering. Independent rear suspension by coil springs and wishbones. Four-wheel disc brakes.

Bodywork: Light-alloy and steel two-door close-coupled four-seater fastback coupe style by Bertone. Length 15ft. 4in.; width 5ft. 11.7in.; height 3ft. 10.9in. Unladen weight (depending on extras fitted) 3740lb.

Performance: Maximum speed 150mph. 0-60mph 7.8sec. Standing ¼-mile 15.7sec. Typical fuel consumption 16mpg.

Lamborghini Jarama

Built: S'Agata, Italy, 1970-1978

In spite of Lamborghini's fine reputation, its front-engined cars were never the most sensational in its range. The original 350GT/400GT cars had been fast, but possessed of rather bulbous styling, while the rebodied cars, called Isleros, were by no means distinctive. Even the Jarama of 1970, which effectively replaced this original strain of Lamborghini, was neither strikingly styled nor outstanding in any way but performance.

Jarama – location not only of a Spanish motor racing circuit, but an important centre for the breeding of Spanish fighting bulls (this theme goes through the short but colourful history of Lamborghini) – was the name given to the new front-engined car to replace the Islero. It did not use a development of that car's chassis, however, but used a shortened derivative of the punt-type steel platform chassis evolved for the four-seater Espada, which had been in production since 1968, along with that car's all-round independent coil spring suspension, and with the same 4-litre engine tune and transmissions. Compared with the Espada, the Jarama offered only 2 + 2 seating, was shorter but rather wider, and had surprisingly undistinguished two-door styling by Bertone, which was by no means as instantly recognisable as that of the Espada. Nevertheless, Ferruccio Lamborghini himself chose a Jarama as personal transport for some years.

Although the body style was by Bertone, body construction was carried out at the Lamborghini factory, and there was some early criticism of poor detail finish and lack of quality, presumably due to the fact that the factory had very little experience of this

Lamborghini Jarama 400GT, 1970

sort of work at the time. 250 of the original 400GT models were built in two years, and from 1972 it became the 400GTS, with a power increase and some styling changes which included a big air intake in the bonnet to funnel more air to the engine bay. There was also a very rare Jarama 'Targa', which had two removable panels above the front passengers' heads. Several hundred 400GTS models were built before production finally ran out in 1978, and it is interesting to note that automatic transmission was available during the last four years of production.

Specification

Engine and transmission: Twelve-cylinders, in 60-degree vee-formation, with twin-overhead-camshaft cylinder heads. Bore, stroke and capacity 82×62mm., 3929cc. **(Early cars)** maximum power 350bhp (DIN) at 7500rpm.; maximum torque 289lb.ft. at 5500rpm. **(Later cars)** 365bhp (DIN) at 7500rpm.; maximum torque 300lb.ft. at 5500rpm. Five-speed manual gearbox in unit with engine. From 1974, Chrysler three-speed Torqueflite automatic transmission became available. Hypoid bevel final drive.
Chassis: Front engine, rear drive. Pressed-steel platform style chassis frame, welded to body on assembly. Independent front suspension by coil springs and wishbones. Worm and sector steering. Independent rear suspension by coil springs and wishbones. Four-wheel disc brakes.
Bodywork: Steel bodywork, in two-door 2 + 2 seater, fastback coupe style, by Bertone. Length 14ft. 8.5in.; width 5ft. 11.6in.; height 3ft. 10.8in. Unladen weight 2960lb.
Performance: Maximum speed 162mph 0-60mph 6.8sec. Standing ¼-mile 14.9sec. Typical fuel consumption 13mpg.

Lamborghini Urraco

Built: S'Agata, Italy, 1970 to date

Although the Urraco is by no means the 'small' Lamborghini which was rumoured throughout the 1960s, it was, and is, rather smaller than any other car to have come from the S'Agata factory since its formation in 1963. The original 'base' Urraco had a 2.5-litre engine, but in response to fuel crises and certain taxation structures a 2-litre car later became available. These units, together with the 3-litre car which also followed, mean that the Urraco is something of a complete model range, which survives into the 1980s.

Philosophically, if not in engineering, the Urraco counts as 'son of Miura', as it was the second mid-engined Lamborghini to be put on the market. The Urraco, however, is distinguished by being the only Lamborghini not to rely on the Bizzarrini-designed vee-12 engine.

The 'little' Urraco — which looked small and neat, because of its remarkably integrated Bertone fastback style, and indeed it was only just over 13-feet long — was announced at the Turin Show in 1970, and in spite of Lamborghini's troubled financial state, and changes of ownership which occurred during the 1970s, still survives. Clearly it was aimed at the same market as cars like the Porsche 911 and Ferrari Dino 246GT were already supplying.

The pressed and fabricated steel platform chassis frame was designed with all the experience of the Miura/Espada/Jarama cars in mind, and was at the same time strong

Lamborghini Urraco by Bertone

yet relatively simple. The all-round independent suspension featured MacPherson strut type layout at front and rear. It was the engine and transmission which were quite new.

For the Urraco, and for other models if only the company's financial position had allowed it, there was a brand new vee-8 engine, with cylinder banks set at 90-degrees, and with single-camshaft cylinder heads and in-line valves. Not even the cylinder bore or the stroke was common to the vee-12 unit, and it was really quite remarkable that a company only seven-years-old had been able to conceive and prepare another new unit for production in – for them – some numbers.

For Bertone, who styled and supplied the production bodies, it had been a difficult job, as Ferruccio Lamborghini had not only wanted a relatively compact four-seater (or, in truth, a generous 2 + 2), but the car also had to have its engine in the mid-mounted position, ahead of the line of the rear wheels. The Urraco, therefore, had to have its cabin placed relatively far forward, with a somewhat stubby nose. Even so, it was a nice integrated style, which obviously found a great deal of favour with the customers. The body, incidentally of steel, is welded to the underframe on initial assembly, and the structure is effectively a monocoque.

The power pack is compact and very nicely detailed, with the transversely-mounted engine driving to a five-speed gearbox, which is all indirect, on the left side of the car, and with the spur gear differential behind the transmission.

The P250 ('P' = posteriore) model went into production in 1971, and was joined at the 1974 Turin Show by the P200 and P300 derivatives which had (as the nomenclature suggests) 2-litre and 3-litre engines respectively. Although the P200 was an interesting attempt to provide 'down market' Lamborghini motoring in view of a petrol supply crisis, it was not a success, and was dropped during 1977, while both the larger engines survive.

Another derivative of the Urraco, on the P300 chassis, is the 3000 Silhouette, with a much-changed bodyshell by Bertone, including a Targa top, only two seats, and more sporting suspension, wheel widths and tyres. Of all the Urracos, this one is for the conspicuous Big Spenders.

Specification

Engine and transmission: Eight-cylinders, in 90-degree vee-formation, with single-overhead-camshaft cylinder heads. Three different engine sizes: **(P200):** Bore, stroke and capacity 77.4×53mm., 1994cc. Maximum power, 182bhp (DIN) at 7500rpm.; maximum torque 130lb.ft. at 3800rpm. **(P250):** Bore, stroke and capacity 86×53mm., 2463cc. Maximum power 220bhp (DIN) at 7500rpm.; maximum torque 166lb.ft. at 5750rpm. **(P300):** Bore, stroke and capacity 86×64.5mm., 2996cc. Maximum power 265bhp (DIN) at 7500rpm.; maximum torque 202lb.ft. at 3500rpm. Five-speed manual gearbox in unit with engine and final drive transaxle. Spur gear final drive.

Chassis: Mid-engine, rear drive. Pressed-steel box section and fabricated platform chassis frame. Independent front suspension by coil springs, MacPherson struts and wishbones. Rack and pinion steering. Independent rear suspension by coil springs, MacPherson struts and wishbones. Four-wheel disc brakes.

Bodywork: Steel body, two-door, close-coupled 2+2 seater, fastback coupe (with removable roof panel on some models) by Bertone. Length 13ft. 1.2in.; width 5ft. 9.3in.; height 3ft. 7.7in. Unladen weight 2885lb.

Performance (250S): Maximum speed 143mph. 0-60mph 8.5sec. Standing ¼-mile 16.6sec. Typical fuel consumption 18mpg. **(P300):** Maximum speed 158mph. 0-60mph 7.6sec. Standing ¼-mile 15.6sec. Typical fuel consumption 15mpg.

Lamborghini Urraco, rear end styling

Lamborghini Countach

Built: S'Agata, Italy, 1974 to date

If any such car is possible, the original Countach was even more extraordinary than the Miura it was to replace. But that was the very first, phenomenally powerful 5-litre prototype. The production car, more civilised and not nearly so extraordinary with its 'normal' 4-litre Lamborghini engine, was rather less stratospheric.

Even so, the Countach, by any standards, is one of the three fastest cars in the world. The combination of Lamborghini chassis engineering, 4-litre vee-12 power, and a dazzlingly individual coupe style by Bertone, makes it a car to remember. For all that, however, those qualified to know — those who can own, and have owned, both types — often suggest that the Miura, on balance, was the better car.

The original Countach was called the LP500, and was shown to a startled world as

an 'ideas car' at the 1971 Geneva Motor Show. 'LP' stands for *Longitudinale Posteriore*, which denotes the engine layout. This was entirely different from that of Miura. Whereas the Miura had a transversely-mounted mid-engine and integral transaxle, the Countach had the vee-12 unit (in 5-litre form in this one car) mounted fore-and-aft, with the five-speed gearbox also in line, and effectively between the two seats, allied to a final driveshaft to the differential unit, which passed through the engine sump.

Faced with this startling sort of layout, which was yet another 'first' for Lamborghini, it is not surprising that all manner of expletives and disbelieving noises were issued. *Countach*, in Italian, can either be construed as a more polite expletive, or more likely as an equivalent of 'splendid', which the car undoubtedly was.

Although the 1971 Geneva Show car was a runner, it was not at all developed, and it is now agreed that the Miura was withdrawn prematurely to make way for it, as development, productionising, and − that modern curse − getting legal approval

Lamborghini Countach LP500 Prototype

Lamborghini Countach LP400 by Bertone   419

from various governments for it to be sold in their territories, took a great deal of time. The first genuine 'production' car was not delivered until the beginning of 1974, and less than 50 cars were completed that year.

The prototype had a simple chassis frame of square-section tubing with some steel reinforcement, but before production began this design was changed completely to a more conventional (by Italian Supercar standards) multi-tube, circular section, frame in three dimensions. The original prototype engine, bored and stroked from the usual 3929cc unit, measured 4971cc, and was claimed to produce the astonishing but quite believable 440bhp at 7400rpm. Customers taking delivery from 1974 on had to make do with 375bhp at 8000rpm. Although there was a lot of talk of 200mph top speeds at first, it is doubtful if such a speed was measured. Even so, production cars can beat 175 to 180mph, which should be quite fast enough for even rich ordinary mortals.

The Bertone body was distinguishable by its noticeably sharp-edge 'wedge' style, and with extensively sculptured tail around the engine bay and rear lamp housings. The windscreen was very sharply angled and almost in line with the front deck, while the doors neither opened outwards nor upwards, but rather were hinged from their front top corners, so that they folded forward rather like the unfurling of the wings of a great bird. These bodies, incidentally, though styled by Bertone, who produced the individual panels, are actually assembled at the Lamborghini factory.

Although the obvious competition comes from Ferrari and the Boxer, the Countach looks more outlandish than any other car on public sale, and is – at one and the same time – less practical and more desirable.

Specification

Engine and transmission: Twelve-cylinders, in 60-degree vee-formation, with twin-overhead-camshaft cylinder heads. Bore, stroke and capacity 82 × 62mm., 3929cc. Maximum power 375bhp (DIN) at 8000rpm.; maximum torque 266lb.ft. at 5500rpm. Five-speed manual gearbox in unit with engine and final drive. Hypoid bevel final drive.

Chassis: Mid-engine, rear drive. Separate multi-tubular chassis frame. Independent front suspension by coil springs and wishbones. Rack and pinion steering. Independent rear suspension by coil springs, wishbones and radius arms. Four-wheel disc brakes.

Bodywork: Light-alloy and steel bodywork, in two-door two-seater fastback coupe style, by Bertone. Length 13ft. 7in.; width 6ft. 6.7in.; height 3ft. 6.1in. Unladen weight 3000lb.

Performance: Maximum speed 175mph. 0-60mph 5.6sec. Standing ¼-mile 14.1sec. Typical fuel consumption 11mpg.

Ligier JS2

Built: Vichy, France, 1971-1976

Guy Ligier was a successful businessman, ex-Rugby international, and no more than an averagely-talented racing driver who bought and campaigned a Cooper-Maserati in the original years of the 3-litre Grand Prix formula. In 1969 he set about producing his own make of competition cars, and in 1971 the first and only Ligier road car appeared. This was the JS2, designed for Ligier by Michel Tetu, in the fashionable mid-engined style.

Ligier JS2, Paris Motor Show 1971

JS stood for 'Jo Schlesser', the great racing-driver friend of Ligier who had been tragically killed in the 1968 French Grand Prix, and '2' meant that it was the second car marketed as a Ligier − the first having been a Cosworth FVC-engined competition coupe.

The JS2 road car was first seen in public at the 1971 Paris Motor Show, having been revealed during the summer. Ligier had done his engine and transmission deal for this car with Citroen, by arranging to take the vee-6 Maserati 2.7-litre engine and five-speed gearbox from the SM Coupe, turn it round through 180 degrees and alter the final drive gearing to suit. This was needed because on the Citroen the Maserati engine was behind the line of the front wheels; in the JS2 it was necessary to put the engine ahead of the rear wheels.

A platform-style chassis in pressed and fabricated steel was chosen − almost in the true Italian Supercar manner − and the two-seater arrangement was topped by a fastback coupe body made in glass-fibre. All independent suspension was very much in the sports-racing category, and performance was certainly in the potential Supercar 421 category. Once the engine had been enlarged to the full three-litres (at the same time as Citroen did this for their own SM model) there was no doubt about it at all.

Ligier was not equipped to make many of these exclusive machines, especially as they had no long-established reputation to back them up, and after production of Citroen SMs was moved to the Ligier factory the opportunities to build JS2s tailed off even further. No more than 100 had been made by July 1974, when Ligier's business was taken over by Citroen. The last was built in 1975/1976.

Specification

Engine and transmission: Six-cylinders, in 90-degree formation, with twin-camshaft cylinder heads, made by Maserati. Bore, stroke and capacity 91.6×75mm., 2965cc. Maximum power 180bhp (DIN) at 6500rpm.; maximum torque 181lb.ft. at 4000rpm. Five-speed gearbox in unit with engine and transaxle. Spiral bevel final drive.
Chassis: Mid-engine, rear drive. Platform-type chassis in pressed-steel. Independent front suspension by coil springs and wishbones. Rack and pinion steering. Independent rear suspension by coil springs and wishbones. Four-wheel disc brakes.
Bodywork: Glass-fibre bodywork, in two-seat fastback coupe style. Length 13ft. 11.3in.; width 5ft. 7.7in.; height 3ft. 9.3in. Unladen weight 2140lb.
Performance (Manufacturer's claim): Maximum speed 150mph. Typical fuel consumption 17mpg.

Maserati 3500GT, GTI and Sebring

Built: Modena, Italy, 1958-1964

Although there had been Maseratis since 1926, the first true road car to be built in any numbers was the 3500GT of 1958. Until then the Orsi family, who had taken over from the Maserati brothers in 1937, concentrated on competition cars and the occasional hand-built road car.

The 3500GT, built round a simple but robust tubular chassis frame, used what was in effect an enlarged derivative of a six-cylinder racing engine introduced in 1952. In 2-litre Formula 2, 2.5-litre Formula 1, 3.0 and 3.5-litre sports-racing form, this engine was progressively developed, then installed in detuned form in the 3500GT.

The chassis was really 'current sporting Italian', which is to say that the tubular chassis was equipped with coil spring independent front suspension and a live rear axle. During the six years this basic car remained in production, the 3500GT gave rise to the 3500GTI, distinguished by the first-ever fitment of Lucas fuel-injection on a road car, and later the Vignale-bodied 3500GTI coupe became known as the Sebring, after the North American racing circuit where Maserati sports cars raced with such distinction.

There were many special bodies, and short-run 'standard' bodies on these cars, none of which were ever erected by Maserati, who did not have the space or ability to

Maserati Sebring by Vignale, 1963

make their own coachwork. 3500GT shells were built by Touring of Milan on the 'Superleggera' principle, and spiders by Vignale. 3500GTIs were by Touring (as before), and both coupes and spiders were built on a shorter wheelbase by Vignale. Even so, specials were also seen by Bertone, Allemano, Frua and Ghia. The vast majority, however, were by Touring, and well over 2000 were built in less than six years.

There were so many variations between bodies that it has only been feasible to quote those of the Vignale 'Sebring', along with that car's mechanical specification. The 3500GT with carburettors was considerably out-numbered by the GTI with injection; the carburettor engine produced 220bhp at 5500rpm.

Specification

Engine and transmission: Six-cylinders, in-line, with twin-overhead-camshaft cylinder head and fuel-injection (carburettors on less-powerful 3500GT). Bore, stroke and capacity 86 × 100mm., 3485cc. Maximum power 235bhp (net) at 5800rpm.; maximum torque 232lb.ft. at 4000rpm. Five-speed ZF manual gearbox or three-speed Borg Warner automatic transmission in unit with engine. Hypoid bevel final drive.

Chassis: Front engine, rear drive. Separate tubular steel chassis frame. Independent front suspension by coil springs and wishbones. Recirculating ball steering. Rear suspension of live axle by half-elliptic leaf springs and torque arms. Four-wheel disc brakes.

Bodywork: Variety of two-door coachwork, coupe or spider, with light-alloy or steel panels according to make. 'Sebring' model exclusively by Vignale. Sebring dimensions: length 14ft. 8in.; width 5ft. 5.3in.; height 4ft. 4in. Unladen weight 3330lb.

Performance (Sebring): Maximum speed 137mph. 0-60mph 8.4sec. Standing ¼-mile 16.0sec. Typical fuel consumption 16mpg.

Maserati 5000GT with body by Ghia

Maserati 5000GT

Built: Modena, Italy, 1959 to 1964

Before Maserati produced their first true 'production' road car, the 3500GT, they had abandoned motor racing, and this left them with a small but valuable stock of the ultra-powerful vee-8 engines. The 5000GT Coupes, of which only 32 examples were built in five years, were effectively 3500GT rolling chassis, with the massive vee-8 engine installed, and with luxurious handbuilt 2 + 2 bodies. All the 32 production cars appear to have been coupes, though a single convertible was reputedly shown at the Turin Show in 1961. The first three cars used out-and-out racing engines, including gear-driven camshafts, while the rest used the more refined version being developed for later production car use, and featured fuel-injection by Lucas. 20 of the cars were bodied by Allemano, but all looked striking, and were undoubtedly rich men's toys. The first customer was the Shah of Iran, and another was Briggs Cunningham.

The 5000GT, however, was really only an indulgence by Maserati, involving them in little more than re-engining the 3500GT frame and suspensions, and was built by hand to keep their richest clients happy.

Specification

Engine and transmission: Eight-cylinders, in 90-degree vee-formation, with twin-overhead-camshaft cylinder heads and fuel-injection. Bore, stroke and capacity 98.5 × 81mm., 4935cc. Maximum power 330bhp at 5700rpm.; maximum torque 330lb.ft. at 3500rpm. Four-speed manual gearbox in unit with engine. Hypoid bevel final drive.

Chassis: Front engine, rear drive. Separate tubular steel chassis frame. Independent front suspension by coil springs, wishbones and anti-roll bar. Recirculating ball steering. Rear suspension of live axle by half-elliptic leaf springs, with anti-roll bar and torque arms. Front wheel disc brakes, and rear drums.

Bodywork: Separate coachbuilt bodyshells in variety of two-door styles, mainly by Allemano (but also by Touring, Ghia, Frua, etc), in notchback coupe 2 + 2 layouts; steel and/or light-alloy depending on style chosen. Typical dimensions: length 15ft. 1in.; width 5ft. 7in.; height 4ft. 4in. Unladen weight 4400lb.

Performance: (Typical) Maximum speed up to 170mph. 0-60mph 6.5sec. Standing ¼-mile 14.0sec. Typical fuel consumption 14mpg.

Maserati Mistrale

Built: Modena, Italy, 1963 to 1969

Once Maserati had found that their 3500GTIs were deservedly popular among wealthy sportsmen, they set about expanding their production car range. In 1963, with the Sebring on the market and already beginning to look a trifle dated, they introduced the Mistrale model at the Turin motor show. This, while using the same basic engineering layout as the Sebring, had a choice of coupe or spider bodies of the same type, built for Maserati by Frua, and it is interesting to note that the coupe had an early example of what we would now call a hatchback.

The Mistrale was distinguished by the use of the two largest-of-all derivatives of the famous Maserati six-cylinder engine. It was offered in 3692cc or 4012cc form, the latter having a bore and stroke of 88×110mm, which compares with the 76×72mm and 1978cc of the original Formula 2 car of 1951/52. However, this was also the end of the development road for the big 'six', and all future Maserati models would use vee-8 or vee-6 engines of the other 1950s racing car design.

By Maserati standards, the Mistrale was a successful model, as 948 examples (of which 120 were spiders) were built in six years.

Specification

The Mistrale was based on GTI Sebring engineering, but with important differences as follows: bore, stroke and capacity 86×106mm., 3692cc. Maximum power 245bhp (net) at 5500rpm.; maximum torque 253lb.ft. at 4000rpm. Two body styles by Frua — two-door two-seater fastback coupe or convertible, were available. Length 14ft. 9in.; width 5ft. 4in.; height 4ft. 3in. Unladen weight 2800lb.

Note: An alternative engine size was 88×110mm., 4012cc. Maximum power 255bhp (net) at 5500rpm.; maximum torque 268lb.ft. at 4000rpm.

Maserati 3500GT Mistrale

Maserati Quattroporte

Built: Modena, Italy, 1963-1970

When first revealed, the Quattroporte caused something of a motoring sensation, not only for its interesting engineering, but for its body layout. *Quattroporte*, incidentally, sounds lyrical and romantic, but means nothing more than 'four-door' in Italian, and it was this factor which made the car unique. Until then, no self-respecting Supercar was ever offered with four doors, and usually not with four full-sized seats either, so Maserati were clearly trying to create an entirely new market sector in super-performance saloon car transport.

The chassis was more complex than previous Maseratis had been. The tubular chassis frame had more complex boxed and fabricated sections to stiffen it, and was distinguished, at first, by a de Dion rear suspension. This feature, however, did not confer the roadholding and practical benefits it should have done, and from 1967 was abandoned in favour of nothing more complex than a live axle and half-elliptic leaf springs.

The Quattroporte, too, was the first proper Maserati road car to use a detuned version of the 4.5-litre vee-8 sports-racing engine which had first been seen in public in the brutish 450S model. (32 hand-built examples of the 5000GT model had already been built, but these were not in serious production). The 450S was of 4477cc, with 93.8 × 81mm bore and stroke, while the detuned Quattroporte road car had 4136cc, and a bore and stroke of 88 × 85mm.

Coachwork was by Frua, who must have had a great deal of influence at Modena at the time, for they were also involved in building the Mistrale bodies.

When the live-axle chassis was introduced in 1967, it was accompanied by an enlarged 4719cc engine (93.9 × 85mm). A total of 679 Quattroportes of both types were built, but the car was not as popular as the company had hoped.

Specification

Engine and transmission: Eight-cylinders, in 90-degree vee-formation, with twin-overhead-camshaft cylinder heads. Bore, stroke and capacity 88 × 85mm., 4136cc. Maximum power 260bhp (net) at 5200rpm.; maximum torque 267lb.ft. at 4000rpm. From 1967, the engine was enlarged to 4719cc, 93.9 × 85mm., with 290bhp at 5500rpm. Five-speed manual ZF gearbox or three-speed automatic Borg Warner transmission, in unit with engine. Hypoid bevel final drive.

Chassis: Front engine, rear drive. Fabricated steel tubular and box-section front chassis frame, bolted to all-steel bodyshell. Independent front suspension by coil springs and wishbones. Recirculating ball steering with optional power-assistance. De Dion rear suspension, by coil springs, radius arms and transverse Watts linkage. From 1967, rear suspension by live axle, half-elliptic leaf springs and radius arms. Four-wheel disc brakes.

Bodywork: Steel four-door four-seater GT saloon style, by Frua. Length 16ft. 4in.; width 5ft. 8in.; height 4ft. 5in. Unladen weight 3810lb.

Performance: Maximum speed 130mph. 0-60mph 8.3sec. Standing ¼-mile 16.4sec. Typical fuel consumption 19mpg.

Maserati Quattroporte by Frua

Maserati Ghibli, 1967

Maserati Mexico & Ghibli

Built: Modena, Italy, 1965 to 1973

Expansion of Maserati road car choice continued in the mid-1960s, and when the 3500GTI Sebring faded away, it was effectively replaced by the new Mexico. Although it is always dangerous to expect logical cross-fertilisation of models in a company making a limited number of cars, there is little doubt that in this case the new model was based on the chassis engineering of the Quattroporte saloon car — and would in fact outlive it.

The Mexico made its bow at the 1965 Turin Show, and though its Quattroporte-based chassis had a live rear axle suspension layout this was not at the time thought to indicate what could happen to the Quattroporte. Throughout the life of the model, it was available with optional vee-8 engine sizes — the 4.2-litre and 4.7-litre derivatives, both of which were in a higher state of tune than those fitted to Quattroporte models.

Mexico coachwork, of a close-coupled four-seater coupe, was by Vignale. By this time, however, competing Supercars from Ferrari, Lamborghini and Iso were making inroads to a limited market, and sales never went ahead very fast. A total of only 250 Mexicos were built. From the Turin show of 1966, however, the Mexico was joined by the sensationally sleek Ghibli model, which was built on the same basic chassis, but with a shorter wheelbase, shorter overall length, and with only two seats. Its body, however — available either as a fastback coupe or as a convertible — was by Ghia, and was quite startlingly beautiful. It had very high performance, particularly when

Maserati Mexico, 1966

fitted with the optional 4.9-litre engine (4930cc, 93.9 × 89mm., 355bhp at 5500rpm), and the clientele was obviously attracted as 1274 cars were built before production finally came to an end ahead of the energy crisis of 1973.

Specification

Engine and transmission: Eight-cylinders, in 90-degree vee-formation, with twin-overhead-camshaft cylinder heads. Choice of two engine sizes: bore, stroke and capacity 88 × 85mm., 4136cc. Maximum power 260bhp (net) at 5800rpm.; maximum torque 268lb.ft. at 4000rpm. Or: bore, stroke and capacity 94 × 85mm., 4719cc. Maximum power 330bhp (net) at 5000rpm.; maximum torque 290lb.ft. at 4000rpm. Five-speed manual ZF gearbox or three-speed automatic Borg Warner transmission, in unit with engine. Hypoid bevel final drive.

Chassis: Front engine, rear drive. Fabricated steel tubular and box section front chassis frame, bolted to steel bodyshell. Independent front suspension by coil springs and wishbones. Recirculating ball steering with power assistance. Rear suspension of live axle by half-elliptic leaf springs, and radius arms. Four-wheel disc brakes.

Bodywork: Steel two-door close-coupled four-seater notchback coupe style by Vignale. Length 15ft. 7.4in.; width 5ft. 8.1in.; height 4ft. 5.1in. Unladen weight 3640lb.

Note: Ghibli was mechanically like the Mexico, but with the following important body differences: two-door, two-seater fastback coupe style by Ghia. Length 15ft. 0.7in.; width 5ft. 10.8in.; height 3ft. 9.6in. Unladen weight 2980lb. Also optional was a 4930cc engine, with 93.9 × 89mm bore and stroke. Maximum power 355bhp (net) at 5500rpm.

Performance (4.7-litre): Maximum speed 154mph. 0-60mph 7.5sec. Standing ¼-mile 15.1sec. Typical fuel consumption 15mpg.

Maserati Indy

Built: Modena, Italy, 1969 to 1975

Unlike most Maseratis, the Indy was first shown as a prototype, on the Vignale stand of the 1968 Turin Motor Show, but it was 'officially' adopted by the time the Geneva Show came around in March 1969. In effect the Indy was a 2 + 2 coupe, falling midway between the Mexico four-seater and the Ghibli two-seater, thus filling a somewhat narrow gap.

In engineering and chassis layout, the Vignale coachwork of the Indy was quite new. For the first time, a Maserati was built, on a small-production basis, as a unit-construction body-chassis unit, which ensured that there would be no major styling changes, no one-off bodies from rival coachbuilders, and no convertible version. In style, the Indy by Vignale was very similar to the Ghibli by Ghia, although − as already made clear − the two bodies were entirely different. Both cars, however, had a shark-like nose, with concealed headlamps above low-mounted air inlets.

The engine and transmission layout was much as used by other Maserati models of the period, except that the Indy was originally introduced as a 4.2-litre model, and the 4.7-litre version with 330bhp was not made available until later.

As with the Ghibli, so with the Indy − the remarkable styling made it easy to sell, and no less than 1136 cars were built before the company changed hands, and the product line was simplified for 1976.

Maserati Indy − cutaway

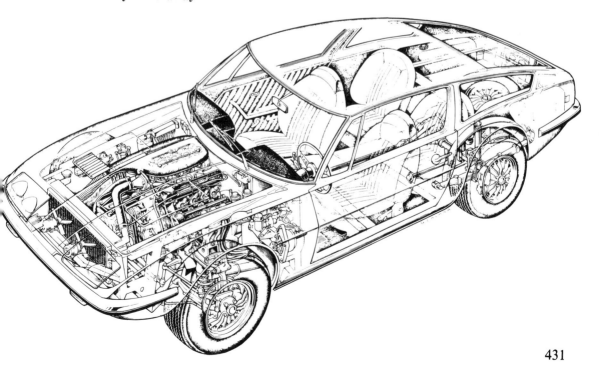

Maserati Indy

Specification

Engine and transmission: Eight-cylinders, in 90-degree vee-formation, with twin-overhead-camshaft cylinder heads. Choice of two engine sizes: bore, stroke and capacity 88 × 85mm., 4136cc. Maximum 260bhp (net) at 5800rpm.; maximum torque 268lb.ft. at 4000rpm. Or: bore, stroke and capacity 94 × 85mm., 4719cc. Maximum power 330bhp (net) at 5000rpm.; maximum torque 290lb.ft. at 4000rpm. Five-speed manual ZF gearbox or three-speed automatic Borg Warner transmission in unit with engine. Hypoid bevel final drive.

Chassis: Front engine, rear drive. Pressed and fabricated steel unit-construction body-chassis unit. Independent front suspension by coil springs and wishbones. Recirculating ball with power assistance. Rear suspension of live axle by half-elliptic leaf springs and radius arms. Four-wheel disc brakes.

Bodywork: Steel two-door close-coupled four-seater fastback coupe style by Vignale. Length 16ft. 0in.; width 5ft. 10in.; height 4ft. 3in. Unladen weight 3640lb.

Performance: (4.7-litre version) Maximum speed 156mph. 0-60mph 7.5sec. Standing ¼-mile 15.6sec. Typical fuel consumption 15mpg.

Maserati Merak & Bora

Built: Modena, Italy, 1971 to date

To be truly modern, every Italian manufacturer of Supercars has to have mid-engined two-seaters with immense performance, and Maserati are no exception. Not one, but two distinctly different models, have been produced on the same basic design. The larger of the two, the Bora, came first, and the slightly less exotic Merak followed considerably later.

When first seen at the Geneva motor show of 1971, in prototype form, with a body style by Ital Design, the Bora caused something of a sensation. It was, after all, Maserati's first mid-engined road car (though who will ever forget the fantastically complex series of 'birdcage' cars of the early 1960s?), and it looked wickedly attractive. It was also, in detail, influenced by Citroen design thinking, and complex hydraulics included seat and pedal adjustment.

Although the steel unit-construction bodyshell was styled by Ital Design, they had no production facilities, so construction was farmed out to the various metal-working sub-contractors who abound in the north of Italy. Shells arrive at Modena to be painted, trimmed, and for final assembly to take place.

All the sound and fury took place behind the driver's head, with that well-known Maserati vee-8 engine in 4.9-litre form producing no less than 330bhp at 6000rpm, with enormously impressive flexibility and torque. Only a ZF gearbox could deal with that sort of power, and a five-speed component from that factory was installed.

Like other exciting cars before it, the prototype looked like nothing more than an indulgent design exercise from Ital Design, but experience on the road proves otherwise. Apart from the remarkable performance to be expected from this specification, there is evidence of Citroen wizardry everywhere, including the use of pressurised hydraulic brake circuits with a 'no travel' brake pedal like DS and SM models. Stowage space, too, is very generous, for this is a front 'boot' and a container above and behind the engine – in effect in the 'dead' space over the transaxle.

The Merak, announced at the Paris Show in 1972, has much in common with the Bora, but has its own important differences. Distinctive cabin and rear quarter styling is made possible because there is a Maserati 90-degree vee-6 engine instead of the vee-8, which has allowed the cabin to be extended and for tiny rear seats to be installed.

The Paris Show launch was chosen by Citroen, as the engine was that of the SM (though built by Maserati), and the rest of the transmission was modified from that used in the front-engine/front-drive SM, though of course the entire assembly had been turned round and re-geared for use in the Merak.

Although the Bora was made without major change following the energy crisis of 1973/1974, the Merak was changed in two ways. To make the car more powerful the SS came along, with 220bhp at 6500rpm instead of the original 190bhp at 6000rpm. On the other hand, to give the nod towards fuel economy, and to countries like Italy with progressive engine size tax structures, Maserati also introduced a 2-litre version of the engine, which nevertheless managed to produce 170bhp at 7000rpm.

Maserati Bora by Ital Design

Specification

Engine and transmission: (Merak) Six-cylinders, in 90-degree vee-formation, with twin-overhead-camshaft cylinder heads. Bore, stroke and capacity 91.6×75.0mm., 2965cc. Maximum power 190bhp (DIN) at 6000rpm.; maximum torque 188lb.ft. at 4000rpm. **(SS derivative)** Maximum power 220bhp (DIN) at 6500rpm.; maximum torque 200lb.ft. at 4500rpm. **(Bora)** Eight-cylinders, in 90-degree vee-formation, with twin-overhead-camshaft cylinder heads. Bore, stroke and capacity 93.9×89mm., 4930cc. Maximum power 330bhp (DIN) at 6000rpm.; maximum torque 340lb.ft. at 4200rpm. Five-speed ZF manual gearbox in unit with engine and transaxle. Spiral bevel final drive.

Chassis: Mid-engine, rear drive. Steel unit-construction body-chassis unit. Independent front suspension by coil springs and wishbones. Rack and pinion steering. Independent rear suspension by coil springs and wishbones. Four-wheel disc brakes.

Bodywork: Steel two-door 2+2-seater (Merak) or two-seater (Bora) fastback coupe style by Giugiaro/Italdesign. Length 14ft. 2.4in.; width 5ft. 8.1in.; height 3ft. 9.5in. Unladen weight (Merak) 3085lb. (Bora) 3210lb.

Performance: (Merak) Maximum speed 135mph. 0-60mph 8.2sec. Standing ¼-mile 16.0sec. Typical fuel consumption 19mpg. **(Bora)** Maximum speed 162mph. 0-60mph 6.5sec. Standing ¼-mile 14.6sec. Typical fuel consumption 12mpg.

Note: Merak is also sold with alternative engine, 80×66.3mm., 1999cc. Maximum power 170bhp (DIN) at 7000rpm.; maximum torque 137lb.ft. at 5000rpm.

Maserati Khamsin

Built: Modena, Italy, 1972 to date

Although the Khamsin was designed to replace the Indy, it had a different coachbuilder (Bertone), and was first seen as a prototype at the Turin Show of 1972, only three years after the Indy had first appeared. Though based on the same basic elements of Maserati engines, transmissions and suspension units, it was different in almost every detail.

The Khamsin is important for being the first Maserati road car by Bertone (who, until then, had been engrossed with Lamborghini and Iso production) and for being the only front-engined survivor of the Citroen-owned regime. Bertone built the combined body/chassis unit in pressed and fabricated steel, ready for completion at Maserati. It is notable that the Indy was also the first front-engined Maserati to have four-wheel independent suspension, this giving the lie to those who suggested that under the skin the Indy and the Khamsin were blood-brothers.

Mechanically, however, there was much close similarity between Ghibli, Indy and Khamsin, as all used derivatives of the race-proved vee-8 engine (usually in 4.2 and 4.7-litre form, though that of the Khamsin was 4.9-litres), all used imported ZF manual or Borg Warner automatic gearboxes, along with British disc brakes and axle components.

Maserati Khamsin by Bertone

Specification

Engine and transmission: Eight-cylinders, in 90-degree vee-formation, with twin-overhead-camshaft cylinder heads. Bore, stroke and capacity 93.9 × 89mm., 4930cc. Maximum power 320bhp (DIN) at 5500rpm.; maximum torque 354lb.ft. at 4000rpm. Five-speed manual ZF gearbox or three-speed automatic Borg Warner transmission, in unit with engine. Hypoid bevel final drive.

Chassis: Front engine, rear drive. Steel unit-construction body-chassis unit. Independent front suspension by coil springs and wishbones. Power-assisted rack and pinion steering. Independent rear suspension by coil springs and wishbones. Four-wheel disc brakes.

Bodywork: Steel two-door, 2 + 2-seater fastback coupe style by Bertone. Length 14ft. 5.2in.; width 5ft. 10.9in.; height 4ft. 1in. Unladen weight 3620lb.

Performance: (Automatic) Maximum speed 130mph. 0-60mph 7.5sec. Standing ¼-mile 15.8sec. Typical fuel consumption 17mpg.

Maserati Kyalami by Frua

Maserati Kyalami & Quattroporte II

Built: Modena, Italy, 1976 to date

For several years in the early 1970s, Maserati had a troubled time, industrially and financially. Taken over by the French concern, Citroen, in 1969, when that firm was also getting close to Fiat, they then suffered badly as a result of the abandonment of the Fiat-Citroen agreement, following which Citroen themselves struck financial trouble. Eventually, in 1975, Citroen abandoned Maserati to their fate, and it was only with the help of Italian state finance that Alejandro de Tomaso was able to merge them with his own Supercar marque.

   The Kyalami, developed very rapidly indeed, was the first fruit of this takeover and rebirth. Maserati themselves make no secret of the fact that the Kyalami is little more than a slightly restyled de Tomaso Longchamps (described elsewhere in this book) with Maserati engine and transmissions.

European Sports & GT Cars

The basic style had been done a few years earlier by Frua, and was a unit-construction pressed-steel body chassis unit of rather boxy and angular type, with 2 + 2 seating. It has all-independent suspension which is, naturally, common with that of the Longchamps, but entirely different from the Khamsin which was the last true 'Maserati' Maserati.

The Kyalami is also significant because it has given rise, directly, to the new Quattroporte II four-door Supersaloon car. This, although a spiritual descendant of the original Quattroporte, was styled by Ital Design, and should not be confused with a Citroen-inspired car of the same name which used much Citroen SM hydraulics and a vee-6 engine. This Quattroporte, like the Kyalami, has the Maserati vee-8 engine and transmissions, and the elements of the Kyalami chassis. Because of its bulk (it is more than 16-feet long) the 4.9-litre engine is also available.

Specification

Engine and transmission: Eight-cylinders, in 90-degree vee-formation, with twin-overhead-camshaft cylinder heads. Bore, stroke and capacity 88 × 85mm., 4136cc. Maximum power 270bhp (DIN) at 6000rpm.; maximum torque 289lb.ft. at 3800rpm. Five-speed ZF manual gearbox or three-speed Borg Warner automatic transmission in unit with engine. Hypoid bevel final drive.

Chassis: Front engine, rear drive. Unit-construction pressed-steel body-chassis unit. Independent front suspension by coil springs and wishbones. Power-assisted rack and pinion steering. Independent rear suspension by double coil springs, fixed length halfshafts, lower links and radius arms. Four-wheel disc brakes.

Bodywork: Steel two-door close-coupled four-seater notchback coupe style by Frua. Length 15ft. 0.25in.; width 6ft. 0.75in.; height 4ft. 1in. Unladen weight 3835lb.

Performance: Maximum speed 147mph. 0-60mph 7.6sec. Standing ¼-mile 15.8sec. Typical fuel consumption 17mpg.

Note: The new Quattroporte model uses Kyalami engineering, but has the following important differences: length 16ft. 0.1in.; height 5ft. 10.4in.; height 4ft. 5.1in. Unladen weight 4340lb. Four-door GT saloon body.

Note: A 4.9-litre engine, 93.9 × 89mm., 4930cc, maximum power 320bhp (DIN) at 5500rpm.; maximum torque 354lb.ft. at 4000rpm., is also available.

Maserati Quattroporte II by Ital Design

Mercedes-Benz 300SL

Built: Stuttgart, Germany, 1954 to 1963

Like the Jaguar E-Type, the 300SL was originally conceived as a racing sports car. Unlike the E-Type, however, it was a successful racer *and* rally car, and a less successful (in terms of numbers built) road car. Prototypes won at Le Mans in 1952, where they astonished the world with their gullwing coupe styling, and production cars followed in February 1954.

It is as well to remember that there were two distinct types of 300SLs – the legendary 'gullwings' of 1954-1957, and the less visually exciting but more practical 300SL Roadsters of 1957-1963. Both used one or other version of the complex and quite unmistakeable space-frame chassis, with its myriad tubes and complex jointings (something never matched by any other car in series production), by all-independent suspension including swing-axle rear suspension (though the Roadster had low-pivot linkage which tamed the roadholding somewhat), and by the use of a fuel-injected three-litre engine, installed at an angle in the chassis.

It was also very fast. By the standards of 1954, only the occasional Ferrari (and Ferraris were not in any scale of quantity production by then) was as fast, so this made the 300SL at once desirable and a potential winner. The problem was that the space frame chassis was difficult to build, fragile when faced by even minor accidents, and extremely complex to repair. It was not, therefore, a car which Mercedes-Benz dealers liked to maintain. This, and the fact that it was extremely expensive, meant that sales were very limited.

There was also the problem of the roadholding. Not even Mercedes-Benz themselves denied that the swing-axle suspension could make it tricky to handle, and a change of mind in mid-corner, on the tyres of the day, usually led (at best) to a spin, and (at worst) to a high-speed accident. This did not stop expert drivers making a winning car out of the 300SL, whether it was in Grand Touring races, or in rallies as arduous as the Liège-Rome-Liège.

The Roadster was an attempt to cure all these problems – the body was simpler and easier to seal against water entry, the roadholding more predictable, and the whole car that much more robust. The fuel-injected engine, which was always a great success, had ten more bhp (250 instead of 240bhp gross, at more than 6000rpm), and was astonishingly flexible.

When we consider the car's high price, and its ferocious performance, it sold remarkably well. More than 3250 examples of both types were built before it was dropped in favour of the new 230SL of 1963. In every way, in marketing approach, in engineering, in complexity, and in its 'image', the 300SL was a unique Mercedes-Benz, which that essentially practical concern is not likely to repeat. It is worth recalling that it had nothing physically in common with the similarly-named 300SLR, which had a straight-eight racing engine and its own brand of space-frame chassis and suspensions, even though the close visual and technical links were obvious. The publicity achieved by the racing successes of the 300SLR certainly helped to sell the less-fierce 300SL.

Mercedes-Benz 300SL, 1958

Specification

Engine and transmission: Six-cylinders, in-line, with single-overhead-camshaft cylinder head, installed at 50-degrees to vertical. Bore, stroke and capacity 85×88mm., 2996cc. Maximum power 240bhp (gross) at 6100rpm.; maximum torque 210lb.ft. at 5000rpm. (From 1957 250bhp (gross) at 6200rpm.; maximum torque 228lb.ft. at 5000rpm). Four-speed manual gearbox in unit with engine. Hypoid bevel final drive.

Chassis: Front engine, rear drive. Small-diameter multi-tubular 'space frame' chassis. Independent front suspension by coil springs and wishbones. Recirculating ball steering. Independent rear suspension by coil springs and swing axles (low-pivot from 1957). Four-wheel drum brakes.

Bodywork: Pressed steel, two-door two-seat shell. From 1954 to 1957 sold only as closed coupe with 'gullwing' doors. From 1957 to 1963 sold only as open sports roadster (with optional hardtop) and conventional doors. Length 15ft. 0in.; width 5ft. 10in.; height 4ft. 3in. Unladen weight (coupe) 2750lb., (Roadster) 3000lb.

Performance: (Coupe) Depending on gearing, but typically, maximum speed 129mph. 0-60mph 8.8sec. Standing ¼-mile 16.1sec. Typical fuel consumption 21mpg.

Monteverdi 375 family

Built: Binningen, Switzerland, 1967-1977

Peter Monteverdi, successful Swiss businessman, BMW importer and maker of the MBM competition cars, decided to go into luxury car manufacture on his own account in the 1960s, and first showed a Chrysler vee-8-engined GT coupe at the 1967 Frankfurt Show. Styled by himself, with much assistance from Frua, he nevertheless arranged to have production shells supplied by Fissore. The 375 series evolved from this original 2 + 2 style, and was made in various forms in the next ten years.

Even though production never exceeded 70 to 80 cars a year, the Monteverdi was nevertheless Switzerland's only motor manufacturer until the Sbarro replicars came along in the mid-1970s. Like the Ferraris, Maseratis and other machines with which they competed, they were designed to sell only to the very rich, and were built accordingly.

The basis of the design, which never changed no matter what the type of body produced – was a tubular steel chassis frame, with coil spring independent front suspension, and with de Dion rear suspension. Engines, as so often to manufacturers of this type, and in this period, came from Chrysler in Detroit. The 7.2-litre engine as fitted to cars like the New Yorkers and large limousines provided up to 380 gross bhp, and was backed either by a Chrysler manual or (more often) by a Chrysler Torqueflite automatic transmission. As a higher-cost option, incidentally, the harsher and more powerful 7-litre Chrysler 'Hemi' engine was available.

As the years developed there were several different types of coachwork on offer – ranging from the 375S and 375C two-seater coupes and convertibles, through the 375L fastback 2 + 2-seater, right up to the vast Monteverdi Limousine, which used a lengthened wheelbase chassis. Later, in 1975, came the subtly different Palm Beach cabriolet, with the shortest wheelbase of all the types, and only three seats.

Specification

Engine and transmission: Eight-cylinders, in 90-degree vee-formation, with pushrod-operated overhead-valve cylinder heads. Bore, stroke and capacity 109.72×95.25mm., 7210cc. Maximum power 380bhp (gross) at 4600rpm.; maximum torque 480lb.ft. at 3200rpm. Four-speed manual gearbox or three-speed Chrysler automatic transmission in unit with engine. Hypoid bevel final drive.

Chassis: Front-engine, rear drive. Separate steel tubular chassis frame. Independent front suspension by coil springs and wishbones. Power-assisted worm and roller steering. De Dion rear suspension by coil springs, radius arms and Watts linkage. Four-wheel disc brakes.

Bodywork: Steel coachbuilt bodyshells, two-door two-seater coupe, two-seater Cabriolet, or long-wheelbase close-coupled four-seater coupe, by Fissore. Length (375S and 375C) 15ft. 1.1in.; (375L) 15ft. 8.9in.; width 5ft. 10.6in.; height (375S and 375C) 3ft. 1.6in, (375L) 4ft. 2in. Unladen weight (375S and 375C) 3345lb. (375L) 3630lb.

Performance: Maximum speed 152mph. 0-60mph 6.3sec. Standing ¼-mile 14.6sec. Typical fuel consumption 14mpg.

Monteverdi 375L

Monteverdi Hai 450SS

Monteverdi Hai 450SS

Built: Binningen, Switzerland, 1970-1976

To follow the established line of sleek front-engined cars, Peter Monteverdi then astonished the world of motoring by announcing a starkly but brutally attractive styled mid-engined car. The Hai 450SS, with its 7-litre Chrysler engine, looked every bit as purposeful as the Lamborghini Miura, even if its maker had no similar reputation to help him sell the cars. The Hai, in fact, was a car of many parts, for although it had true Supercar performance, it was also air-conditioned and given a great deal of 'comfort' equipment.

The layout was conceived in 1969, and the first prototype was ready for the 1970 Geneva Show. Monteverdi's intention was merely to make one Hai every month, if the demand should justify it, though he wanted to use as much as possible of the engineering already found in the 375 series cars.

The chassis, like many of those fitted to similar Italian cars of the 1960s, was a multi-tube frame with rectangular-section tubes and suitable cross-bracing. Front suspension from the 375 series was specified, and much of the de Dion layout at the

rear was also shared with the front engined cars. The engine, also shared with the 375 series Monteverdis, was a Chrysler 'Hemi' unit of 6974cc, producing no less than a claimed 450bhp (gross), which partly defines the reason for the car's name. The rest of the name, incidentally, comes from the German word for 'shark', while 'SS' merely stood for 'Super Sports', which it most assuredly was.

The bulky vee-8 engine, which was really as wide as it was long, was mounted longitudinally in the chassis, and mated to the ubiquitous five-speed ZF manual transmission and final drive unit, the same type also to be found in Maseratis and de Tomasos of the period. The engine was mounted so far forward that the two passenger seats had to be widely separated, being positioned on each side of the 'power bulge' where the engine protruded into the cockpit.

To clothe this exciting, if simple, structure, Monteverdi commissioned Fissore to build the shells which he had already styled. Because Peter Monteverdi styled all his own products, there was an obvious family resemblance, even though the general shape was entirely different. The nose of the 'shark' was so low that there was no space ahead of the occupants for anything other than a large fuel tank and the radiator. When originally announced there was no spare wheel at all, as front and rear wheels were of different rim widths, and as there was simply no space for one to be included. Customers did *not* approve of that.

The 450SS was not a great success – customers preferring to look for a car like the Miura or the Ferrari Boxer – and it was withdrawn in 1976.

Specification

Engine and transmission: Eight-cylinders, in 90-degree vee-formation, with pushrod-operated overhead-valve cylinder heads, built by Chrysler USA. Bore, stroke and capacity (450SS model) 107.95 × 92.95mm., 6974cc. Maximum power 450bhp (gross) at 5000rpm.; maximum torque 489lb.ft. at 4000rpm. Bore, stroke and capacity (375SS model) 109.72 × 95.25mm., 7210cc. Maximum power 380bhp (gross) at 4600rpm.; maximum torque 480lb.ft. at 3200rpm. Five-speed manual ZF gearbox in unit with engine and spiral bevel final drive.
Chassis: Mid-engine, rear drive. Separate steel tubular chassis frame. Independent front suspension by coil springs and wishbones. Worm and roller steering. De Dion rear suspension by coil springs, radius arms and Watts linkage. Four-wheel disc brakes.
Bodywork: Light-alloy two-door two-seater fastback coupe style by Monteverdi, built by Fissore. Length 14ft. 0.5in.; width 5ft. 10.7in.; height 3ft. 4.9in. Unladen weight 3310lb.
Performance (Manufacturer's claim): Maximum speed 169mph.

Monteverdi Sierra

Monteverdi Sierra

Built: Binningen, Switzerland, 1977 to date

As the popularity of his long-running '375' family of cars dropped away, Peter Monteverdi bravely decided to introduce an entirely new range of cars, using smaller Chrysler engines than before. The Sierra cars − a four-door saloon looking rather like an early 1970s BMW or Peugeot, and a two-door four-seater Cabriolet − were the only cars listed by the Swiss concern as the 1970s drew to a close.

By comparison with the obsolete four-door 375/4 limousine, the Sierra was no less than 17-inches shorter, and could make do with one of two Chrysler engines − 5.2-litre or 5.9-litre, though it retained suspension elements (including the well-known de Dion layout) of the 375 family.

The Sierra's structure was of steel unit-construction type, made on rudimentary tooling by Fissore of Turin, which by then had been taken over financially by Monteverdi.

By this time, however, Monteverdi were also making substantial numbers of a 'Range Rover look-alike' cross-country vehicle, and could not find the space nor the funds to make the Sierra cars in any quantity.

Specification

Engine and transmission: Eight-cylinders, in 90-degree vee-formation, with pushrod-operated overhead-valve cylinder heads. Bore, stroke and capacity 101.6 × 90.93mm., 5898cc. Maximum power 180bhp (DIN) at 4000rpm.; maximum torque 288lb.ft. at 1600rpm. Three-speed Chrysler automatic transmission, in unit with engine. Hypoid bevel final drive.
Chassis: Front engine, rear drive. Pressed-steel unit-construction platform-style frame. Independent front suspension by coil springs and wishbones. Power-assisted worm and roller steering. Rear suspension of live axle by coil springs, radius arms and transverse links. Four-wheel disc brakes.
Bodywork: Steel two-door four-seater Cabriolet body style. Length 15ft. 4in.; width 5ft. 11.6in.; height 4ft. 2.4in. Unladen weight 3090lb.

445

Porsche 911 family

Built: Stuttgart, Germany, 1964 to date

Porsche's 911 is probably the most successful Supercar of all time — there is not likely to be much argument about that. Apart from the four-cylinder 912 models, described elsewhere, every 911, of whatever type, has had Supercar performance, and in later years there have been Supercar road manners to match.

The 911 was conceived at the end of the 1950s to supplant, and soon to replace the 356 models, which were beginning to look their age. As a design, its philosophy followed that of the 356, and therefore that of Dr. Porsche himself, but in detail it was entirely different. This time there was no need to adhere to the use of any VW parts, and the car could be specifically designed for its purpose.

As with the 356, the 911 had a pressed-steel monocoque, styled as a two-door 2 + 2-seater coupe, with a wedge nose, faired-in headlamps, and a fastback style. There was an aircooled engine, this time a flat-six, originally of 1991cc, but obviously with space for 'stretching' in due course, and four-speed or five-speed gearboxes ahead of the line of the rear wheels. The engine, as with that of the 356, was hung out in the tail, where it affected the car's stability and weight distribution somewhat. Four-wheel independent suspension (by torsion bars all round) and four-wheel disc brakes, all

helped to complete an ambitious and carefully-made motor car.

While there is now no denying that early 911s had wheels and tyres which were far too narrow, and roadholding that in the wet could be most disconcerting (it was a combination of front brakes which might lock on, and a tail which could become very wayward if pushed too far), later cars improved rapidly.

A fairly regular feature of 911 development has been that the engines have repeatedly been enlarged. Without diverting from the aircooled flat-six installation, there have now been six different swept volumes in little more than 10-years, and the 3.3-litre unit now displaces 66-percent more than the 1991cc unit of 1966. That the chassis and the rest of the car can still cope is a great credit to its designers and development engineers.

In the same period that engines have grown more powerful and wheel/tyre widths have increased, there has been one minor increase in wheelbase (in 1968, coincident with introducing the first enlarged – 2.2-litre – engine), and body changes to suit both fatter wheels, North American regulations ('5mph' bumpers have been styled cleverly into place without disturbing the basic line) and aerodynamic stability. A feature of later models has been the use of an engine lid spoiler, of which there have been several shapes, sizes and types, starting with the Carrera of 1972.

In addition, Porsche introduced their clever 'Targa' body style in 1967, which retained the strength of a roll-over hoop, but with a removable roof panel and a fabric

Porsche 911 Carrera 3 Sport & Turbo, 1976

Porsche 911SC

rear section which could also be removed in good weather conditions.

Semi-automatic (Sportomatic) transmission, designed and built for Porsche by Fichtel und Sachs, was introduced on some models from the end of 1967, and use of this even extends to the most sporting models of all. At one point Porsche made a point of entering Sportomatic-equipped cars for the 84 hour Nurburgring Marathon, and proved it, because their cars won the event.

As each engine, larger than the last, came along, so Porsche detuned the basic concept. The result was that although a 3.3-litre car is more flexible, and indeed faster, than the original 911S (which was the most powerful − 160bhp − of the original engines), it runs on 2-star fuel (unleaded fuel in the United States), and is not proportionately more powerful in terms of peak bhp developed.

The most exciting of all Porsches, of course, are the Turbos, introduced in 1975 as 2993cc cars, and built since 1977 as 3299cc cars. Quieter, even, than normally aspirated Porsches, and much more powerful, they need only four-speed gearboxes to extract their best performance.

The cars continue in production, which is now on its way towards the 200 000 mark. Few doubt that this will be achieved before the car is retired sometime in the 1980s.

Porsche 911 'Family' 1975/6

Specification

Engine and transmission: Six-cylinders, aircooled, horizontally-opposed, with single-overhead-camshaft cylinder heads. Following engine sizes used over the years: **(1964-1969)** 80 × 66mm., 1991cc. **(1969-1971)** 84 × 66mm., 2195cc. **(1971-1973)** 84 × 70.4mm., 2341cc. **(1973-1977)** 90 × 70.4mm., 2687cc. **(1975 to date)** 95 × 70.4mm., 2993cc (Normal or Turbocharged). **(1977 to date)** 97 × 74.4mm., 3299cc. (Normal or Turbocharged).

Many different power ratings have been used, ranging from the original 1991cc engine, with 130bhp (DIN) at 6100rpm.; maximum torque 128lb.ft. at 4200rpm, to 1979 Turbo model, with maximum power of 300bhp (DIN) at 5500rpm.; maximum torque 303lb.ft. at 4000rpm. Turbocharging on 3-litre Turbo (1975 to 1977), and on 3.3-litre Turbo (1977 to date). Four-speed or five-speed manual transmission, or Sportomatic semi-automatic transmission in unit with engine and transaxle. Spiral bevel final drive.

Chassis: Rear engine, rear drive. Unit-construction, pressed-steel body-chassis unit. Independent front suspension by torsion bars and wishbones. Rack and pinion steering. Independent rear suspension by transverse torsion bars, and semi-trailing wishbones. Four-wheel disc brakes.

Bodywork: Pressed-steel (light alloy panels on some models) body in two-door, 2 + 2 seater, fastback coupe or 'Targa' convertible styles. (Original model) length 13ft. 8in.; width 5ft. 3.5in.; height 4ft. 4in. Unladen weight 2200lb. (Latest wide-track Turbo models) length 14ft. 0.9in.; width 5ft. 9.9in.; height 4ft. 4in. Unladen weight 2635lb.

Performance: (selection) **(911S 1991cc, 1966)** maximum speed 137mph. 0-60mph 8.0sec. Standing ¼-mile 15.8sec. Typical fuel consumption 18mpg. **(911E 2341cc)** maximum speed 139mph. 0-60mph 6.4sec. Standing ¼-mile 14.4sec. Typical fuel consumption 17mpg. **(911S 2687cc 1974)** Maximum speed 142mph. 0-60mph 6.1sec. Standing ¼-mile 15.0sec. Typical fuel consumption 25mpg. **(911SC 2993cc, 1978)** Maximum speed 141mph. 0-60mph 6.5sec. Standing ¼-mile 15.1sec. Typical fuel consumption 20mpg. **(Turbo 2993cc 1976)** maximum speed 153mph. 0-60mph 6.1sec. Standing ¼-mile 14.7sec. Typical fuel consumption 20mpg.

Porsche 928

Porsche 928 and 928S

Built: Stuttgart, Germany, 1977 to date

German engineers have a reputation of being incredibly thorough in their design and development work, and there is much evidence to show that the fabulous Porsche 928 cars are among the most carefully studied designs anywhere in the world. And so they should be, for the 928 family, which will surely proliferate through the 1980s and 1990s, is effectively only the fifth new structural design produced by Porsche since they started building cars in the 1940s (the others are the 356, 911, 914 and 924 ranges).

If it had not been beaten to public announcement by the Porsche 924 (which was, in fact, designed later!) the 928 would have caused a complete sensation by being the first-ever Porsche with a water-cooled engine and 'classic' front engine/rear drive layout. It took nothing less than the safety, legislation and changing fashion developments of the 1970s to cause this. However, as one might expect of Porsche, the result is neither the same as that produced by everyone else, nor is it in any way disappointing.

Work on a new car actually began at the beginning of the 1970s, but was frozen out for a time by the 1973/1974 energy crisis. Almost immediately, too, Porsche were commissioned by VW-Audi to design and develop a new coupe for their use, and as already made clear elsewhere this car finally became the Porsche 924. Only then was worked picked up again on the 928, and its public announcement was delayed until the spring of 1977.

Not surprisingly, the *general* layout of the 928 is like that of the 924 — which is to say that the front-mounted engine is linked to a rear-mounted gearbox and final drive unit by a rigid steel tube — but absolutely nothing is the same in detail, and there are no shared components. The engine, a light-alloy 90-degree vee-8 of 4.5-litres, is brand new and something of an engineering masterpiece, for it combines single-overhead-camshafts, Bosch fuel-injection, and a very 'lazy' power output of 240bhp at a mere 5500rpm. The transmission can either be a five-speed manual or a three-speed (Mercedes-Benz manufactured) automatic gearbox.

The most advanced single feature, if not immediately obvious to the casual inspection, is the new form of independent rear suspension. Called the 'Weissach' axle, after the proving grounds where it was developed, the geometry is arranged so that if the driver releases the throttle in mid-corner, the torque reaction allows the rear wheel to toe-in slightly and counteract any tendency for the car to spin off the road. This is not an idle gimmick, as road experience shows that the 928 is almost embarrassingly stable, and refuses to be 'unstuck' even by the most brutally bad driving.

The fastback 2 + 2 seater hatchback style, by comparison with all this engineering excellence, is at the same time impressively plain and very disappointing. It is smooth and carefully contoured, but has none of the obvious character of any of the old model Porsches. Nevertheless, the steel monocoque (there are light-alloy doors, detachable panels and opening panels) is immensely strong and practical, and designed with every known and projected safety requirement in mind.

In original form, and compared with some early 911 Porsche cars, the 928 is still something of a disappointment, but there seems to be little doubt that the engine's output could be boosted to much greater levels (especially with turbocharging) if the market demands it. The 928S derivative, announced late in 1979, with a slightly enlarged engine of 4664cc, and no less than 300bhp (DIN), is the first of those improvements. We must expect the car, and all its derivatives, to be with us until the 1990s at least, and maybe beyond.

Never forget that a Porsche has something often found lacking in other Supercars. It is manufactured in considerable numbers, it is fully and meticulously tooled, and is built with an eye to long-life and quality matched by very few other car makers. There is also that little matter of a six-year guarantee against body rot which is great comfort to anyone living in less than perfect climes!

Specification

Engine and transmission: Eight-cylinders, in 90-degree vee-formation, with single-overhead-camshaft cylinder heads. **(928):** Bore, stroke and capacity 95×78.9mm., 4474cc. Maximum power 240bhp (DIN) at 5500rpm.; maximum torque 267lb.ft. at 3600rpm. **(928S):** Bore, stroke and capacity 97×78.8mm., 4664cc. Maximum power 300bhp (DIN) at 5900rpm.; maximum torque 283lb.ft. at 4500rpm. Five-speed manual gearbox or three-speed automatic gearbox. Hypoid bevel final drive.
Chassis: Front engine, rear drive. Unit-construction pressed-steel body-chassis unit. Independent front suspension by coil springs and wishbones. Power-assisted rack and pinion steering. Independent rear suspension by coil springs and semi-trailing wishbones. Four-wheel disc brakes.

451

Bodywork: Pressed-steel two-door (with hatchback), 2 + 2 seater, fastback coupe style. Length 14ft. 7.1in.; width 6ft. 0.3in.; height 4ft. 3.7in. Unladen weight 3200lb.
Performance (928): Maximum speed 142mph. 0-60mph 7.5sec. Standing ¼-mile 15.7sec. Typical fuel consumption 18mpg. **(928S):** Maximum speed 152mph. 0-60mph 6.2sec. Standing ¼-mile 14.3sec. Typical fuel consumption 19mpg.

Rolls-Royce Camargue

Rolls-Royce Camargue

Built: London and Crewe, England, 1975 to date

In many ways, the Rolls-Royce Carmargue is one of the most super Supercars of all time. It is enormously expensive – more than £60,000 in Britain, in mid-1979 – very exclusive, and with a long waiting list which almost guarantees demand and a stable specification for years to come. By comparison with Ferraris and other such Italian performance machinery, its performance potential is somewhat limited – 125mph is its maximum speed, and with an unladen weight of more than 5000lb it does not feature flashing acceleration either – but of its prestige, and its qualification for inclusion here, there is no doubt.

The Camargue is also the first Rolls-Royce to be styled by an outside consultant for many years. Up to the outbreak of the second world war, Rolls-Royce never made coachwork at all, but gave their considered approval to the products of a handful of noted British coachbuilders. After the war, they began marketing 'standard steel' saloon versions of their cars – Silver Dawn, then Silver Cloud, and latterly the Silver

Shadow. The Camargue, conceived in 1969 by Rolls-Royce, is a product of the Pininfarina styling house in Italy.

Because Rolls-Royce struck financial trouble in 1971, and because it took some time for the car division to be hived off from the troubled aero-engine business, the launch of the Camargue was delayed. It was not until the spring of 1975 (after a long and particularly damaging strike at the Mulliner Park Ward works had held things up yet again) that the Camargue was first revealed to the public.

Its 'chassis' and mechanical engineering is almost identical with that of the Rolls-Royce Silver Shadow four-door saloon which is — if such a description is possible — the 'bread and butter' model in the range. The same pressed-steel floorpan (built and supplied by the Pressed Steel Fisher division of British Leyland, whose forebears had supplied standard steel coachwork since 1946), with its 120in. wheelbase, is used, along with the same all-independent suspension, steering, engine and transmission assemblies which are used in the Silver Shadow. Like the Shadow, too, the 'chassis' was thoroughly revised in the spring of 1977, where one of the most important changes was to the steering, and when power-assisted rack-and-pinion was installed.

That renowned 6.75-litre light-alloy vee-8 is used in higher-powered 'Corniche' tune, and has a single four-choke Solex carburettor (Silver Shadows have always had twin SUs). Although we know that it is more powerful than the Shadow, Rolls-Royce do not, and never have, quote maximum power and torque figures. The magnificently refined engine is matched to the latest (and very well thought of) General Motors automatic transmission.

Construction of the bodywork has changed in procedure since the Camargue was announced. At first the pressed-steel underpans were supplied to Mulliner Park Ward, who built up the bare shell, shipped it to the main works at Crewe, then took it back for internal trimming and finishing. After a hiatus in 1977, when the car was actually out of production, the new arrangement was that Motor Panels of Coventry built up the bare shell on the floorpan, after which Crewe completed the car themselves.

Like the Silver Shadow series from which the car is derived, the emphasis, above all things, is on quality of engineering, careful assembly, and the most rigid inspection of every conceivable feature before the car is delivered to its new owner. Silence, refinement, and long-term reliability, are thought to be of more importance than high performance and spirited road behaviour. Even so, the Camargue, which has much of the character of the old Bentley Continentals in its nature, is much the best-handling Rolls-Royce yet built, and has a 'presence' which no other Supercar can match.

Rolls-Royce are understandably coy about releasing production data on this model, but is likely that less than 150 cars were built in the first four years of its production life.

Specification

Engine and transmission: Eight-cylinders, in 90-degree vee-formation, with pushrod-operated overhead-valve cylinder heads. Bore, stroke and capacity 104.1 × 99.1mm., 6750cc. Maximum power and maximum torque not quoted. Three speed automatic General Motors gearbox, in unit with engine. Hypoid bevel final drive.

Chassis: Front engine, rear drive. Pressed-steel, unit construction, body/chassis unit. Independent front suspension by coil springs and wishbones. Power-assisted rack and pinion steering (power-assisted recirculating ball steering on 1975-1977 models). Independent rear suspension by coil springs and semi-trailing wishbones, and self-levelling. Four-wheel disc brakes.

Bodywork: Two-door four-seater notchback coupe body style by Pininfarina, panelling produced by Mulliner Park Ward at first, since 1977/1978 by Motor Panels, final assembly by Rolls-Royce. Length 16ft. 11.5in.; width 6ft. 3.5in.; height 4ft. 10.2in. Unladen weight 5135lb.

Performance: Maximum speed approx 125mph. Typical fuel consumption 12mpg.

European Sports & GT Cars

De Tomaso Mangusta

Built: Modena, Italy, 1967 to 1971

In the first few years of the 1960s, Alejandro de Tomaso, an Argentinian who settled in Italy, produced a whole series of interesting and exciting prototypes, most of which were promised for production, but few of which ever got further than the one-off stage. Not only cars, but racing engines (including Formula 1 and 2 units) were produced. By the mid-1960s, observers had come to expect a new de Tomaso folly at every Turin Motor Show, and they were rarely disappointed.

In November 1966, therefore, when a prototype mid-engined two-seater coupe was shown, with a massive and powerful Ford vee-8 engine providing the performance, no-one really thought that the genial Arngentinian was serious. They were wrong. Aided by the enterprise of Ghia, an Italian styling house which he had just purchased, de Tomaso managed to put this car into production, as the first truly 'series production' de Tomaso of all.

De Tomaso Mangusta, 1969

The 'Mangusta' (which, in English, means 'Mongoose') was a refined and developed version of the Vallelunga sports car, which had been shown a year earlier, and which had also been Ford-powered, but only by a British four-cylinder Ford Cortina engine. Complete with around 300bhp, of course, the Mangusta was completely different.

In layout it was really a classic statement of the new mid-engined theme which was sweeping through the world of motor racing. The big Detroit-produced 4.7-litre vee-8 engine was mounted longitudinally behind the two rather cramped seats, but ahead of the line of the rear wheels, and was matched (as so often with this layout) to a proprietary five-speed ZF gearbox and transaxle.

456

The chassis layout used a pressed-steel backbone frame, with box-section and tubular super-structures to carry the engine/transmission unit, the suspensions, and provision for seats. Suspension – all-independent, by coil springs and wishbones – is also in the racing car mould, while front and rear tyres are of 15in. rim diameter but different sizes (185 front section, 235 rear section).

It was the body style however, which Ghia had evolved, which caused the greatest stir. Sleek, clean, and wickedly attractive, it was very striking in conception. Not only did the huge engine lid/rear suspension covers hinge up from a centre spine located on the cage behind the seats and at the very tail, but the long doors opened wide to reveal a really functional and purposeful interior.

The Mangusta's two principal drawbacks were that it was really a detuned sports-racing car concept, and that (allied to this) it did not provide enough space for passengers, and extremely limited stowage accommodation. In addition, the rear-bias to the weight distribution (68-percent of the weight was over the rear wheels) made high-speed handling a very perilous business, particularly in wet and slippery conditions.

The Pantera, which came along in 1970, was a better car in all respects, and once in production in 1971 replaced the Mangusta completely.

Specification

Engine and transmission: Eight-cylinders, in 90-degree vee-formation, with pushrod-operated overhead-valve cylinder heads. Bore, stroke and capacity 101.6×72.89mm., 4727cc. Maximum power 305bhp (DIN) at 6200rpm.; maximum torque 392lb.ft. at 3500rpm. Five-speed manual ZF gearbox in unit with engine and transaxle. Spiral bevel final drive.

Chassis: Mid-engine, rear drive. Pressed-steel backbone and box-section separate chassis frame. Independent front suspension by coil springs and wishbones. Rack and pinion steering. Independent rear suspension by coil springs, wishbones and radius arms. Four-wheel disc brakes.

Bodywork: Light-alloy and steel coachbuilt body, in two-door two-seater, fastback coupe style, by Ghia. Length 14ft. 0.3in.; width 6ft. 0.2in.; height 3ft. 7.3in. Unladen weight 2175lb.

Performance: Maximum speed (claimed) 155mph.

De Tomaso Pantera

Built: Modena, Italy, 1971 to date

De Tomaso's replacement for the rather specialised Mangusta was the Pantera (Panther), which made its bow at the New York Show in March 1970, and went into production in 1971. The most significant feature of that New York launch was not the car itself, its styling, and its specification, but the fact that it was shown not by de Tomaso, but by Ford of North America. In a complicated deal which would eventually lead to de Tomaso selling the Ghia business to Ford, the Detroit monolith agreed to market the Pantera in North America through their Lincoln-Mercury chain, who were also dealing with such goodies as the European Ford Capris.

Unlike the Mangusta, the Pantera was based around a unit-construction pressed steel and fabricated body/chassis unit. As with the Maserati Merak/Bora concept, this was possible with limited tooling, due to the particular expertise of the chassis and body builders in and around the Italian 'supercar' industry. This unit-construction fixed-head coupe shell was to be built in considerably larger quantities than the Mangusta – thousands rather than hundreds – and once again it benefitted from a sharp and delicately-detailed shape by Ghia.

Mechanically, however, the Pantera was a good deal more standardised than the Mangusta had been. Ford, who were anxious to sell this car at attractive prices throughout North America, had given a great deal of cost-saving advice. The engine, for example, was as powerful as that installed in the Mangusta, but was – at the same time – of larger capacity and of a completely standard Ford USA production tune. The ZF five-speed transmission and the transaxle were of the same type as used by the Mangusta, and the same as that used in the Maserati Bora, which was convenient when de Tomaso and Maserati came to merge in 1975/1976.

Most importantly, the weight distribution had been improved (nearly 42-percent of the considerable weight was now on the front wheels), the tyre size imbalance had been improved (185 front section, 215 rear section), and there was a great deal more accommodation, both for passengers and for their luggage. Performance, too, in spite of a very 'soft' engine tune, was also improved, and any customer's Pantera was capable of exceeding 160mph in any but the most adverse conditions. To pander to the tastes of wealthy North American customers, too, there was the astonishing provision (for such an out-and-out Supercar) of full air-conditioning. The body construction, incidentally, was somewhat more conventional than on the Mangusta, with a large but simple engine lid, hinged at the cockpit end, replacing the flamboyant gullwing variety of the Mangusta.

Although the Pantera was still listed by de Tomaso as the 1970s drew to a close, this was not because it had been a great success in North America, where its marketing had been so aggressive. In June 1974 Ford announced that it had stopped taking Pantera supplies, after about 4000 cars had been sold. This was a combination of factors – of which the combined legislative/emission control burden was the most serious – but which also included the after effects of the energy crisis of 1973/1974, and the fact that considerable quality and reliability problems were being experienced.

Several varieties of Pantera, in terms of power output and performance, have been sold since 1971. The most glamorous and powerful of these is the Pantera GTS, where the 5.7-litre Ford engine is boosted to produce 290bhp (DIN) at a high-revving

5800rpm.

Specification

Engine and transmission: Eight-cylinders, in 90-degree vee-formation, with pushrod-operated overhead-valve cylinder heads, made by Ford USA. Bore, stroke and capacity 101.6 × 88.9mm., 5763cc. Maximum power 330bhp (gross) at 5400rpm.; maximum torque 325lb.ft. at 3600rpm. Five-speed manual ZF gearbox in unit with engine and transaxle. Hypoid bevel final drive.

Chassis: Mid-engine, rear drive. Unit-construction pressed and fabricated chassis/body unit. Independent front suspension by coil springs and wishbones. Rack and pinion steering. Independent rear suspension by coil springs and wishbones. Four-wheel disc brakes.

Bodywork: Steel two-door, two-seater, fastback closed coupe style. Length 13ft. 11.5in.; width 6ft. 0in.; height 3ft. 7in. Unladen weight 3110lb.

Performance: Maximum speed 159mph. 0-60mph 6.2sec. Standing ¼-mile 14.4sec. Typical fuel consumption 14mpg.

De Tomaso Longchamps

Built: Modena, Italy, 1972 to date

Once de Tomaso had forged links with Ford in North America, and expanded their production facilities accordingly, they began to get more ambitious in terms of new models. Immediately after the launch of the mid-engined Pantera, they showed the Deauville four-door saloon at the Turin Show of November 1970. Although this was virtually a line-for-line copy of Jaguar's stupendously popular XJ6, Ghia took the credit for its shape. On announcement, it was supposed to be having a de Tomaso-designed overhead-camshaft derivative of a big Ford vee-8 engine, but this feature proved to be nothing more than wishful thinking, like many other concepts from this fertile-minded but infuriating concern. Two years later, in November 1972, the Longchamps – a shortened-chassis, two-door coupe version – was launched.

The Longchamps, by Ghia, was formed on the limited-tooling unit-construction floorpan, dash, engine bay, bulkhead structure already set up to make the Deauville, but with the pan shortened by 6.7-inches. Both cars shared the same four-wheel independent suspension, which was by coil springs and wishbones at front and rear. The rack and pinion steering was power-assisted.

Both cars had the same mass-production Ford of Detroit 5.77-litre vee-8 engine, in each case exactly as was being used in the mid-engined Pantera sports car. There was a choice of transmissions – a five-speed ZF box of the type often used by manufacturers of this type of car, or – equally as often – a three-speed Ford automatic transmission with which the engine would normally be matched in North American Cars.

By de Tomaso's standards, the Longchamps was successful, though it did not sell so well as the Pantera. Alejandro de Tomaso himself must have been happy with it, because following the take over of Maserati, one of his first moves was to marry Longchamps engineering with a Maserati vee-8 engine, and call the result a Maserati Kyalami. Both cars were in production at the close of 1979, and it is also interesting to note that the Maserati Quattroporte is derived from both, on a Deauville wheelbase.

Specification

Engine and transmission: Eight-cylinders, in 90-degree vee-formation, with pushrod-operated overhead-valve cylinder heads. Bore, stroke and capacity 101.6 × 88.9mm., 5769cc, built by Ford USA. Maximum power 330bhp (gross) at 6000rpm.; maximum torque 325lb.ft. at 3500rpm. Five-speed ZF manual gearbox or three-speed Ford automatic transmission in unit with engine. Hypoid bevel final drive.
Chassis: Front engine, rear drive. Unit construction pressed-steel body/chassis unit. Independent front suspension by coil springs and wishbones. Power-assisted rack and pinion steering. Independent rear suspension by coil springs and wishbones. Four-wheel disc brakes.
Bodywork: Light-alloy and steel two-door 2 + 2 notchback coupe body style by Ghia. Length 14ft. 10in.; width 6ft. 0.4in.; height 4ft. 4.4in. Unladen weight 4000lb.
Performance:

De Tomaso Longchamps

Index

Note: Numbers in bold print indicate the page on which the analysis of that particular car begins.

A

B

C

G

H

I

M

N

O

Z